Microsoft 365 Compliance

A Practical Guide to Managing Risk

Erica Toelle

Apress®

Microsoft 365 Compliance: A Practical Guide to Managing Risk

Erica Toelle
Seattle, WA, USA

ISBN-13 (pbk): 978-1-4842-5777-7   ISBN-13 (electronic): 978-1-4842-5778-4
https://doi.org/10.1007/978-1-4842-5778-4

Copyright © 2021 by Erica Toelle

Managing Director, Apress Media LLC: Welmoed Spahr
Acquisitions Editor: Joan Murray
Development Editor: Laura Berendson
Coordinating Editor: Jill Balzano

Cover image designed by Freepik (www.freepik.com)

Distributed to the book trade worldwide by Springer Science+Business Media LLC, 1 New York Plaza, Suite 4600, New York, NY 10004. Phone 1-800-SPRINGER, fax (201) 348-4505, email orders-ny@springer-sbm. com, or visit www.springeronline.com. Apress Media, LLC is a California LLC and the sole member (owner) is Springer Science + Business Media Finance Inc (SSBM Finance Inc). SSBM Finance Inc is a **Delaware** corporation.

For information on translations, please e-mail booktranslations@springernature.com; for reprint, paperback, or audio rights, please e-mail bookpermissions@springernature.com.

Apress titles may be purchased in bulk for academic, corporate, or promotional use. eBook versions and licenses are also available for most titles. For more information, reference our Print and eBook Bulk Sales web page at http://www.apress.com/bulk-sales.

Any source code or other supplementary material referenced by the author in this book is available to readers on GitHub via the book's product page, located at www.apress.com/9781484257777. For more detailed information, please visit http://www.apress.com/source-code.

Printed on acid-free paper

This book is dedicated to my best friend and sister, Lisa Volkening. Without her encouragement and support, this book would not exist.

Table of Contents

About the Author

 **Erica Toelle** is a Microsoft MVP in Office Apps and Services. She is an internationally recognized speaker on compliance, Office 365, and SharePoint. Erica has been working with customers to deploy these solutions since 2004 and has been hired as an expert by over 75 Fortune 500 companies, several Microsoft Product Teams, and Microsoft IT. Erica was voted by her peers as one of the top 15 International SharePoint Influencers from 2016 to present.

Contact Erica on LinkedIn at `www.linkedin.com/in/ericatoelle/`.

About the Technical Reviewer

Ryan Sturm has worked in the information technology industry for over 18 years. He is currently working as a Microsoft 365 Compliance SME in a consulting capacity. Prior to his current role, he worked in the financial services industry for 11+ years as a director of IT managing data center and M365 operations with direct responsibility for security and compliance. He also spent several years working in the healthcare industry and before that in IT services and agriculture.

More info can be found on his LinkedIn profile at http://linkedin.com/in/ryan-sturm.

About the Technical Reviewer

Acknowledgments

I was the person to write this book, but the knowledge it contains represents an entire community's effort. Without their expertise and experiences, this book would not exist.

First, I would like to thank the Microsoft FastTrack Compliance SME team. I was honored to be a member of this team over the past year. Together we learned every aspect of the Microsoft compliance solutions and helped many customers on their deployment journeys. I specifically want to thank Chris Staab, Ryan Sturm, and Leandro Ramirez. They were never too busy to help me when I couldn't figure something out alone.

Next, I would like to thank a few Microsoft employees for always answering my email when I want to understand something undocumented. Roberto Yglesias, Nick Robinson, and Stefanie Bier, I couldn't have written this book without you.

I have been fortunate to be a member of the SharePoint community for the past 15 years of my career. The people I've met have become my extended family and have been an endless source of support. When I decided to switch my focus to 100% compliance a few years ago, the community gave me a platform for opportunities to speak, blog, podcast, and make videos, even though the topic was not yet popular.

And finally, I have to thank my #1 source of compliance inspiration, Joanne Klein. She pushes our industry forward with her innovative and creative compliance solutions, which she captures in her blog at `https://joannecklein.com`. Thank you for being my friend and confidant and for inspiring all of us.

Introduction

Microsoft 365 Compliance is a book for anyone interested in Microsoft's Office 365 compliance solutions. It doesn't matter if you are technical or not; you will understand the content in this book. I have scoped these solutions to anything located in the Microsoft Compliance Center, focusing on what you can accomplish through the user interface. Compliance is always a joint effort between the business and IT, and I hope that this book helps both audiences implement Microsoft compliance solutions.

Each chapter begins with an overview of the business reasons for the compliance solution. It answers the "why" behind the solution. I hope that this information will help you to understand if the solution meets your business needs.

Next, I cover licensing and permissions for each solution. The licensing for compliance is complex, and you need to know up front if your organization can use the solution with the licenses you own. Permissions for compliance can also be complicated. More organizations are beginning to follow the security best practice of least permissions, meaning people only have the minimum access they need to perform their jobs. My goal is to help you follow the least permissions model with the Microsoft compliance solutions.

Then, we go over the "how" for each solution. This section covers the technical details for implementing compliance solutions. I explain every button, setting, and option for each solution. Again, I focus on what you can do through the user interface since that is what 95% of the customers I speak with want. I mention where you can use PowerShell and APIs with the solutions, but don't cover it in this book.

I end each chapter with a summary of what we learned and briefly introduce the next chapter.

Throughout the book, I use short URLs to direct you to additional resources. These URLs are case sensitive.

Finally, the information covered in this book changed weekly while I was writing. If you find an inaccuracy, please let me know so I can correct it in the next version. You can find me on LinkedIn at `www.linkedin.com/in/ericatoelle/`.

CHAPTER 1

An Introduction to Compliance in Microsoft 365

Why do we care about compliance? Compliance refers to relevant laws, regulations, and any internal or external standards. Organization compliance is the process of making sure your company and employees follow the rules, regulations, standards, policies, and ethical practices.

Effective corporate compliance covers internal policies and rules and international, federal, state/providence, and local standards and laws. Enforcing compliance through corporate policy will help your company prevent and detect violations of these rules. Adherence can save your organization from fines, lawsuits, and a poor public image.

Corporate compliance also defines expectations for employee behavior. It helps employees stay focused on your organization's broader goals and mission and allows operations to run smoothly. Compliance is an ongoing process. Most organizations have a corporate compliance program to help set, guide, and maintain their compliance policies.

Compliance mitigates risk, and it makes sure everyone follows the rules. What is not simple is understanding laws and regulations and knowing what rules to create. You can break compliance down into two main areas:

1. **Regulatory compliance**: Regulatory compliance ensures that a company's business or action is within legal parameters and that you have taken all reasonable measures to prevent incidents.

2. **Internal compliance**: Internal compliance focuses on internal policies and standards in ensuring that a company operates according to its own culture.

© Erica Toelle 2021
E. Toelle, *Microsoft 365 Compliance*, https://doi.org/10.1007/978-1-4842-5778-4_1

Another reason compliance is important is related to litigation and legal proceedings. By managing compliance in your organization, we can reduce the risk of lawsuits and criminal investigations. When it does happen, we can provide evidence that we have taken reasonable actions to prevent an incident. For example, let us say an employee gets injured at a manufacturing plant. Can we prove that we performed all machine maintenance correctly and on schedule? Do we have proof that the employee took the required safety training course?

Compliance activities can include internal audits, third-party audits, security procedures, handling private data, preparing reports, supporting documentation, and developing and implementing policies and procedures to ensure compliance.

There are many benefits of having a transparent and controlled compliance process in your organization:

- Avoids criminal charges

- Prevents fines from noncompliance

- Builds a positive reputation for your organization

- Reduces legal risks and avoids future costs

- Builds trust with your customers

- Reduces organizational and individual risk

- Helps employees make better decisions

- Helps to realize the company's mission

- Helps to attract and retain talent

To further complicate compliance programs, data is exploding. Information is created, stored, and shared everywhere. There are many platforms and software-as-a-service (SaaS) tools used by businesses. It is challenging to understand where you store data in your organization and what tools and platforms your employees are using to conduct their work. It can be even more challenging to create compliance processes and controls across all these locations.

Managing this data overload and the variety of devices that create the data is complicated. Many companies are struggling to decide how many of these solutions they need and where to start. Using multiple solutions means integration and a management challenge.

First and foremost, the compliance landscape is continually evolving. If you are a global organization or even one operating in one or two countries, the number of regulations to which you are subject is always changing. A recent study indicated there are over 200 updates per day from 750 regulatory bodies worldwide. Electronic data continues to grow at an exponential rate and is increasing in complexity. Whereas before you were primarily dealing with documents and email, now you are also dealing with instant messages, text messages, video files, images, audio files, and more. Understanding what data you have, what information is sensitive, what is business critical, what you need to keep, how long, and what you can delete is of utmost importance to maintaining compliance.

Data is also your most significant compliance risk. Data is no longer only an IT asset. It is a core strategic asset. Some data types are more valuable than others. Confidential business information, which encompasses company financials and customer and employee data, is a highly strategic asset and equally a high-value target. Protecting and managing this data is essential.

Finally, the cost of compliance continues to increase year over year, not only in terms of processes, people, and technologies you need to be compliant with but also the cost of noncompliance. The challenge in compliance is that the market is very fragmented and very confusing. There are dozens of requirements and dozens of categories of solutions. Within each one of these categories, there are hundreds of solutions from which to choose. Identifying where to start and what can do can be a daunting task.

Data regulations are increasing around the world. In the past few years, we have added the following privacy regulations:

- California Consumer Privacy Act (CCPA)

- EU General Data Protection Regulation (GDPR)

- Canadian Personal Information Protection and Electronic Documents Act (PIPEDA)

Several more pieces of critical legislation are pending implementation. With the advent of data and privacy concerns, these regulations and laws are only going to increase.

When it comes to compliance, Microsoft will manage your data according to the law of the land – for example, your region or country. Microsoft helps you comply with national, regional, and industry-specific requirements governing individual data collection and use. They offer the most comprehensive set of compliance offerings of any cloud service provider.

What does it mean to manage content for compliance in Microsoft 365? Microsoft has trust principles that run their business. These principles are security, privacy, transparency, and compliance. They take a very principled approach to running their business and what they will fight to protect with their customers.

Microsoft leverages a shared responsibility model for compliance. This model shows what compliance risks Microsoft manages and what risks are managed by your organization. When customers use only on-premises IT infrastructure, they have complete responsibility to protect their data and implement their controls to comply with regulatory standards.

The cloud represents a shared responsibility between the customer and the cloud service provider. For example, if you use a SaaS solution, like Microsoft 365, Microsoft helps you take care of network controls and host infrastructure, shown in Figure 1-1. Customers do not need to spend resources building their data center or setting up the infrastructure.

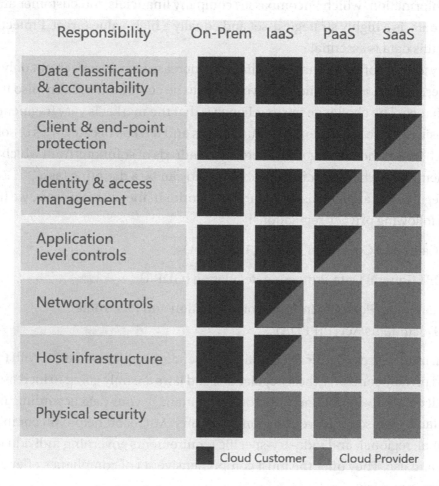

Figure 1-1. *An example cloud shared responsibility model*

For example, Microsoft will take care of your data's physical security risk, meaning nobody can enter the data center and perform a malicious or unintentional action against the computer's hardware. Microsoft also handles application-level controls to ensure compliance. However, it will always be the customer's responsibility to manage data classification and accountability, and they share responsibility with Microsoft for client and endpoint protection.

Let us look at an example of shared responsibility. One of the most stringent security and privacy control frameworks used by the US government is NIST 800-53. NIST 800-53 defines federal agencies' standards and guidelines to architect and manage their information security systems. When you use Microsoft 365, Microsoft helps you manage 79% of the 1,201 NIST controls, so you only need to focus on implementing and maintaining the remaining 21% of the rules. You can save a lot of time and effort and benefit from the shared responsibility model in cloud compliance. Imagine if you are using on-premises services, then you would need to implement and maintain all 1,201 controls by yourself.

Even more compelling is that Microsoft takes care of its responsibilities and provides customers with tools and features to help them cover theirs. However, before you can embrace these benefits, you need to know how Microsoft implemented and tested 79% of the controls. We will cover this information in detail in Chapter 2.

Microsoft Compliance Pillars

Microsoft is in a unique position to help you with intelligent compliance and risk management solutions. First, they understand compliance can have different meanings to various teams across your organization. Compliance typically involves compliance, risk, legal, privacy, security, IT, and even HR and finance teams. It requires an integrated approach to managing risk. Microsoft offers four key solution areas for compliance that we will review in this book.

Compliance Manager

Compliance Manager simplifies risk assessment and mitigation in an automated way. This solution provides visibility, insights, and checklists to help meet compliance regulations. Microsoft has assessment templates for over 240 regulations worldwide. These assessments provide a list of the tasks you need to complete to ensure your Microsoft infrastructure's compliance with the regulation. The template also shows the Microsoft completed tasks and how they tested and implemented the controls.

The Microsoft Service Trust Portal is a resource for information about Microsoft's audit reports, penetration tests, and security assessments. It includes industry-specific compliance information, regional compliance information, Microsoft services risk assessment information, and other resources. These documents can help you to prepare for an external audit.

We will cover both Compliance Manager and the Service Trust Portal in Chapter 2.

Information Protection and Governance

Microsoft can protect and govern data throughout its life cycle. This option is often the critical starting point for many organizations in their modern compliance journey. It is essential to know what sensitive data you have in your organization. Information Protection provides flexible and user-friendly policies for both security and compliance outcomes using automation and intelligence. We cover Information Protection in Chapter 5.

Information Governance helps you to manage the life cycle of your data and files. It allows you to keep what information you need and delete what information you do not need. Records Management helps you comply with regulations, laws, and internal policies about keeping and deleting data. We cover Information Governance in Chapter 8 and Records Management in Chapter 9.

Microsoft 365 can archive data from third-party solutions for compliance purposes. These solutions include platforms such as Bloomberg Messenger, Slack, text messaging services, and much more. We will look at this archiving functionality, called Data Connectors, in Chapter 4.

Data Loss Prevention (DLP) helps identify sensitive information across many Microsoft 365 locations such as Exchange Online, SharePoint Online, OneDrive for Business, and Microsoft Teams. DLP policies prevent accidental sharing of sensitive information. They monitor and protect sensitive information in the desktop versions of Excel, PowerPoint, and Word. They can help monitor message traffic to comply with regulations. We will review the Data Loss Prevention solution in Chapter 6.

There are some foundational components used throughout the information protection and governance solutions. These components include

- **Sensitive information types**: Define sensitive data patterns so we can identify sensitive data using Microsoft compliance solutions.

- **Trainable classifiers**: Use machine learning to find and classify common data types in your organization, such as a contract.

- **Content explorer**: Understand what documents contain sensitive data and have a sensitivity or retention label.

- **Activity explorer**: See the user and admin activity around your sensitivity and retention labels, DLP policies, and more.

We review these foundational components in Chapter 3 on Data Classification.

Insider Risk Management

Internal risks are what keep business leaders up at night. Regardless of whether the action is negligent or malicious, identifying and acting on internal threats is critical. Insiders are employees or contractors with corporate access. Insider risks can include stealing or leaking data or sending an email with inappropriate or harassing language.

The Insider Risk Management (IR) solution looks for patterns of risky behavior from your employees and contractors. It can recognize deviations from normal behavior and flag them using an alert. You can choose to investigate these alerts in a case focused on the user. We discuss insider risk in Chapter 10.

Communication Compliance monitors communications for inappropriate behavior or sensitive information or to meet compliance regulations. You can monitor emails, Teams chats and messages, Yammer, and third-party data such as Bloomberg Messenger and Slack. We review Communication Compliance in Chapter 11.

Information Barriers (IB) can block or allow communication and collaboration between two groups of users in your organization. Typically, this is done for regulatory reasons. We discuss Information Barriers in Chapter 7.

Discover and Respond

Discover and respond solutions help you to locate and preserve compliance content. These solutions include Compliance Search, eDiscovery, and the audit log. The audit log helps you monitor actions taken by administrators and end users.

Content search allows you to search for most content in Microsoft 365 and export it. We cover Compliance Search in Chapter 12.

Core and Advanced eDiscovery help you identify and deliver electronic information that can be used as evidence in legal cases. We discuss Core eDiscovery in Chapter 13 and Advanced eDiscovery in Chapter 14.

Data Investigations help you to conduct internal investigations that involve Microsoft 365 content as evidence. These investigations can cover things like data leaks, poor behavior, or data subject requests. We cover Data Investigations in Chapter 15.

Lastly, use the Microsoft 365 audit log to determine what the users and admins in your organization have been doing. You will be able to find activities related to email, groups, documents, permissions, directory services, and much more. We discuss the audit log in Chapter 16.

Microsoft 365 Compliance Licensing

Microsoft licensing can be confusing. Not only is it difficult to understand what compliance features your organization owns but licensing changes frequently, at least every year. There is a high chance that the licensing information in this book has changed since publishing. Here are two excellent resources for Microsoft compliance licensing information:

- The official Microsoft 365 licensing guidance for security and compliance: `http://erica.news/ComplianceLicensing`.

- Aaron Dinnage, a Microsoft sales employee, created these fantastic visual diagrams for all Microsoft licensing. I would not understand licensing myself if it were not for this resource: `http://erica.news/AaronDinnage`.

This section is intended to guide typical Microsoft licensing so you can understand what compliance features in this book are available to you. It also provides a foundation of understanding for when I refer to license options later in this book.

This is intended to be guidance only and is not a comprehensive guide to Microsoft licensing. Please consult with your IT department or your Microsoft account representative for more information about your specific licensing situation.

First, I generally think of compliance licensing as core or advanced. Microsoft includes core features in most licenses. Advanced features require additional licensing.

Second, there are a few definitions we should review before we dive into compliance licensing:

- A SKU is a type of license.

- Microsoft 365 SKUs include Office 365, Enterprise Mobility + Security, and Windows 10 licenses.

- An Office 365 SKU includes only Office 365 functionality.

- "E" SKUs are the standard commercial tenants.

- "A" SKUs are for education.

- "G" SKUs are for the US government clouds.

- "F" SKUs are for frontline and shift workers.

Third, Microsoft has a lot of options for purchasing compliance solutions. It is possible only to buy the functionality you intend to use. Let us go through these available options. I made up these categories based on what makes sense to me, and Microsoft does not use them:

- **Buy everything**: These SKUs include all the advanced compliance features.

    - Microsoft 365 E5/A5/G5

    - Microsoft 365 E5/A5/G5 Compliance

    - Office 365 E5/A5/G5

- **Purchase only the compliance solutions you need**: These SKUs include the advanced compliance features for one of the pillars we reviewed in the preceding section. You must purchase them as an add-on to a Microsoft or Office 365 E3 license.

    - Microsoft 365 E5/A5 Information Protection and Governance

    - Microsoft 365 E5/A5 Insider Risk Management

    - Microsoft 365 E5/A5 eDiscovery and Audit

- **Core compliance features**: These licenses provide access to core compliance features.

    - Microsoft 365 E3/A3/G3

    - Microsoft 365 F3

    - Office 365 E3/A3/G3

    - Office 365 F3

- **More limited features**: These licenses provide access to a subset of compliance features. I recommend looking at the official Microsoft 365 licensing guidance for security and compliance linked in the preceding text for the specifics.

  - Microsoft 365 F1

  - Microsoft 365 Business Premium

  - Office 365 E1/A1/G1

- **Retired licenses**: This license is retired, meaning you can no longer purchase it. However, if you previously purchased this license, it provides access to some advanced compliance features. Please look at the official Microsoft 365 licensing guidance for security and compliance linked in the preceding text for this license's specifics.

  - Office 365 Advanced Compliance

The Compliance Center

Microsoft 365 or the Microsoft 365 Compliance Center is the portal to administer and maintain your Microsoft compliance solutions. You can find it at `https://compliance.microsoft.com`.

On the portal's homepage, you can see various widgets containing information about your compliance solutions. These widgets show you things like your Microsoft Compliance Score, links to your solution catalog, information about retention label usage, pending disposition information, DLP policy matches, externally shared files, and much more.

You can customize this view for your purposes. Customizing this view will only personalize it for you and not for other people in your organization. To do this, on the right-hand side of the page, click Add cards.

Here, you can add or remove cards to or from your homepage. There are a variety of cards covering all the different compliance solutions available in the Compliance Center. These include things like

- Active alerts

- Cloud app compliance

- DLP policy matches

- Discover shadow IT

- High-risk apps

- Microsoft Compliance Score

- Pending dispositions

- Retention label usage

- Files shared outside your organization

- The compliance solution catalog

- Third-party DLP policy matches

- Users with the most shared files

Going back to the homepage, let us look at the left-hand navigation to understand better what you can do inside the Microsoft 365 Compliance Center. I have matched the chapter names to the solution names listed in the left navigation, focusing on the navigation items not mentioned elsewhere.

First, we have our Home button. This button will always take you back to the dashboard view.

Figure 1-2. *The Alerts dashboard in the Microsoft Compliance Center*

Then, we have Alerts. This view will show you alerts from compliance solutions such as Data Loss Prevention and Communication Compliance, shown in Figure 1-2.

Next, we have Reports. Reports allow you to view status and trends for the compliance of your Microsoft 365 devices, data, identities, apps, and infrastructure. The reports are divided into various areas, such as labels, organizational data, compliance, and more.

The Policies navigation item contains links to other areas of the Compliance Center. It is not very useful, in my opinion.

The Permissions navigation item brings you to a page containing the types and number of admins assigned across security and compliance. You can click an item to open a pane listing the name of the admins. More useful is the description at the top of the page. It says, "To view and manage roles in Office 365, please go here." Click "here" to go to the page to manage the Compliance Center permissions. We will discuss permissions later in this chapter and then again within each chapter.

Next, we have the catalog. The catalog is a way to find and use the Microsoft 365 Compliance Center solutions. They are divided into three sections: information protection and governance, insider risk management, and discover and respond.

Figure 1-3. *A solution in the catalog in the Compliance Center*

Under each heading are the solutions that correspond to that area and a description of each solution. Click one of the solutions. Here you can see the solution details such as an overview, benefits of the solution, and what is new in the most recent release of the solution, shown in Figure 1-3. You can also see how the solution impacts your Compliance Score and then requirements for the solution, such as the subscription you need, links to documentation, and helpful how-to videos to help you learn more about the solution. You can click Show in navigation for the solution to appear in your left-hand navigation or click Share to share the solution with a colleague.

The Settings navigation item provides access to some global settings for compliance solutions. As of the time of writing, this includes global settings for Compliance Manager, which we describe in Chapter 2. It also provides device onboarding for Endpoint DLP (Data Loss Prevention), briefly reviewed in Chapter 6.

Next, we have More Resources. Compliance is a vast topic. Sometimes, actions need to be performed outside the Microsoft 365 Compliance Center, such as working with security information, the Service Trust Portal, or solutions in the legacy Security and Compliance Center. You can access those resources in the More Resources link.

The Customize navigation item allows you to change the left navigation. You can show or hide navigation items, and other people will not see your changes. Click Customize Navigation to bring up a screen where you can select the solutions you want to show in the left-hand navigation.

Tip   If you are a compliance admin or using a test tenant, choose Select all at the top of the navigation item list to always see all the compliance solutions.

That is it for the Microsoft 365 Compliance Center. As somebody working with compliance in your organization, this portal will become your best friend, so please bookmark it.

Compliance Permissions

Compliance permissions can be complicated, especially if you want to follow the security best practice of least permissions. Least permissions mean that all users should log on with a user account with the absolute minimum permissions necessary to complete the current task and nothing more. For example, you could give someone permission to search but not export the data from the search. Or a paralegal could manage custodian communications but not be allowed to perform any other tasks. This approach works well when you want to increase security and reduce risk.

Microsoft 365 manages permissions using roles and role groups. Roles are what grant permission to perform the task. You add a role or roles to a role group and then add people to the role group to permit them to complete a task. Microsoft has provided several default role groups. Some of them work well for a least permissions approach, and some of them do not.

If you have a small, centralized compliance team, then the default role groups may work for you. But I see most large organizations creating custom role groups that meet their needs.

To grant someone permission through a default role group, follow these steps:

1. Visit `https://protection.office.com/permissions`.

2. Search for the name of the role group and click it.

3. Click Edit role group.

4. Click Choose Members in the left navigation of the pop-up window.

5. Click Choose members ➤ Add.

6. Search for the name of the person you want to add and check the box next to their name.

7. Click Add, then Done, and then Save.

To create a new custom role group, follow these steps:

1. Visit `https://protection.office.com/permissions`.

2. Click Create.

3. Name your role group. Click Next.

4. Click Choose roles ➤ Add. Pick from the default list of roles described in the next section. You can choose one or all the roles. Click Done and then Next.

5. Click Choose Members in the left navigation of the pop-up window.

6. Click Choose members ➤Add.

7. Search for the name of the person you want to add and check the box next to their name.

8. Click Add, then Done, and then Next.

9. Review your settings and click Create role group.

Tip   If you evaluate the compliance solutions in a dev or test environment and do not need to test permissions, create a default role group that contains all the roles and add evaluators to that role group.

At the beginning of each chapter, I will review the permission roles needed for that specific solution and the default role groups that contain the roles. This way, you can understand what permissions you need for that solution.

The remainder of this section reviews the default roles in the Compliance Center and the default role groups. You can use this information as a reference as you build your permissions model for compliance.

I can best explain the roles and role groups in an Excel table, rather than a list. I created a compliance permission planning spreadsheet, which I will keep up to date as the permission roles and groups change: `http://erica.news/CompliancePermissions`.

Roles

- **Audit Logs**: Turn on and configure auditing for the organization, view the organization's audit reports, and then export them to a file.

- **Case Management**: Create, edit, delete, and control access to eDiscovery cases.

- **Communication**: Manage all communications with the custodians.

- **Communication Compliance Admin**: Used to manage policies in the Communication Compliance feature.

- **Communication Compliance Analysis**: Used to perform an investigation and remediation of the message violations in the Communication Compliance feature. Can only view message metadata.

- **Communication Compliance Case Management**: Used to access Communication Compliance cases.

- **Communication Compliance Investigation**: Used to perform investigation, remediation, and review of message violations in the Communication Compliance feature. Can view message metadata and messages.

- **Communication Compliance Viewer**: Used to access reports and widgets in the Communication Compliance feature.

- **Compliance Administrator**: View and edit settings and reports for compliance features.

- **Compliance Manager Administration**: Manage assessments and template and tenant data.

- **Compliance Manager Assessment**: Create assessments, implement improvement actions, and update test status for improvement actions.

- **Compliance Manager Contribution**: Create assessments and perform work to implement improvement actions.

- **Compliance Manager Reader**: View all Compliance Manager content except for administrator functions.

- **Compliance Search**: Perform searches across mailboxes and get an estimate of the results.

- **Custodian**: Identify and manage custodians for Advanced eDiscovery cases.

- **Data Classification Content Viewer**: View in-place rendering of files in content explorer.

- **Data Classification Feedback Provider**: Allows providing feedback to classifiers in content explorer.

- **Data Classification Feedback Reviewer**: Allows reviewing feedback from classifiers in feedback explorer.

- **Data Classification List Viewer**: View the list of files in content explorer.

- **Data Investigation Management**: Create, edit, delete, and control access to data investigations.

- **Device Management**: View and edit settings and reports for device management features.

- **Disposition Management**: Control permissions for accessing Manual Disposition in the Security and Compliance Center.

- **DLP Compliance Management**: View and edit settings and reports for data loss prevention (DLP) policies.

- **Export**: Export mailbox and site content that is returned from searches.

- **Hold**: Place content in mailboxes, sites, and public folders on hold.

- **IB Compliance Management**: View, create, remove, modify, and test Information Barrier policies.

- **Insider Risk Management Admin**: Create, edit, delete, and control access to the Insider Risk Management feature.

- **Insider Risk Management Analysis**: Access all insider risk management alerts, cases, and notice templates.

- **Insider Risk Management Investigation**: Access all insider risk management alerts, cases, and notice templates and content explorer for all cases.

- **Insider Risk Management Permanent Contribution**: This role group is visible but used by background services only.

- **Insider Risk Management Temporary Contribution**: This role group is visible but used by background services only.

- **Manage Alerts**: View and edit settings and reports for alerts.

- **Organization Configuration**: Run, view, and export audit reports and manage compliance policies for DLP, devices, and preservation.

- **Preview**: View a list of items returned from content searches and open each item from the list to view its contents.

- **Quarantine**: Allows viewing and releasing quarantined emails.

- **RecordManagement**: View and edit the configuration and reports for the Records Management feature.

- **Retention Management**: Manage retention policies.

- **Review**: Use Advanced eDiscovery to track, tag, analyze, and test documents assigned to the reviewer.

- **RMS Decrypt**: Decrypt RMS-protected content when exporting search results.

- **Role Management**: Manage role group membership and create or delete custom role groups.

- **Search and Purge**: Lets people bulk-remove data that match the criteria of a content search.

- **Security Administrator**: View and edit the configuration and reports for security features.

- **Security Reader**: View the configuration and reports for security features.

- **Sensitivity Label Administrator**: View, create, modify, and remove sensitivity labels.

- **Sensitivity Label Reader**: View the configuration and usage of sensitivity labels.

- **Service Assurance View**: Download the available documents from the Service Assurance section.

- **Supervisory Review Administrator**: Manage supervisory review policies, including which communications to review and who should perform the review.

- **View-Only Audit Logs**: View and export audit reports. Because these reports might contain sensitive information, you should only assign this role to people with a clear need to view this information.

- **View-Only Device Management**: View the configuration and reports for the Device Management feature.

- **View-Only DLP Compliance Management**: View the settings and reports for data loss prevention (DLP) policies.

- **View-Only IB Compliance Management**: View the configuration and reports for the Information Barriers feature.

- **View-Only Manage Alerts**: View the configuration and reports for the Manage Alerts feature.

- **View-Only Recipients**: View information about users and groups.

- **View-Only Record Management**: View the configuration and reports for the Records Management feature.

- **View-Only Retention Management**: View the configuration and reports for the Retention Management feature.

Default Role Groups

In this section, we review the purpose of the default role groups and then list their roles.

- **Communication Compliance**: Provides permission to all the communication compliance roles: administrator, analyst, investigator, and viewer.

  - Case Management

  - Communication Compliance Admin

  - Communication Compliance Analysis

  - Communication Compliance Case Management

  - Communication Compliance Investigation

  - Communication Compliance Viewer

  - Data Classification Feedback Provider

  - View-Only Case

- **Communication Compliance Administrators**: Administrators of communication compliance can create/edit policies and define global settings.

  - Communication Compliance Admin

  - Communication Compliance Case Management

- **Communication Compliance Analysts**: Analysts of communication compliance can investigate policy matches, view message metadata, and take remediation actions.

    - Communication Compliance Analysis

    - Communication Compliance Case Management

- **Communication Compliance Investigators**: Investigators of communication compliance can investigate policy matches, view message content, and take remediation actions.

    - Case Management

    - Communication Compliance Analysis

    - Communication Compliance Case Management

    - Communication Compliance Investigation

    - Data Classification Feedback Provider

    - View-Only Case

- **Communication Compliance Viewers**: Viewers of communication compliance can access the available reports and widgets.

    - Communication Compliance Case Management

    - Communication Compliance Viewer

- **Compliance Administrator**: Members can manage settings for device management, data loss prevention, reports, and preservation.

    - Case Management

    - Communication Compliance Admin

    - Communication Compliance Analysis

    - Communication Compliance Case Management

    - Communication Compliance Investigation

    - Communication Compliance Viewer

    - Compliance Administrator

    - Compliance Manager Administration

- Compliance Manager Assessment

- Compliance Search

- Data Classification Feedback Provider

- Data Classification Feedback Reviewer

- Data Investigation Management

- Device Management

- Disposition Management

- DLP Compliance Management

- Hold

- IB Compliance Manager

- Manage Alerts

- Organization Configuration

- RecordManagement

- Retention Management

- View-Only Audit Logs

- View-Only Device Management

- View-Only DLP Compliance Management

- View-Only IB Compliance Management

- View-Only Manage Alerts

- View-Only Recipients

- View-Only Record Management

- View-Only Retention Management

- **Compliance Data Administrator:** Members can manage settings for device management, data protection, data loss prevention, reports, and preservation.

  - Compliance Administrator

  - Compliance Manager Administer

- Compliance Search

- Device Management

- Disposition Management

- DLP Compliance Management

- IB Compliance Manager

- Manage Alerts

- Organization Configuration

- RecordManagement

- Retention Management

- Sensitivity Label Administrator

- View-Only Audit Logs

- View-Only Device Management

- View-Only DLP Compliance Management

- View-Only IB Compliance Management

- View-Only Manage Alerts

- View-Only Recipients

- View-Only Record Management

- View-Only Retention Management

- **Compliance Manager Administrators**: Manage template creation and modification.

  - Compliance Manager Administration

  - Compliance Manager Assessment

  - Compliance Manager Contribution

  - Compliance Manager Reader

- **Compliance Manager Assessors**: Create assessments, implement improvement actions, and update test status for improvement actions.

- Compliance Manager Assessment
- Compliance Manager Contribution
- Compliance Manager Reader

- **Compliance Manager Contributors**: Create assessments and perform work to implement improvement actions.

  - Compliance Manager Contribution

  - Compliance Manager Reader

- **Compliance Manager Readers**: View all Compliance Manager content except for administrator functions.

  - Compliance Manager Reader

- **Content Explorer Content Viewer**: View the contents of files in content explorer.

  - Data Classification Content Viewer

- **Content Explorer List Viewer**: View all items in content explorer in list format only.

  - Data Classification List Viewer

- **Data Investigator**: Members can perform searches on mailboxes, SharePoint sites, and OneDrive accounts.

  - Communication

  - Compliance Search

  - Custodian

  - Data Investigation Management

  - Export

  - Preview

  - Review

  - RMS Decrypt

  - Search and Purge

- **eDiscovery Manager**: Members can perform searches and place holds on mailboxes, SharePoint online sites, and OneDrive for Business locations. Members can also create and manage eDiscovery cases, add and remove members to and from a case, create and edit content searches associated with a case, and access case data in Advanced eDiscovery.

  - Case Management

  - Communication

  - Compliance Search

  - Custodian

  - Export

  - Hold

  - Preview

  - Review

  - RMS Decrypt

- **Global Reader**: Members have read-only access to reports and alerts and can see all the configuration and settings.

  - Security Reader

  - Sensitivity Label Reader

  - Service Assurance View

  - View-Only Audit Logs

  - View-Only Device Management

  - View-Only DLP Compliance Management

  - View-Only IB Compliance Management

  - View-Only Manage Alerts

  - View-Only Recipients

  - View-Only Record Management

  - View-Only Retention Management

- **Insider Risk Management**: Use this role group to manage your organization's insider risks in a single group.

  - Case Management
  - Insider Risk Management Admin
  - Insider Risk Management Analysis
  - Insider Risk Management Investigation
  - Insider Risk Management Temporary Contribution

- **Insider Risk Management Admins**: Use this role group to configure insider risk management and later segregate insider risk administrators into a defined group.

  - Case Management
  - Insider Risk Management Admin

- **Insider Risk Management Analysts**: Use this group to assign permissions to users who will act as insider risk case analysts.

  - Case Management
  - Insider Risk Management Analysis

- **Insider Risk Management Investigators**: Use this group to assign permissions to users who will act as insider risk data investigators.

  - Case Management
  - Insider Risk Management Investigation

- **IRM Contributors**: This role group is visible but used by background services only.

  - Insider Risk Management Temporary Contribution

- **MailFlow Administrator**: Members can monitor and view mail flow insights and reports in the Security and Compliance Center.

  - View-Only Recipients

- **Organization Management**: Members can monitor and view mail flow insights and reports in the Security and Compliance Center. Members can control permissions for accessing features in the Security and Compliance Center and manage settings for device management, data loss prevention, reports, and preservation.

  - Audit Logs

  - Case Management

  - Compliance Administrator

  - Device Management

  - DLP Compliance Management

  - Hold

  - IB Compliance Manager

  - Manage Alerts

  - Organization Configuration

  - Quarantine

  - RecordManagement

  - Retention Management

  - Role Management

  - Search and Purge

  - Security Administrator

  - Security Reader

  - Sensitivity Label Administrator

  - Sensitivity Label Reader

  - Service Assurance Viewer

  - View-Only Audit Logs

  - View-Only Device Management

  - View-Only DLP Compliance Management

- View-Only IB Compliance Management

- View-Only Manage Alerts

- View-Only Recipients

- View-Only Record Management

- View-Only Retention Management

- **Quarantine Administrator**: Manage and control quarantined messages.

  - Quarantine

- **Records Management**: Members can manage and dispose of record content.

  - RecordManagement

- **Reviewer**: Members can only view the list of cases on the eDiscovery Cases page in the Security and Compliance Center.

  - Review

- **Security Administrator**: Members have access to many security features of the Identity Protection Center, Privileged Identity Management, Monitor Microsoft 365 Service Health, and Security and Compliance Center.

  - Audit Logs

  - Compliance Manager Administration

  - Device Management

  - DLP Compliance Management

  - IB Compliance Management

  - Manage Alerts

  - Quarantine

  - Security Administrator

  - Sensitivity Label Administrator

  - View-Only Audit Logs

- View-Only Device Management

- View-Only DLP Compliance Management

- View-Only IB Compliance Management

- View-Only Manage Alerts

- **Security Operator**: Members can manage security alerts and view reports and settings of security features.

  - Compliance Search

  - Compliance Manager Administration

  - Device Management

  - DLP Compliance Management

  - IB Compliance Management

  - Manage Alerts

  - Quarantine

  - Security Administrator

  - Sensitivity Label Administrator

  - View-Only Audit Logs

  - View-Only Device Management

  - View-Only DLP Compliance Management

  - View-Only IB Compliance Management

  - View-Only Manage Alerts

- **Security Reader**: Members have read-only access to many security features of the Identity Protection Center, Privileged Identity Management, Monitor Microsoft 365 Service Health, and Security and Compliance Center.

  - Security Reader

  - Sensitivity Label Reader

  - View-Only Device Management

- View-Only DLP Compliance Management

- View-Only IB Compliance Management

- View-Only Manage Alerts

- **Service Assurance User**: Members can access the Service Assurance section in the Security and Compliance Center.

  - Service Assurance Viewer

- **Supervisory Review**: Members can create and manage the policies that define which communications are subject to review in an organization.

  - Supervisory Review Administrator

Where Microsoft 365 Stores Content

In the upcoming chapters, you will see some of the compliance features rely on understanding where Microsoft 365 stores content. For example, you may need to understand where Microsoft 365 stores the compliance records for Teams chats to find them in an eDiscovery search.

All files in Microsoft 365 get stored in either SharePoint or OneDrive. SharePoint is typically the location for collaborative documents, while OneDrive is for personal documents or files shared with a small group of people. I find that people will store documents in SharePoint when there is an obvious place to put them and put them in OneDrive when they do not know where else to save something.

The system stores files shared in Microsoft Teams in SharePoint or OneDrive. It stores files shared in 1:1 or 1:Many chats in a folder in OneDrive called Microsoft Teams Chat Files. Files shared through a Microsoft Team, either in a message or in the files tab, get stored in the SharePoint site's document library. The system automatically creates this site along with the Team. Each Team's channel gets a folder in the document library.

Microsoft Teams chat and channel messages get stored in the Azure chat substrate, which is not accessible through the compliance tools. A copy of each message or chat is created and stored in Exchange mailboxes to enable compliance solutions, such as retention, eDiscovery, and Communication Compliance. The compliance copy of chat messages is stored in a hidden folder in each participant's user mailbox. When you create a Team, an Exchange group mailbox is created for that Team. The compliance copy of channel messages is kept in a hidden folder in that group mailbox.

Microsoft Teams private channels are a bit different. Teams creates a new SharePoint site for each private channel to store files. Messages sent in a private channel are stored in each user's mailbox instead of the group mailbox.

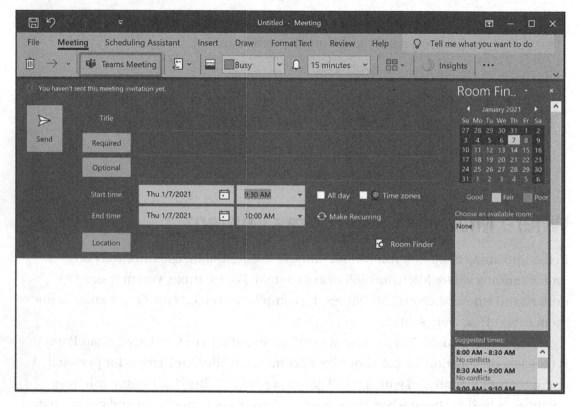

Figure 1-4. *The Teams Meeting button in a new Outlook meeting*

When you record a meeting using Microsoft Teams, it gets stored in either SharePoint or OneDrive as a file. If you scheduled the meeting using the Microsoft Teams interface and specified a channel, the meeting recording is stored in the associated Team SharePoint site. If the meeting was created using Outlook and the Teams Meeting button, shown in Figure 1-4, then the recording and related meeting chats are stored in OneDrive.

Items such as email messages, calendar items, Outlook tasks, and traditional email attachments are stored in Exchange, in either a user or group mailbox.

If you want Yammer messages and files to be available for compliance solutions, your network needs to be running in native mode. If you created your Yammer network before January 2020, you would need to transition to native mode. Networks created after January 2020 are already running in native mode.

Yammer content is stored like how Microsoft 365 stores Teams content. For example, a copy of the Yammer group's posts gets stored in the Exchange group mailbox associated with the Yammer group for compliance purposes. Files shared in a group are stored in SharePoint. A copy of Yammer private messages is stored in individual mailboxes. Users cannot share files in a private Yammer message.

Chapter 1 went through introducing compliance solutions, why they exist, and their value to an organization. We went over the Microsoft compliance solutions at a high level. We also reviewed permissions and licensing for the Microsoft 365 compliance solutions. We introduced the Compliance Center and discussed where compliance content is stored in Microsoft 365.

In the next chapter, we will review the Compliance Manager solution. This solution is a great place to start with compliance, especially if you are interested in being compliant with a specific regulation.

CHAPTER 2

Compliance Manager

Compliance Manager simplifies compliance and reduces risk. It offers continuous assessments to detect and monitor the effectiveness of compliance controls with a risk-based score. Compliance Manager provides recommended actions to reduce compliance risks with actionable guidance. Compliance Manager also has built-in control mapping to scale your compliance efforts with built-in mapping across regulations and standards.

This chapter will help you understand why you should use Compliance Manager to assess your organization's compliance and risk posture. We will talk about how to use each component of Compliance Manager and how Microsoft calculates the score. Finally, we will also look at the Service Trust Portal and how you can access Microsoft audit reports, information on controls, and more.

IT and cybersecurity risks are a big concern for risk management. Amid all the challenges in risk management, identifying and assessing risk continues to be a time-consuming task. Many companies rely on point-in-time assessments like auditing, which are manual and can quickly go out of date. This situation exposes companies to unidentified risks in between audits.

It is essential to equip IT professionals with the knowledge and tools to work with compliance and risk teams to assess and monitor risks effectively. Compliance Manager helps you to simplify compliance and reduce risk.

I typically see customers using Compliance Manager to help track their compliance efforts toward a goal like being GDPR or CCPA compliant. Compliance Manager is beneficial for mapping controls from those regulations, which are the steps you need to complete to be compliant, directly to the actions you can take in Microsoft 365 to accomplish those goals.

E. Toelle, *Microsoft 365 Compliance*, https://doi.org/10.1007/978-1-4842-5778-4_2

An Overview of Compliance Manager

Compliance Manager is a solution in the Office 365 Compliance Center. It makes it easy for IT admins and compliance stakeholders to help their organizations manage data protection controls and meet compliance requirements.

With Compliance Manager, even if you are not an expert in complex regulations, you can still quickly learn the actions recommended to help you progress toward compliance. You can continuously assess and monitor data protection controls. It provides clear guidance on how to improve your score by implementing Microsoft solutions and thus reduce compliance risks. You can leverage the built-in control mapping to scale your compliance efforts across global industrial and regional standards. Here are some of the features and benefits of Compliance Manager:

Scan and detect system settings: Compliance Manager can scan your Microsoft 365 environment and discover your system's settings. It continuously and automatically updates your technical control status. For example, if you configured a compliance policy for Windows devices in the Azure AD (Active Directory) portal, Compliance Manager can detect the setting and reflect that in your score. Conversely, if you have not created the policy, Compliance Manager can flag that as a recommended action for you to take. With the ongoing control assessment, you can proactively maintain compliance instead of reactively fixing settings following an audit.

Improve your score with recommended actions and solutions: Compliance Manager provides you with improvement actions in different areas such as information protection, information governance, device management, and more. These actions allow you to quickly understand the contribution you are making toward organizational compliance by category.

Each recommended action has a different impact on your score, depending on the potential risk involved. This way, you can prioritize essential activities accordingly. You can assess controls using the Assessments View, which shows you the scores of things like GDPR, ISO 27001, HIPAA, and more. Compliance Manager helps make connections between each regulatory requirement and the solutions that can enhance your controls, thus increasing your overall score.

Built-in control mapping: With more than 220 updates from 1,000 regulatory bodies every day around the world, it's overwhelming for organizations to keep up to date with the evolving compliance landscape. Microsoft has more than 1,000 compliance experts building out and maintaining a common control framework to scale their compliance effort. They share this knowledge with organizations to help them scale their compliance program across global industrial and regional regulations and standards with Compliance Manager's built-in control mapping.

Keep in mind that Compliance Manager does not express an absolute measure of organizational compliance with any standard or regulation. It shows the extent to which you have adopted controls, reducing the risks to personal data and individual privacy. You should not interpret recommendations from Compliance Manager as a guarantee of compliance. I recommend that you work with your legal and compliance teams to ensure that your organization meets its compliance requirements.

Compliance Manager supports global, regional, and industrial regulations and standards. As of the writing of this chapter, there are 243 pre-built assessments available in Compliance Manager. Microsoft frequently adds new assessments. Compliance Manager helps make connections between each regulatory requirement and the Microsoft solutions to enhance your controls, thus increasing your overall score. Only the assessments for Data Protection Baseline, GDPR, NIST 800-53, and ISO 27001 are available with your license. Additional assessments are available for purchase as described in the next section.

Permissions and Licensing

Compliance Manager was previously available to all Office 365 subscriptions. However, a recent license change means Compliance Manager is now available only with these licenses:

- Office 365 E5/A5

- Microsoft 365 E5/A5

As mentioned in the preceding text, only the assessments for Data Protection Baseline, GDPR, NIST 800-53, and ISO 27001 are available with these licenses. Additional assessments are considered to be "premium," and you can purchase them individually. As of this writing, Microsoft has not announced the costs for these premium assessments.

To use Compliance Manager, you need to have the correct permissions. Your organization's global administrator can set user permissions in the Microsoft 365 Compliance Center or Azure Active Directory (AAD). Once they set permissions in either of these locations, users will be able to access Compliance Manager. Figure 2-1 below lists the permissions you will need for various tasks.

User can:	Compliance Manager role	Azure AD role
Read but not edit data	Compliance Manager Reader	Azure AD Global Reader, Security Reader
Edit data	Compliance Manager Contribution	Compliance Administrator
Edit test results	Compliance Manager Assessment	Compliance Administrator
Manage assessments and template and tenant data	Compliance Manager Administration	Compliance Administrator, Compliance Data Administrator, Security Administrator
Assign users	Global Administrator	Global Administrator

Figure 2-1. *Compliance Manager permission roles*

Use the preceding chart to determine which permission roles to assign.

How to Use Compliance Manager

Now let us look at how you can use Compliance Manager to assess your organization's compliance posture. Navigate to the Microsoft 365 Compliance Center at `https://compliance.microsoft.com`. On the left-hand side of the page, click Compliance Manager.

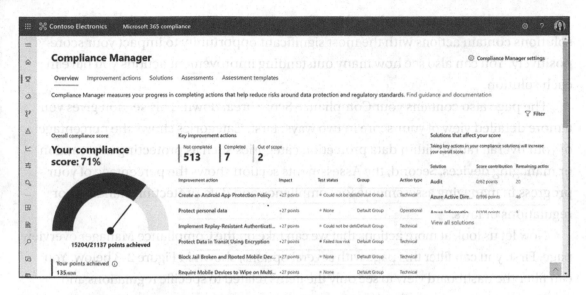

Figure 2-2. *The Compliance Manager dashboard*

This page is the Compliance Manager dashboard, shown in Figure 2-2 above. Your Compliance Score is featured prominently at the top and shows a percentage based on points achievable for completing improvement actions and addressing essential data protection standards and regulations.

When you visit Compliance Manager for the first time, Microsoft bases your initial score on the built-in Microsoft 365 Data Protection Baseline. This baseline is a set of controls that include common industry regulations and standards.

The Data Protection Baseline draws elements primarily from NIST CSF, the National Institute of Standards and Technology Cybersecurity Framework. It also draws from ISO, the International Organization for Standardization, and FedRAMP, the Federal Risk and Authorization Management Program. Lastly, it covers some elements of GDPR, which is the General Data Protection Regulation of the European Union.

Compliance Manager scans your system for existing Microsoft 365 solutions and gives an initial assessment of your compliance posture based on the privacy and security settings currently enabled by your organization. As you add assessments that are relevant to your organization, your score becomes more meaningful.

Also on this page are key improvement actions. This section lists the top improvement actions you can take right now to make the most significant positive impact on your overall Compliance Score. It contains activities that are not completed or failed with the assessment with high risks.

Next on this page are solutions that affect your score. This section shows which solutions contain actions with the most significant opportunity to impact your score positively. You can also see how many outstanding improvement actions you have in each solution.

The page also contains your Compliance Score breakdown. This section gives you a more detailed view of your score in two ways: First, Categories shows the percentage of your overall rating within data protection categories such as protecting information or managing devices. Second, the Assessments section shows the percentage of your progress in managing assessments for compliance and data protection standards or regulations or laws.

Now let us look at more actions that we can take on the Compliance Manager overview page. First, you can filter this page with several options, shown in Figure 2-3 below. You can filter the dashboard view to see only the items related to specific regulations and standards, solutions, type of action, groups, or data protection categories. Filtering your view in this way will also filter the score on your dashboard, showing how many points you've achieved out of total possible points based on your filter criteria.

To apply filters

1. Select Filter on the upper-right side of the dashboard.

2. Select your filter criteria from the fly-out filters pane and then select Apply.

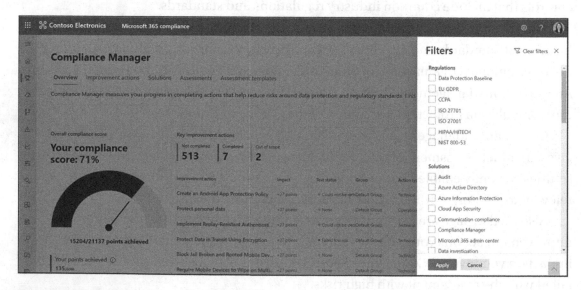

Figure 2-3. *Compliance Manager filters*

You will see your Compliance Score adjusted in real time, and you will only see improvement actions, solutions, and score breakdown information that corresponds to your filter criteria. If you sign out of Compliance Manager, your filter view will remain when you sign back in.

To remove filters, at the Applied Filters heading above your Compliance Score, select the X next to the individual filter you want to delete or choose a filter on the upper-right side of your dashboard and then select Clear filters.

The option to cover on this page is the Compliance Manager settings. You can find these settings in the upper right of the page. Click this text to visit the settings area. Your first option in the settings is Automated testing. You can set up automated testing for your Compliance Manager improvement actions that are jointly monitored by Secure Score. If this option is on, an action tested and updated in Secure Score will sync with the same action in Compliance Manager and update your Compliance Score. Choose to turn on automated testing for all such actions, turn off for all actions, or turn on for individual actions.

The second settings option is the Manage user history. Use these settings to manage the data of users who work with improvement actions. You can export a report of user data, delete user data, and reassign improvement actions to different users. This setting helps you to comply with GDPR and work with natural attrition.

Now let us look at the other tabs in Compliance Manager. We will go through each one of these in detail later in the chapter. Click the Improvement actions tab. This view contains the actions you can take to improve the overall Compliance Score. It lists activities that are not completed or have failed. You can group or filter the view or search for specific items. The filter options are the same as on the previous page.

Tip   The Improvement actions tab shows you the highest-priority items for improving your Compliance Score. This view is a great place to start exploring compliance recommendations for your organization.

Next, let's click the Solutions tab. The Solutions page shows the share of earned and potential points as organized by a solution. Viewing your remaining points and improvement actions from this view helps you understand which solutions need more immediate attention. Again, the filters are the same as the other pages.

Now let's click the Assessments tab. The Assessments page lists the assessments you select to track for your organization. Microsoft determines your Compliance Score denominator from all your tracked assessments. The more assessments you add, the more improvement actions you see on your Improvement actions page and the higher your score denominator.

Each assessment measures the compliance readiness of a product against a regulation or a standard. You can also see a clear view of the number of actions managed by customers and by Microsoft. By default, you will see the Microsoft 365 Data Protection Baseline assessment on the Assessments page. Here I have added more assessments to customize my Compliance Score.

How Microsoft Calculates the Compliance Score

The Compliance Manager dashboard displays a score that measures your progress toward completing improvement actions within controls. Points accrue when you complete activities. Your score is calculated based on the completion of Microsoft-managed actions and customer-managed actions. Each action has a different impact on your score, depending on the potential risks involved. The score can help prioritize which activities to focus on to improve your overall compliance posture.

The displayed Compliance Score values for the controls are applied in their entirety to your total score on a pass-fail basis. Either the control is implemented and passes the subsequent assessment test, or it does not.

Assigned points are added to the Compliance Score when the control has implementation status equal to implemented or alternative implementation and test result equals passed. The sum of points earned by taking improvement actions is the control score. The sum of your control scores is the assessment score. The sum of your assessment scores is your overall Compliance Score.

We will look at each of the Compliance Manager tabs in detail, starting with Improvement actions, then Solutions, and Assessments.

Continuous Assessment of Controls

Compliance Manager automatically scans through your Microsoft 365 environment and detects your system settings. It continuously and automatically updates your technical control status. For example, if you turned on multifactor authentication (MFA) in the Azure AD portal, Compliance Manager detects the setting and reflects that in the controlled access solution details.

Conversely, if you didn't turn on MFA, Compliance Manager flags that as a recommended action for you to take. Compliance Manager updates your control status every 24 hours. Once you follow a recommendation to implement a control, you will see the control status updated the next day.

Compliance Manager tracks two types of actions: Microsoft-managed actions and customer-managed actions. Each of these has points that contribute to your overall score. Customer-managed actions add to your Compliance Score based on controls managed by your organization. Microsoft-managed actions contribute to your Compliance Score based on Microsoft's controls as a cloud service provider.

Actions are assigned a score value based on whether they are mandatory or discretionary and whether they are preventative, detective, or corrective, as described in Table 2-1.

Table 2-1. *Assigned scores of the actions*

Type	Assigned score
Preventative mandatory	27
Preventative discretionary	9
Detective mandatory	3
Detective discretionary	1
Corrective mandatory	3
Corrective discretionary	1

- Mandatory actions cannot be bypassed either intentionally or accidentally. An example is multifactor authentication. Users must comply with using multifactor authentication to access the system.

- Discretionary actions rely on users to understand the policy and act accordingly. For example, a policy requiring users to classify sensitive information manually relies on the end user taking the correct action.

- Preventative actions address specific risks. For example, blocking risky OAuth applications can prevent unintentional data leaks through these applications.

- Detective actions actively monitor systems to identify irregular conditions or behaviors representing a risk or that the system can use to detect intrusions or determine if a breach occurs. An example is to enable auditing in Office 365 to monitor administrator and user actions.

- Corrective actions try to keep the adverse effects of security incidents to a minimum. An example is to review your malware detections report weekly. This report gives you a sense of the overall volume of malware targeted at your users.

Now let us look at improvement actions, which you can complete to improve your Compliance Score. These improvement actions are categorized as mandatory or discretionary and as preventative, detective, or corrective. Its point value is assigned accordingly.

Improvement Actions

First, let's look at the suggested improvement actions. To do that, click the Improvement actions tab.

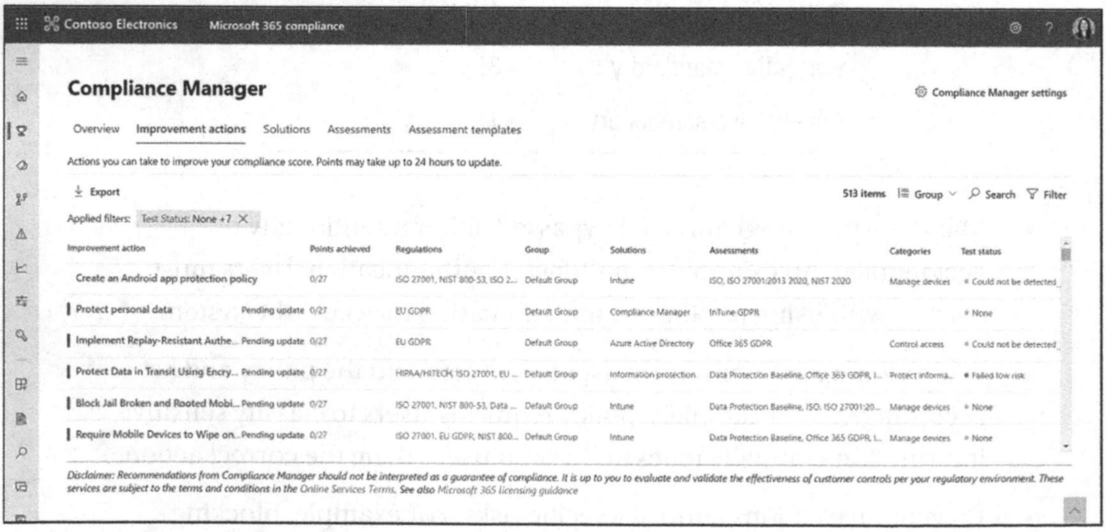

Figure 2-4. *Compliance Manager improvement actions*

Here, you'll see a list of the recommended improvement actions that you can do to increase your compliance posture, shown in Figure 2-4. You can configure this view in a few ways: First, you can group the items by solution category, action type, or status. The view also allows you to search for all the information on this list. A second option is to filter the view based on specific regulations or specific Microsoft solutions. Finally, you can also filter on a group that you've designated, the test status, or the category.

In this view, you can see the improvement action, the points that are achievable or achieved, and the specific regulations that map to this improvement action. This group is something that you designate for your organization, the solution that is involved with the improvement action, the assessments you have added that map to the improvement action, the category, and the test status. Please note that when you complete an activity, points may take up to 24 hours to update. You can also export a list of improvement actions in the filtered view that you've selected.

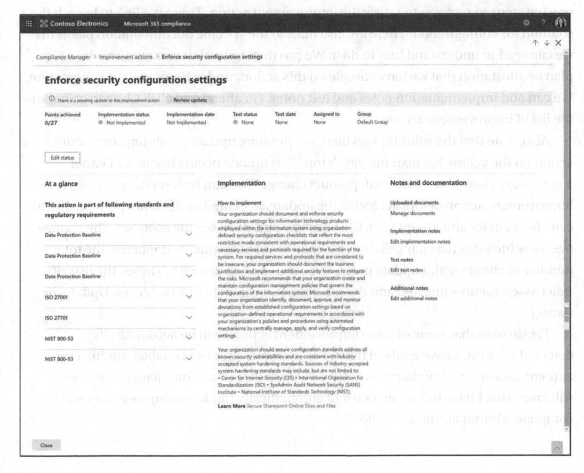

Figure 2-5. *Improvement action details*

Click one of the improvement actions. For example, I'm going to select Enforce security configuration settings. When I click that control, it shows me a variety of information, show in Figure 2-5 above. First, we can see the number of points that we can achieve for Enforce security configuration settings. We can see the current implementation status, implementation date, current test status, test date, person assigned to complete this item, and assigned group. Click Edit status to change any of these fields.

Additionally, we can see that this action is part of specific standards and regulatory requirements, and we can see a list of the rules and regulations. If we expand one of these areas, it shows us the exact control ID, control title, control family, and description from that specific regulation or regulatory requirement. This way, we can know exactly how this action fulfills the condition of that regulation.

We have instructions on implementation that tell us how to implement this action or what steps to perform to satisfy the improvement action. There is a link to launch the solution for configuration. There are also links to the specific documentation pages that we can read to understand how to do it. We can then upload documents, maybe a test plan or attestation that we have completed this action, under Notes and documentation. We can add implementation notes and test notes. Go ahead and click Close to go back to the list of improvement actions.

Also, note that the solution says there is a pending update to this improvement action on the yellow bar near the page's top. This update occurs because of either a regulatory change or a Microsoft product change. You can review changes to this improvement action before accepting the update. Accepted updates are permanent. You can always defer and accept later. Click Review update to see the specifics. The change overview includes the change's date, the number of assessments impacted, the total number of changes, and update notes. Click the Change details tab to see the lists of exact assessments impacted and the specific action changes. Click Accept, Update, or Cancel.

Please note that some of these improvement actions will be automatically detected when you have enabled them. For example, suppose I enabled multifactor authentication for administrators in Office 365. In that case, Compliance Manager will know that I have turned that on and automatically mark this improvement action complete without any manual effort.

Solutions

The solution view is simple, shown in Figure 2-6 below. It lists all the Microsoft technology solutions involved with Compliance Manager. You can filter the list using the usual options. If you'd like to view only the actions for a specific solution, click the blue number at the end of the solution's row.

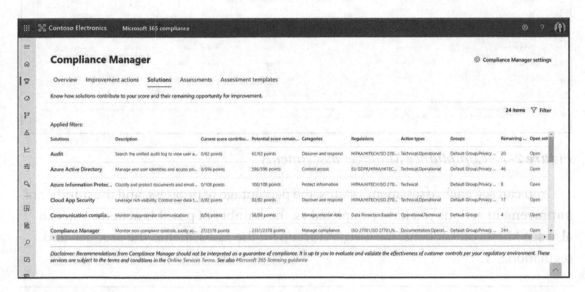

Figure 2-6. *Compliance Manager solutions*

Assessments

The Assessments tab lists all the assessments that you have created for your organization, shown in Figure 2-7 below. You can search, filter, and group your assessments to customize the view.

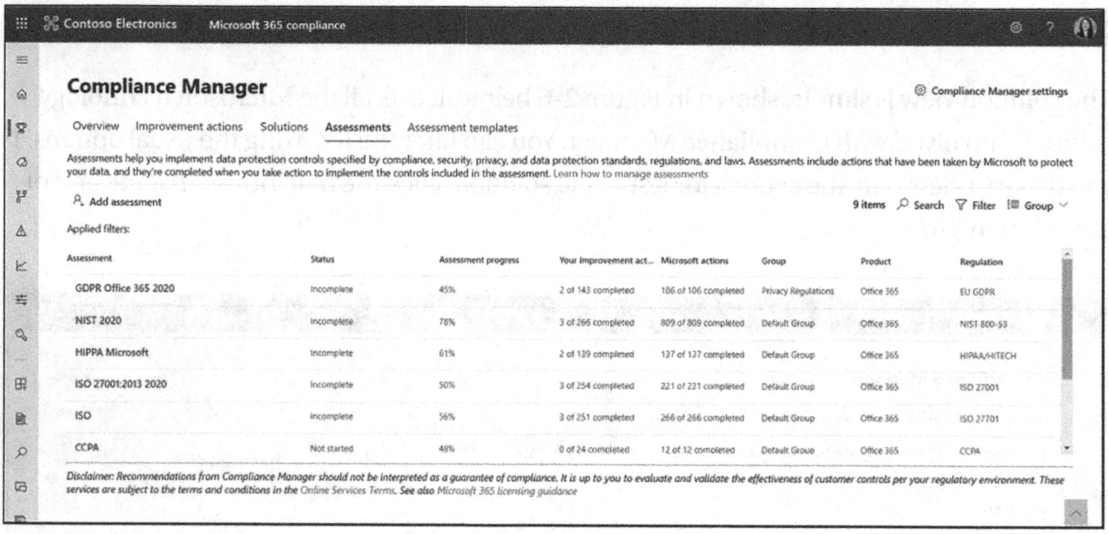

Figure 2-7. *Compliance Manager assessments*

You can see each assessment's status, the percentage of progress, and the number of improvement actions you have completed vs. the number of possible actions. You can also see Microsoft's actions, the assigned group for the assessments, the product, and regulation.

Tip   Adding additional assessments allows you to personalize your organization's Compliance Score, reflecting your compliance goals.

To create a new assessment using one of Microsoft's pre-built templates, click Add assessment.

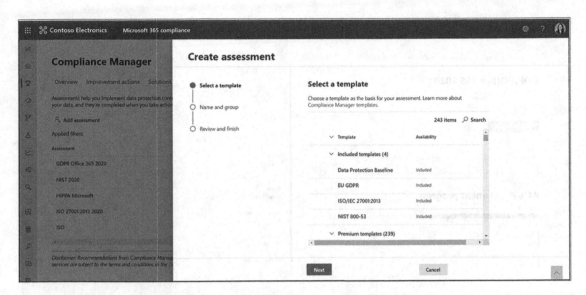

Figure 2-8. *Create a new Compliance Manager assessment*

The first step in the wizard asks you to select a template. It groups the templates by those included in your subscription and premium templates requiring an additional license. Select a template and click Next.

The next screen asks you to name your assessment and select a group. For example, if you need to do a GDPR assessment every year, you might call your assessment GDPR 2021. The group is purely for organization purposes. Click Next. Finally, it asks you to review your settings and click Create Assessment.

Assessment Details

To view the details of a specific assessment, click the name of the assessment. This click will bring you to a dashboard to review the assessment information and understand your progress toward completion.

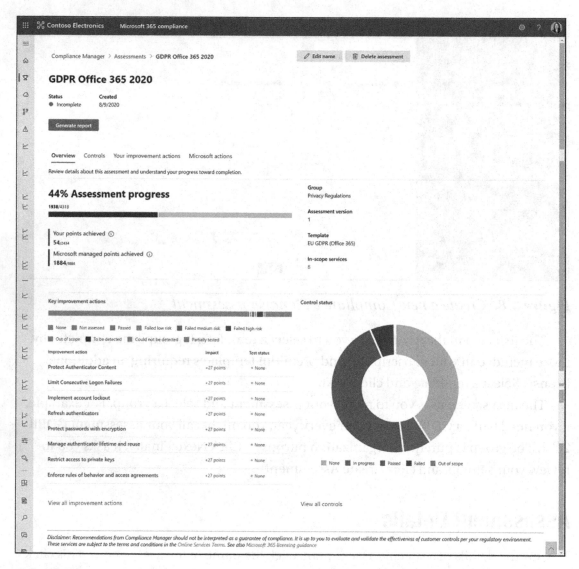

Figure 2-9. *The detailed overview of a Compliance Manager assessment*

On this page, you can see

- The assessment status, which is whether the assessment is marked as incomplete or complete

- The creation date of the assessment

- An option to delete the assessment

- The percentage of assessment progress, including your points achieved and Microsoft managed points achieved

- The assessment group and version

- The template used to create the assessment

- In-scope services

- A graph of key improvement actions and their status

- A list of the highest-value improvement actions

- A graph of the status of controls and a link to view all controls

Additionally, on this page, you can generate a report for the assessment. This report downloads the assessment information as a CSV file. It includes all the information you entered in the actions. You can give this report to an external party, such as internal audit. Also, on the page, you can rename or delete the assessment.

If you click the Controls tab, you will see one of my favorite pages in the Compliance Manager solution. It is my favorite because it is the most accessible view of how you can fulfill the specific requirements for a regulation. It is also where you can see details for the Microsoft completed actions. In our example, the Controls page shows the requirements for meeting GDPR.

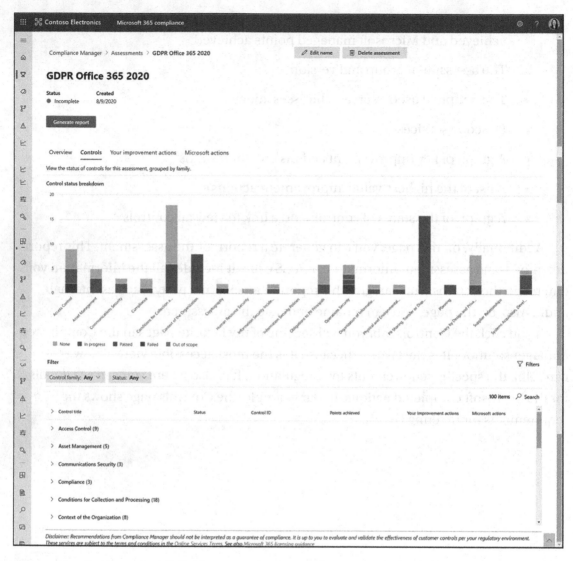

Figure 2-10. *The details of the controls included in your compliance assessment*

Figure 2-10 shows the Controls page. You can see the status of controls, such as communications security, operations security, and so on. Below the graph, you will see a list of the controls. You can filter the list by control family or status.

Click one of the controls to see the description of the control directly from the regulation. Scroll down to see the list of your key improvement actions for that control. You can also see Microsoft's actions.

Figure 2-11. *The details of a Microsoft-managed action*

Click one of the Microsoft actions. Here you can see all the information about the action, such as the implementation and test dates, shown in Figure 2-11 above. You can also view notes about how Microsoft implemented and tested the action.

Create a Custom Assessment

If the built-in assessments do not meet all your requirements or needs, you can create a custom assessment or modify one of the built-in assessments. This feature is useful if your organization has already developed assessments for on-premises or non-Microsoft applications. Compliance Manager can act as a central repository for all assessments. Note that only users who hold a Global Administrator or Compliance Manager Administration role can create and modify assessments.

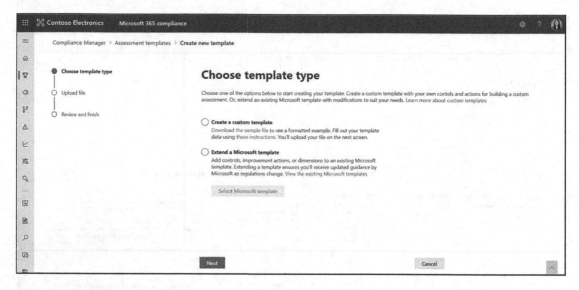

Figure 2-12. *Add a compliance assessment*

Before you start, if you would like to extend an existing assessment, click the assessment, and click Generate report to download the CSV of the existing assessment.

To add a new assessment, click Assessment templates. Click Create new template. Decide whether you want to create a custom template or extend a Microsoft template, shown in Figure 2-12. If you extend an existing template, click Select Microsoft template, and choose from the list. Suppose you create a custom template. Download the sample file, and fill it out using the linked instructions. Make your selection and click Next.

The next step asks you to upload the CSV file you create based on the sample file. It will add this information to an existing Microsoft template or create a new assessment using the information.

Note   Exporting the CSV file of an existing assessment is a great way to get examples and ideas for creating a custom assessment.

The resulting CSV file has four tabs. You must keep the tabs in this order. The following is the information about the tabs and the fields on each tab:

- **Template** (required): The information on this tab provides metadata about the template.

    - **title:** This is the title for your template, which must be unique.

- **product**: List the product associated with the template.

- **certification**: This is the regulation you're using for the template.

- **inScopeServices**: These are the services within the product that this assessment addresses (e.g., if you listed Office 365 as the product, SharePoint could be an in-scope service). You can list multiple services separated by two semicolons.

- **Control Family** (required): This is the information that ties the improvement action to the standard, regulation, or law.

  - **controlName**: This is the control name from the certification, standard, or regulation, typically some type of ID. Control names must be unique within a template. You can't have multiple controls with the same name in the spreadsheet.

  - **controlFamily**: Provide a word or phrase for the controlFamily, which identifies a broad grouping of controls.

  - **controlTitle**: Provide a title for the control. Whereas the controlName is a reference code, the title is a rich text format typically seen in the regulations.

  - **controlDescription**: Describe the control.

  - **controlActionTitle**: This is the title of an action that you want to relate to this control. You can add multiple actions by separating them with two semicolons and no space in between. Every control you list must include at least one action, and the action must exist somewhere. The action could be an action that you list on the Actions tab of this spreadsheet, an action in a different template, or an action created by Microsoft. Different controls can reference the same action.

- **Actions** (required): It designates your organization's actions that you must take to fulfill the requirements of the controls.

  - **actionTitle**: This is the title for your action and is a required field. The title you provide must be unique.

- **implementationType**: List one of the following three implementation types.

  i.   **Operational**: Actions implemented by people and processes

  ii.   **Technical**: Actions completed using technology

  iii. **Documentation**: Actions implemented through documented policies and procedures

- **actionScore**: In this required field, provide a numeric score value for your action. I recommend following the same scoring system described in the previous section on how the Compliance Score is calculated.

- **actionDescriptionTitle**: This is the title of the description and is required. This description title allows you to have the same action in multiple templates and surface a different description in each template.

- **actionDescription**: Describe the action.

- **dimension-Action Purpose**: This is an optional field. If you include it, the header must consist of the "dimension-" prefix. Any dimensions you add here will be used as filters in Compliance Manager and appear on the Compliance Manager's improvement action details page.

- **Dimensions** (optional): If you reference a dimension elsewhere, you need to specify it here if it does not exist in a template you've already created or in a Microsoft template.

  - **dimensionKey**: List as "product," "certifications," or "action purpose."

  - **dimensionValue**: Examples are Office 365, HIPAA, Preventative, and Detective.

Once you finish creating your template, upload it into Compliance Manager by browsing the file and clicking Add to Dashboard.

If you would like to modify your custom assessment later, follow the instructions here: http://erica.news/ModifyAssessment.

In the next section, we will review the Microsoft Service Trust Portal, which provides the documentation for how Microsoft meets compliance requirements.

The Service Trust Portal

The Service Trust Portal contains information about Microsoft's audit reports, penetration tests and security assessments, industry-specific compliance information, regional compliance information, Azure security and compliance blueprints, Microsoft services, risks, assessment information, and other document resources. You can access the portal at `https://servicetrust.microsoft.com`. Users with any Office 365 license can access the portal, and it doesn't require special permissions.

This portal is beneficial for preparing for an audit. It gives the auditor the details of the controls in place on the Microsoft data platforms to which you subscribe. It also provides the results of penetration tests and security assessments. You can also view Azure blueprints and other whitepapers. Additionally, there is a step-by-step risk assessment for Microsoft's platform that you can complete.

You can access audit reports by clicking Trust Documents ➤ Audit Reports in the top navigation. Audit reports contain information about the specific audits conducted on behalf of Microsoft. For example, you can access the latest assessment report demonstrating Microsoft Azure, Dynamics 365, and other online services' compliance with the ISO 9001 frameworks to show your auditor. It lists a description of the document and the date on which the audit occurred, shown in Figure 2-13 below.

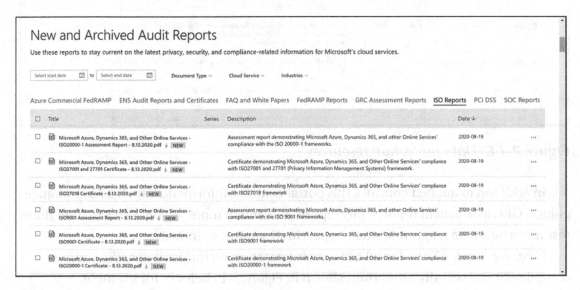

Figure 2-13. Examples of available audit reports

You can filter by audit date, document type, cloud services such as Azure or Office 365, or industries on the page. There are tabs for common types of audit reports.

Next, let's look at the data protection resources, shown in Figure 2-14 below. In the navigation at the top of the page, click Trust Documents and then Data Protection. The data protection resources contain information about how Microsoft cloud services protect your data and how you can manage cloud data security and compliance for your organization. For example, if you're interested in GDPR, there are reports on how GDPR controls map to various services such as Office 365. It shows the audited controls for also different types of regulations.

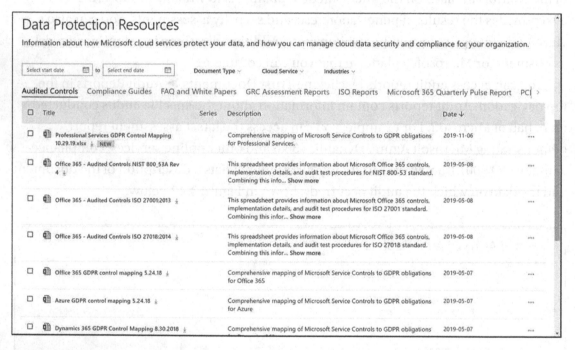

Figure 2-14. *Data protection resources*

In addition to audited controls, this portal contains information such as compliance guides, GRC assessment reports, ISO reports, and much more. Again, you can filter these resources by a date range, document type, cloud service, or industry.

Next, the Service Trust Portal contains information on industry-specific Azure compliance and security blueprints, shown in Figure 2-15 below – for example, blueprints for governments, such as FedRAMP or UK official blueprint, and blueprints for industries such as finance and healthcare or retail. There's also information on industry compliance solutions, so if you're in a specific sector such as financial services, this page can guide you toward information that applies to your organization.

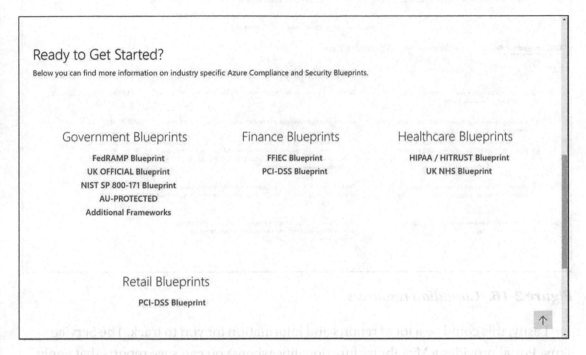

Ready to Get Started?
Below you can find more information on industry specific Azure Compliance and Security Blueprints.

Government Blueprints   Finance Blueprints   Healthcare Blueprints

FedRAMP Blueprint   FFIEC Blueprint   HIPAA / HITRUST Blueprint
UK OFFICIAL Blueprint   PCI-DSS Blueprint   UK NHS Blueprint
NIST SP 800-171 Blueprint
AU-PROTECTED
Additional Frameworks

Retail Blueprints

PCI-DSS Blueprint

Figure 2-15.   Available Azure blueprints

There are also pages for regional compliance resources. For example, if you are a company in Canada, a page lists documents describing how Microsoft's cloud services comply with Canadian policy, regulatory, and legislative requirements, shown in Figure 2-16 below. It provides a filtered view of resources specific to Canadian companies.

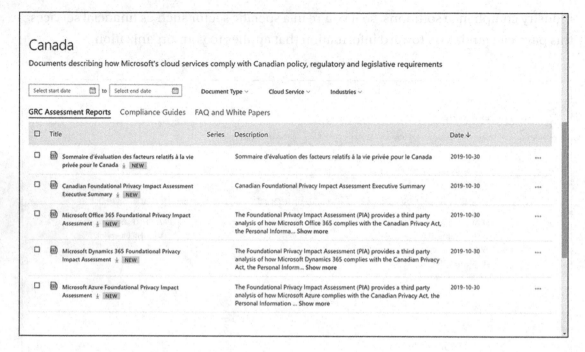

Figure 2-16. *Canadian resources*

Lastly, this could be a lot of reports and information for you to track. The Service Trust Portal provides a My Library functionality, where you can save reports that apply to your organization, shown in Figure 2-17 below. You can even get a notification when updated reports are available via email on a daily, weekly, or monthly digest.

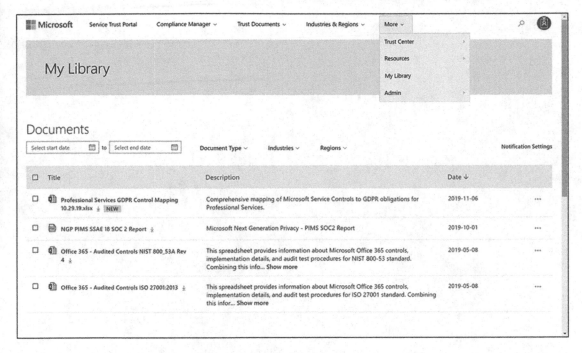

Figure 2-17. *My Library in the Service Trust Portal*

In this chapter, we went over the following topics:

1. What Compliance Manager is and how you use it to understand the compliance risks in your organization.

2. How Microsoft calculates the Compliance Score.

3. How to create and use an assessment.

4. Information about the Service Trust Portal and the content the portal contains.

In the next chapter, we will talk about data classification and how the Compliance Center allows you to create trainable classifiers and sensitive information types and view reports on your sensitivity and retention labels' content and activity.

CHAPTER 3

Data Classification

The Data Classification solutions provide the mechanisms needed to categorize and tag content across all the compliance solutions in Microsoft 365. Microsoft designed the Compliance Center's solutions to govern, protect, and search for information in different ways, depending on your business requirements. The Data Classification solutions provide the foundational features across all the solutions.

Data Classification includes:

1. **Trainable classifiers**: Use machine learning to classify content.

2. **Sensitive information types**: Define patterns of sensitive information like Social Security, credit card, or bank account numbers.

3. **Content explorer**: It shows information that may contain a sensitive information type and content with a sensitivity label or a retention label.

4. **Activity explorer**: It gives you visibility into discovered content, labels, and its location.

For example, the patterns identified using sensitive information types are leveraged by Data Loss Prevention policies, sensitivity labels, retention labels, Communication Compliance, and more. When one of these solutions finds a sensitive information type, you can automatically apply protections.

In this chapter, we will have a section on each of the preceding solutions. In each section, I will discuss why you would use a given solution, including business scenarios as examples. I will also cover licensing and permissions. Then we will go through step-by-step instructions for how to set up and use the solution. Of course, I will mention any best practices and lessons learned along the way.

© Erica Toelle 2021
E. Toelle, *Microsoft 365 Compliance*, https://doi.org/10.1007/978-1-4842-5778-4_3

Trainable Classifiers

Trainable classifiers use machine learning to classify content. They are an excellent option for unstructured data, which is challenging to categorize manually or with automated methods based on content properties. It is easy to classify data in a perfect Microsoft 365 environment, with every document precisely in the right place, with the correct labels or metadata. What is challenging is categorizing content when you do not have any clues about the document contents. Microsoft's trainable classifiers solve this problem using machine learning to find and match patterns in the material. They allow you to find the data that matches the classifier, no matter where it lives.

Once a classifier finds matching information, it can categorize it with a high level of accuracy. After the classifiers are enabled or created, they are low maintenance. You can just let them run, find content, and label it appropriately.

You can use trainable classifiers in the following compliance solutions:

- **Retention labels**: Retain and delete content in Microsoft 365. See Chapters 8 and 9.

- **Sensitivity labels**: Classify and protect your organization's data. See Chapter 5.

- **Communication Compliance**: Minimize communication risks by helping you detect, capture, and take remediation actions for inappropriate messages in your organization. Learn more in Chapter 11.

Licensing and Permissions

Microsoft includes trainable classifiers in the following licenses:

- Microsoft 365 E5

- Microsoft 365 E5 Compliance

- Microsoft 365 E5/A5 Information Protection and Governance

Note   Microsoft does not include trainable classifiers in the Office 365 E5 SKU.

Before you begin, a Microsoft 365 global administrator will need to opt in to trainable classifiers in the tenant. Figure 3-1 shows what a user logged in as a global admin vs. someone who is not a global admin would see.

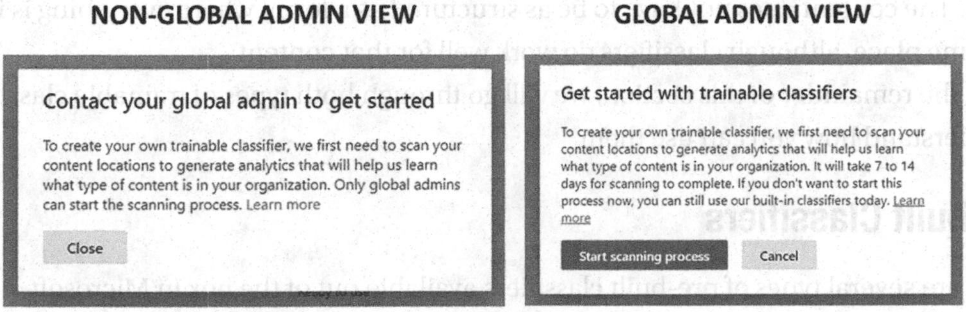

NON-GLOBAL ADMIN VIEW   **GLOBAL ADMIN VIEW**

Contact your global admin to get started

To create your own trainable classifier, we first need to scan your content locations to generate analytics that will help us learn what type of content is in your organization. Only global admins can start the scanning process. Learn more

Close

Get started with trainable classifiers

To create your own trainable classifier, we first need to scan your content locations to generate analytics that will help us learn what type of content is in your organization. It will take 7 to 14 days for scanning to complete. If you don't want to start this process now, you can still use our built-in classifiers today. Learn more

Start scanning process   Cancel

Figure 3-1. *Opt in to the use of trainable classifiers*

Here are the steps:

1. Visit `https://compliance.microsoft.com/` and log in with a global admin account.

2. On the left navigation, click Data classification.

3. Click the Trainable classifiers tab.

To create and train a custom classifier, you need to be a member of one of the following roles:

-   Compliance Administrator

-   Compliance Data Administrator

How to Use Trainable Classifiers

There are two types of trainable classifiers available in Microsoft 365:

1. **Microsoft provides pre-built classifiers** to cover common types of content. You cannot customize them.

2. **Custom classifiers** allow you to create and train a new classifier that is specific to your organization.

Pre-built classifiers are easy to set up and use. They require much less content to test, and they either work for you or they do not.

I have found that custom classifiers work well for somewhat structured content. For example, a proposal uses a standard template, including the same headers, sections, and tables. The content does not have to be as structured as a form, where everything is in the same place, although classifiers do work well for that content.

In the remainder of this section, we will go through both types of trainable classifiers to understand how you can use them.

Pre-built Classifiers

There are several types of pre-built classifiers available out of the box in Microsoft 365. You can access them from the Microsoft Compliance Center. You can use these classifiers right away.

To access trainable classifiers, in the Compliance Center left navigation, click Data classification and the Trainable classifiers tab.

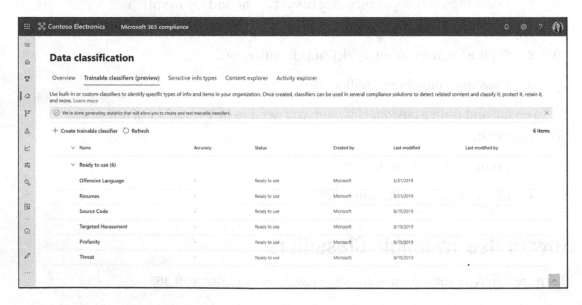

Figure 3-2. *Trainable classifiers*

These are the pre-built classifiers available today (March 2021), shown in Figure 3-2:

- **Offensive Language**: Don't use this classifier. Microsoft is deprecating this built-in classifier because it has been producing a high number of false positives.

- **Resumes**: Detects items that are a textual account of an applicant's personal, educational, and professional qualifications, work experience, and other personally identifiable information. This classifier is especially useful for EU citizens who are subject to the GDPR.

- **Source Code**: This classifier detects items that contain a set of instructions and statements written in widely used computer programming languages. Note that it detects when the bulk of the text is source code. It does not recognize source code interspersed with plain text.

- **Targeted Harassment**: Detects offensive language targeting one or multiple individuals based on the following traits: race, ethnicity, religion, national origin, gender, sexual orientation, age, or disability.

- **Profanity**: This classifier detects text items that contain expressions that would embarrass most people.

- **Threat**: Detects text items related to threats to commit violence or do physical harm or damage to a person or property.

Microsoft announced they would continue to develop additional out-of-the-box classifiers. The preceding pre-built classifiers were available at publishing. Please check the Trainable classifiers tab to see what new classifiers Microsoft has added since the publishing date! Please also note that Microsoft reserves the right to update these classifiers at its discretion.

My customers always start their journey into trainable classifiers by using one of the pre-built classifiers first. Most organizations I work with use the Targeted Harassment, Threat, and Profanity classifiers to monitor code of conduct violations in Communication Compliance. They will start by testing the Resumes pre-built classifier to understand better how the classifiers work for information protection and governance.

In this section, we will use an example of using the Resumes pre-built classifier. If you want to monitor code of conduct violations using Communication Compliance, we will go through that example in Chapter 11.

IMPLEMENT A PRE-BUILT CLASSIFIER

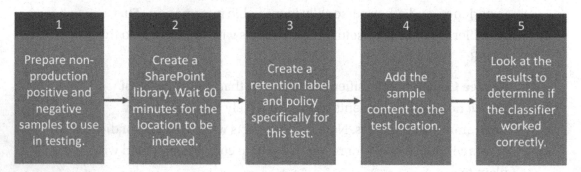

1	2	3	4	5
Prepare non-production positive and negative samples to use in testing.	Create a SharePoint library. Wait 60 minutes for the location to be indexed.	Create a retention label and policy specifically for this test.	Add the sample content to the test location.	Look at the results to determine if the classifier worked correctly.

Figure 3-3. *How to implement a pre-built classifier*

There are five steps to implement a pre-built classifier, shown in Figure 3-3:

1. Prepare non-production positive and negative resumes to use in testing. We will need to have great examples of content in this category and instances of content that we should not include in the group.

2. Create a SharePoint library in a SharePoint site used only to test the Resumes classifier. A best practice is to have one folder in the library for the positive examples and one folder for the negative examples.

3. Create a retention label and policy specifically for this test.

4. Add the sample content to the SharePoint library and folders.

5. Review the results of the pre-built classifier to determine if the classifier worked correctly.

Now, let us go into each one of these steps in detail. For step 1, we will prepare disposable positive and negative resumes to use in testing. These documents can be a copy of real resumes but should not be your essential production copies! We will want to include actual resumes and content that are not resumes but may contain similar information. The goal is to make sure the pre-built classifier can differentiate between what is and is not a resume. You will need a minimum of 200 content pieces for testing, 100 positive and 100 negative samples.

Next, create a new SharePoint library that is used only to test the Resumes classifier. You do not want to reuse an existing SharePoint library or folder for this purpose. Create two folders: one called Positive and one called Negative. Wait one hour until the search index processes the SharePoint library before proceeding to the next step. Do not add content to the folders yet.

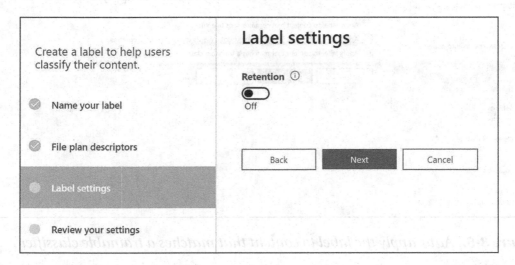

Figure 3-4. Retention label settings

Now, we want to create a retention label. This step is so we can tell if the classifier worked. If the resume samples have the retention label and the negative examples do not, our test was a success. I will go over the settings quickly here, but we describe retention labels in detail in Chapter 8:

1. In the Compliance Center, click Records Management in the left navigation.

2. Click File plan ➤ Create a label ➤ Retention label.

3. Choose a name for the label. Pick a name that you would never want to reuse. Click Next.

4. On the file plan descriptors page, click Next without completing any information.

5. For label settings, keep retention turned off, as shown in Figure 3-4. Click Next.

6. Click Create this label.

7. For the label settings, be sure to keep retention turned off. We do
   not want to apply retention using this label yet, as we are only
   training the classifier.

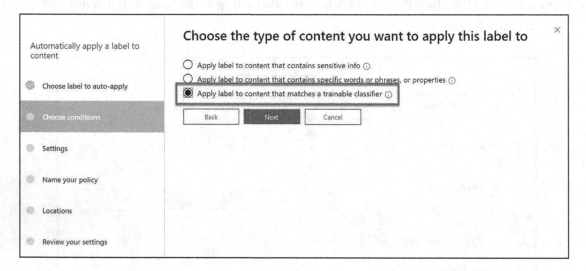

Figure 3-5. *Auto-apply the label to content that matches a trainable classifier*

Then, we need to deploy the label, which tells the label how and where to apply
the label settings. We do that using an auto-applied retention policy. We will go over
retention label policies in detail in Chapters 8 and 9. Here are the steps to complete now:

1. In the same Records Management solution, click the Label
   policies tab. Click Auto-apply a label.

2. Click Choose a label to auto-apply. Check the box next to the label
   you just created. Click Add and then Next.

3. On the Choose conditions screen, select Apply label to content
   that matches a trainable classifier, which is the third option,
   shown in Figure 3-5. Click Next.

4. Select the radio button next to Resumes. Click Next.

5. Name your policy. Again, use a name you will not want to reuse in
   the future.

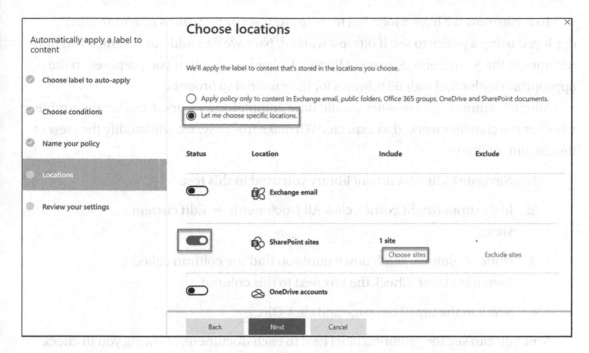

Figure 3-6. *Choose SharePoint as the location and choose your test site*

6. Next, on the Locations screen, select Let me choose specific locations. Turn off all the locations except for SharePoint, as shown in Figure 3-6.

7. Next to SharePoint sites, click Choose sites. Click the Choose sites button again in the new window.

8. In the box that says Type site, paste the URL for the SharePoint site from the first step in this process. Do not include the document library portion of the URL, only the site.

Tip   The URL for your SharePoint site will look like `https://[tenantname].sharepoint.com/sites/[sitename]`. Do not add any additional information after the site name.

---

9. Click the plus sign next to the URL box, and then check the box next to the site below.

10. Click Choose, Done, and Next.

11. Review your settings and click Auto-apply.

To recap, now we have a location to store our test content and a retention label deployed using a policy to see if our test worked. Now we can add our resumes and non-resumes to the SharePoint document library. Upload the content you prepared to the appropriate folder and wait 60 minutes for the material to process.

After 60 minutes, the classifier should have completed its work. Now, we determine whether the classifier worked as expected. To make this easy, we will modify the view of the document library:

1. Navigate to the document library you used in this test.

2. In the upper-right corner, click All Documents ➤ Edit current view.

3. Under Columns, scroll down until you find the column called Retention label. Check the box next to this column.

4. Scroll to the top of the page and click OK.

Now you can see the retention label next to each document, allowing you to check your work quickly. Every resume in the Positive folder should have a retention label, and every document in the Negative folder should not have a label. If this is the case, then congratulations! The built-in classifier worked for you!

If your organization is mature in its use of retention labels, then there is a small chance that a different retention label might be auto-applied to the content. To find out why this occurred, please see the section "The Principles of Retention Policies" in Chapter 8.

If the content was not labeled as expected, please investigate creating a custom classifier instead, which we cover in the next section. You cannot modify a pre-built classifier. It either works for you, or it does not.

Create a Custom Classifier

Next, let us look at how custom classifiers work. Custom classifiers classify content based on what it is, for example, a contract, rather than what it contains, for example, sensitive information or metadata.

As I mentioned in the preceding text, most of my customers start with testing the Resumes pre-built classifier. Once they have gone through that process, they usually have a list of ideas for their custom classifiers. Creating a custom classifier requires a lot of sample content, so they typically choose the classifiers to build based on the availability of seed and test content.

Custom classifiers work best with content that has a similar structure – for example, a contract that has the same sections and headers. It also works with highly structured content, such as a form where content is in the exact place every time.

These custom classifiers are relatively new, released into preview in January 2020. Currently, my customers have only used the classifiers for common, templatized information because it is sure that it will work. It is quite a time investment to train a custom classifier. I have not gotten the opportunity to test the boundaries of how well they work with less structured content. I would love to hear about your experiences using custom classifiers, so please reach out on social media!

A custom classifier learns how to identify a type of content by following two process phases:

- **Seed content**: Looks at hundreds of examples of the documents that you want to classify. Start by feeding it content that are good examples of the content category.

- **Test content**: Once the custom classifier processes the seed data, you can test the classifier's accuracy by providing a mix of both matching and nonmatching samples.

Each process phase has more detailed steps, which we will review in the next sections. However, before you begin to create a custom classifier, it is essential to understand the custom classifier training timeline, which we detail in Figure 3-7.

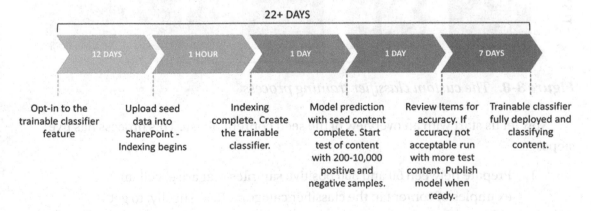

Figure 3-7. *The custom classifier training timeline*

The overall timeline to create your first custom classifier is 22+ days. Subsequent custom classifiers will take a minimum of 10 days. Here is why:

1. After your global admin opts into using classifiers, there is a pre-processing step that runs. This process analyzes all the content in your environment. The analysis will take 7–12 days to complete. Once the process completes, you will see a message at the top of the Trainable Classifiers page that says: We're done generating analytics that will allow you to create and test trainable classifiers.

2. We explain the next steps in detail in the following. Use Figure 3-8 as a quick reference for the timing of each step.

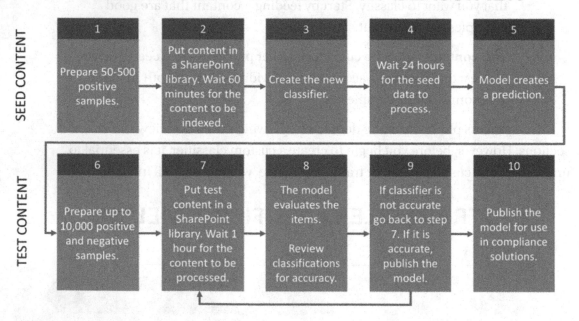

Figure 3-8. The custom classifier training process

Now let us start with an overview of the seed content phase. This process has five steps:

1. Prepare between 50 and 500 positive samples that are excellent examples of content in the classifier category. Realistically, to get the best results, you will need over 200 positive samples.

2. Put the seed content into a SharePoint library. Wait 60 minutes for the content to be indexed.

3. Create the new custom classifier.

4. Wait 24 hours for the seed data to process.

5. The classifier will generate a prediction model.

Next, we start the test content phase. This process also has five steps:

1. Prepare up to 10,000 positive and negative samples. Start with what you can manage, maybe 200 positive and 200 negative documents. You can always add more test content later.

2. Place test content in a SharePoint library.

3. The model evaluates the items. Wait one hour, and then you can review the classifications for accuracy.

4. If a classifier is not accurate, then go back to step 2 of the test content phase. Add more test content to the library, wait an hour for it to be processed, and reevaluate the items. If the classifier is accurate, then you can publish the model.

5. Publish the model for use in compliance solutions.

Now, let us go into more detail about the seed content and test content processes.

The Seed Content Process

First, provide between 50 and 500 positive samples of the content category. The classifier will create the model based on these examples, so make sure they are strong examples of the content. I have found the best results with 200 or more positive samples, and of course, more is better. Be sure to include various file types such as Word, PowerPoint, PDF, and text files if that applies to your category.

Create a new SharePoint library that you use only to train this custom classifier. Do not repurpose an existing SharePoint library, especially one with production data. Wait 60 minutes for the new location to be indexed.

Next, we will want to create the classifier. To do this, visit the Microsoft 365 Compliance Center. In the left-hand navigation, click Data classification. From there, click the Trainable classifiers tab and then Create trainable classifier.

A wizard will start that asks you to name your new trainable classifier. Remember that this is the name that everyone who uses the classifier will see for all time. You cannot change the name later. I recommend using a name that best describes the category of content you want to classify, for example, employment agreement or project contract. Also, enter a description for your new classifier.

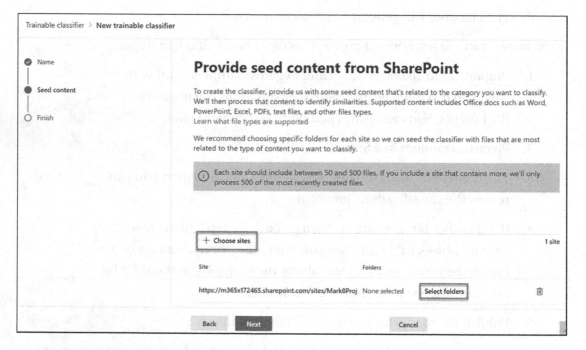

Figure 3-9.   Select your seed content

Next, you will go to a screen that asks you to provide seed content from SharePoint. Click Choose sites, shown in Figure 3-9, and check the box next to the site that contains the seed content. The list will show every site in your organization, so you can search for the site to find it more quickly.

Then click Select folders, also shown in Figure 3-9. The list will show all the libraries in the site. Check the box next to the plus sign to find the folders that contain the seed content. Click Next and then Create trainable classifier.

Now we wait 24 hours for the classifier to process the data. After 24 hours, the seed content model creates a baseline prediction for what content fits in that category. However, we still need to train the model. The test content process teaches the custom classifier more about how to recognize content in the category. If you want to get technical about it, we consider the seed content phase as machine learning, while the test content process is called machine teaching. Now let us review the details of the test content phase!

The Test Content Process

From the Data classification ➤ Trainable classifiers tab, click the name of your custom classifier.

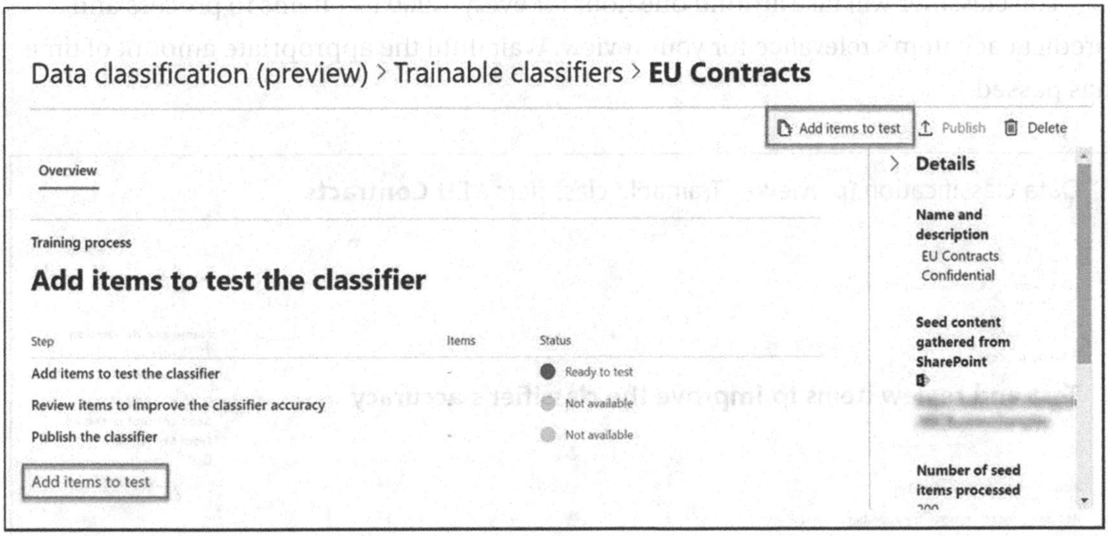

Figure 3-10. *The custom classifier status screen*

This click will bring you to your classifier's status page, as shown in Figure 3-10. The status page shows you the steps you need to complete to teach your classifier and highlights the next step in the process. It also shows you details about the classifier, including the name and description, location of seed content, and the number of items processed in the seed phase.

As you can see in Figure 3-10, the next step is to Add items to test. Prepare a minimum of 200 but up to 10,000 positive and negative samples of your content category. Make sure the sample contains a mix of definite positives, strong negatives, and then some less obvious examples. This way, your classifier will be the most accurate possible. You can have any mix of bad and good examples – for instance, a ratio of 50:50 or 80:20, if you have a minimum of 200 items.

The sample items must not be encrypted and are currently only supported in English. Create a new folder in your SharePoint document library and upload the samples. Wait 60 minutes for the content to be indexed.

Now we will add the test data to the model. Go to the classifier status page. There is a link to Add items to test on this page, as shown in Figure 3-10. Click that link, which will take you to a screen where you can input the document library or folder that contains your test data.

The classifier will take around one hour for every 1,000 test items to process and predict each item's relevance for your review. Wait until the appropriate amount of time has passed.

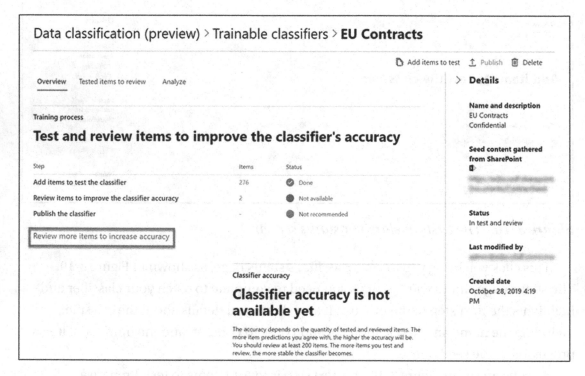

Figure 3-11. *Review more items to increase the classifier accuracy*

Now go back to the trainable classifier status page. In Figure 3-11, you will see that the option to review items to improve the accuracy is available. Also, note that the classifier accuracy is not available until you review at least 200 documents. Click Review more items to increase accuracy. This click takes you to a list of all the items in your test data.

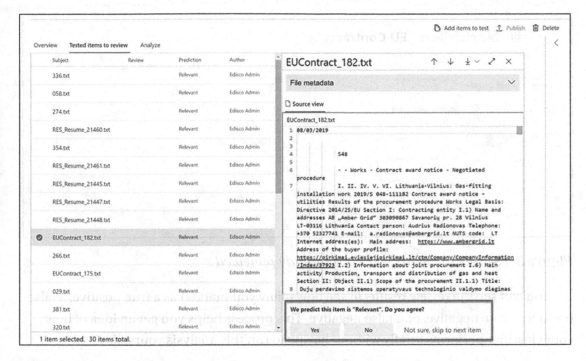

Figure 3-12. *Review your test items for accuracy*

Check the circle next to an item to view the document text, metadata, and prediction model. The prediction states whether the model thinks the item is relevant or irrelevant:

- **Relevant** items are positive examples of the content you would like to categorize. The classifier should mark them as a member of the content category.

- **Irrelevant** items are negative examples of the category, and the classifier should not mark them with the content category.

For each document, the process will ask if you agree with the model's prediction. Figure 3-12 says, "We predict this item is "Relevant". Do you agree?" You can mark Yes, No, or Not sure, skip to next item. You then proceed with each item individually to tell the model whether you agree with its relevancy. This machine teaching process increases the accuracy of the model.

The system will update the accuracy of the model for every 25 items you review. As a part of this process, you can also view the items that you have already reviewed. To do this, click the Analyze tab, as shown in Figure 3-13. You can see the items that you have reviewed and the items that you have not evaluated.

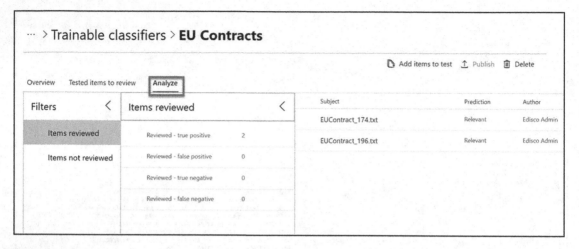

Figure 3-13. *See the items you have already reviewed*

You can see the review results to see how many you marked as a true positive, a false positive, a true negative, or a false negative. This process helps you get an idea of how your classifier performs briefly without having to run this analysis yourself.

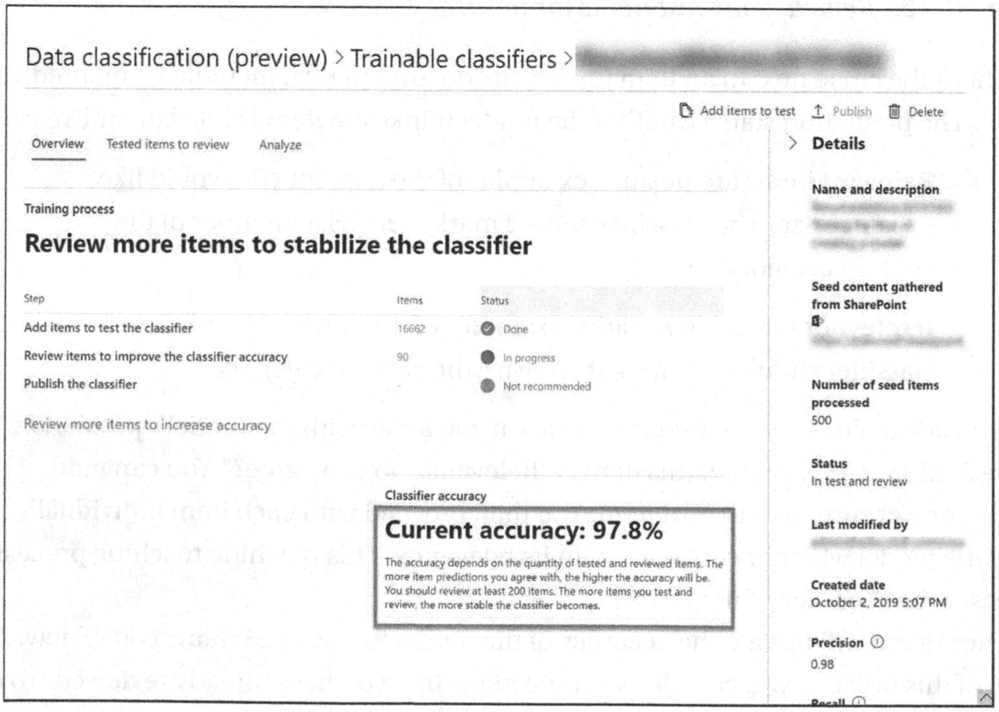

Figure 3-14. *Classifier accuracy*

Keep adding more test documents to the model and reviewing the content as described in the preceding text until you are happy with the model's accuracy. You can view the current accuracy on the classifier status page, shown in Figure 3-14.

The trainable classifier solution will not let you publish the model until the accuracy is at least 70%. Once you publish the classifier, currently, you cannot modify it or review additional items to increase accuracy. However, Microsoft has announced that they will add this ability soon. Make sure that you are pleased with the current accuracy, and then publish your custom classifier!

Voila! You can now use your custom classifier to categorize content for retention, sensitivity, or communication compliance policies. Next, we will look at how we can automatically identify sensitive information in content, such as documents, emails, and Microsoft Teams chats and conversations. All these methods use the same thing to identify sensitive content, called sensitive information types.

Sensitive Information Types

Sensitive information includes bank account numbers, passport numbers, national identity numbers, and other business-critical data. From my experience, there is almost a guarantee that you have sensitive information in your organization in places that you do not realize. Microsoft 365 helps you identify and protect sensitive information using something called a sensitive information type.

Sensitive information types help to identify patterns that indicate that content contains this type of information. They look for things like formats, patterns, proximity to other information, keywords, and more. Microsoft has provided 100 common sensitive information types with Microsoft 365 to get you started, shown in Figure 3-15. You can also create a custom sensitive information type for sensitive information that is unique to your organization.

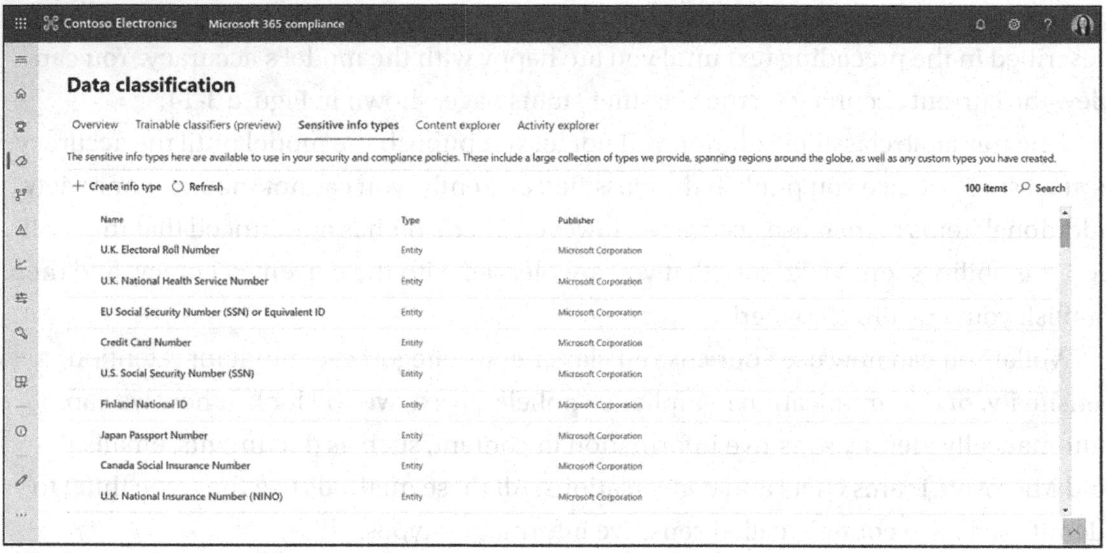

Figure 3-15. *Pre-built sensitive information types from Microsoft*

We use these sensitive information types in other Microsoft 365 compliance solutions – for example, Data Loss Prevention, sensitivity labels, retention labels, Azure information protection, and Microsoft Cloud App Security.

Here are some examples of how I have seen organizations use sensitive information types:

- Block people from sharing sensitive information in emails and Teams chats and channel messages.

- Prevent access to sensitive information by external users, who are people outside of your organization.

- Warn people when they share sensitive information to be sure they are doing the right thing and following corporate policies.

- Encrypt documents that contain sensitive information.

- You could remove sensitive data from Microsoft 365 altogether.

I could easily list 50 more examples of how you can use sensitive information types, but you get the idea. Protection of sensitive data is usually one of the first solutions organizations begin with on their compliance journey.

Licensing and Permissions

Microsoft includes sensitive information types in almost every enterprise Microsoft 365 license type. However, some of the options for using sensitive information types to protect content are only available in some license types. Of course, I will point out these cases in their respective sections of the book. Here are the licenses that include the ability to use the Microsoft-provided sensitive information types and create a custom type:

- Microsoft 365 E5/A5/G5/E3/A3/G3/F1/F3/Business Premium

- Enterprise Mobility + Security F3/E3/E5

- Office 365 E5/A5/E3/A3/F3

You should have global administration or compliance administration access to create, test, and deploy a custom sensitive information type through the user interface.

The permissions needed to use a pre-built sensitive information type will depend on how you are using the type.

How Is a Sensitive Information Type Structured?

What is in a sensitive information type, and how does it recognize information accurately? The first thing to realize is that locating sensitive information is more of an art than a science. You will never be 100% accurate. The goal is to balance the risk of unnecessary exposure of sensitive information with end user productivity. Where is this balance? That is something that you must determine for your organization. It will be the subject of many meetings with your legal and compliance teams.

Any solution that finds and protects sensitive information will require a long period of testing, adjustments to improve accuracy, and more testing. It is essential to understand how we structure sensitive information types so you know how to adjust them properly.

SENSITIVE INFORMATION TYPE

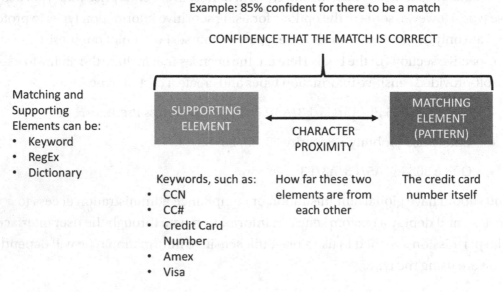

Example: 85% confident for there to be a match

CONFIDENCE THAT THE MATCH IS CORRECT

Matching and
Supporting
Elements can be:
- Keyword
- RegEx
- Dictionary

SUPPORTING ELEMENT

CHARACTER PROXIMITY

MATCHING ELEMENT (PATTERN)

Keywords, such as:
- CCN
- CC#
- Credit Card Number
- Amex
- Visa

How far these two elements are from each other

The credit card number itself

Figure 3-16. *The structure of a sensitive information type*

There are four sections to a sensitive information type, as shown in Figure 3-16:

1. **Matching element**: The pattern of the data itself.

2. **Supporting element**: Increases the likelihood we have found a match when we see this near the matching element.

3. **Character proximity**: The distance between the matching and supporting elements.

4. **Confidence**: A percentage of how sure we are that we have found a correct match.

The first piece of a sensitive information type is the matching element or pattern. This pattern is the data itself, for example, a credit card number or US Social Security number. It will designate whether the pattern contains letters, numbers, spaces, a certain number of characters, dashes, and more. We usually write this pattern as a regular expression (regex), so it is very exact. You could use keywords or a keyword dictionary as your matching elements, but this will have low accuracy, and I do not recommend it.

The second part is the supporting element. The supporting element is additional evidence for your match and can be keywords, regular expressions, or a dictionary of keywords. For example, suppose you were searching for credit card numbers. In that case, the supporting element might be keywords such as CCN, CC#, credit card number, Amex, Visa, or other keywords that designate a credit card number.

Before we get into the third and fourth parts of a sensitive information type, I think this is an excellent time to define keywords, regular expressions, or a keyword dictionary:

- A **regular expression** (regex) is a sequence of characters that define a search pattern. Programmers frequently use them when writing code, and I recommend reaching out to your programming team if you need help writing one.

- **Keyword lists** are text words 1–50 characters in length, containing no special characters. You should place a multi-word keyword between double quotations ("). These lists are limited in size and require modifying XML to create or edit them.

- A **keyword dictionary** allows up to 100,000 terms per dictionary. Dictionaries are modified using PowerShell, so they are easier to edit than keyword lists. We will cover how to create a keyword dictionary in a later section in this chapter.

The third element of a sensitive information type is the character proximity between the matching element and the supporting element. The character proximity defines how far apart these two elements can be to qualify as a match. For example, with a credit card number, one of the supporting elements needs to be within a hundred characters of the matching element. These two elements together give us confidence that we found an actual credit card number.

The fourth part of an info type is the confidence that the match is correct. For example, to be considered a match, you might want to be 85% confident that you found a match before applying protection necessary to manage risk but hinder the end user. The confidence is based on the pattern or matching element, the supporting element, and character proximity.

The output of the sensitive information type is a percent confidence level that the match is correct, plus the number of matches found in the document. The confidence and number of matches are elements we can use later to utilize the sensitive information types to reduce false matches.

What Are Pre-built Sensitive Information Types?

Microsoft provides 100 pre-built sensitive information types that you can immediately use in your environment. The pre-built types have already defined the pattern, supporting elements, character proximity, and confidence for each info type. The content explorer solution, discussed in the next section of this chapter, uses these built-in types to scan for sensitive information in your Microsoft 365 environment proactively.

You can find sensitive information types in the Microsoft 365 Compliance Center. In the left-hand navigation, click Data classification. Then click the Sensitive info types tab. Here you see a list of all the Microsoft-provided sensitive information types. You can also view any information types that have been created by your organization. You can also search to find a specific sensitive information type.

I recommend that you start using the pre-built sensitive information types until there is some reason not to use them. You cannot modify the pre-built information types through the UI. You can still adjust the confidence and frequency information in some of the protection solutions if you get too many false positives.

You may be wondering about the specific details of each pre-built sensitive information type. Fortunately, Microsoft has extensive documentation for what each of these info types contains. You can find the documentation here: `https://erica.news/SensitiveInfoEntityDefinition`. I would also recommend looking at this documentation before building a custom sensitive info type to get ideas about structuring your data. Next, we are covering how to create custom sensitive information types.

Create a Custom Sensitive Information Type

Sometimes the pre-built sensitive information types will not meet the needs of your organization. For example, they might not mirror your sensitive information structure, or you might have unique business-critical information that you would like to protect. In these cases, you can create a custom sensitive information type.

There are four ways that you can create a custom sensitive information type:

1. **Use the user interface**. You can set up a custom sensitive information type using the Compliance Center UI.

2. **Customize a built-in sensitive information type** using PowerShell. You are taking a copy of the pre-built type, modifying it, and publishing a new custom info type.

3. **Use PowerShell**. You can set up custom sensitive information types using PowerShell. Although this method is more complicated than using the UI, you have more configuration options.

4. **Use Exact Data Match (EDM).** You can set up a custom sensitive information type using Exact Data Match–based classification. This method enables you to create a dynamic sensitive information type using a secure database that you refresh periodically.

Let us look at each of these options in more detail.

Create a Sensitive Information Type Using the Compliance Center

Creating a custom sensitive information type via the UI is the easiest of the customization options. It does not require any custom code beyond an optional regex pattern to define the matching element. To create a custom info type, go to the Microsoft 365 Compliance Center. In the left navigation, click Data classification. Next, click the Sensitive info types tab. On this page, click Create info type. This click will open the creation wizard.

On the first screen, choose a name and description. This information will show in the list of sensitive information types, and we will see it throughout other solutions, so choose wisely. Click Next.

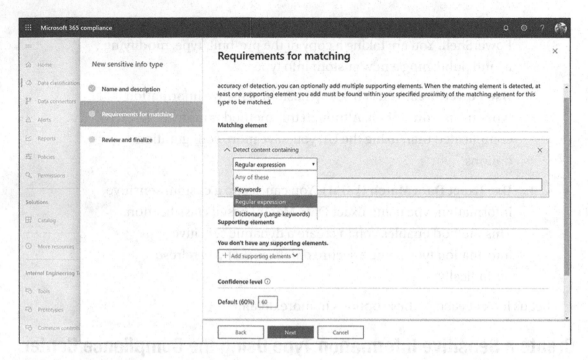

Figure 3-17. *Requirements for matching screen*

On the screen shown in Figure 3-17, we designate the matching elements, supporting elements, confidence level, and proximity for your custom sensitive information type. We went over these in detail in the section "How Is a Sensitive Information Type Structured," so if you skipped it, please go back and take a look.

Here are some tips for completing the information that is unique to creating a sensitive info type via the UI:

- **Keyword**: If it finds any of the keywords, it will be considered a match. You will need to specify the minimum number of keywords found in the pattern to be considered a match. Strings should be in quotes ("").

- **Dictionaries** (large keywords): The instructions for creating a keyword dictionary are covered later in this chapter. Please review that section if you want to use this option.

- I would leave the default confidence (60%) and character proximity (300) unless you have a logical reason to change them. As you test your custom info type, you can increase the confidence or decrease the character proximity as needed if you received too many false positives.

- Custom sensitive information types are generally more successful when the matching element is a regular expression. Keywords or dictionaries work best as supporting elements. Your situation might be different, but use this advice as a starting point and only change it if there is a good reason.

When you have completed these fields, click Next. Review your settings and click Finish. Your sensitive information type will be available to use immediately.

What happens if you try one of the built-in sensitive information types, but it just isn't quite working with you? In the next section, we cover how to modify the built-in sensitive information types.

Customize a Built-In Sensitive Information Type

A few times, I have run into a situation where a customer tested one of the pre-built sensitive information types, but it just did not work for them. They wanted to leverage Microsoft's work but customize it a bit for their organization. This section is a brief introduction on how to do that using PowerShell.

Unfortunately, I will not be going into depth about using PowerShell to customize a pre-built information type. As I said in the introduction, 99% of the questions I get from customers involve what you can do in the UI. And this book is already very long without covering all the cool things you can do with PowerShell. But I want you to know what options exist, which is why I briefly mention it.

Here is a brief overview of how to customize one of the sensitive information types with Microsoft 365:

1. Export all the built-in sensitive information types via PowerShell.

2. Find the XML for the specific rule in the export that you would like to modify.

3. Modify the XML to meet your needs

4. Create a new sensitive information type via PowerShell.

For more detailed instructions on how to customize built-in sensitive information types, see this documentation: https://erica.news/CustomBuiltinInfoType.

Use PowerShell to Create a Custom Sensitive Information Type

Creating a custom sensitive information type using PowerShell is much more powerful than building one in the UI. Here are some examples of why you might use PowerShell:

- Create keywords and sensitive information types in multiple languages.

- Use multiple patterns with corresponding low, medium, and high confidence levels.

- Specify elements that cause false positives, so the info type ignores them.

- Use combinations of evidence to find a match, including child match elements.

For more information about how to use PowerShell to create a sensitive information type, please see this article: `https://erica.news/PowerShellCustomInfoType`.

Use Exact Data Match–Based Classification

What if you want a custom sensitive information type that uses exact data values instead of matching only generic patterns? With Exact Data Match–based classification, you can create a custom sensitive information type designed to be dynamic and refreshable. EDM can be more scalable, result in fewer false positives, work with structured sensitive data, and handle sensitive information more securely. You can also use EDM with several Microsoft cloud services.

EDM-based classification enables you to create custom sensitive information types that refer to exact values in a database of sensitive information. You can refresh the database daily or weekly, and it can contain up to 100 million rows of data. As customers, employees, patients, or students change, your custom sensitive information type remains current and applicable.

For example, let us say that you are a professional services organization with a list of confidential clients. You can search for these exact client names and protect any document or email that mentions them. Your employees do not even have to think about it, which reduces your risk of unintentional disclosure.

EDM-based classification is considered a premium feature. Microsoft includes EDM in these subscriptions:

- Office 365 E5

- Microsoft 365 E5

- Microsoft 365 E5 Compliance

- Microsoft E5/A5 Information Protection and Governance

You configure and deploy Exact Data Match–based classification using PowerShell, so, unfortunately, we will not cover the details here. But you can find the details here: https://erica.news/ExactDataMatchClassification. Note: Since authoring this chapter, Microsoft has added Exact Data Match to the UI. Unfortunately, it was too late to add it to this book. You can find the tab called Exact data matches in the Data Classification solution area.

Create a Custom Keyword Dictionary

A custom keyword dictionary stores many keywords. We use them in a sensitive information type or other areas of Microsoft 365. Keyword lists are limited in quantity, and you need to modify the XML of a sensitive information type to update them. A keyword dictionary allows you up to 100,000 terms per dictionary.

The keywords for your dictionary could come from a variety of sources. Most commonly, we import them from a file such as a CSV or TXT list. We import this through the UI or by using a PowerShell cmdlet. When you want to update the terms, you will need to do that via PowerShell.

We create a custom keyword dictionary as a part of the custom sensitive information type process. Go to the Microsoft 365 Compliance Center. In the left-hand navigation, click Data classification and the Sensitive info types tab. Click Create info type. Fill out a name and description for your new sensitive information type and click Next.

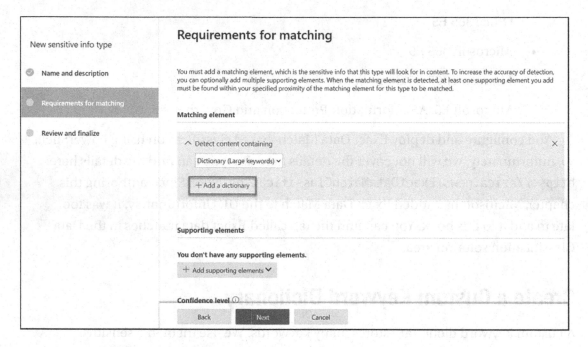

Figure 3-18. *Add a keyword dictionary*

On the Requirements for matching screen, under Matching element, select
Dictionary (Large keywords). Then click + Add a dictionary, as shown in Figure 3-18.
This option will allow you to select an existing keyword dictionary.

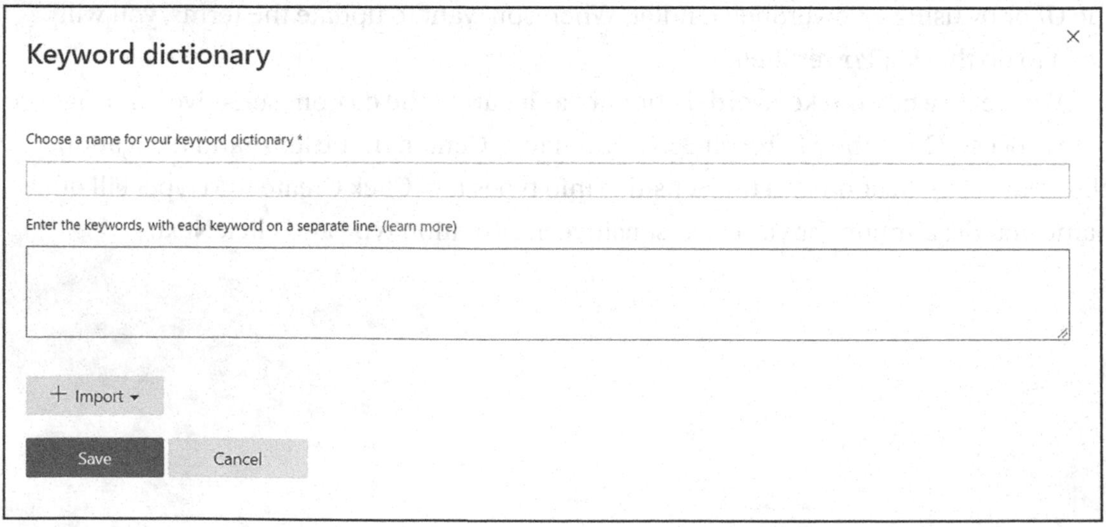

Keyword dictionary

Choose a name for your keyword dictionary *

Enter the keywords, with each keyword on a separate line. (learn more)

+ Import ▾

Save   Cancel

Figure 3-19. *Create a custom keyword dictionary*

If you would like to create a new keyword dictionary, click the Create new keyword dictionaries link. That will bring you to a screen where you can name your new keyword dictionary, shown in Figure 3-19. You can either paste the keywords with each keyword on a separate line or import a text or CSV file. Click Done, then Add, and then Finish to complete your custom keyword dictionary.

If you want to edit the keyword dictionary, please see these instructions: `https://erica.news/ModifyKeywordDictionary`.

If you edit the keyword dictionary often and have the right licensing, it might be better to use Exact Data Match instead.

We have discussed several ways to create and use sensitive information types to identify sensitive data in your Microsoft 365 environment. Now let us look at how we can put these info types to use and monitor the ongoing adoption of our information protection and governance labels using content and activity explorers. We will discuss how to create and use information protection and governance labels in upcoming chapters.

Content and Activity Explorers

Content and activity explorers are a set of tools that allow you to view retention and sensitivity label usage across SharePoint, OneDrive, and Exchange. They also allow you to view other file details, such as whether the system found sensitive information in a file. With the correct permissions, you can see these files' content to determine how to protect the content that contains sensitive information.

There are a few ways that content and activity explorers can make an administrator's life easier. First, content explorer proactively scans all your Microsoft 365 content for sensitive information. This functionality is useful when you start to plan for information protection and want to get a better idea of what sensitive data exists in your environment.

Next, content explorer shows what content has an associated retention or sensitivity label. When a record manager asks me how they can easily see the retention labels' usage, I always point them to content explorer. Or, if you deployed sensitivity labels for Office documents, you could see how people use them.

The last scenario is monitoring audit activity around labels. Activity explorer shows you user activities around labels, such as when someone applies, changes, or removes a label. A common concern I hear from records managers is that they are worried site owners will change record labels. With activity explorer, you can see when someone changes or removes a record label. Let us look at these scenarios and others in the remainder of this section.

How to Use Content Explorer

Content explorer enables you to do a few things for files located in SharePoint, OneDrive, or Exchange. We will go over each of them in this section:

- See the locations of content that potentially contains sensitive information.

- See the locations of content with a sensitivity label.

- See the location of content with a retention label.

- View the content of a document that falls into one of the preceding categories.

- View the metadata of a document in one of the preceding categories.

- Export a list of documents and locations for executing the preceding abilities.

- Search for specific files or email addresses.

- View additional details about sensitive information types found in files.

Before we dive into those, let us get licensing and permissions out of the way.

Licensing and Permissions

Each person who uses content explorer needs to have one of these licenses:

- Microsoft 365 E5

- Microsoft 365 E5 Compliance

- Microsoft 365 E5/A5 Information Protection and Governance

- Office 365 E5

- Office 365 Advanced Compliance

Content explorer has two roles associated with its use. They are:

- The **Content Explorer List Viewer role**, which allows people to see each item in the location.

- The **Content Explorer Content Viewer role**, which allows people to view the contents of each item in the list.

If you want people to be able to see the locations of documents but not the contents of the files, you could give them the Content Explorer List Viewer role only, as an example.

View Content Locations and Export a List

First, open the Microsoft 365 Compliance Center and click the Data classification solution in the left navigation. Next, click the Content explorer tab.

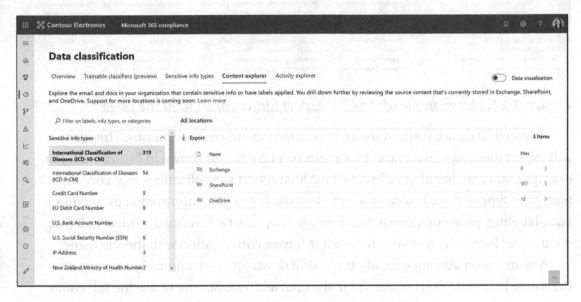

Figure 3-20. *The content explorer landing page*

As shown in Figure 3-20, you can see a list of sensitive info types, sensitivity labels, and retention labels currently applied to content on the left side. You can click the category names to collapse and expand them. On the right side, you can see the available content locations: Exchange, SharePoint, and OneDrive. If you know the name of the label or sensitive information type you would like to find, you can type it into the search box. Alternatively, you can browse for the item by expanding the label type and selecting the label from the list.

Click one of the sensitive information types or labels on the left side of the screen. The All locations area automatically filters to show only locations that contain that info type or label. Double-click one of the locations to drill down into that area. Keep double-clicking a location to drill down until you see a list of documents or emails.

	A		B		C		D		E
1	Name		Sensitive info type		User created		User modified		Retention label
2	Introducing the Contoso Mark 8 3D.pptx		[{"name":"International		Brad McCabe;Megan Bowen		Brad McCabe		Project Contract
3	Creating the Contoso Mark 8.pptx		[{"name":"International		Sonia Dara;Megan Bowen		Megan Bowen		Personal Financial PII
4	Building the Contoso Mark 8 (ProPlus).pptx		[{"name":"International		Sonia Dara;Megan Bowen		Peter Kelly		One Day Retention
5	Building the Contoso Mark 8.pptx		[{"name":"International		Sonia Dara;Megan Bowen		Simon Huang		Employee Records
6	Building the Contoso Mark 8.pptx		[{"name":"International		Sonia Dara;Megan Bowen		Simon Huang		One Day Retention
7	Introducing the Contoso Mark 8 3D.pptx		[{"name":"Internationa.		Brad McCabe;Megan Bowen		Brad McCabe		One Day Retention
8	Creating the Contoso Mark 8.pptx		[{"name":"Internationa		Sonia Dara;Megan Bowen		Megan Bowen		One Day Retention
9	Building the Contoso Mark 8 (ProPlus).pptx		[{"name":"Internation		Sonia Dara;Megan Bowen		Peter Kelly		Employee Records
10	Engine Perf.xlsx		[{"name":"Internation		nt Megan Bowen		Megan Bowen		Project Contract
11	Introducing the Mark 8.pptx		[{"name":"Internation		Brad McCabe;Megan Bowen;Erica Toelle		Josh Addison (Xtreme Co		Employee Records
12	Usability Testing Priorities.docx		[{"name":"Internation		Bryon Mascher;Megan Bowen;Erica Toel		Bryon Mascher		EU Contract
13	Mark 8 - FAQ.docx		[{"name":"Internation		Megan Bowen		Megan Bowen		Project Deliverable
14	Marketing Deck v1.pptx		[{"name":"Internationa.		garthf@spc14a.ccsctp.net;Megan Bowe		Garth		One Day Retention
15	XT1050 Marketing Collateral Timelines_V2.docx		[{"name":"Internationa		Alex Darrow;Megan Bowen;Erica Toelle		Terry Wilson		EU Contract
16	Adventure Works Copter Camera Overview.docx		[{"name":"Internationa		Josh Addison (Xtreme Consulting Group		Catherine Boeger		Project Contract
17	CR -227 Camera briefing.docx		[{"name":"Internationa		.":"Brett Polen (Xtreme Consulting Group In		Brett Polen (Xtreme Cons		One Day Retention
18	R and D Presentation.pptx		[{"name":"Internationa		garthf@spc14a.ccsctp.net;Megan Bowe		Garth		Project Contract
19	XT1050 Usability test 2.3.docx		[{"name":"Internationa		Junmin Hao;Megan Bowen;Erica Toelle		Terry Wilson		Product Retired
20	Introducing the Mark 8.pptx		[{"name":"Internationa.		Brad McCabe;Erica Toelle		Josh Addison (Xtreme Co		One Day Retention
21	Campaign Sales Data.xlsx		[{"name":"Internationa		."In Nataly Vaisman (MGS);Erica Toelle		Erica Toelle		Project Deliverable
22	Brussels Proposal.docx		[{"name":"Internation.		Roberto Yglesias;Allan Deyoung		Roberto Yglesias		
23	2019 France-Paris- Facade work.docx		[{"name":"Internationa.		Roberto Yglesias;Erica Toelle		Roberto Yglesias		EU Contract
24	Contract Notice.docx		[{"name":"Internationa.		Roberto Yglesias;Allan Deyoung		Roberto Yglesias		
25									

Figure 3-21. *An example of the CSV export file, cropped to fit the page*

As you drill down, you can see an Export button above the locations. This button will export the view of the current locations to a CSV file, as shown in Figure 3-21. For example, you can download a list of all the SharePoint site collections that contain a particular type of data. You can then use this site list to plan information protection auto-labeling, protecting sensitive information by site. Or you can download a list of documents located in one site and use it to have a conversation with the site owner.

A search icon also appears when you drill down into a location. If you are in an Exchange location, you can search for an email address. Be sure to use the full email address, such as etoelle@contoso.com. If you are in SharePoint or OneDrive, you have the following options for search:

- **Full site name**: https://contoso.onmicrosoft.com/sites/Mark8

- **Root folder name** (gets all subfolders): /sites

- **File name**: Resume_Erica_v1.docx

- **Text at the beginning of a file name**: Resume

- **Text after an underscore character (_) in a file name**: Erica or v1

- **File extension**: docx

Next, let us discuss what we can do with individual files in content explorer.

View the Content and Metadata of a Document

Now we have drilled down into our content locations until we only have a list of files. Double-click a document to open it in the viewer. In this view of individual documents, there is some useful information, shown in Figure 3-22.

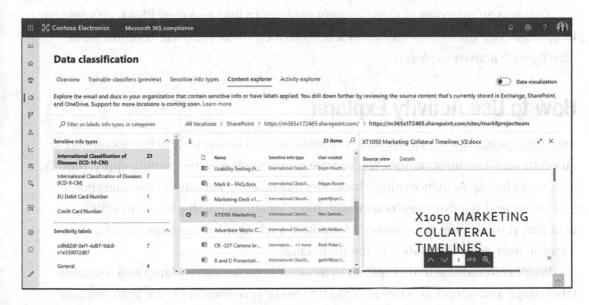

Figure 3-22. *The document view in content explorer*

The document viewer allows you to navigate the content of a document in its native format. You can view the document in full screen by clicking the diagonal arrows next to the title. Arrows allow you to navigate through the pages, and a magnifying glass lets you zoom in and out. To view the file's metadata, click the Details tab next to the Source view tab. Click the X in the upper-right corner of the document to close it.

CR -227 Camera briefing.docx

Sensitive info type	Count	Confidence
International Classification of Diseases (ICD-10-CM)	12	55%
International Classification of Diseases (ICD-9-CM)	3	55%

Figure 3-23. *Sensitive information type details*

Another feature of the document list is the ability to view additional details about the sensitive information types found in a document, shown in Figure 3-23. In the Sensitive info type column, click the blue text with an info type. This click will bring up a box listing all the sensitive info types found in the document. It also states how many times it found the info type and the confidence level of the matches.

That was an overview of using content explorer to find and view files with sensitive info, sensitivity labels, or retention labels. Next, let us look at how to monitor label activity with activity explorer.

How to Use Activity Explorer

Activity explorer displays a subset of the audit log and shows only activities related to labels or sensitive information. You can see events such as when people apply, modify, or remove labels. Activity explorer monitors this labeling activity across SharePoint, OneDrive, and Windows endpoints, with more locations coming soon. In activity explorer, you can filter the data on information such as the date range, activity type, location user, sensitivity label, or retention label.

People often use activity explorer to monitor both sensitivity label and retention label usage and adoption. They also use it to make sure that labels are auto-applied correctly. If your retention or sensitivity labels are manually applied, you can check that users did this successfully. We will go into detail about sensitivity labels in Chapter 5 and retention labels in Chapter 8.

Another scenario that I briefly mentioned earlier is around record labels. I often hear concerns from records managers that SharePoint site collection administrators can remove and change record labels. They would prefer that no changes are allowed once we declare them as a record. Activity explorer enables you to monitor this behavior, so you can catch it if someone makes a mistake.

Licensing and Permissions

Every user who accesses and uses activity explorer must have a license assigned from one of these subscriptions:

- Microsoft 365 (E5)

- Office 365 (E5)

- Advanced Compliance (E5) add-on

- Advanced Threat Intelligence (E5) add-on

An account must be assigned membership in any one of these role groups:

- Global Administrator

- Compliance Administrator

- Security Administrator

- Compliance Data Administrator

Now let us get into how to use the data displayed in activity explorer.

Work with Activity Explorer Data

Microsoft 365 monitors and reports on 12 types of activities across SharePoint Online, OneDrive, and Windows 10 endpoints. You will need to configure Endpoint Data Loss Prevention to get the Windows 10 endpoint events into activity explorer. Microsoft has said that more event types will come soon.

The types of activities monitored include

- File created

- File modified

- File renamed

- File copied to the cloud

- File accessed by unallowed app

- File printed

- File copied to removable media

- File copied to network share

- File read

- File copied to clipboard

- Label applied

- Label changed, such as if the label has been upgraded, downgraded, or removed

To access activity explorer, visit the Microsoft 365 Compliance Center. On the left side, click Data classification. Click the Activity explorer tab.

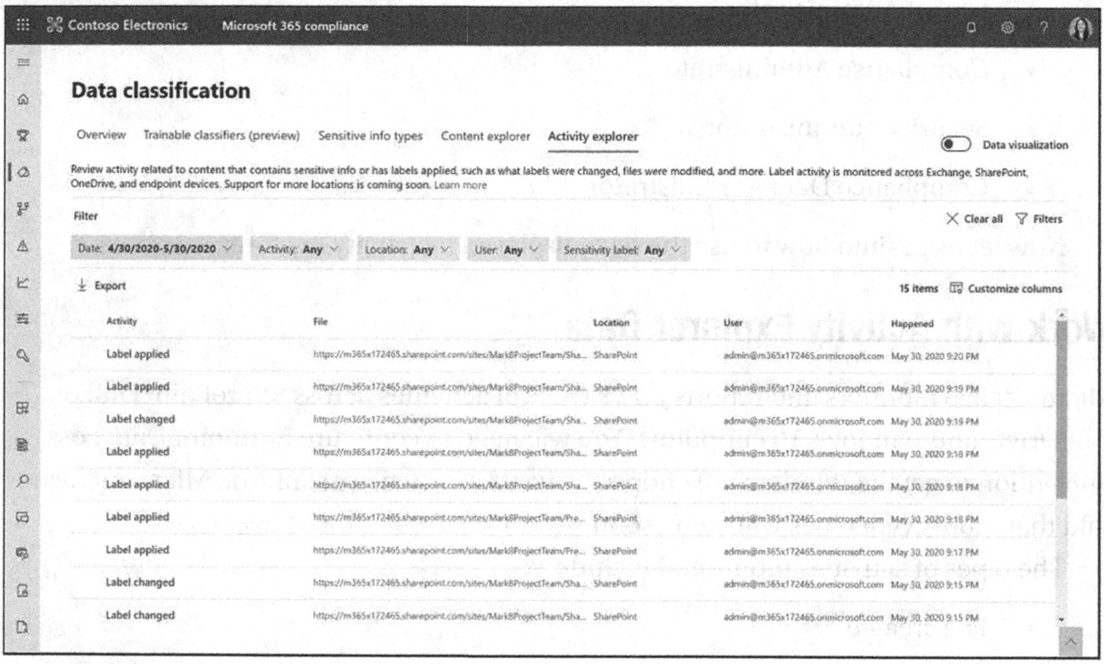

Figure 3-24. *The activity explorer page*

On the activity explorer page, shown in Figure 3-24, you will see a list of all the events from your organization. You have the option to turn on a data visualization of these activities. Also shown is a set of filters. You also can export the events shown in the view.

First, let us customize our view of the activities. Do this by selecting columns to show in the view. We can also select filters for the data. The default filters include date, activity, location, user, and sensitivity label. Click the filters on the right-hand side of that area to view. Here you will see a list of the available filter options. Click Done when you complete your selection of filters.

Next, we will customize the columns displayed in activity explorer. From the activity explorer homepage, click Customize columns. Check the boxes next to the columns you would like to show. Click Apply when you complete your selection.

You can also export all the activities for the selected period. Choose your date range and click the Export button. The export includes all the columns and their data.

Finally, you can view all the metadata for a single activity. Click an event, and an information box will appear. Additional activity details include the specific activity name, the client IP, and the label event type. The information also includes when the event happened and how the label was applied. It also tells you information about the item, including the file name, the user, the file extension, the retention label, the old retention label, and any sensitive information types. Lastly, the box shows location details such as the location type, the parent location, and the file path.

Activity explorer is a simple but powerful tool for monitoring security and compliance events. In this section, we learned about what events the activity explorer monitors. We also learned how to customize our view and export the view to a CSV file.

This chapter covered a lot of information. First, we reviewed trainable classifiers, including the built-in classifiers and the process for creating a custom trainable classifier. Then, we looked at sensitive information types and how to create your own. Lastly, we reviewed content and activity explorers, describing how to use the tools to monitor sensitive information and label usage.

The next chapter will cover compliance data connectors, which allow you to archive data in Microsoft 365. Examples of the types of data you can archive include social media platforms, Slack, Zoom, Bloomberg, and other popular applications. By importing the data, you can manage it using Microsoft 365 tools. For example, you can retain the data or find it using eDiscovery.

CHAPTER 4

Data Connectors

Compliance data connectors allow you to import and archive data from sources outside of Microsoft 365. For example, you could import content from your company's Facebook page, your LinkedIn company account, or your Twitter company account. You could also import data from internal sources, such as Bloomberg Mail, Bloomberg Messenger, an HR system, or Slack.

After you set up and configure a data connector, it connects to the third-party source regularly and converts that content into an email message format. Microsoft then imports these email messages into user mailboxes in Microsoft 365. After we store the data in user mailboxes, you can use Microsoft 365 compliance features to manage the third-party data.

What are some ways in which these connectors might be useful? Using a connector to import and archive data in Microsoft 365 can help your organization stay compliant with government and regulatory policies. Data connectors can also be useful if you want to manage your data using one set of compliance tools and solutions.

The proliferation of cloud services means most organizations are storing data in a lot of different locations. It's not practical to build separate compliance solutions for all these cloud services. Data connectors allow you to have one place to administer and maintain compliance across all these cloud solutions. Finally, you can reduce costs by replacing other point compliance solutions with the features available in Microsoft 365.

The data from the connectors work seamlessly with the compliance solutions in Microsoft 365. For example, Communication Compliance allows you to monitor communications, such as Slack or Bloomberg Messenger, to make sure that the messaging is in line with company policies and outside regulations. You can make sure that no harassment occurs through corporate messaging solutions. Communication Compliance can also monitor for sensitive information shared in messages or to comply with regulations that require you to watch certain communications.

© Erica Toelle 2021
E. Toelle, *Microsoft 365 Compliance*, https://doi.org/10.1007/978-1-4842-5778-4_4

You can find content from third-party sources using eDiscovery and content search. Because content is associated with a user account, you can search on the data source, the sender, the content of the message, and other properties. With eDiscovery, you can put third-party content on legal hold and export messages.

Data connectors also work with information governance and records management retention policies. These policies allow you to govern connector content, so you maintain a copy of the data according to laws and regulations. You can also defensibly dispose of content when the retention period has passed.

Finally, you can use the Insider Risk Management solution to identify risky behavior from employees, such as data theft, security policy violations, and other types of malicious and non-malicious behavior. Insider Risk Management can monitor these third-party solutions for these risks, so you can further investigate and act on violations.

Please note that not every connector works with every compliance solution. For example, in Table 4-1, you can see the Slack Connector works with Communication Compliance, eDiscovery, and Information Governance, whereas the HR Connector only works with Insider Risk Management. This table shows each of the available data connectors, whether they are Microsoft or partner owned, and the compliance solutions they support.

- CC = Communication Compliance

- eDisc = eDiscovery

- IG + RM = Information Governance and Records Management

- IR = Insider Risk Management

Table 4-1. *Available data connectors in the Microsoft Compliance Center*

Connector name	Created by	CC	eDisc	IG + RM	IR
Android Archiver	TeleMessage	X	X	X	
AT&T SMS/MMS	TeleMessage	X	X	X	
Bell SMS/MMS (Canada)	TeleMessage	X	X	X	
Bloomberg Instant Message	Microsoft	X	X	X	
Bloomberg Mail	Microsoft	X	X	X	

(*continued*)

Table 4-1. (*continued*)

Connector name	Created by	CC	eDisc	IG + RM	IR
CellTrust	Globanet	X	X	X	
Cisco Jabber	Globanet	X	X	X	
EML	Globanet		X	X	
Enterprise Number Archiver	TeleMessage	X	X	X	
Facebook Page	Microsoft	X	X	X	
FX Connect	Globanet	X	X	X	
Human Resources	Microsoft				X
ICE Chat	Microsoft	X	X	X	
Jive					
LinkedIn	Microsoft	X	X	X	
MS SQL Database	Globanet		X	X	
O2 Telefonica (UK)	TeleMessage	X	X	X	
Physical Badging Systems	Microsoft				X
Pivot	Globanet	X	X	X	
Reuters Dealing	Globanet	X	X	X	
Reuters Eikon	Globanet	X	X	X	
Reuters FX	Globanet	X	X	X	
Slack	Globanet	X	X	X	
Symphony	Globanet	X	X	X	
Telus Network (Canada)	TeleMessage	X	X	X	
Text-Delimited	Globanet	X	X	X	
Twitter	Microsoft	X	X	X	
Verizon Network	TeleMessage	X	X	X	
Webex Teams	Globanet	X	X	X	

(*continued*)

Table 4-1. (*continued*)

Connector name	Created by	CC	eDisc	IG + RM	IR
Web pages	Globanet	X	X	X	
WhatsApp	TeleMessage	X	X	X	
Workplace from Facebook	Globanet	X	X	X	
XIP	Globanet	X	X	X	
XSLT/XML	Globanet	X	X	X	
Zoom (IM Only)	Globanet	X	X	X	

Table 4-1 shows a list of currently available compliance connectors, as of December 2020. New connectors are released every month, so please see the Microsoft documentation for a current list of connectors: `https://erica.news/Connectors`.

Both Microsoft and Microsoft partners develop data connectors. Microsoft-built connectors are available with the licenses outlined in the next section. Connectors created by partners will require additional licensing, and you should contact the partner for licensing information.

Permissions and Licensing

Data connectors require the following permissions:

- A global admin must opt into the use of third-party connectors. When you set up a connector, the wizard will prompt you for this approval.

- A user must be assigned the Mailbox Import Export role in Exchange Online to set up the connector. An Exchange admin will need to grant this permission. Visit the Exchange admin center ➤ Permissions ➤ Admin roles ➤ New. Complete the information and choose the Mailbox Import Export role.

For licensing, compliance connectors are available with these SKUs:

- Office 365 E5

- Microsoft 365 E5

- Microsoft 365 E5 Information Protection and Governance

- Microsoft 365 E5 Compliance

Some connectors, like the Facebook and Twitter connectors, will require an Azure subscription in addition to the preceding licensing.

Additionally, some of the connectors are developed by Microsoft partners and require an additional license from those partners.

How to Use Compliance Connectors

To access data connectors, visit the Microsoft 365 Compliance Center. In the left-hand navigation, click Data connectors.

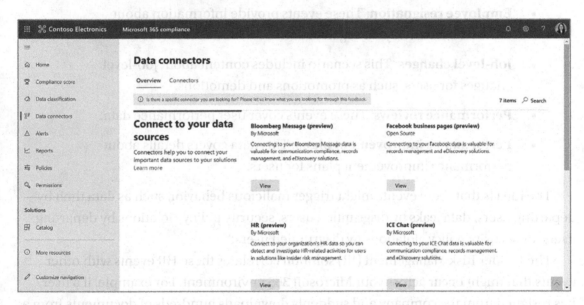

Figure 4-1. *The Data connectors overview page in the Microsoft 365 Compliance Center*

Figure 4-1 shows the overview page for data connectors. Here you will see all the connectors available for use in your environment. Click the Connectors tab. This tab shows you a list of all the connectors that you've already set up in your environment.

Now, let's go through how to set up some of these connectors. First, we will start with the HR Data Connector. We will talk about why you would use the connector, configuration options, and how to set it up. Then, we will archive content from LinkedIn company pages. These two connectors are a good representation of the type of configuration you will encounter for connectors. One connector requires an Azure account and configuration, and one does not.

HR Data Connector

We use data from the HR Data Connector with the Insider Risk Management solution, which I cover in detail in Chapter 10. The HR Connector brings employee-related events into Insider Risk Management, such as

- **Employee resignation**: These events provide information about users who have left your organization.

- **Job-level changes**: This scenario includes content about job-level changes for users, such as promotions and demotions.

- **Performance reviews**: These events cover user performance data.

- **Performance improvement plans**: This data covers details about performance improvement plans for users.

The idea is that these events might trigger malicious behavior, such as data theft by departing users, data leaks by disgruntled users, security policy violations by departing users, or security policy violations by disgruntled users.

The Insider Risk Management (IR) solution correlates these HR events with other events that might occur across your Microsoft 365 environment. For example, if a user has resigned from the company and suddenly downloads hundreds of documents from a SharePoint site to a flash drive, those three events together are suspicious. IR would flag that as risk, and a human can examine the triggers more closely and act if necessary.

Table 4-2. *IR policies mapped to HR data types*

IRM policy template	HR data type
Data theft by departing users	Employee resignation
Data leaks by disgruntled users	Job-level changes, performance reviews, performance improvement plans
Security policy violations by departing users	Employee resignation
Security policy violations by disgruntled users	Job-level changes, performance reviews, performance improvement plans

Insider Risk Management has several policy templates available for your use. Table 4-2 shows the IR policy templates that use HR data and what HR data types you need to enable them. For example, if you want to use the data leaks by disgruntled users policy template, you would use the HR Connector to import job-level changes, performance reviews, and performance improvement plans data types.

Set Up the HR Connector

There are five steps to set up the HR Data Connector:

1. Create a CSV file to map the HR Connector data.

2. Create an Azure Active Directory app registration.

3. Create the HR Connector in the Compliance Center.

4. Build a solution to sync your HR system data with the CSV file.

5. Create a scheduled task to sync the CSV file with the connector regularly.

Thank you to Ryan Sturm for clarifying the HR Connector process for all of us.

I do not have access to an HR system without confidential data to provide real screenshots of this process. So instead, I'm going to explain how to set up fake HR data for an Insider Risk Management demo or evaluation. I think this is useful because when most people trial Insider Risk Management, they don't want to use production data.

Create a CSV File to Map the HR Connector Data

	A	B	C	D	E	F	G	H
1	HRScenario	EmailAddressResignation	ResignationDate	LastWorkingDate	EmailAddressJobChange	EffectiveDate	OldLevel	NewLevel
2	Resignation	MiriamG@M365x172465.OnMicrosoft.com	2020-07-23T15:18:02.4675041+05:30	2020-07-29T15:18:02.4675041+05:30				
3	Resignation	JoniS@M365x172465.OnMicrosoft.com	2020-07-23T15:18:02.4675041+05:30	2020-07-29T15:18:02.7117540				
4	Demotion				PradeepG@M365x172465.OnMicrosoft.com	2020-07-23T15:18:02.4675041+05:30	Level 61 – Sr. Manager	Level 60-Manager
5	Demotion				PattiF@M365x172465.OnMicrosoft.com	2020-07-23T15:18:02.4675041+05:30	Level 62 – Sr. Director	Level 60-Manager

Figure 4-2. *Sample CSV file for the HR Connector*

Firstly, we need to create a CSV file for the HR Connector data. To make this process easier, I've created a sample CSV file for the HR Connector, shown in Figure 4-2, that you can download here: `https://erica.news/HRCSV`.

Here is how I created this spreadsheet. Each of the HR data types has required and optional information. We list this information as a column in the spreadsheet. The information we need for each type is in the following list. Starred fields are required:

- Employee resignation
  - User email address*
  - Date and time of the resignation*
  - The date and time of the employee's last day of work*
- Job-level changes
  - User email address*
  - Effective date and time*
  - Old job level
  - New job level
- Performance reviews
  - User email address*

- • Review effective date and time*

- • Remarks

- • Rating

- • Performance improvement plans

  - • User email address*

  - • Effective date*

  - • Remarks

  - • Rating

You can name the columns whatever you want if the names are unique. If you are using one spreadsheet for multiple scenarios, add one column to designate which scenario corresponds to the row of data. In Figure 4-2, I called the column HRScenario. At this point, you should also update the dummy data for your environment. You need to update the email addresses of users in your environment and optionally update the dates. Only complete the columns related to the scenario for that row. After you create the CSV file with the required HR data, store it on the local computer where you plan to run the script.

Note   Email addresses must have the same capitalization or letter case as the UPN field in Azure Active Directory, or the data import will fail.

Create an Azure Active Directory App Registration

Now we have our CSV file with sample data created, and we can move on to the next step. In this step, we will register an Azure Active Directory app. Here are the steps:

1. Visit https://portal.azure.com.

2. Click the menu button in the upper-left corner, and click Azure Active Directory.

3. In the left-hand navigation, click App Registration.

4. Click + New Registration.

5. Create a user-facing display name for this application. I called my app HR Data Connector.

6. For Who can use this application or access this API? choose Accounts in this organizational directory only.

7. Leave the Redirect URI blank.

8. Click Register.

9. This click will bring you to a screen with information for your completed app, shown in Figure 4-3. Note the Application (client) ID and the Directory (tenant) ID. I like to paste them into the Notepad app.

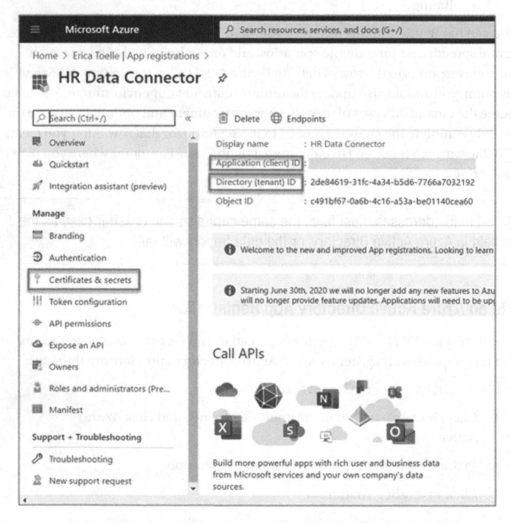

Figure 4-3. *The Application (client) ID for your registered AAD app*

Next, we need to create a secret. This secret is like a password, and we will need it to sync the data in the next step. Click Certificates & secrets in the left navigation. In the Client secrets section, click New client secret. Type a description for the secret, such as HR Connector, and choose the expiration of one or two years or never expires. Your IT department will usually have a policy for which one you should select. Click Add. Write down the Value somewhere secure. You won't be able to see it again once you close this page. You will need this Value in the next step.

Create the HR Connector in the Compliance Center

That completes the app registration step. Keep this window open as we will need some information in the next step. Next, we will create the HR Connector in the Compliance Center. Navigate to the Microsoft 365 Compliance Center. In the left navigation, click Data connectors. Find the HR Connector and click View and then Add connector. This click will bring us to the wizard to set up the new HR Connector.

First, accept the Terms of Service. Second, we add credentials for connecting to our data source. Enter the Application (client) ID in the first field. Choose a unique name for the connector in the second field. I called mine HR Data Connector. Click Next.

Third, we'll choose the HR scenarios that we want to include in this connector. Our example CSV file contains all the scenarios, so check all four boxes. Click Next. Select the radio button next to Upload a sample file. Click the blue text that says Upload a sample file. Navigate to the example CSV file we created in step #1 and upload it. Click Next.

This screen asks us to map the columns in our spreadsheet to the types of data they contain, shown in Figure 4-4. If you didn't modify the sample file, then the columns should appear in the same order as the page lists them.

Map the HR scenarios to the columns in your file

The HR scenarios you selected appear below. Select
the scenarios and columns from your sample file that
correspond with the required details. If the correct
data isn't listed, you might need to edit your sample
file according to the guidelines.

Column in sample file where scenarios are listed

Because you selected multiple scenarios, let us know
which column in your sample file contains the related
scenarios so we know where to look.

HRScenario	⌄

Employee resignation   ⌃

　Entry for this scenario *

Employee resignations

　Microsoft 365 user email address *

EmailAddressResignation	⌄

　Resignation submitted date (UTC time) *

ResignationDate	⌄

　Last working date (UTC time) *

LastWorkingDate	⌄

Job level changes   ⌄

Performance reviews   ⌄

Performance improvement plans   ⌄

Back	Next		Cancel

Figure 4-4.   Map the CSV file to the types of HR data it represents

The first dropdown asks us to specify which column contains the HR scenario
name. Then, we map the columns for employee resignation. The first field asks about
your entry for this scenario. This field is where you enter the name of your resignation
scenario from the CSV file. In the example, I called this Employee resignations. Then you
complete the dropdowns for the other three columns, which should be self-explanatory.
Follow the same process for the remaining scenarios and click Next.

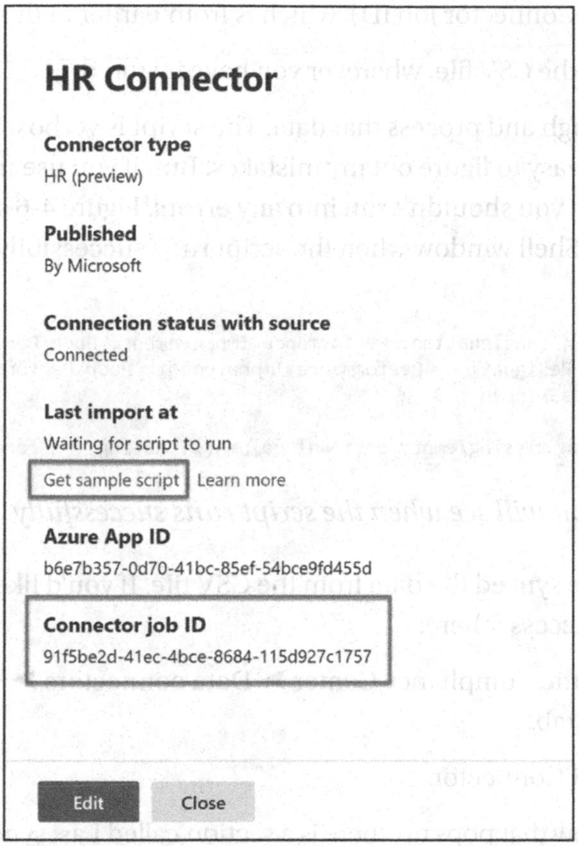

HR Connector

Connector type
HR (preview)

Published
By Microsoft

Connection status with source
Connected

Last import at
Waiting for script to run
Get sample script | Learn more

Azure App ID
b6e7b357-0d70-41bc-85ef-54bce9fd455d

Connector job ID
91f5be2d-41ec-4bce-8684-115d927c1757

Edit   Close

Figure 4-5. *Information about the new HR Connector*

On the next screen, review the details of the connector and click Finish. The resulting screen gives us some information about our new HR Connector. Specifically, it provides us with a link to the script, shown in Figure 4-5, that we need to run to import the data now that we've created the data mappings. It also displays the Connector Job ID, which we will need later in the process, so keep the window open to use then.

Click Get sample script to go to the GitHub site with the data for the HR data sync. Click Raw, located in the upper-right corner of the page. Select all the text on this page and copy it to your clipboard. To run the script, open PowerShell, paste the script in the window, and press Enter. PowerShell will prompt you for information, specifically the following:

- The Tenant ID [Directory (tenant) ID], the App ID [Application (client) ID], and the client secret, which all came from the Azure app we created in the previous step

113

- The Job ID (Connector Job ID), which is from earlier in this step

- The path to the CSV file, wherever you have it stored

Then, it'll go through and process that data. The script is verbose about any error details, and I found it easy to figure out my mistakes. But, if you use my CSV template and follow these steps, you shouldn't run into any errors. Figure 4-6 shows the text you will see in your PowerShell window when the script runs successfully.

```
Data types configured : 4 (Resignation, Performance Improvement, Poor Performance, Demotion)
Data types identified : Resignation, Performance Improvement, Poor Performance, Demotion
RecordsSaved : 8, RecordsSkipped : 0

2 records were saved with missing/empty optional column(s) Rating, PerformanceRating
```

Figure 4-6. *What you will see when the script runs successfully*

At this point, we've synced the data from the CSV file. If you'd like to view the log file for the sync, you can access it here:

1. Navigate to the Compliance Center ➤ Data connectors ➤ Connectors tab.

2. Click the HR Connector.

3. In the window that pops up, there is a section called Last synced at [Date]. Next to this section, there is a blue link called Download Log.

If you are configuring this connector for an IR evaluation, you can stop here. However, if you want to use the HR Connector in production, you need to complete two additional steps. First, we need a solution to sync the data from your HR system to the CSV file regularly. Second, we need to schedule a task to synchronize the CSV file with the connector, like we just did manually.

Build a Solution to Sync Your HR System Data with the CSV File

This step is an area where I can't be much help. The instructions for how to do this will vary widely depending on your HR system. You may need to pull data from multiple HR systems, depending on your organization. I will say that every well-known HR system should have a way to export data out of the system. Often that data can be exported directly to a CSV file. If it can't, then there are standard ways of transforming the data into a CSV format. If you need help with this step, I would advise looking for a consultant who can help.

Create a Scheduled Task to Sync the CSV File with the Connector Regularly

The Task Scheduler app in Windows is a common way to run a PowerShell script every day automatically. IT departments that use PowerShell will be familiar with this approach. There are a few things you will need to do to run this specific solution using Task Scheduler. For full instructions, go here: https://erica.news/HRTask.

1. Take the PowerShell script that we got from GitHub in the previous step and paste it into Notepad or a text editor. Save it and change the file extension to .ps1, so the system recognizes it as a PowerShell script.

2. Create a script command using this format. Remove the brackets, but keep the quotes. This information is the same as you used to run the preceding script manually:

   ```
   .\HRConnector.ps1 -tenantId "[enter tenant ID]" -appId "[enter
   app ID]" -appSecret "[enter your secret]" -jobId "[enter Job ID]"
   -csvFilePath "[enter CSV file path]"
   ```

Now you have a functioning connector to bring in your HR data to use in the Insider Risk Management solution. You either use fake data for an IRM evaluation, or you have your real HR system connected and scheduled to update daily.

Now let's set up a connector to import the LinkedIn posts from your public company page.

LinkedIn Connector

Internal policies or compliance regulations may require your organization to archive public social media posts. They are a record of what your company has stated publicly and might need to be discoverable for litigation purposes or archived as a historical record. I've noticed many records managers haven't thought about how to maintain social media posts for recordkeeping purposes, so bring it up to them!

LinkedIn facilitates public company social media posts using a company page. Microsoft 365 makes archiving these posts easy through the LinkedIn Data Connector. Please note that the connector only works with company pages and not personal profiles or LinkedIn groups. Let's see how to set up the connector.

Set Up the LinkedIn Connector

Setting up the LinkedIn Connector is very easy, as long as you have the correct permissions to your LinkedIn company page. Here are the steps to configure the connector:

1. Get administrator access to your LinkedIn company page.

2. Create the LinkedIn Data Connector.

Administrator Access to the LinkedIn Company Page

To configure the connector, someone must log in as a page admin during the configuration process. The data connector will use this person's credentials to read the LinkedIn posts and copy them to Microsoft 365.

Here is how you can request access to be an administrator for your LinkedIn company page:

1. List your current position with the organization on your profile.

2. Go to the page you'd like admin access to.

3. Click the More icon and select Request admin access from the dropdown.

4. Click the checkbox to verify that you're authorized to become an admin of the page.

5. Click Request access. You'll see a notification indicating that your request was successfully sent.

6. Note: This grants all current designated admins' access to your public profile information.

7. You'll receive an email notification once you've been granted page admin access.

Note   The page admin must be one of your LinkedIn connections for them to grant your request.

Create the LinkedIn Data Connector

First, navigate to the Microsoft 365 Compliance Center. On the left-hand side, click Data connectors. Scroll down the page to find the LinkedIn Company Pages Connector and click View. On the next page, click Add connector. This click will bring up the wizard to create the connector.

The first step in the wizard asks you to agree to the Terms of Service. Next, choose a unique name for the connector, and click Sign In with LinkedIn. This click will pop open the Authentication window, where you enter the information for your personal LinkedIn account, including your email and password. Click Sign In. The Microsoft 365 Import Connector will display a set of permissions that the data connector needs to work correctly. Click Allow to agree to the permissions. If you are an admin for multiple LinkedIn company pages, the next screen will ask you to choose which LinkedIn company page you would like to use for this connector. Click Next.

The next screen asks you to choose where to store the LinkedIn company information. The storage location must be a mailbox, but it can be an active, inactive, or archived mailbox. Type the name of the person and select them from the list, and click Next.

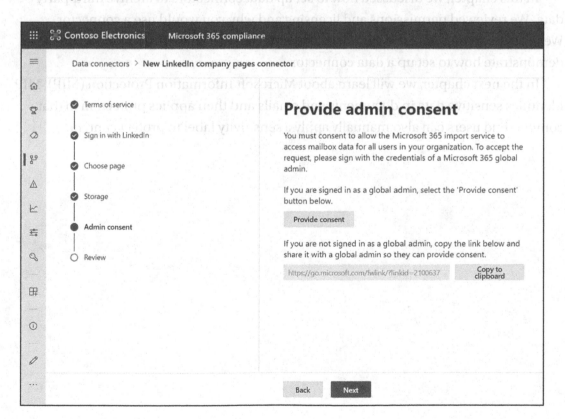

Finally, you need to provide global administrator consent for this connector to work. So there are two ways to do that. First, if you're logged in as a global admin, you'll see a button that says Provide consent. Click that and you are done. Second, if you're not the global admin, you have a link that you can copy and send to your global admin. They can click the link to provide their consent. Once the admin grants consent, click the Next button.

The next screen allows you to review the details of your connector. If you're happy with the configuration, click Finish. Now you'll see the LinkedIn Connector on the Connectors tab, and it will import your data daily. To view the import status, click the connector and view the date and time under the Last imported at text. You can also download a log of the sync information.

That was an example of how to set up a LinkedIn data connector. As you can see, some connectors are very easy to set up. Some connectors are more complex and require an Azure subscription or a partner license. Microsoft has said they will invest heavily in data connectors in the coming year. Watch for announcements about new connectors and enjoy managing all your content in one place.

In this chapter, we discussed how to set up data connectors to archive third-party data. We reviewed permissions and licensing and why you would use a connector. We used the examples of the HR Data Connector and the LinkedIn Connector to demonstrate how to set up a data connector.

In the next chapter, we will learn about Microsoft Information Protection (MIP). MIP identifies sensitive data in documents and emails and then applies protection to that content. End users can also manually apply a sensitivity label to protect content.

CHAPTER 5

Information Protection

Microsoft Information Protection allows you to add protections to documents and emails that stay with the content, wherever it is located. For example, the protections will remain with a file, whether someone emails it outside the organization, downloads it to a device, takes it offline, or stores it in a file share. Information protection also has a lot of options for what types of protections it applies. You can use encryption, headers, or specific permissions. Other options include applying protections automatically to files or enforcing settings for SharePoint sites, Microsoft 365 groups, and Microsoft Teams.

Microsoft information protection uses sensitivity labels to apply these protections. There are quite a few ways to use sensitivity labels, which we will review in this chapter:

- Apply sensitivity labels to files and add protections to the data itself.

    - Manually classify and protect emails and documents in the Office client.

    - Auto-apply sensitivity labels to Office documents that contain sensitive information.

    - Auto-label content located in email, SharePoint sites, or OneDrive that contains sensitive information.

- Sensitivity labels that enforce settings on containers, such as SharePoint sites, Microsoft Teams, and Microsoft 365 groups. For example, any site with a highly confidential sensitivity label would not allow external users.

Most organizations use sensitivity labels that follow an existing data classification schema. For example, you might have highly confidential, confidential, general, and public labels with varying protection levels.

© Erica Toelle 2021
E. Toelle, *Microsoft 365 Compliance*, https://doi.org/10.1007/978-1-4842-5778-4_5

Here are some examples of how you might use sensitivity labels to protect content:

- Encrypt documents that contain sensitive data, such as a bank account number or national identification number.

- Automatically assign specific permissions to content that includes types of sensitive information, for example, if you have a customer number that is considered sensitive and only a particular group in your organization should see content with a customer number.

- You could also use sensitivity labels in conjunction with retention labels to automatically apply a specific retention period to content that contains sensitive information.

- Ensure that only users within your organization and not external users can open a confidential document or email.

- Use a sensitivity label so that only users in the marketing department can edit and print a price sheet, whereas salespeople can distribute it.

- Set an expiration for that price sheet at the end of the quarter so that nobody can open it and use outdated information once you have released the new pricing information.

You can also use a sensitivity label to protect a container, such as a SharePoint site, Microsoft Team, or Microsoft 365 group. The protections on the container can include things like allowing or disallowing external users. They also can allow or disallow users from accessing the container using unmanaged devices. Container labels can set the group's privacy, such as public, where it is available to everyone in the organization, vs. private, where only members of the group can see the content.

You can also apply a label automatically to Office documents and emails based on properties or other criteria of the document. You could also recommend that users label a document, and they can choose whether to apply it. You can also target the label to specific users or groups. For example, suppose you have one set of labels for the general user base in your organization, but then a different set of labels for the finance organization. In that case, it is possible to do that through this user group targeting. You can also apply a default label to new documents and emails to use a base level of protection. Users can then apply more strict classification labels to these documents as needed. Finally, you can require a justification for a user to change a label to understand why they made that decision.

In addition to protecting files and enforcing settings on a container, you can leverage sensitivity labels in other Microsoft solutions. We will not be covering these solutions in this book, but I want you to be aware that they exist.

You can protect content in third-party apps and services using sensitivity labels in the Microsoft Cloud App Security solution. With Cloud App Security, you can detect, classify, label, and protect content in third-party apps and services such as Salesforce, Box, or Dropbox. You can also extend sensitivity labels to third-party apps and services using the Microsoft Information Protection SDK. A third-party app can read these sensitivity labels and apply protection settings.

Another way you could use sensitivity labels is to classify content without using any protection settings. You could simply assign a classification to content that persists and roams with the content as it is used and shared. You can use this classification information to generate usage reports and see activity for your sensitive files. This report is often used in a pilot phase to understand the behavior of sensitive information in your organization so you can plan and implement the right protection for this data.

Please note that a solution called Azure Information Protection (AIP) is related but different from sensitivity labels. I will not be covering Azure Information Protection (AIP) in this chapter because Microsoft is deprecating label management for AIP on March 31, 2021. You cannot use both AIP labels and sensitivity labels together. If you have not started using AIP labels, please begin with using sensitivity labels instead.

Now let us look at how we create sensitivity labels and the available protection options.

Sensitivity Labels

Classifying content with a sensitivity label allows you to apply the protections we have mentioned in the preceding text. These labels are completely customizable for your organization, so you can create categories that match your existing information protection policies. Sensitivity labels store the label in clear text, so it is seen as metadata and travels with the file. Files can have only one sensitivity label applied at a time.

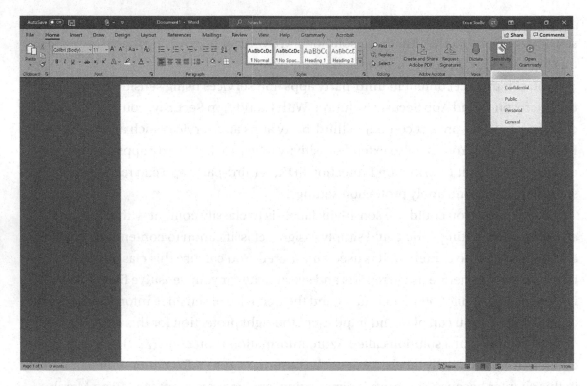

Figure 5-1. *Manually apply a sensitivity label in Word*

Next, let us look at sensitivity labels from the end user perspective. First, sensitivity labels can be available for manual labeling within Office documents. For example, Figure 5-1 shows a Word document. On the Home tab in the ribbon, there is a dropdown for sensitivity labels. This dropdown allows me to label the file as a confidential, public, personal, or general document. A similar labeling schema is available in Exchange as well, and these labels are also available in the Office mobile apps.

When you use the option to auto-apply sensitivity labels to Office documents that contain sensitive information, the end user will see a yellow ribbon notifying them of the applied label. If you choose to prompt them to apply a label, a banner will ask them to confirm it.

Now let us discuss licensing for sensitivity labels.

Licensing and Permissions

If you have not noticed, Microsoft compliance permissions are complicated. And out of all the features, information protection (sensitivity labels) is the most complex. Sensitivity label licensing depends on how you will use the sensitivity labels. I have tried my hardest to sum it up as simply as possible in a format that fits in a book (a giant spreadsheet is out).

I think of the licensing as falling into two general buckets: manual labeling and automatic labeling. As in other solution areas, manual labeling is available with most licenses, while automatic is available only in advanced licenses. The exact details are as follows.

If you want to apply labels manually in the following ways

- Apply sensitivity labels manually in Microsoft 365 apps (Office 365 ProPlus/Business client apps) using built-in labeling.

- Apply and view sensitivity labels in Power BI and protect data when it is exported to Excel, PowerPoint, or PDF:

  - Not included in Office 365 E3

- Apply sensitivity labels manually to data in third-party clouds (must also own Cloud App Security):

  - Not included in Office 365 E3 or Office 365 E5

Then you need one of the following licenses:

- Azure Info Protection (AIP) Plan 1

- AIP Plan 2 (retired)

- EMS E3

- Enterprise Mobility + Security (EMS) E5

- Office 365 E3

- Office 365 E5

- Microsoft 365 Business Premium

- Microsoft 365 F1

- Microsoft 365 F3

- Microsoft 365 E3

- Microsoft 365 E5/A5 Information Protection and Governance

- Microsoft 365 E5 Compliance

- Microsoft 365 E5

There are some exceptions for manual labeling when you involve containers. If you want to apply labels manually in the following ways

- Apply sensitivity labels manually in Office for the Web and Office Mobile:

  - Included in Microsoft 365 Business Premium and Microsoft 365 F3

- Apply sensitivity labels manually for SharePoint sites, Teams, and Microsoft 365 groups.

Then you need one of the following licenses:

- Office 365 E3 (requires Azure Active Directory Premium Plan 1)

- Office 365 E5 (requires Azure Active Directory Premium Plan 1)

- Microsoft 365 E3

- Microsoft 365 E5

If you want to apply labels automatically in the following ways

- Apply sensitivity labels automatically in Microsoft 365 apps (Office 365 ProPlus/Business client apps), Office for the Web, and Office Mobile based on sensitive information types.

- Apply sensitivity labels automatically to files in SPO or EXO email.

- Auto-labeling policy simulation.

Then you need one of the following licenses:

- Office 365 Advanced Compliance (retired)

- Office 365 E5

- Microsoft 365 E5/A5 Information Protection and Governance

- Microsoft 365 E5 Compliance

- Microsoft 365 E5

I know that was a lot, so I will remind you of the licensing requirements as we talk about each area.

For permissions, you will need to be a member of one of the following roles to create new sensitivity labels in your organization. If you want somebody to read labels but not modify them, use the Sensitivity Label Reader role:

- Sensitivity Label Administrator

- Organization Configuration

If you would like to utilize an existing role group, the following role groups are pre-configured with the proper permissions:

- Compliance Data Administrator

- Compliance Administrator

- Security Administrator

Please note these roles are not required for end users to use labels; it is only for people performing administration functions on the labels.

Create a Sensitivity Label

Now let us look at how we can create and use a sensitivity label. First, visit the Microsoft 365 Compliance Center. On the left-hand navigation, click Information protection.

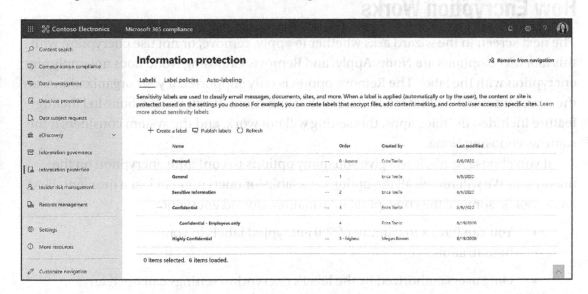

Figure 5-2. The Information protection overview page

This click will bring you to an overview of any labels that already exist in your organization, shown in Figure 5-2. The Label policies tab lists policies used to deploy a label to specific users, groups, or sites. The Auto-labeling tab lists policies for automatically applying a sensitivity label to content in SharePoint and OneDrive.

Please note that this is one section where I expect the user interface to change a bit right after publication. Microsoft has announced they will add some additional capabilities around defining whether a label is associated with files or with containers like SharePoint sites or Microsoft Teams. The UI will look a bit different soon after the book is published. However, the functionality described in this chapter will still be the same; Microsoft is merely rearranging the UI to make it easier to use.

To create a sensitivity label, visit the Labels tab. Click + Create a label. This click brings you to the new sensitivity label wizard. The first step asks you to name your label. Create a unique name and a description that helps end users. The description should allow them to understand when and how they might use this label. It will show as a tooltip to users in Office apps and other locations. You can also add a description for admins. I have seen people use the admin description to help remember the label's business purpose, but you can use it for any purpose. Then click Next.

How Encryption Works

The next screen in the wizard asks whether to apply, remove, or not use encryption with this label. The options are None, Apply, and Remove. Choosing None does not apply any encryption with the label. The Remove option is only supported if your organization uses the Azure Information Protection unified labeling client. If you use the built-in labeling feature included in Office apps, this setting will not work, and the system considers it the same as choosing None.

If you choose Apply, it will give you many options to configure encryption on the document. We will review all the options available for encryption in just a moment. First, let us look at some of the conceptual information around encryption:

- You can have a maximum of 500 encrypted labels in your organization.

- Only users authorized by the label's encryption settings can open an encrypted document, meaning the label enforces permissions about who can read, edit, or perform other actions on the file.

- Content remains encrypted no matter where it resides, either inside or outside your organization.

- A renamed file will remain encrypted.

- Encryption applies both at rest, for example, in a OneDrive account, and in transit, for example, a sent email.

There are many nuances when it comes to encryption, and the topic could probably fill an entire book, so I am only providing a high-level overview of encryption in the section. I encourage you to do some additional research about how encryption works to make the right decisions for your organization.

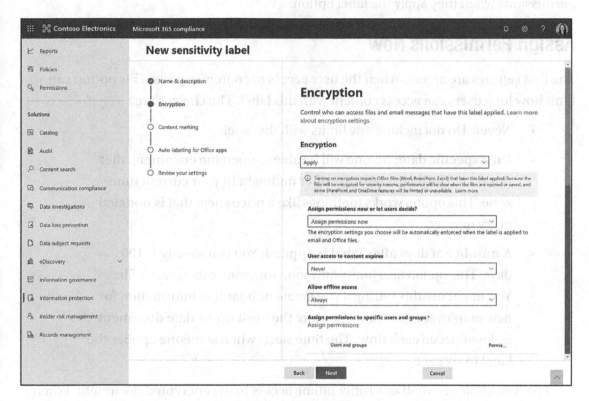

Figure 5-3. *Encryption options for sensitivity labels*

If you want to apply encryption using this label, click the dropdown menu on the screen, and choose Apply. This choice causes several options to appear:

1. Assign permissions now or let users decide?

2. User access to content expires

3. Allow offline access

4. Assign permissions to specific users and groups

These options will change as we choose the various options on the page. The options shown in Figure 5-3 appear when you select Assign permissions now as the first option. Next, we will examine each one of these options shown in this view in detail. Later, we will look at the possibilities for the other choice in the dropdown called Let users assign permissions when they apply the label option.

Assign Permissions Now

The first settings are around when the user access to content expires. This option can limit how long users can access content with this label. The choices are

- **Never**: Do not include any limits with the label.

- **On a specific date**: No one will be able to open the document after this date. The date is effective after midnight in your current time zone. This option works for things like a price sheet that is updated every quarter.

- **A number of days after label is applied**: You can specify 1–100 days. This option also limits how long someone can access a file. You might use this setting if you create onboarding information for new employees and want to ensure the most up-to-date document is downloaded each time. The time starts when someone applies the label to content.

The next choice is whether to offer offline access to the encrypted document. When we encrypt a file, each user gets a use license that contains the user's usage rights to the document. If you do not select an expiration date, then by default, the use license is only reauthorized to access the file every 30 days. The user can access the content even when not connected to the Internet for that time. The choices for this setting are

- **Always**: Uses the tenant default of 30 days.

- **Never**: Requires the system to check the use rights every time someone interacts with the document. This check requires an Internet connection. I see people use this option for highly confidential documents.

- **Only for a number of days**: You can specify 1–100 days. I see people use this option for two reasons:

- You want to allow offline access for less than 30 days. For example, if people need to access a highly confidential document offline, you could sometimes set this to 1–2 days to allow flexibility.

- You want to allow offline access for more than 30 days. For example, you have trainers who rarely have access to the Internet at a client site. You want the training materials to expire every 90 days (using the User access to content expires setting), forcing them to download the new materials. You would set this field to 90 days to have offline access to the materials for the entire time.

The last option is to assign permissions to specific users and groups. This option allows you to define who can interact with content classified by the label. For example, you might want to enable HR to edit onboarding materials, but everyone else can only read the document. You set these permissions in two steps: First, select the group of users, such as HR. Then define what actions this group can perform, such as edit.

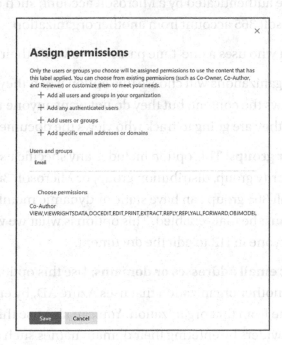

Figure 5-4. The Assign permissions options

Click the blue link that says Assign permissions. This click will open the dialog box shown in Figure 5-4. Choose one of the user or group options. Do this by clicking one or more of the options and then specifying any required information. You will want to work with one permission level at a time, such as everyone who can co-author a document.

These options for users and groups are

- **Add all users and groups in your organization**: This option includes anyone in your organization with a Microsoft 365 account. It excludes guest accounts.

- **Add any authenticated users**: This setting is the least restrictive. It does not restrict who can access the content that the label encrypts. Anyone who can authenticate with your organization is included in this group, such as

  - A person with an email account authenticated by Azure AD or a federated social provider like Google or Facebook

  - Someone authenticated by a Microsoft account, such as a Live ID or Microsoft 365 account from another organization

  - A person who uses a one-time passcode to verify their email address

  Typically, organizations will choose this option when they do not care who views the content, but they do not want anyone to edit or print it, or if they are going to track who views the document.

- **Add users or groups**: This option includes any specific user or email-enabled security group, distribution group, or Microsoft 365 group. The Microsoft 365 group can have static or dynamic membership. The group must be mail-enabled. This option is what we would use to allow everyone in HR to edit the document.

- **Add specific email addresses or domains**: Use this option to specify all users in another organization that uses Azure AD, by entering any domain name from that organization. You can also use this option for social providers by entering their domain names such as gmail. com, hotmail.com, or outlook.com. You might use this option when sharing partner materials with another organization while ensuring a competitor cannot open them.

Now that we have specified the users or groups, we can define what permissions they receive. The permissions you choose will apply to all the groups you have selected in the previous step. Click the blue link that says Choose permissions.

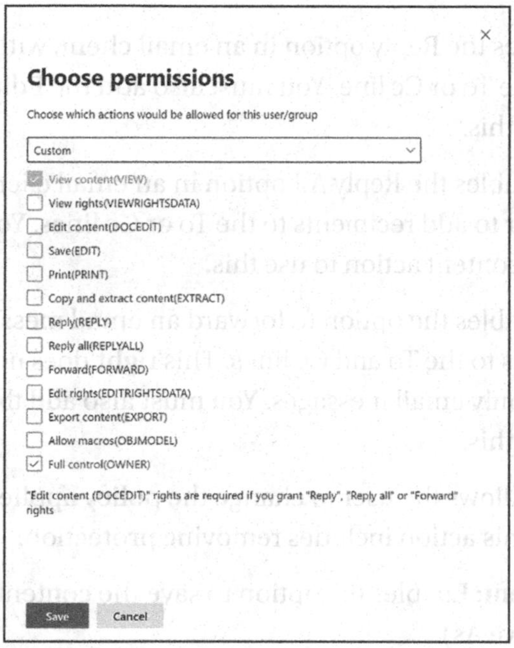

Choose permissions

Choose which actions would be allowed for this user/group

Custom

☑ View content(VIEW)
☐ View rights(VIEWRIGHTSDATA)
☐ Edit content(DOCEDIT)
☐ Save(EDIT)
☐ Print(PRINT)
☐ Copy and extract content(EXTRACT)
☐ Reply(REPLY)
☐ Reply all(REPLYALL)
☐ Forward(FORWARD)
☐ Edit rights(EDITRIGHTSDATA)
☐ Export content(EXPORT)
☐ Allow macros(OBJMODEL)
☑ Full control(OWNER)

"Edit content (DOCEDIT)" rights are required if you grant "Reply", "Reply all" or "Forward" rights

[Save] [Cancel]

Figure 5-5. The custom permission actions

One option is to set custom permission actions. The actions available, shown in Figure 5-5, include

- **View content**: This allows the user to open the document and see the content. This action is always selected because you must view the content to perform other actions.

- **View rights**: This allows the user to see the policy applied to the document. This option does not work in Office apps.

- **Edit content**: This allows the user to modify, rearrange, format, or sort the application's content. It does not grant the right to save the edited copy. You must include this option if you give Reply, Reply all, or Forward rights.

- **Save**: Allows the user to save the document to the current location. They can also save Office documents to a new place, with a new name.

131

- **Print**: Enables the option to print the content.

- **Copy and extract content**: Enables options to copy data (including screen captures) from the document into the same or another document.

- **Reply**: Enables the Reply option in an email client, without allowing changes in the To or Cc line. You must also add the Edit content action to use this.

- **Reply all**: Enables the Reply All option in an email client but does not allow the user to add recipients to the To or Cc lines. You must also add the Edit content action to use this.

- **Forward**: Enables the option to forward an email message and add recipients to the To and Cc lines. This right does not apply to documents, only email messages. You must also add the Edit content action to use this.

- **Edit rights**: Allows the user to change the policy applied to the document. This action includes removing protection.

- **Export content**: Enables the option to save the content to a different file name (Save As).

- **Allow macros**: Enables the option to run macros or perform other programmatic or remote access to a document's content.

- **Full control**: Grants all rights to the document, and the users can perform all available actions.

With the custom permission level, you can turn any of those options on or off. There are also pre-configured permission actions available for the following permission levels. These permission levels have the recommended actions selected for you and cannot be modified:

- **Co-owner:** All the actions listed in the preceding text are selected.

- **Co-author**: View content, View rights, Edit content, Save, Print, Copy and extract content, Reply, Reply all, Forward, Allow macros.

- **Reviewer**: View content, View rights, Edit content, Save, Reply, Reply all, Forward, Allow macros.

- **Viewer**: View content, View rights, Allow macros. Do not use this option for email.

This section explained all the options available when selecting "Assign permissions now" for the "Assign permissions now or let users decide?" option. Next, we will examine the options for choosing the Let users assign permissions when they apply the label option.

Let Users Assign Permissions When They Apply the Label

A sensitivity label that lets users assign permissions can only be applied to content manually by users. It cannot be auto-applied or used as a recommended label. There are only two options available for this selection:

- **In Outlook, enforce restrictions equivalent to the Do Not Forward option**: This setting means recipients can view it but cannot forward, print, or copy the content when someone manually applies this label to an email. If this is the only box checked, this label will not appear in Word, Excel, and PowerPoint.

- **In Word, PowerPoint, and Excel, prompt users to specify permissions**: This option allows users to select from a predefined list of permission levels. They then choose the groups to which the permission level applies. Finally, they have an option to select an expiration date. If this is the only box checked, this label will not appear in Outlook.

When both options are selected, the label is visible in Outlook, Word, Excel, and PowerPoint.

Now that we have configured everything in the encryption step in the label wizard, we can finally click Next and continue configuring our sensitivity label.

Content Marking

Content marking allows you to place text inside of an Office document or email. The content marking step has three options, shown in Figure 5-6. You can add one of the following to content classified with your sensitivity label:

1. Add a watermark

2. Add a header

3. Add a footer

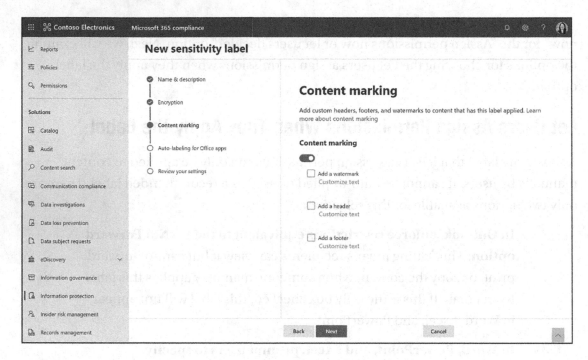

Figure 5-6. *Content marking options for sensitivity labels*

A watermark is a faint text placed behind the text in the body of a document. To add a watermark, check the box next to Add a watermark. Click the blue Customize text link:

- Type the word you wish to display as a watermark text. Watermarks are limited to 255 characters.

- Set the font size. There do not seem to be any limits on the font size you can select.

- Choose the watermark color. It can be black, yellow, blue, green, or red.

- Select the text layout for the watermark. Your choices are diagonal and horizontal.

Watermarks are applied to documents but not to email. When you complete the watermark settings, click Save, and it will take you back to the wizard screen.

Your next content marking option is for a header. The header will automatically inject text to the top of the email messages and documents with this sensitivity label:

- Specify the header text. The header can be up to 1,024 characters except for Excel, which has a limit of 255 characters.

- Set the font size. There do not seem to be any limits on the font size you can select.

- Choose the font color. It can be black, yellow, blue, green, or red.

- Decide whether you want the text to be aligned left, right, or center.

You can apply headers to emails or documents. The content marking footer settings are the same as the header options. The difference is the footer appears at the bottom of the document instead of at the top. When you complete the configuration of the content marking options, click Next.

If your organization has enabled sensitivity labels for sites and groups, the next screen will show those options. We will cover this functionality a section later in this chapter called "Use Sensitivity Labels with Containers." If you have not enabled this feature in your organization, you will see the next screen.

Auto-label Office Documents

You will only see the auto-labeling for Office apps step if you have the proper license. I will cover the license needed in just a moment. If you do not have the appropriate license, then the next screen you see will be the Review your settings screen, which we cover at the end of this section.

Assuming you have the right license, this screen shows you the auto-labeling options for Office apps. Microsoft 365 supports auto-labeling in Office apps for users who have either Office 365 ProPlus or the Azure Information Protection unified labeling client installed. When it detects sensitive content in an email or document matching the conditions you choose, the system can automatically apply this label or show a message to users recommending they use it themselves.

Note   This feature works for client-side labeling when users edit documents or compose emails. Auto-labeling for content stored in SharePoint, OneDrive, and Exchange is covered later in this chapter.

I see companies using this feature to protect sensitive information so that end users do not have to worry about doing the right thing. They use the conditions to look for sensitive information types, such as a bank account number. If a bank account number is found more than four times in a document and we are 80% sure that it is, in fact, a bank account number, then it will automatically classify the file using the label that protects the content.

As a reminder, auto-labeling for Office apps is available with the following licenses:

- Microsoft 365 E5

- Microsoft 365 E5 Compliance

- Microsoft 365 E5 Information Protection and Governance

- Office 365 E5

- Office 365 Advanced Compliance (retired)

Now let us discuss the options for auto-labeling Office apps. First, toggle on the feature.

Second, decide the condition that you would like to match. Our only option is Content contains. Then click Add. You can choose to classify content based on a sensitive info type or a trainable classifier, both of which we covered in-depth in Chapter 3.

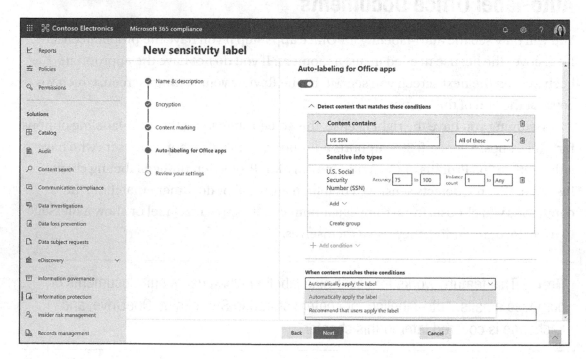

Figure 5-7. *Auto-labeling for Office apps options*

If you choose sensitive info types, it will bring you to a screen displaying all the available info types in alphabetical order. You can also search for info types. Select the info types you want to use and click Add. The screen will display each sensitive info type in a row, shown in Figure 5-7. For each info type, you can set the accuracy and instance count. If you get too many false positives or negatives in your testing of auto-labeling for Office apps, try adjusting these settings.

If you choose trainable classifiers, the screen will display a list of your organization's available classifiers. Select one or more classifiers and click Add.

There is a text box that says Default where you can name your condition group. You can also choose to match all the conditions or any of the conditions. Additionally, you can click Create group to add another group for conditions. You can join these two groups by an AND or OR operator.

When you complete your conditions' configuration, scroll down to decide what happens when content matches these conditions. Your choices are

- Automatically apply the label

- Recommend that users apply the label

In both cases, the user decides whether to accept or reject the label to ensure correct content labeling.

Finally, you can enter text for "Display this message to users when the label is applied." You can display the default message or create your own. If you choose to recommend labeling, the message will include users' option to dismiss the recommendation. If they do this, the message will appear again the next time someone opens the file. This message appears under the Office ribbon of the email or document.

Now that the auto-label settings are complete, click Next. The next screen asks you to review your label settings. If you are happy, click Submit. Congratulations! You have finished setting up your sensitivity label!

Sensitivity Label Priority

After you click Submit, you will be brought back to the Information protection solution and the Labels tab. Once you create a few labels, you will notice that the screen lists them in an order. This order is important. You want your highest-priority labels, such as highly confidential, to be at the bottom of this list. The least important labels, such as personal, appear at the top. Zero is the lowest priority, and the highest number is the highest priority. This order is important because you can apply just one sensitivity label to a document or email. If there is a conflict between options, then the system will use the highest-priority label. If you set an option that requires your users to justify changing a label to a lower classification, it is this order that identifies what label is a lower classification.

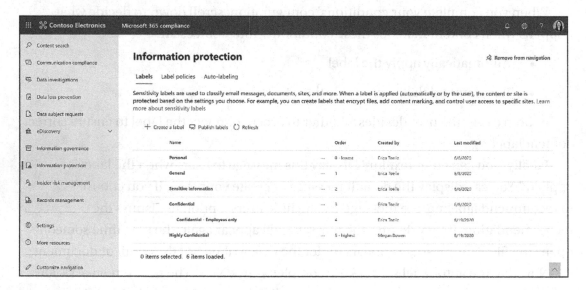

Figure 5-8. *Sensitivity label order and hierarchy*

You can also create a two-level hierarchy of labels, shown in Figure 5-8. This hierarchy allows you to have parent labels and sub-labels. Sub-labels can be a logical way to present sensitivity labels to end users in groups. Sub-labels do not inherit any settings from their parent label; it is just an easy way for end users to think about them.

Modifying and Deleting Sensitivity Labels

If you want to edit or delete labels, you need to be careful. If you delete a sensitivity label, the system does not remove that label from the content. It will still enforce the protection settings from the deleted label. If you edit a label, you do not need to republish the label, but it can take up to 24 hours for changes to take effect. But edited sensitivity labels enforce the original label settings.

I do not recommend that you ever delete a label. If you would like to stop using a label, remove it from the label policy, so it is not active. We will cover label policies in the next section. This way, you can keep track of your label history. This procedure is especially essential for labels that apply encryption. You always want to have a record of that label to not accidentally lose the encryption key. If you do delete a label with encryption, the encryption template is archived. You will not be able to reuse that label name because of the archived encryption template. You can technically delete an encryption template by using PowerShell. But please do not do that unless you are sure that you have no content that still uses that encryption key.

If you want to remove a label from a policy, this is a much less risky option than deleting a label. And this way, you can always add it back to a label policy later if needed. When you remove a label from a label policy, the end users can no longer utilize it. The next time the label policies refresh, users will no longer see it as an option in their Office apps. For documents classified with the removed label, users will still see the label name in the status bar for Word, Excel, and PowerPoint. Similarly, for removed labels applied to SharePoint files, they will still see the label name in the sensitivity column.

Now that we have covered everything related to the creation and maintenance of sensitivity labels, let us discuss how we can deploy them for end users. In our next section, we are going to talk about sensitivity label policies.

Sensitivity Label Policies

Sensitivity label policies are how we deploy labels to end users so they can manually apply them to documents. We can choose to deploy a label to specific users or groups or the entire organization. Once we deploy the labels through a policy, they will appear in Office apps, such as Outlook, Excel, PowerPoint, and Word. With a sensitivity label policy, you can choose which users and groups see the labels. You can apply a default label to documents, require a justification for changing a label, require users to use a label to their emails and files, or provide a help link to a custom help page. You can also use labels in more than one policy.

Note   It could take up to 24 hours for labels to appear to users after publishing
them through a policy.

How to Create Sensitivity Label Policies

To publish a label, visit the Microsoft 365 Compliance Center. In the left navigation, click
Information protection and then the Label policies tab.

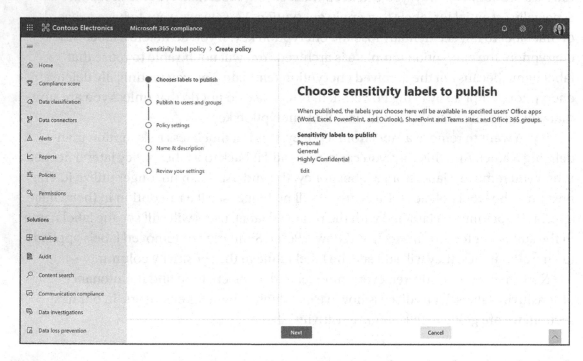

Figure 5-9. *Choose the sensitivity labels to publish*

Click Publish labels. The wizard that appears, shown in Figure 5-9, will first ask you
to choose which sensitivity labels you would like to publish. You would choose from your
existing list of sensitivity labels that you have already created. Click Choose sensitivity
labels to publish and then check the boxes next to your label selections and click Add. If
you select a sub-label, make sure you also choose its parent label. Click Next when done.

The next screen asks you to select the users and groups to which the labels should
appear. You can publish labels to everyone in your organization or specific users or
specific Microsoft 365 groups. You can also publish them to distribution lists and mail-
enabled security groups.

If you want to deploy the labels to everyone in the organization, click Next. Otherwise, click the blue text that says Choose users or groups. Click Add and check the boxes next to the users or groups you would like to select. You can also use the search bar to narrow down the list, but it will only find items that begin with the term you enter. You cannot search for users or groups that contain the phrase. Once you have finished with your selection, click Add, then Done, and then Next.

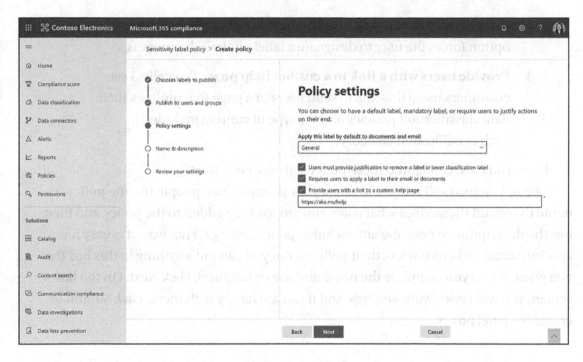

Figure 5-10.   Policy settings options

The next step is to choose the policy settings. This screen allows you to choose to have a default label or a mandatory label or require users to justify their actions, shown in Figure 5-10. For example, the first field asks you if you want to apply a label by default to documents and emails. You have a dropdown menu that will allow you to choose any of the labels you designated in this wizard's first step. As a reminder, this default will only apply to the users and groups you selected in the previous step. If a user has two default labels assigned, the higher-priority label will take precedence.

The next options allow you to do the following:

1. **Users must provide justification to remove a label or lower classification label**: If chosen, if the user assigns a lower-priority label to an item or removes the label, a box will pop up, asking them to type a justification. This action will trigger an alert for subscribed admins that includes this justification.

2. **Require users to apply a label to their email or documents**: This option forces the user to designate a label on their documents.

3. **Provide users with a link to a custom help page**: Typically, I see customers using this link to send users to a page that outlines their data classification policies and the type of content included in each classification category.

Once you have configured these policy settings, click Next.

The next screen will ask you to name your policy. Often, people use the policy name to remind themselves what users and groups they added to the policy and then use the description to describe any included policy settings. That way, it is easy for administrators to keep track of their policies. But you can put anything in this box that you want. When you complete the name and the description, click Next. On the last screen, you will review your settings, and if you are happy with them, click Submit to create the label policy.

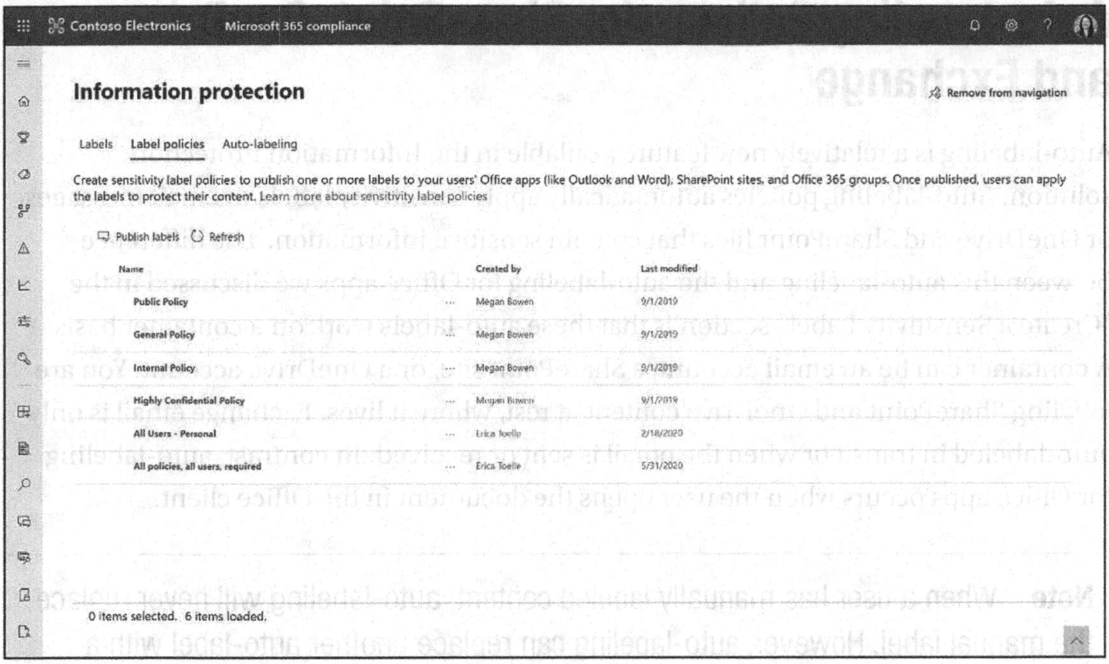

Figure 5-11. Sensitivity label policy priority

This click will bring you back to the Label policies screen, shown in Figure 5-11. Like sensitivity labels, the sensitivity label policies' order is essential because it reflects their priority. The label policy with the lowest priority is at the top. The label policy with the highest priority displays at the bottom. This priority is not apparent because there is not a priority column like in the Labels screen.

You can include one user and multiple label policies, and the user will see all the sensitivity labels from those policies. However, a user gets the policy settings from only the label policy with the highest priority. If you are not seeing the label or label policy setting that you expect for a user or a group and you have waited 24 hours for any new policies or changes to propagate, check the sensitivity label policies' order. If you would like to reorder the label policies, select one of the policies, choose the ellipsis on the right, and choose to move up or move down.

Auto-labeling Policies for SharePoint, OneDrive, and Exchange

Auto-labeling is a relatively new feature available in the Information Protection solution. Auto-labeling policies automatically apply sensitivity labels to email messages or OneDrive and SharePoint files that contain sensitive information. The difference between this auto-labeling and the auto-labeling for Office apps we discussed in the "Create a Sensitivity Label" section is that these auto-labels work on a container basis. A container can be an email account, a SharePoint site, or a OneDrive account. You are labeling SharePoint and OneDrive content at rest, where it lives. Exchange email is only auto-labeled in transit or when the email is sent or received. In contrast, auto-labeling for Office apps occurs when the user opens the document in the Office client.

Note   When a user has manually labeled content, auto-labeling will never replace the manual label. However, auto-labeling can replace another auto-label with a lower priority.

Given that auto-labeling is a new feature, there are some limitations at the time of writing, of which you should be aware.

For SharePoint and OneDrive:

- There is a maximum of 25,000 automatically labeled files in your tenant per day.

- There is a maximum of ten auto-labeling policies per tenant. Each policy can target up to ten sites (SharePoint or OneDrive).

- The existing values for modified, modified by, and the date will not change due to auto-labeling policies.

For Exchange:

- Manual labeling or auto-labeling for Office apps does not scan Office attachments (Word, Excel, and PowerPoint files) and PDF attachments. Auto-labeling for containers does scan attachments. When there is a match, the email is labeled but not the attachment.

- Auto-label container policies, Exchange mail flow rules, and Data Loss Prevention (DLP) policies all can apply encryption. When content satisfies the conditions for encryption, the auto-labeling policy will apply encryption settings first. The system will ignore the encryption settings from the Exchange mail flow rules or DLP policies. However, if the sensitivity label does not apply encryption, the encryption settings from the mail flow rules or DLP policies are applied in addition to the label.

- For an email that has encryption with no label, this encryption will be replaced by a label with any encryption settings when there is a match by using auto-labeling.

- Incoming email is labeled when there is a match with your auto-labeling conditions. However, if the label has encryption, that encryption is not applied.

As a reminder, auto-labeling policies for containers require one of the following licenses:

- Office 365 Advanced Compliance (retired)

- Office 365 E5

- Microsoft 365 E5/A5 Information Protection and Governance

- Microsoft 365 E5 Compliance

- Microsoft 365 E5

How to Use Auto-labeling

To create an auto-labeling policy, visit the Microsoft 365 Compliance Center. On the left side, click Information protection and then the Auto-labeling tab.

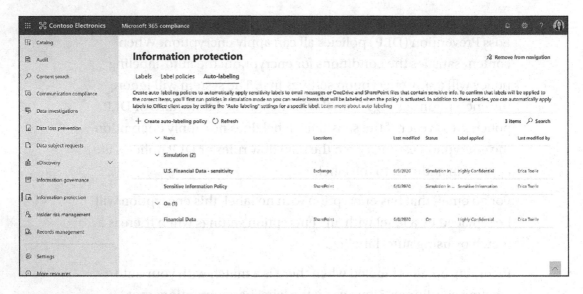

Figure 5-12. *The auto-labeling policies overview page*

Here, you will see a list of all your existing auto-labeling policies, shown in Figure 5-12. To create a new policy, click the + Create auto-labeling policy button. The first screen will ask you to choose the type of sensitive information you would like to protect.

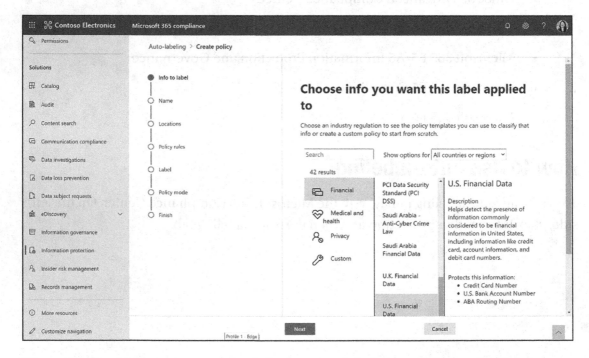

Figure 5-13. *Choose the sensitive info the auto-labeling policy should protect*

Microsoft has grouped some of the most common sensitive information types into templates. For example, if you choose Financial and then US Financial Data as shown in Figure 5-13, it will include info types like a US bank account number, US bank routing number, and credit card number. It can be convenient to group those types into one template.

You can also choose to create a custom policy by choosing Custom and then Custom policy to choose from the 150+ built-in sensitive information types and any custom sensitive information types that your company created. Once you have selected the correct template, click Next.

The next screen will ask you to choose a name for your auto-labeling policy. If you chose one of the previous step's templates, the label name populates automatically for you, such as US Financial Data. Or, if you chose a custom policy, you would create the name yourself. Again, please add some information in the description about how you have configured this auto-labeling policy so you can quickly see that later. Click Next.

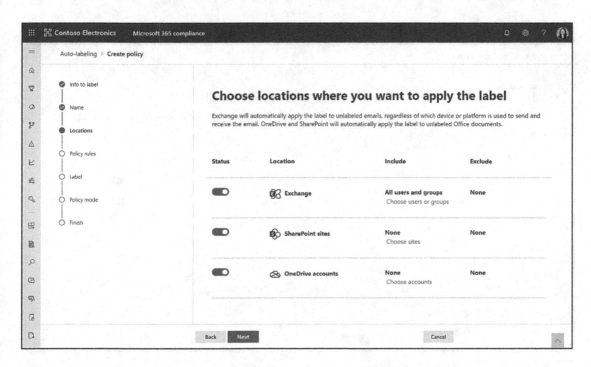

Figure 5-14. *Available locations for container auto-labeling*

The screen in Figure 5-14 will ask you to which locations you want to apply the label. You have the option of choosing Exchange, SharePoint sites, or OneDrive accounts. You can select these entire locations or choose to include or exclude specific people, groups, or sites to or from the policy. If you would like to add specific people to Exchange, turn on the Exchange location and click the blue link that says Choose users or groups. This click brings you to a screen that lists all the users and groups in your organization. Check the box next to an account to add it to the policy. Or you can search for an account by typing at least three letters of the user or group name. When finished, click Done. When you are happy with all the locations you have chosen, click Next.

The next screen allows you to set the policy rules. If you chose to use a template in the first step, you could use the default settings to find content that contains the specified information in the template. If you would like to use advanced settings, this option allows you to create different policy rules for locations, such as OneDrive and SharePoint vs. email and Exchange. Click Advanced settings to see all the available options and click Next.

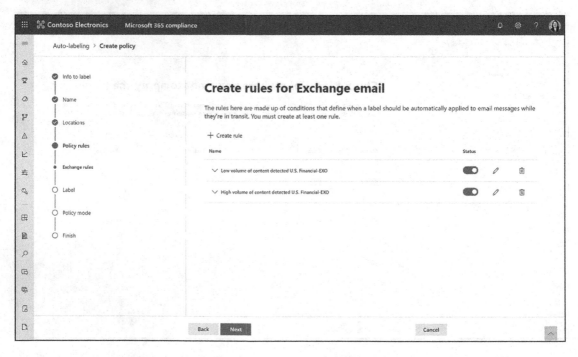

Figure 5-15. *Default Exchange rules for US Financial Data*

The screen in Figure 5-15 shows you the default Exchange rules for the US Financial Data template. We started with a template, so it populated the rules for us. Otherwise, if you chose a custom template, you would need to create these rules yourself.

Typically, most organizations would have different rules for a low volume of sensitive information in content vs. a higher number of matches. This logic is because, for example, content with a high volume of financial information is usually riskier and should have more strict protections than documents with a low amount of financial data. The low volume of financial data could also be a false positive, in which case we do not want to block people from doing their work.

You can also use rules to test out different matching scenarios. Later, when we run our auto-labeling policy in simulation mode, we will get the number of matches per rule in our simulation report. This report allows you to see which rules triggered the matches and whether the results match your hypothesis.

Let us click + Create rule. First, you will need to name the rule and provide a description.

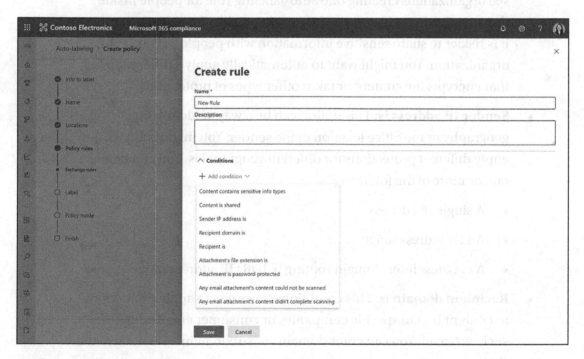

Figure 5-16. *Rule condition options*

Then, you will add a condition. Each rule you create for Exchange must have one or more of the following conditions, shown in Figure 5-16:

- **Content contains sensitive info types**: In our example, we have chosen US Financial Data, such as bank account and credit card information.

- **Any email attachment's content could not be scanned**: If the system cannot scan an attachment, we do not know if it contains sensitive information. Therefore, you might want to apply extra protection to be safe.

- **Any email attachment's content did not complete scanning**: This logic is the same as the previous bullet.

These are optional conditions that you can use:

- **Content is shared**: The two options are With people outside my organization and Only with people inside my organization. I often see organizations creating one auto-labeling rule for people inside the organization and another for people outside. The idea is that it is riskier to share sensitive information with people outside your organization. You might want to automatically apply a different label that encrypts the content or takes other types of protections.

- **Sender IP address is**: This option can be a way of identifying geography or the office location of the sender. You might want to apply different protections for different geographies. You can enter one or more of the following:

  - A single IP address

  - An IP address range

  - A classless inter-domain routing (CIDR) IP address range

- **Recipient domain is**: This condition allows you to apply protections to content sent to specific companies or consumer email addresses, such as Gmail. You can enter domains or subdomains. Do not use the @ sign.

- **Recipient is**: You can enter up to 50 email addresses. Each email address has a limit of 256 characters.

- **Attachment's file extension is**: The period is optional. You can enter these as ".exe" or "exe." Enter the extensions one at a time, clicking Add between each entry.

- **Attachment is password protected**: If an attachment is password protected, then the system cannot scan it.

When you are happy with the logic of your rule, click Save.

Next, the system will ask you to make rules for SharePoint sites, and then the following screen will ask about OneDrive. The options for SharePoint and OneDrive are the same, so I will explain them together. Like Exchange, since we started with a template, it populated the rules for us. Otherwise, if you chose a custom template, you would need to create these rules yourself.

Let us click New rule. First, you will need to name the rule and provide a description. Then, you will add conditions. These are the condition options available for SharePoint:

- Content contains sensitive info types (required).

- Content is shared.

Once you have finished with your rules, click Save.

The next step in the wizard asks you to choose the sensitivity label. Click the blue text that says Choose a label. This list shows sensitivity labels that are available in your organization. This selection will designate the applied sensitivity label if the file meets the conditions you selected in the previous policy rule steps. Remember, you cannot use a parent label (a label with sub-labels) to apply to content. Make sure that you do not configure a parent label for an auto-labeling policy. If you do, the system will not apply the parent label to content. Select the radio button next to one of the labels and click Add and then Next.

Your last choice is whether you would like to run the policy in simulation mode now or leave the policy turned off. Simulation mode allows you to test what would happen after you deploy the policy. This test helps you check for things like false positives or changes you want to make to your configuration before rolling it out to all users. The simulation results are only available to the administrators of the information protection solution, and it will not impact users.

Make your selection and click Next. The next screen is going to show you a summary of your settings for this auto-labeling policy. If you are happy with the settings, click Submit. Then you will get a screen saying it created your auto-labeling policy, and you can click Done to go back to the overview screen.

Next, we will review the label policy simulator, which you would use to run the policy in the previous step in simulation mode.

Label Policy Simulator

The policy simulator shows you how the system will apply labels once you turn on the auto-labeling policy. This test confirms that the policy applies labels to the correct items and that there will not be too many false positives or false negatives. We first run these policies in simulation mode to review items labeled when the policy activates. When we start the simulation, it will take at least 24 hours for the policy to complete the simulation.

The permissions for the label policy simulator are the same as auto-labeling policies for SharePoint, OneDrive, and Exchange.

How to Use the Label Policy Simulator

After you wait 24 hours, you can view the simulation results. Go to the auto-labeling screen and double-click the policies to see how the simulation turned out.

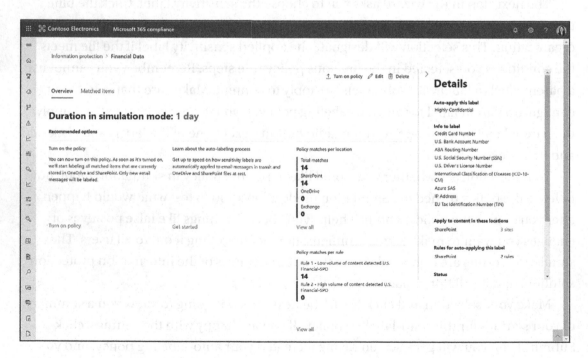

Figure 5-17. *An auto-label policy in simulation mode*

After the simulation has been running for at least one day, we can see a few things on the dashboard shown in Figure 5-17. First, under Recommended options, we can turn on the policy by clicking the blue Turn on policy link. We could learn more about the auto-labeling process and read the documentation by clicking Get started. We can see the number of policy matches per location, including the total matches, in SharePoint, OneDrive, and Exchange.

I also can see the number of policy matches per rule. Remember, we set up our rules during the creation of the auto-label policy. Here we can see which rule triggered the policy. This view is helpful because if you want to try out multiple hypotheses for labeling your content, you can create a rule for each one. Keep in mind that the first matched rule will trigger the policy. The report shows this first rule as a match and will not evaluate additional rules.

You can also overview details of your auto-label policy configuration on the simulation overview page, including what label is auto-applied, what sensitive info it labels, and what content locations and rules it will use to label the content.

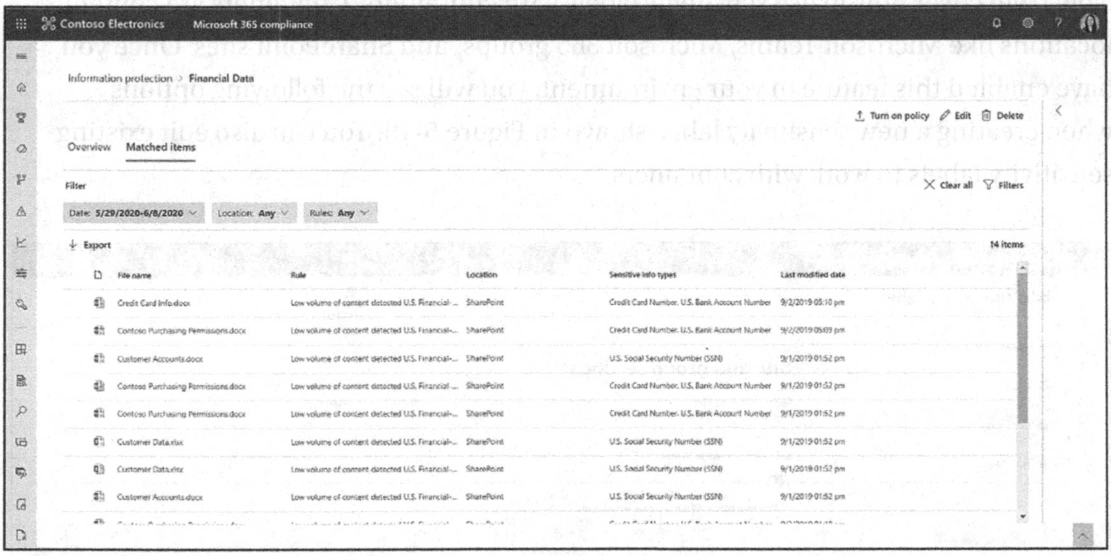

Figure 5-18. *Items matched by the auto-label policy in simulation mode*

Now let us look at the specific items that matched the policy. Click the Matched items tab. In Figure 5-18, you see a list of all the documents that would be labeled by this policy if you turned it on. The view shows you information like the file name, the type of file, the rule that it matched, the content location, what sensitive information types it found, and the last modified date of the information.

Additionally, you can filter the content by a date range, a location, or rules. If you would like to see more details about the matched sensitive information types, click that column's information. This click will bring up a screen that will show you the count of each type of sensitive information it finds and the confidence level that there was a match.

If you need to modify your policy, you can click Edit policy and rerun the simulation. When you are happy with the results, click Turn on policy.

We could use auto-labeling in the policy simulator to set up our policies correctly to ensure they are not too broad or too restrictive. It also helps us understand if we will get false positives and false negatives to adjust our policy's rules and logic accordingly.

In the next section, we will discuss using sensitivity labels with containers such as Microsoft Teams, SharePoint, and Microsoft 365 groups.

Use Sensitivity Labels with Containers

Now I will cover how to use sensitivity labels with containers. Containers are content locations like Microsoft Teams, Microsoft 365 groups, and SharePoint sites. Once you have enabled this feature in your environment, you will see the following options when creating a new sensitivity label, shown in Figure 5-19. You can also edit existing sensitivity labels to work with containers.

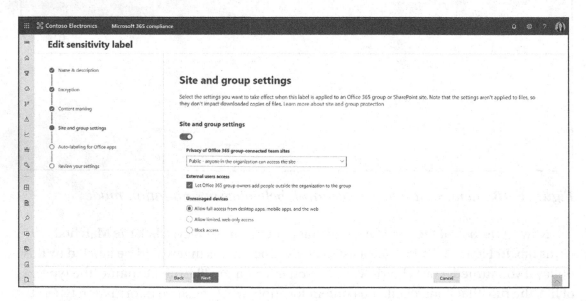

Figure 5-19. *Container options for a sensitivity label*

Containers allow you to control container settings, specifically the following:

- **Privacy of Office 365 group-connected team sites**: Anyone in the organization can find and access public containers, while only those with permission can access private containers.

- **External users access**: This setting determines whether the site admin can add external users or guests as site members.

- **Unmanaged devices**: Device management enables organizations to protect and secure their resources and data from different devices. The idea is that it is riskier to allow access to sensitive information from unmanaged devices. Microsoft Intune offers mobile device management. The options are:

  - Allow full access from desktop apps, mobile apps, and the web

  - Allow limited, web-only access

  - Block access

When you apply a sensitivity label to a supported container, the label automatically applies the configured options to the connected site or group. Figure 5-20 shows the end user view of a SharePoint container label. Content in these containers does not inherit the labels; you will need to add labels to content in the containers using another method.

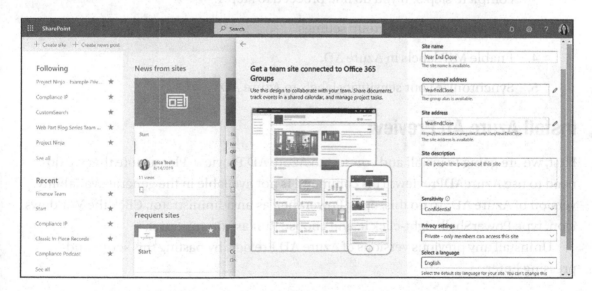

Figure 5-20. *Apply a confidential label to a new SharePoint site*

As a reminder, you need one of the following licenses to use this feature:

- Office 365 E3 (requires Azure Active Directory Premium Plan 1)

- Office 365 E5 (requires Azure Active Directory Premium Plan 1)

- Microsoft 365 E3

- Microsoft 365 E5

How to Use Sensitivity Labels on Containers

By default, this feature will not be available in your environment. You will need to enable it using PowerShell. This part of the book is one of the few places where I will break my no PowerShell rule because the documentation around enabling sensitivity labels with containers is very confusing. The steps are presented in an illogical order, and they are quite challenging to follow. I am going to explain the actions in a more logical order and with more detail. Here are the steps to enable sensitivity labels for containers.

Thank you to Ryan Sturm for helping me make sense of the documentation for enabling sensitivity labels with containers.

1. Install Azure AD Preview, run it, and log into Azure as an admin.

2. Try to access group settings in Azure AD. If you get an error, complete step 3. If you do not, proceed to step 4.

3. Configure Azure AD group settings.

4. Enable MIP labels in Azure AD.

5. Synchronize your sensitivity labels to Azure AD.

Install Azure AD Preview

First, we are going to install and connect to Azure AD Preview. Please note that we do need to use AzureADPreview. This command is not available in the general availability version of Azure AD. To do this, open PowerShell as an administrator. Click the Windows icon, type PowerShell, right-click it, and choose Run as administrator.

Uninstall any previous versions of Azure AD Preview by pasting this script and pressing Enter:

```
Uninstall-Module AzureADPreview
Uninstall-Module azuread
```

Next, we are going to install the latest version of Azure AD Preview:

```
Install-Module AzureADPreview
```

Then we are going to run the import module and connect to Azure AD:

```
Import-Module AzureADPreview
Connect-AzureAD
```

It will then ask you to log into your Azure environment with an admin account. Enter your credentials into the pop-up.

Next, we are going to get our unified group properties by running this command:

```
$Setting = Get-AzureADDirectorySetting -Id (Get-AzureADDirectorySetting |
where -Property DisplayName -Value "Group.Unified" -EQ).id
```

If you get the error shown in Figure 5-21, go ahead and continue with the steps. If you do not get an error, jump to the section "Enable MIP Labels in Azure AD."

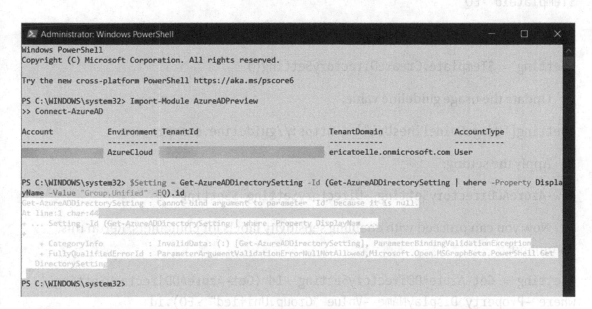

Figure 5-21. *The error you receive when Microsoft 365 group settings are not enabled in your environment*

Configure Azure AD Group Settings

If you do get the error in Figure 5-21, this next step has nothing to do with using sensitivity labels on containers. It is due to the architecture of Azure AD. You must sync one property with the unified group template that the system uses to create a Microsoft 365 group before any other properties such as sensitivity labels can be enabled and synced.

We will use the usage guideline value to trigger this sync because many organizations do not use it. However, if you are using this field in your organization, you could use any other property to trigger the sync. Paste the following PowerShell script and press Enter:

```
Get-AzureADDirectorySettingTemplate
```

This command will return a list of all the available templates. Use this script to select the unified group template, which we will eventually use with sensitivity labels:

```
$TemplateId = (Get-AzureADDirectorySettingTemplate | where { $_.DisplayName
-eq "Group.Unified" }).Id
$Template = Get-AzureADDirectorySettingTemplate | where -Property Id -Value
$TemplateId -EQ
```

Create a new setting object based on the unified group template:

```
$Setting = $Template.CreateDirectorySetting()
```

Update the usage guideline value:

```
$Setting["UsageGuidelinesUrl"] = https://guideline.example.com
```

Apply the setting:

```
New-AzureADDirectorySetting -DirectorySetting $Setting
```

Now you can proceed with enabling sensitivity labels for containers. Rerun this command:

```
$Setting = Get-AzureADDirectorySetting -Id (Get-AzureADDirectorySetting |
where -Property DisplayName -Value "Group.Unified" -EQ).id
```

Enable MIP Labels in Azure AD

Next, we want to display the group settings:

```
$Setting.Values
```

Enable sensitivity labels, so they work in the unified group template:

```
$Setting["EnableMIPLabels"] = "True"
```

Save your changes:

```
Set-AzureADDirectorySetting -Id $Setting.Id -DirectorySetting $Setting
```

Synchronize Your Sensitivity Labels to Azure AD

At this point, we have enabled sensitivity labels for use with our Azure AD groups. We need to sync our sensitivity labels from the Microsoft 365 Compliance Center to Azure AD groups in this step. First, we will connect to the security and compliance PowerShell module.

If you do not already have the EXO v2 module installed, please follow the instructions here: `http://erica.news/EXOv2`.

Execute the following command:

```
Import-Module ExchangeOnlineManagement
```

If you do not use multifactor authentication (you should), run the following command. If you do use MFA, follow these instructions: `http://erica.news/CC-Connect-MFA`.

```
$UserCredential = Get-Credential
Connect-IPPSSession -Credential $UserCredential
```

Type in the credentials for a Microsoft 365 global administrator.

Then, we will run the following command to sync the sensitivity labels:

```
Execute-AzureAdLabelSync
```

Then, remember to end your PowerShell session:

```
Disconnect-ExchangeOnline
```

Now that we synced the labels, we need to wait 24 hours before showing Microsoft 365 groups, SharePoint sites, and Microsoft Teams in the user interface. After 24 hours, you can visit `https://portal.azure.com`.

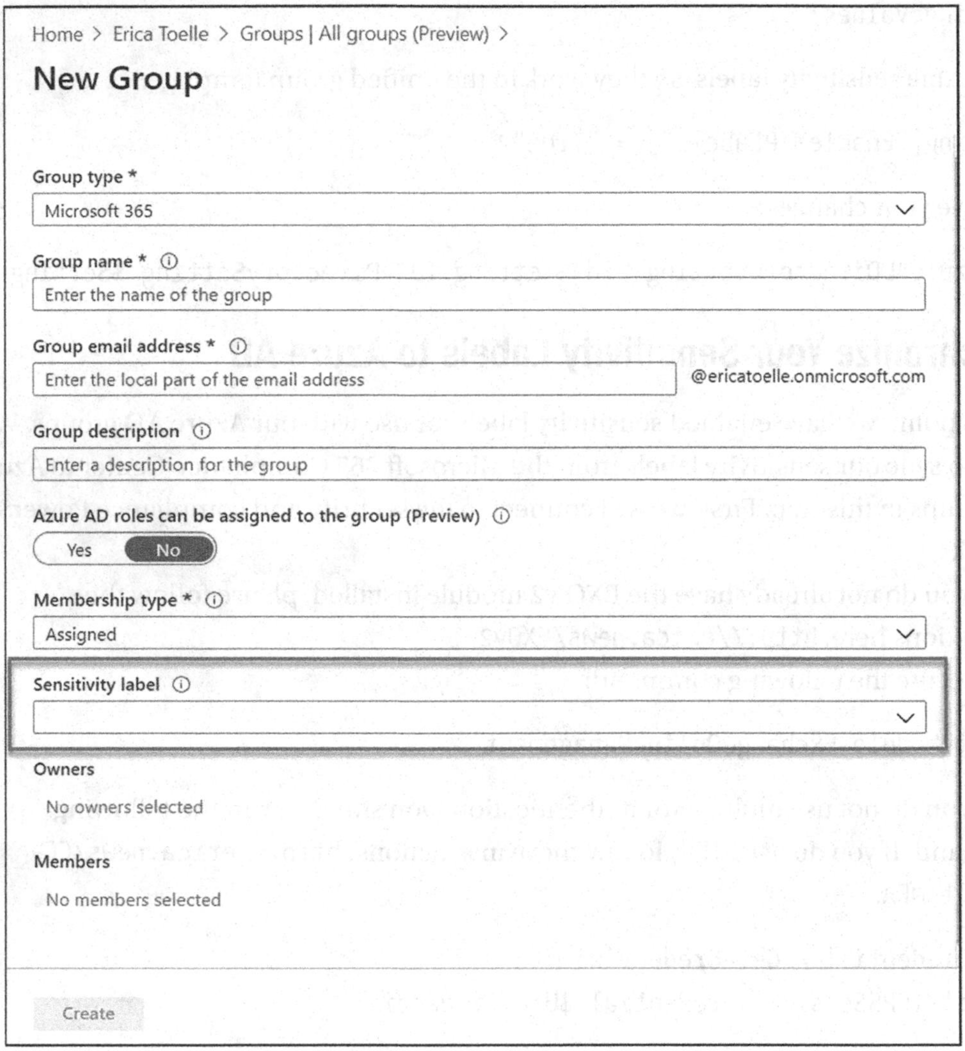

Home > Erica Toelle > Groups | All groups (Preview) >

New Group

Group type *

Microsoft 365

Group name * ⓘ

Enter the name of the group

Group email address * ⓘ

Enter the local part of the email address   @ericatoelle.onmicrosoft.com

Group description ⓘ

Enter a description for the group

Azure AD roles can be assigned to the group (Preview) ⓘ

Yes   **No**

Membership type * ⓘ

Assigned

Sensitivity label ⓘ

Owners

No owners selected

Members

No members selected

Create

Figure 5-22.   You will see the sensitivity label option if you have successfully enabled container labels

Click Azure Active Directory, click Groups, click New Group, and select Microsoft 365 from the Group type dropdown. You should see a field for a sensitivity label. If you see this field, shown in Figure 5-22, you have successfully enabled sensitivity labels for Microsoft 365 groups, SharePoint sites, and Microsoft Teams. If you do not see it, please go back and revisit the configuration steps.

New Features for Using Sensitivity Labels for Containers

Microsoft has announced a couple of additional features for sensitivity labels on containers. As of this book's writing, they were not available yet in my environment to try out and get screenshots, but they are close enough to public preview that I feel comfortable talking about them. Please keep an eye out for these additions.

First is the ability to control external sharing links for sites via sensitivity labels on containers. This feature allows you to define what happens when someone tries to share a file that lives in a container. You can determine what options are available for sharing links and whether you can share with people outside your organization. You can also choose whether you must authenticate external users before they can access a link. Another option is whether you can use anonymous access links, called Anyone with the link. I show the choices in Figure 5-23, and you can turn on or off any of these options.

Figure 5-23. *Sharing link options*

The next change is when we create a new sensitivity label; instead of just creating one label used for both files and containers, you will be able to define whether the label is for files, for containers, or both. Then the label creation wizard will change accordingly to show the appropriate options for your selection.

Another upcoming feature is the ability to set conditional access policies per site. For example, suppose you want to apply terms of use policy or a multifactor authentication policy using an Azure AD conditional access policy. In that case, you will be able to attach that to a container sensitivity label. This feature will be available to advanced compliance licenses only.

This last feature is not coming soon, but Microsoft has publicly announced that it is top of mind. A common request from organizations is that when you apply a label to a container, they want that label to apply to all the documents that live in that site. For example, if you mark a site as confidential, it will also mark all the site files as confidential. Microsoft has not announced a release timeline for this feature.

The last topic in this chapter is storing encrypted files in SharePoint and OneDrive. In the past, encrypted Office documents in SharePoint did not allow co-authoring, search, and eDiscovery, and you could not use DLP with these files. However, that has changed with the release of sensitivity labels for Office files in SharePoint and OneDrive.

Store Documents with Sensitivity Labels in SharePoint and OneDrive

Enabling sensitivity labels for Office files in SharePoint and OneDrive allows you to get around many of the previous limitations of storing encrypted files in these locations. By enabling this feature, you can co-author files in the browser version of Microsoft 365 applications. However, you still will not be able to co-author when editing those files in the Office client.

This feature will also allow you to find encrypted documents in an eDiscovery search and place content on hold. Data loss prevention will be able to scan the files to apply protections to sensitive information. However, this solution will not work well if you are using your own key or double key encryption.

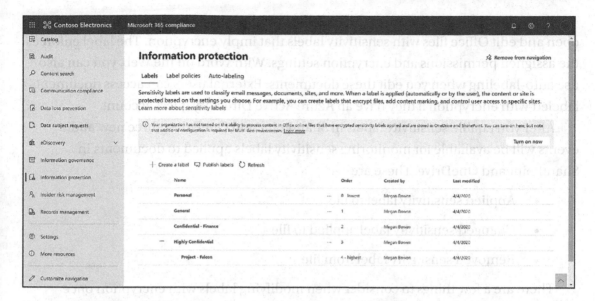

Figure 5-24. *Turn on the ability to process content in Office online files stored in OneDrive and SharePoint that have encrypted sensitivity labels applied*

The great news is that this feature is easy to enable. Simply visit the information protection solution and the Labels tab. A yellow box on the page asks if you would like to turn on this feature, shown in Figure 5-24. Click Turn on now. If you want to disable this feature, you will need to do that via PowerShell.

When you enable the ability to use encrypted sensitivity labels in SharePoint and OneDrive, here is what happens. First, it allows a sensitivity button on the Office client app ribbon, or it will show you the applied label name in the status bar. For Word, Excel, and PowerPoint files, SharePoint does recognize the label and is now able to process the contents of the encrypted data.

When you download or access these files from SharePoint or OneDrive, the sensitivity label and any encryption settings from the label are enforced and remained with the content, wherever it is stored. When users upload labeled and encrypted documents to SharePoint, they must have at least view rights to those files. If they do not have this minimum usage right, the upload would be successful, but then SharePoint would not recognize the label, and it would not be able to process the file contents for search and other purposes.

You will need to use Office on the Web, specifically Word, Excel, and PowerPoint, to open and edit Office files with sensitivity labels that imply encryption. The label enforces the assigned permissions and encryption settings. With Word on the Web, you can also use auto-labeling when you edit these documents. External users can access documents labeled with encryption if they have an Azure Active Directory guest account.

After you enable sensitivity labels in SharePoint and OneDrive, three new audit events will be available for monitoring sensitivity labels applied to documents in SharePoint and OneDrive. These are

- Applied sensitivity label to file

- Changed sensitivity label applied to file

- Removed sensitivity label from file

There are a few things to consider when modifying labels with encryption once you enable the ability to process content in Office online files stored in OneDrive and SharePoint that have encrypted sensitivity labels applied. We will go over them in the next section.

Changing Labels for Documents in SharePoint and OneDrive

Let us say you create and publish a new sensitivity label that applies encryption. It will appear within one hour, but sometimes much faster, in the user's desktop app. The user then applies this label to a document and uploads it to SharePoint and OneDrive. If the system has not completed label replication, encryption will not apply to that document on upload. So, as a result, it will not return the document in search or eDiscovery. You cannot open the document in Office for the Web. The document will not get evaluated by DLP policies.

Here are how fast changes to sensitivity labels replicate:

- **1 hour**: New and deleted sensitivity labels

- **1 hour**: Sensitivity label policy settings that include which labels are in the policy

- **24 hours**: Changes to the sensitivity level settings for existing labels

Because of the difference in the replication times, please keep the following in mind. First, I recommend publishing new labels to only a few test users. Wait for an hour and verify that the label properly encrypts documents in SharePoint and OneDrive. Once you have verified this behavior, make the label available to more users by either adding people to the existing label policy or adding the label to an existing label policy. This way, when your users see the label, the encryption and settings have already been synchronized to SharePoint and OneDrive, and you do not run the risk of not having it work properly.

In this chapter, we learned the following:

1. How to create a new sensitivity label

2. Licensing and permissions for sensitivity labels

3. How to configure encryption for a sensitivity label

4. How to set up content marking

5. How to auto-label Office documents

6. Setting a priority for sensitivity labels and label policies

7. Considerations for modifying and deleting sensitivity labels

8. How to deploy labels to users and groups using a sensitivity label policy

9. How to auto-label content in SharePoint, OneDrive, and Exchange

10. How to use the label policy simulator to test auto-label policies

11. How to enable sensitivity labels with containers

12. How to enable the ability to process content in Office online files stored in OneDrive and SharePoint with encrypted sensitivity labels applied

In the next chapter, we will learn about Data Loss Prevention (DLP) policies. DLP policies are complementary to sensitivity labels. Sensitivity labels apply protections to content and still allow it to move around. DLP policies entirely block the sharing of content that contains sensitive information.

CHAPTER 6

Data Loss Prevention Policies

Data Loss Prevention (DLP) helps identify sensitive information across many Microsoft 365 locations such as Exchange Online, SharePoint Online, OneDrive for Business, and Microsoft Teams. DLP policies prevent accidental sharing of sensitive information. They monitor and protect sensitive information in the desktop versions of Excel, PowerPoint, and Word. They can help monitor message traffic to comply with regulations.

DLP policies also help users to learn how to stay compliant without interrupting their workflow. DLP policies can protect your data, such as blocking people from sharing sensitive information in email and Teams chats and channel messages. They can also prevent sensitive information from being accessed by or shared with external users. You can also use DLP policies to warn people when they share sensitive information to ensure they are doing the right thing.

Compliance standards outline how an organization should safeguard personally identifiable information (PII) and other sensitive data. DLP policies, used together with Microsoft Information Protection sensitivity labels (discussed in Chapter 5), provide a well-rounded solution for protecting sensitive data. DLP policies can identify sensitive information and block its movement. Sensitivity labels can protect content in place, using encryption and other methods.

Before you begin to use DLP policies, you should take steps to plan for their use. First, determine what data needs to be protected. Define the sensitive information types you want to protect and include examples.

Next, decide how you should protect the data. Should the information be encrypted, blocked, or prevented from sharing with external users, or should all access be removed?

Now, decide if there should be different protections for small vs. large amounts of data. For example, you might have less strict protections if you find one piece of sensitive information vs. 15 pieces of sensitive information.

© Erica Toelle 2021
E. Toelle, *Microsoft 365 Compliance*, https://doi.org/10.1007/978-1-4842-5778-4_6

Lastly, decide on your reporting requirements. Would you like an alert to happen when an item meets the policy conditions? When we find sensitive information in small or large amounts, should an email be sent to certain people?

As always, let us look at permissions and licensing before we dive into the specifics of Data Loss Prevention.

Permissions and Licensing

To create DLP policies, users need to have the DLP Compliance Management role. Microsoft includes this role in the following role groups:

- Compliance Administrator

- Compliance Data Administrator

- Organization Management

- Security Administrator

People who can only view DLP policies will need to have the View-Only DLP Compliance Management role. Microsoft includes this role in the following role groups:

- Compliance Administrator

- Compliance Data Administrator

- Organization Management

- Security Administrator

- Security Operator

- Security Reader

Microsoft 365 DLP is available in the following subscriptions:

- Office 365 E3

- Office 365 E5

- Microsoft 365 E3

- Microsoft 365 E5

- Office 365 Data Loss Prevention (DLP)

The exception is Teams DLP, also known as communications DLP, which is only possible with the E5 licenses.

Contents of a DLP Policy

A DLP policy has two elements. First, you need to decide on the locations where you will apply the policy. These locations could be SharePoint, OneDrive for Business, Teams chats and conversations, Exchange email, devices (onboarded through Microsoft Defender Advanced Threat Protection), or Microsoft Cloud App Security locations.

Second, you need to define the rules that will provide matches for your policy. A rule consists of a condition plus an action. For example, you may have a rule that detects large amounts of Social Security numbers. The condition is if it finds more than ten instances of the sensitive information type "Social Security numbers." The action is to block it from being emailed or shared with external users. The condition and the action together make up the rule around how to handle large amounts of Social Security numbers. You can have multiple rules within one DLP policy. Content can match one or several rules depending on the settings of your policy.

Create a New DLP Policy Using a Microsoft 365 Template

First, we will create a DLP policy using one of the standard out-of-the-box templates. And then, in the next section, we will look at the advanced options you can use when creating your DLP policy.

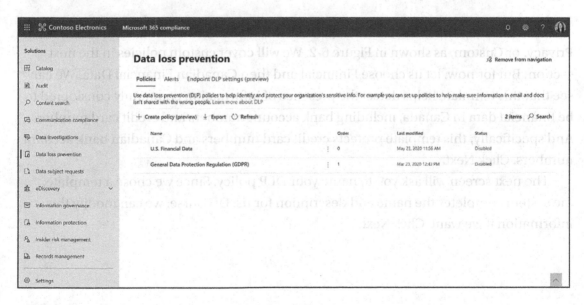

Figure 6-1. *Data Loss Prevention policy list*

To create a new DLP policy, visit the Microsoft Compliance Center. On the left side of the page, find Data loss prevention. Clicking it takes you to the DLP overview page shown in Figure 6-1. Click the + Create policy button. This click will bring you to a screen where you can first choose the information to protect. On the screen, you can see several templates available.

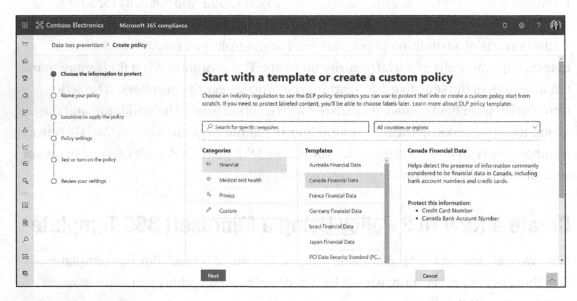

Figure 6-2. *DLP policy templates*

We can choose from template categories, such as Financial, Medical and health, Privacy, or Custom, as shown in Figure 6-2. We will cover custom policies in the next section. But for now, let us choose Financial and then Canadian Financial Data. We can see that this template helps detect the presence of information commonly considered to be financial data in Canada, including bank account numbers and credit card numbers. And specifically, this template protects credit card numbers and Canadian bank account numbers. Click Next.

The next screen will ask you to name your DLP policy. Since we chose a template, the system completes the name and description for us. Of course, we can modify this information if we want. Click Next.

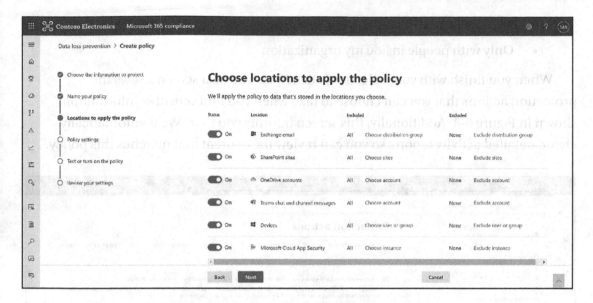

Figure 6-3. *Locations where you can apply DLP policies*

Now we will choose the locations to apply our policy, shown in Figure 6-3. Our options are Exchange email, SharePoint sites, OneDrive accounts, Teams chat and channel messages, Devices, and Microsoft Cloud App Security. The choices we have later in the process will depend on the locations chosen. For this reason, I recommend creating separate DLP policies for Exchange content and other types of content. The options available for Exchange are much more extensive than other locations. Some of the Exchange options will only show if you select Exchange only. For this example, select Exchange as the only location. Click Next.

The next screen will ask you to define our policy settings. We have two choices:

1. Review and customize default settings from the template.

2. Create or customize advanced DLP settings.

In this case, let us choose the first option. In the next section, we will look at the second option. Click Next.

The next screen asks you about the info you would like to protect. First, we have the option to add other sensitive information types by clicking the Edit button. This click allows you to choose from the over 130 built-in sensitive information types or other sensitive information types that have been created by your company. Alternatively, you could remove sensitive information types in this step.

We can also decide whether we want to detect when a user shares this content from Microsoft 365. Our choices are

- With people outside my organization

- Only with people inside my organization

When you finish with your selection, click Next. The next screen shows the protection actions that you can choose to take when you find sensitive information, shown in Figure 6-4. Additionally, this screen informs you that "We'll automatically create detailed activity reports so you can review the content that matches this policy."

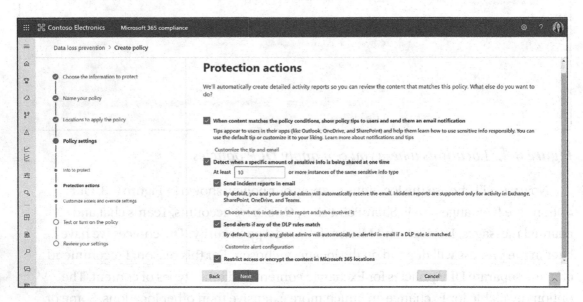

Figure 6-4. *Protection actions for DLP policies*

Our first choice is to show policy tips to users and send them an email when their content matches the policy rules. Tips appear to users in their apps (like Outlook, OneDrive, and SharePoint) and help them learn how to use sensitive info responsibly. You can use the default settings or click the blue text that says "Customize the tip and email to make changes. This click brings you to the same settings for customized policy tips and email notifications that we will cover in the next section. Check the box to select this option.

Our next choice is whether we want to detect when someone shares a specific amount of sensitive information at one time. For example, we can trigger the alert when at least ten or more instances of the same sensitive information type are shared. This setting helps us reduce false positives by creating alerts for higher-risk situations. Check the box to select this option.

When we reach this threshold, we can choose to send an incident report in an email. By default, you and your global admin will automatically receive the email. Incident reports are supported only for activity in Exchange, SharePoint, OneDrive, and Teams. We can click the link to choose what to include in the report and add additional recipients. We will cover these settings in the next section. Check the box to select this option.

We can also choose to send alerts if any of the DLP rules match. By default, you and any global admins will automatically be alerted in an email if something matches a DLP rule. Click the blue text to customize the alert configuration. We will cover these settings in the next section. Check the box to select this option.

Lastly, we can decide to restrict access or encrypt the content that is in Microsoft 365 locations. The next screen will have the settings for this option. Check the box to select this option. Click Next, when you finish your selection.

The next screen allows you to customize access and override settings, shown in Figure 6-5. By default, it blocks users from sending email and Teams chat and channel messages that contain the type of content you are protecting. You cannot override this setting.

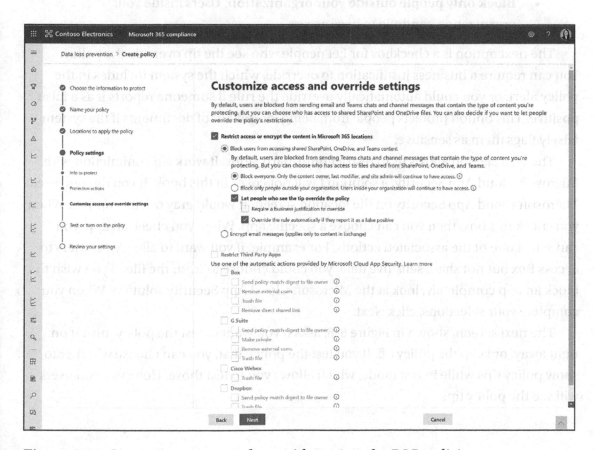

Figure 6-5. Customize access and override settings for DLP policies

You can choose who has access to SharePoint and OneDrive files. You can also decide if you want to let people override the policy's restrictions. Choose if you wish to restrict access or encrypt Microsoft 365 locations. If you do, check that box. This checkbox reveals additional options. Your first choice is whether you want to "Block users from accessing shared SharePoint, OneDrive, and Teams content or use the policy to encrypt email messages." You cannot do both using one DLP policy, which is why I recommend creating separate policies for Exchange content. If you choose to encrypt email messages, a dropdown will appear to select protection settings. You can select Encrypt, Do Not Forward, or a sensitivity label.

If you choose to "Block users from accessing shared SharePoint, OneDrive, and Teams content," additional options will appear to change permissions on the document.

- **Block everyone**: Only the content owner, last modifier, and site admin will continue to have access.

- **Block only people outside your organization**: Users inside your organization continue to have access.

The next option is a checkbox for Let people who see the tip override the policy. You can require a business justification to override, which the system includes in the policy alert, or you could automatically override the rule if someone reports it as a false positive. This option protects people from being locked out of documents if the system falsely flags them as sensitive.

The next section allows us to restrict third-party apps. It works in conjunction with Microsoft Cloud App Security, a solution I will not cover in this book. If you did not select Microsoft Cloud App Security on the location screen, it would gray out this option. When you check this box, then you can choose a specific app. When you check an app, you can select one of the associated actions. For example, if you want to allow your users to access Box but not share sensitive data, you could choose to trash the file. If you wish to block an app completely, look at the Microsoft Cloud App Security solution. When you complete your selections, click Next.

The next screen, shown in Figure 6-6, asks if you want to test the policy, turn it on right away, or keep the policy off. If you test the policy first, you can choose whether to show policy tips while in test mode, which allows you to test those. However, end users will see the policy tips.

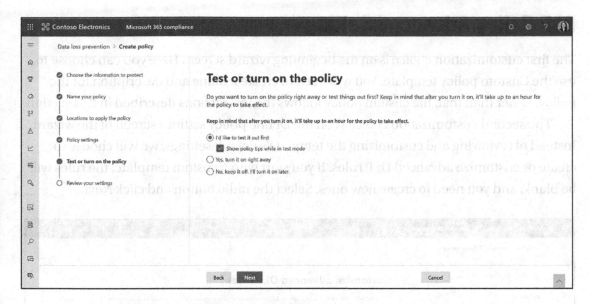

Figure 6-6. *Test or turn on the DLP policy*

If you turn the policy on right away, it will take up to an hour for the policy to take effect. You can always choose to turn the policy on later if you want to save the configuration. I highly recommend that you test your DLP policy first without policy tips, refine it to find the right amount of data, and then turn it on with policy tips in test mode. Once you are satisfied that your policy is working correctly and is not negatively impacting your end users, you can completely turn it on. Click Next, when you finish your selection.

The last page asks you to review your DLP policy settings. This page is a summary of all the decisions you made in the previous steps. Click Submit when you are happy with your choices.

This section described a basic DLP policy using the default settings from a template. In the next section, we will look at the advanced settings you can use to customize your DLP policies further. You can customize a template or start with a blank custom template.

DLP Policy Advanced Settings

The first customization choice is on the beginning wizard screen. Here you can choose to use the Custom policy template. You will need to create a name and description for the policy. Other than that, the custom policy follows the instructions described in this section.

The second customization choice is on the Define policy settings screen of the wizard. Instead of reviewing and customizing the template's default settings, we will choose to create or customize advanced DLP rules. If you start with a custom template, the rules will be blank, and you need to create new ones. Select the radio button and click Next.

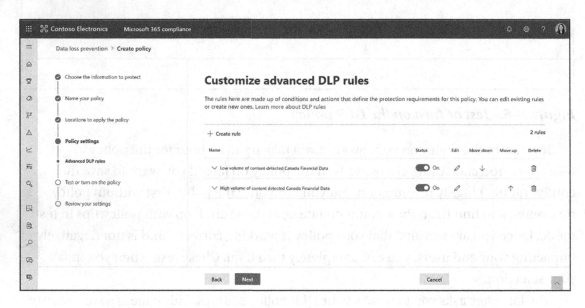

Figure 6-7. *Customize advanced DLP rules*

This screen allows you to customize advanced DLP rules or create new rules, shown in Figure 6-7. The rules here consist of conditions and actions that define the protection requirements for this policy. We can either edit existing rules or create new ones. As an example, the Canada Financial Data template includes two pre-created rules. One rule detects a low volume of content, and the next rule detects a high amount of content. These two rules apply different protections depending on which is triggered.

This difference is because a high volume of detected data is much riskier, so we want to lock down that data more strictly. In contrast, a low amount of content presents less risk to the organization, so we want to provide less strict protections. We do not want to hinder the collaboration process if there is a legitimate business need to work with a low volume of Canadian financial data.

For our example, we will create a new rule, but you could also modify an existing rule. Please click the Create rule button. This click will bring up the Create rule wizard. For this wizard, we will first type in a name for the rule and a description. The description field is a great place to summarize information about the conditions, exceptions, and actions that you have taken on the data.

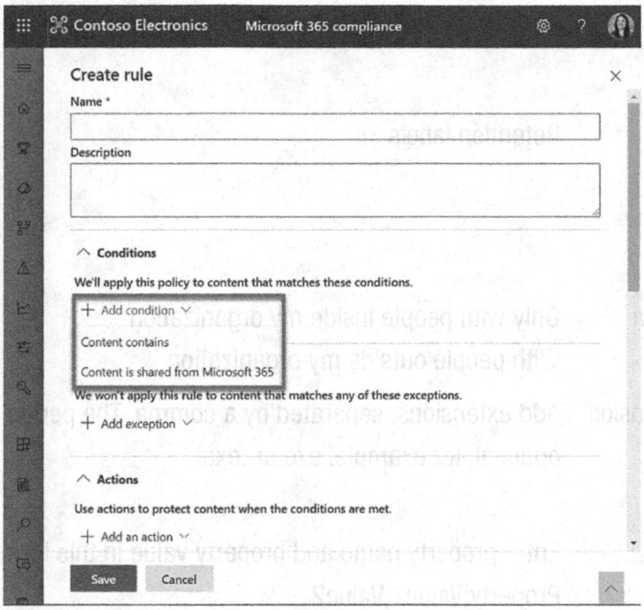

Figure 6-8. *DLP conditions for all locations*

Depending on the locations you chose in the previous step, you will have different conditions and actions. The following table provides the condition, a condition description, and the location where you can use it. For example, if you choose Exchange as a location, all the Exchange conditions will show options. But, if you choose Exchange and SharePoint, then only all location options will appear.

Condition	Options	Locations
Content contains	Sensitive information types	All
Content contains	Sensitivity labels	Exchange Cloud App Security SharePoint OneDrive
Content contains	Retention labels	Cloud App Security SharePoint OneDrive
Content is shared from Microsoft 365	Only with people inside my organization With people outside my organization	All
Attachment's file extension is	Add extensions, separated by a comma. The period is optional, for example, exe or .exe	Exchange SharePoint OneDrive
Document property is	Enter property name and property value in this format: Property:Value1,Value2	Exchange SharePoint OneDrive
Sender IP address is	Single IP address IP address range Classless inter-domain routing IP address range	Exchange
Sender is	Add or remove people	Exchange
Sender domain is	Domain or subdomain Omit the @ before the domain	Exchange
Sender address contains words	Use up to 50 words or phrases, up to 128 characters each. Separate with commas	Exchange
Sender address matches patterns	Enter a regular expression to match a pattern. Up to ten regular expressions, max 128 characters each	Exchange

(continued)

Condition	Options	Locations
Any email attachment's content could not be scanned	N/A	Exchange
Any email attachment's content didn't complete scanning	N/A	Exchange
Attachment is password protected	N/A	Exchange
Recipient is a member of	Add or remove distribution groups	Exchange
Recipient domain is	Domain or subdomain Omit the @ before the domain	Exchange
Recipient is	Up to 50 email addresses. No address can exceed 256 characters	Exchange
Recipient address contains words	Up to 50 words or phrases. Up to 128 characters each. Separate with commas.	Exchange
Recipient address matches patterns	Enter a regular expression to match a pattern. Up to ten regular expressions, max 128 characters each	Exchange
Document name contains words or phrases	Up to 50 words or phrases, max 128 characters each. Separate with commas	Exchange
Document name matches patterns	Enter a regular expression to match a pattern. Up to ten regular expressions, max 128 characters each	Exchange
Subject contains words or phrases	Up to 50 words or phrases, max 128 characters each. Separate with commas	Exchange
Header contains words or phrases	Enter a header name and then words or phrases separated by commas	Exchange
Header matches pattern	Enter a regular expression to match a pattern. Up to ten regular expressions, max 128 characters each	Exchange

(continued)

Condition	Options	Locations
Subject matches patterns	Enter a regular expression to match a pattern. Up to ten regular expressions, max 128 characters each	Exchange
Message type is	Automatic Replies, Automatic Forwarded, Encrypted, Meeting Request or Response, Permission Controlled, Voicemail, Approval Request, Read Receipt	Exchange

After you chose the conditions, the next section asks you to add any exceptions. The exception options are essentially the same as the conditions, with "except" in front. For example, "Except when content contains." There are a few differences:

- The Exchange location has an extra exception: "Except if attachment is un-scannable and has extension."

- For "Content contains," you cannot use a retention label as a trigger.

- For "Content contains," you cannot use a sensitivity label as a trigger for the Cloud App Security and Microsoft Teams locations.

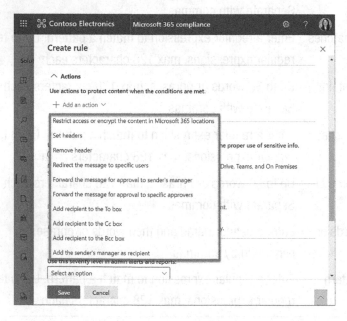

Figure 6-9. *DLP actions available for the Exchange location*

After the exceptions section, we move on to actions. For actions, all locations have the choice to restrict access or encrypt the content in Microsoft 365 locations. If you select this box, some additional options appear. These options are

- Block users from accessing shared SharePoint, OneDrive, and Teams content

    - Block everyone. Only the content owner, last modifier, and site admin will continue to have access. For Teams messages, only the author will see the content.

    - Block only people outside your organization. Users inside your organization will continue to have access.

    - Block only people who were given access to the content through the "Anyone with the link" option. Note: This option will only show when you choose SharePoint or OneDrive as your only location.

- Encrypt email messages (applies only to content in Exchange). Note: This option will only appear when you select the Exchange location.

Additionally, if you chose the Cloud App Security location, the option to restrict third-party apps is available. This option is the same as described in the previous section. When you check this box, then you can select a specific app. When you check an app, you can choose one of the associated actions. For example, allow your users to access G Suite but prevent external sharing when it meets the policy conditions.

If you select only the Exchange location, you will have many more action options, shown in Table 6-1.

Table 6-1. *DLP actions available for the Exchange location*

Action	Options
Set headers	Enter property name and value – up to 64 characters. The header name should not be reserved for internal use only
Remove headers	Enter the names of the headers you want to remove
Redirect the message to specific users	Add or remove people
Forward the message for approval to sender's manager	N/A
Forward the message for approval to specific approvers	Add or remove people
Add recipient to the To box	Add or remove people
Add recipient to the Cc box	Add or remove people
Add recipient to the Bcc box	Add or remove people
Add the sender's manager as recipient	To, Cc, Bcc

Select the actions you would like to take on the content. If you only choose the Exchange location, you can add multiple actions.

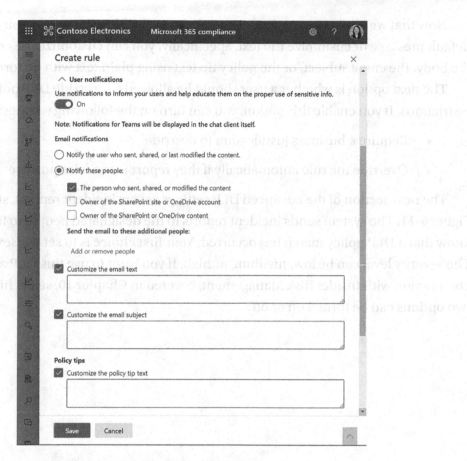

Figure 6-10. *User notification options in a DLP policy*

The next advanced DLP configuration option you have is for user notifications. You can turn them on or off, shown in Figure 6-10. The system sends notifications as emails when the content meets the policy conditions. If you turn on user notifications, you will need to make one choice:

- Notify the user who sent, shared, or last modified the content.

- Notify these people (select all or one):

  - The person who sent, shared, or modified the content

  - Owner of the SharePoint site or OneDrive account

  - Owner of the SharePoint or OneDrive content

  - Send the email to these additional people (add or remove people)

Now that we have chosen whom to notify, let us decide what to say. You can use the default message or customize the text. Specifically, you can customize the email text in the body, the email subject, or the policy tip text using plain text with no formatting.

The next option is whether a user should be allowed to override DLP policy restrictions. If you enable this option, you can turn on the following settings:

- Require a business justification to override

- Override the rule automatically if they report it as a false positive

The next section of the advanced DLP settings covers incident reports, shown in Figure 6-11. The system sends incident reports to the designated people to let them know that a DLP policy match has occurred. Your first choice is to set the severity. The severity level can be low, medium, or high. If you want to use this DLP alert in conjunction with Insider Risk Management, covered in Chapter 10, select high. The next two options can be turned on or off:

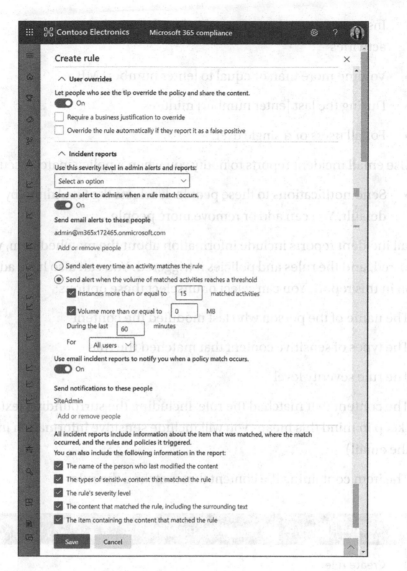

Figure 6-11. Incident report options

- Send an alert to admins when a rule match occurs. Choose one of the following options:

  - Send alert every time an activity matches the rule.

  - Send alert when the volume of matched activities reaches a threshold. If you choose this option, you can configure these settings:

- Instances more than or equal to [set the number] matched activities

- Volume more than or equal to [enter number] MB

- During the last [enter number] minutes

- For all users or a single user

- Use email incident reports to notify you when a policy match occurs.

  - Send notifications to these people. It selects the SiteAdmin by default. You can add or remove more people.

All email incident reports include information about the matched item, where the match occurred, and the rules and policies it triggered. You can also have additional information in this report. You can select or unselect these options:

- The name of the person who last modified the content

- The types of sensitive content that matched the rule

- The rule severity level

- The content that matched the rule, including the surrounding text (keep in mind this means you will include sensitive information in the email)

- The item containing the content that matched the rule

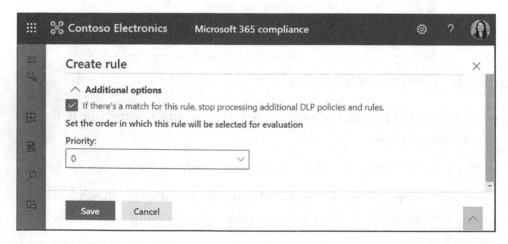

Figure 6-12. *Additional options for DLP policies*

The last section for the advanced DLP settings is the Additional options. Here, if there is a match for this rule, we have the option to stop processing additional DLP policies and rules. You can turn this option on or off, shown in Figure 6-12. Then, we can set the order in which we evaluate the rule. This evaluation occurs in relation to the other rules that are a part of the policy. So as an example, in this case, we already had options for a low amount of Canadian financial data and high amounts of data. Here, we are setting the priority against those other two policies and saying if it matches one of those other higher-priority policies, stop pressing the additional rules or continue to process them.

Those are the options available in DLP policy advanced configurations. The rest of the options are the same as we described in the "Create a New DLP Policy Using a Microsoft 365 Template" section. Next, let us cover how to edit an existing DLP policy.

Edit a DLP Policy

When you finish creating a policy, it brings you back to the Policies tab, which lists all your existing policies. The order of the policies matters. If there are any conflicts, Microsoft 365 uses this order to determine which policy to apply. Priority 0 is the highest. You can also export a list of policies from this page.

To edit a DLP policy, check the box next to the policy you wish to modify. Click the Edit policy button on the toolbar. This click brings you back to the policy creation wizard, where you can edit any of the settings except the DLP policy name.

Alerts

A DLP policy alert gets generated whenever there is an event that matches one of your policies. At the time of writing, only email events show in the dashboard, but I am sure other alerts will get added over time. This dashboard allows you to investigate the details of what triggered the policy.

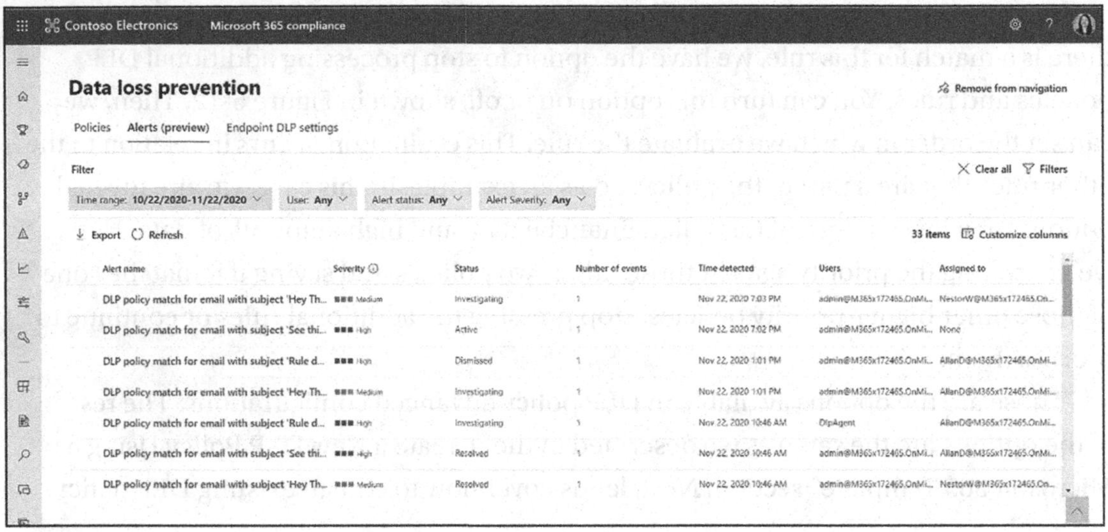

Figure 6-13. *Data Loss Prevention Alerts overview page*

On the Alerts overview page, you can see a list of alerts from your DLP policies. For each alert, you see the alert name, the severity of the alert, the current status, the number of events, the time detected, the user involved in the alert, and whom we have assigned to the alert.

You can filter the alerts by a date range, user, alert status, or alert severity. You can also choose what columns to show. In Figure 6-13, I have shown all the available columns. Lastly, you can export a list of all the alerts in the current view to a CSV file and refresh the list.

Look at the details of an alert by clicking the title. This click brings up a new screen that lists the same details shown on the page, such as the alert status and who is assigned to it. Click Manage alert to make an assignment, change the status, or add any comments about the status. Be sure to save any changes. Click the Management log tab to see a history of status changes for the alert. Back on the details page, there is a button to notify users. This button opens an email with the details of the alert that you can send to anyone.

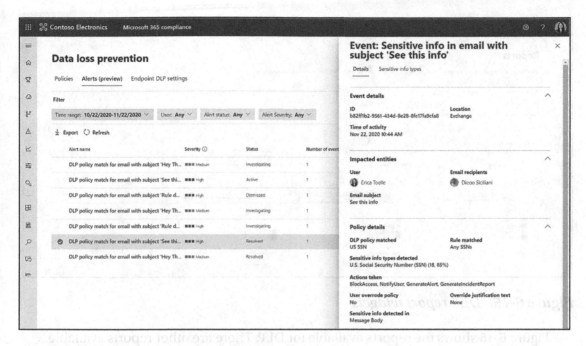

Figure 6-14. *DLP policy alert detail*

Click the Events tab on the alert details page. This tab shows all the events included in the alert. Click one of the events. This click brings you to the details of the alert event, shown in Figure 6-14. Specifically, you can see information such as who sent and received the message, what DLP policy was matched, what sensitive information was detected, the confidence level, the override justification from the user, and more. Click the Sensitive info types tab. This view shows you the types of sensitive data found, the number of incidents, and the confidence level.

Next, we will look at DLP policy reports, which show us trends over time.

DLP Reports

To access DLP trend reports, click the Reports solution in the Compliance Center's left navigation. The DLP reports are in the Organizational data section, about halfway down the page.

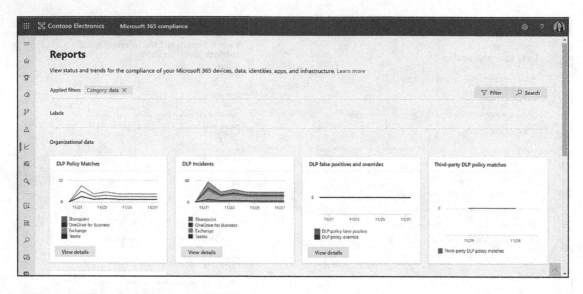

Figure 6-15. *DLP report widgets*

Figure 6-15 shows the reports available for DLP. There are other reports available from this page, but I have filtered the widgets on the organizational data category to focus on DLP reports only. You could also filter the report widgets on the data source: Office 365 or Microsoft Cloud App Security. You can search for a specific widget by clicking the search button.

To view DLP reports in the Security and Compliance Center, you have to be assigned the

- Security Reader role in the Exchange admin center. By default, this role is assigned to the Organization Management and Security Reader role groups in the Exchange admin center.

- View-Only DLP Compliance Management role in the Security and Compliance Center. By default, this role is assigned to the Compliance Administrator, Organization Management, Security Administrator, and Security Reader role groups in the Security and Compliance Center.

- View-Only Recipients role in the Exchange admin center. By default, this role is assigned to the Compliance Management, Organization Management, and View-Only Organization Management role groups in the Exchange admin center.

All DLP reports can show data from the most recent four-month time period. The most recent data can take up to 24 hours to appear in the reports. To access the details for one of the widgets, click the View details button on your desired widget.

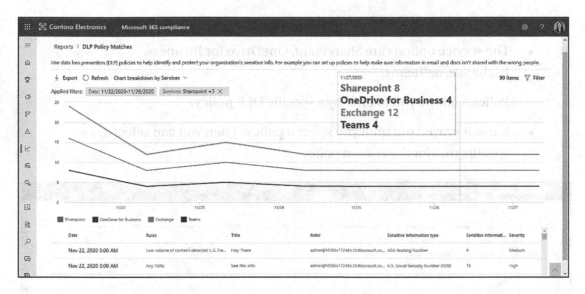

Figure 6-16. *The DLP policy matches report*

Figure 6-16 shows a detailed report for the DLP policy matches widget. This report illustrates the count of DLP policy matches over time. The DLP policy matches report can help you with the following:

- When you run your DLP policies in test mode, any matches will show here. You can view the details of a match to see which exact policy and policy rule was matched. This data can help you tune your DLP policies.

- See why there are spikes and trends over time or within a specific period.

- Look for business processes that repeatedly cause violations so you can address them.

- Understand what actions are applied to content.

- View a list of top users and repeat users who are contributing to incidents in your organization.

- Understand the top types of sensitive information in your organization.

You can filter the report by date, service, policies, or action:

- The date history goes back 30 days.

- The service options are SharePoint, OneDrive for Business, Exchange, or Teams.

- Policies allows you to filter by a specific DLP policy.

- Rules is grayed out until you select a policy. Then you can select a specific rule for the chosen policy.

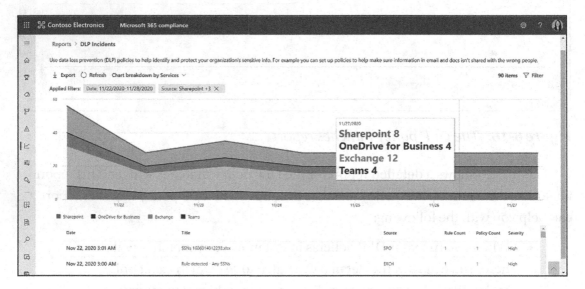

Figure 6-17. *DLP report widget*

Figure 6-17 shows the DLP report widget. This report also indicates policy matches over time. However, it shows matches at a rule level. For example, if an email matched three different rules, the policy matches report shows three line items. By contrast, the incident report shows matches at an item level; for example, if an email matched three different rules, the incident report shows a single line item for that piece of content.

Because it aggregates the report counts differently, the policy matches report is better for identifying matches with specific rules and fine-tuning DLP policies. The incident report is better for identifying particular pieces of content that are problematic for your DLP policies.

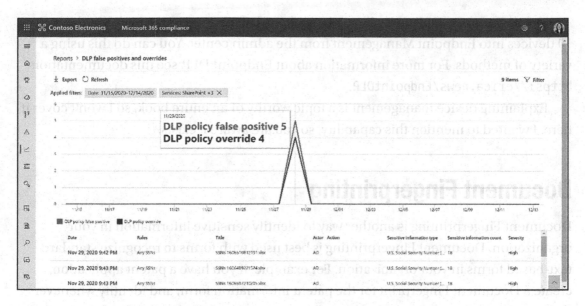

Figure 6-18. *DLP report widgets*

If your DLP policy allows users to override it or report a false positive, this report, shown in Figure 6-18, shows a count of such instances over time. You can filter the information by date, location, or policy. You can use this report to

- Tune or refine your DLP policies by seeing which policies incur a high number of false positives.

- View the justifications submitted by users when they resolve a policy tip by overriding the policy.

- Discover where DLP policies conflict with valid business processes by incurring a high number of user overrides.

Endpoint DLP

Endpoint DLP is a new capability that Microsoft launched in the fall of 2020. It extends the activity monitoring and protection capabilities of DLP to sensitive items that are on Windows 10 devices. For example, you can alert admins when a user copies or prints content containing sensitive information on their work computer.

To use Endpoint DLP, you will need to onboard all your organization's Windows 10 devices into Endpoint Management from the admin center. You can do this using a variety of methods. For more information about Endpoint DLP, see this documentation: `https://erica.news/EndpointDLP`.

Explaining device management is a topic worthy of an entire book, so I won't cover it here. I wanted to mention this capability, so you are aware it exists.

Document Fingerprinting

Document Fingerprinting is another way to identify sensitive information in your organization. Document Fingerprinting is best used with forms to recognize standard text-based forms in your organization. For example, if you have a patent application, create a Document Fingerprint for the patent information form, and identify whenever someone sends it in an email, even if they have completed the form.

Document Fingerprinting is a Data Loss Prevention feature. It converts a standard form into a sensitive information type, but you can then use your DLP policies' rules.

Scenarios create a Document Fingerprint based on a blank patent template and then create a DLP policy that detects and blocks all outgoing patent templates with sensitive content filled in. Block an employee review from being shared with external users. Add a policy tip to warn users that they are sending a patient visit report and remind them of the recipient policy. Here are examples of types of forms that we can use with Document Fingerprinting:

- Government forms

- Health Insurance Portability and Accountability Act (HIPAA) compliance forms

- Employee information forms for human resources departments

- Custom forms created specifically for your organization

How Does Document Fingerprinting Work?

First, the Document Fingerprint looks for a unique word pattern in the document. For example, it looks at what types of words are in the file. It can also look at how we place words with one another and where we located the terms. Document Fingerprinting then looks for outbound documents with the same pattern. These files can only be sent via Exchange online as attachments. The content can't be password protected.

They must contain all the same words as the original form, but it is acceptable to add additional info to the form, such as a completed form. Document Fingerprinting converts the word pattern into a Document Fingerprint, a small Unicode XML file containing a unique hash value, representing the original text. We save the Document Fingerprint as a data classification in the active directory. The fingerprint then becomes a sensitive information type that you can associate with a DLP policy. You create a Document Fingerprint using PowerShell. For more information, please visit this link: `https://erica.news/Fingerprinting`.

This chapter reviewed Data Loss Prevention (DLP) policies, which protect sensitive data in your organization while it is in transit, such as when someone sends an email or shares a document. We reviewed the permissions and licensing needed to use DLP. We also discussed creating a new DLP policy by using a pre-built template or creating a custom policy. We also reviewed how to monitor DLP policies using alerts and reports and evaluate your policy's effectiveness. Lastly, we briefly introduced Endpoint DLP to protect devices and Document Fingerprinting, which protects standardized forms.

In the next chapter, we will look at how you can use Information Barriers to create ethical walls or policies to allow individuals or groups to communicate or prevent individuals or groups from communicating with one another. We often use Information Barriers to comply with financial regulations or protect students in education environments.

CHAPTER 7

Information Barriers

Information barriers are ethical walls or policies that an admin can configure to allow individuals or groups to communicate or prevent individuals or groups from communicating with one another. For example, in a school environment, you might have primary school students who are the younger children and secondary school students who are the older children. You want to prevent the younger children from speaking or communicating with the older children, but you still wish both groups to talk with teachers. Figure 7-1 visualizes the relationship.

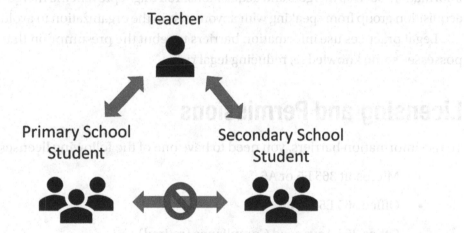

Figure 7-1. *The information barrier relationship between teachers and students*

© Erica Toelle 2021
E. Toelle, *Microsoft 365 Compliance*, https://doi.org/10.1007/978-1-4842-5778-4_7

Information barriers are how you can enforce these relationships in Microsoft 365. Information barriers are policies that an admin can configure to prevent individuals or groups from communicating with each other. Or information barriers can explicitly allow two groups to communicate with one another. These groups of users are called information barrier segments.

Currently, information barriers support Microsoft Teams, SharePoint, and OneDrive. They do not apply to email communications. Microsoft Teams private channels do work with information barrier policies.

Why Use Information Barriers?

Information barriers help organizations avoid a conflict of interest. For example, FINRA, a US financial services regulation, prevents investment bankers from speaking with compliance or research departments. This type of policy helps to avoid conflicts of interest.

Another way to use information barriers is to safeguard highly confidential internal information, such as mergers and acquisitions. You might prevent the merger and acquisition group from speaking with anyone else in the organization to avoid any data leaks.

Legal practices use information barriers to rebut the presumption that an employee possesses some knowledge, reducing legal risk.

Licensing and Permissions

To use information barriers, you need to have one of the following licenses:

- Microsoft 365 E5 or A5

- Office 365 E5 or A5

- Office 365 Advanced Compliance (retired)

- Microsoft 365 Compliance E5 or A5

- Microsoft 365 Insider Risk Management

To set up information barriers, you need to have one of the following permission levels:

- Microsoft 365 Global Administrator

- Office 365 Global Administrator

- Compliance Administrator

- IB Compliance Management, where IB stands for Information Barriers

Information Barriers in Microsoft Teams

You can use information barriers to prevent users from communicating with one another in Microsoft Teams. The Information Barrier Policy Evaluation Service finds and stops the following kinds of unauthorized communications in Teams:

- Searching for a user

- Adding a member to a team

- Starting a chat session with someone

- Starting a chat group session

- Inviting someone to join a meeting

- Sharing a screen

- Placing a call

When is the information barrier checked? The system checks for information barriers periodically to ensure that there have been no changes to the group membership or the barriers themselves. The system monitors the barriers when the following actions occur:

- New members are added to a Microsoft Team.

- A new chat is started.

- Either a one-to-one or group chat is created.

- A member is invited to a meeting when someone initiates a screen sharing session.

- Somebody makes a phone call over VOIP in Teams.

- Somebody tries to open a SharePoint site file or access a SharePoint site.

Figure 7-2. *Trying to start a chat with a user blocked by an information barrier policy*

Figure 7-2 shows an example of a one-to-one chat with users in a conflicting segment. Here, I'm trying to start a chat with somebody who is blocked by a policy. When I search for them on the To line, I get an error that "We didn't find any matches. Talk to your IT admin about expanding the scope of your search."

Next, let us look at a group chat between segmented users. If you attempt to start a chat between segmented users, it will keep the first user you add but automatically remove the user from the blocked segment before anyone can send a message.

Figure 7-3. *Message displayed when a blocked user tries to join a call*

Try to join a meeting, and you are not allowed to attend due to your information barrier segmentation. You will get a message that says, "Sorry, your company policy prevents you from joining this call," as shown in Figure 7-3. Note that a blocked user will not receive the meeting invite, but this screen appears if they try to join the meeting directly with a link.

Let us say a user changes segments. This change results in blocking the user from an existing chat. The next time they try to send a message, the system will automatically remove them from the chat or Team.

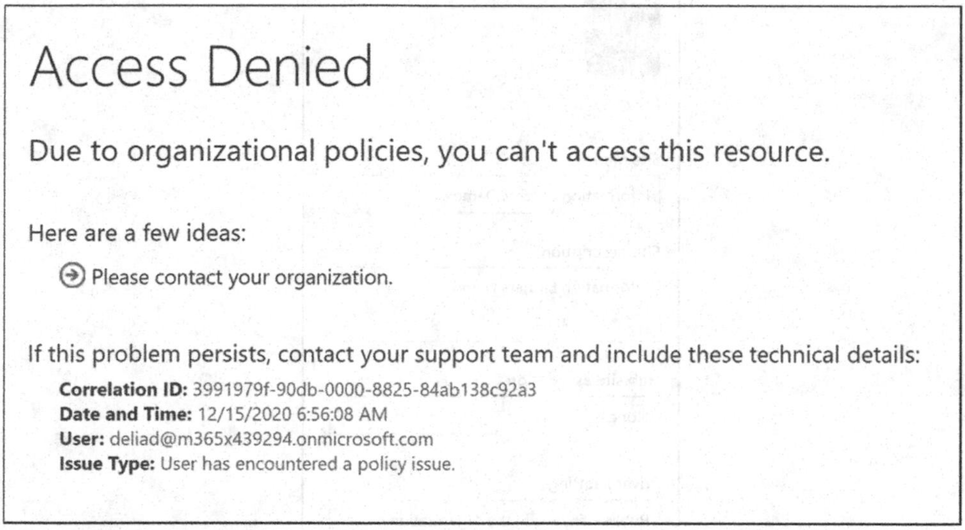

Access Denied

Due to organizational policies, you can't access this resource.

Here are a few ideas:

⊙ Please contact your organization.

If this problem persists, contact your support team and include these technical details:
Correlation ID: 3991979f-90db-0000-8825-84ab138c92a3
Date and Time: 12/15/2020 6:56:08 AM
User: deliad@m365x439294.onmicrosoft.com
Issue Type: User has encountered a policy issue.

Figure 7-4. *The message shown to a blocked user who tries to access a SharePoint file*

Finally, suppose the person attempts to access a file stored in a SharePoint site subject to a Team's information barriers. In that case, they will see the message displayed in Figure 7-4 that says, "Access Denied. Due to organizational policies, you cannot access this resource."

As you can see, information barrier policies prevent blocked users from interacting with one another in Microsoft Teams. The system enforces this barrier in Teams conversations, 1:1 or group chats, meetings, the search directory, and accessing Team files.

Next, let's look at how information barriers work in SharePoint sites unconnected to a Microsoft Team.

Information Barriers in SharePoint

SharePoint enforces information barriers by assigning a user segment and associating it with a SharePoint site, shown in Figure 7-5. Information barriers work at the site level rather than at the individual level. You can associate up to ten segments with one SharePoint site.

Figure 7-5. *A SharePoint site using information barriers*

For a user to access a SharePoint site with segments associated with it, the user's segment must match a segment associated with the site. Non-segment users cannot access a site associated with segments even if they have permission to access the site. To state this more plainly, you either restrict a SharePoint site to up to ten segments, or it is a standard SharePoint site.

Additionally, the user must have the right permissions to the site. If a user is a member of the segment but does not have permissions, they will not access it.

When a segment is associated with a site, the option to share a document with anyone with the link is disabled. A user can only share the site and its content with users whose segment matches the site. For example, if the site is associated only with secondary school students, you can only share the site with other secondary students. This statement is true even though the secondary student segment is compatible with the teacher segment as well, so we need to add both the secondary student and teacher segments to the site for both to access it. Once a site has a segment, new users can only be added to the site as members if their segment matches the site.

When a site has no segments associated with it, the site and its contents can be shared based on the information barrier policy applied to the user. For example, if a secondary school user can communicate with teachers, they can share the site with teachers. They cannot be able to share the site with a primary school student.

Users will see search results from sites with an associated segment that matches the user segment if they have permission. Essentially, the search will follow standard security trimming with the search results.

Note   When you create a Microsoft Team, the system automatically creates a SharePoint site for the Team's files. The SharePoint site created by the Team is always going to follow the information barrier policies of the Team.

SharePoint admins can't change the segments associated with a SharePoint site when it's connected to a Team. It can take up to 24 hours for the segments related to the Team's members to be automatically associated with the site.

SharePoint Behavior When Modifying Information Barriers

Now let's talk about what happens to SharePoint when we make changes to information barriers. Barriers will always override permissions. If a user has permission to the site but isn't a member of the segment, they can't view site contents, even if they previously had access. This rule includes site admins. If you change an information barrier policy and the admin is no longer a member of the segment, they will lose their access. Be careful when making changes to an information barrier policy!

I have also noticed that when you first associate a SharePoint site with a barrier, it blocks all users from having access to the site for about 15 minutes. Make sure you wait for a bit before troubleshooting any access issues.

Information Barriers in OneDrive

OneDrive also uses segments, applied to a OneDrive location, similar to SharePoint. When we apply an information barrier segment to a user, within 24 hours, the system automatically associates that segment with the user's OneDrive. Because a user can only be a member of one segment, their OneDrive can only be a member of one segment. At this point, only members of the same segment can access files in the user's OneDrive. Non-segment users do not have access.

Let's say we set up a segment, so it explicitly allows communication with other segments. Those segments will get associated with the OneDrive so they can access content and collaborate. However, a OneDrive can only have up to ten segments associated with it.

In our example, from the beginning of the chapter, teachers can communicate with both primary and secondary students. The system blocks primary and secondary students from communicating with each other. In this case

- Primary students can access the OneDrive of other primary students but cannot access the teacher's OneDrive.

- Secondary students can access the OneDrive of other secondary students but cannot access the teacher's OneDrive.

- A teacher can access the OneDrive of other teachers, primary students, or secondary students.

Students cannot access a teacher's OneDrive because the primary and secondary students are not compatible with each other. We don't want them to communicate or collaborate through a teacher's OneDrive.

How OneDrive Segments Work

When a segment is associated with a OneDrive, the option to share a file with anyone with the link is disabled. You can only share files and folders with users whose segment matches that of the OneDrive. When a OneDrive has no segments associated, the user can share files and folders based on the information barrier policy applied to the user and the sharing settings for the OneDrive.

For a user to access content in a OneDrive that has segments associated, the user's segment must match a segment that's associated with the OneDrive, and you must share the files with the user. Non-segment users can access OneDrive files only from non-segment users. They cannot access shared OneDrive files from users who have a segment applied.

How to Set Up Information Barriers

You can only set up information barriers by using PowerShell. There are also several prerequisites that you must enable. Here are the steps to set up information barriers:

1. Check that your directory includes data for segmenting users.

2. Enable scoped directory search for Microsoft Teams.

3. Enable the Compliance Center audit log.

4. Make sure there are no Exchange address book policies in place.

5. Complete the information barrier planning spreadsheet.

6. Run the PowerShell scripts.

7. Provide admin consent for Microsoft Teams.

First, make sure that the data you plan to use to segment users is complete in Azure Active Directory (AAD). We'll go over the attributes that you can use to segment users in just a moment. For example, if you want to segment users based on their department, that attribute must be complete in everyone's AAD profile.

Microsoft Teams Scoped Directory Search

Next, let's enable the scoped directory search. Microsoft Teams scoped directory search is the feature that allows organizations to create virtual boundaries that control how users can find and communicate with other users. A scoped directory search provides custom views of the organization's directory to users. Microsoft Teams uses information barrier policies to support these custom views. Once the information barrier policies are enabled, the system scopes the results when you search for users according to the configured policies. FYI, any user data cached before the enforcement of new or updated address book policies will remain available to users for up to 30 days.

To enable scoped directory search, visit the Microsoft 365 admin center. On the left-hand side, under Admin Centers, click Teams. This click brings you to the Microsoft Teams admin center. On the left-hand side, expand the item for org-wide settings, and then click Teams settings.

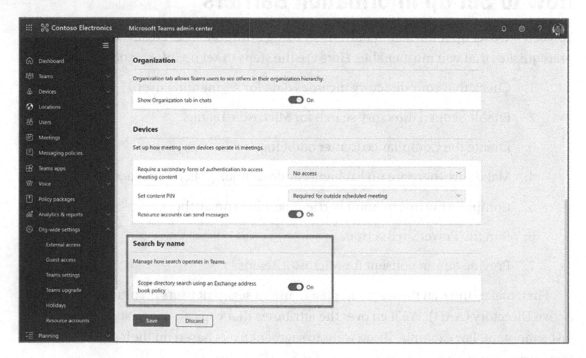

Figure 7-6. *Enable Microsoft Teams scoped directory search*

About halfway down the page, you'll see the heading "Search by name," with a toggle switch, shown in Figure 7-6. Click the toggle switch to on.

Next, we will need to remove any existing Exchange address book policies. Here are the instructions: `https://erica.news/ExchangeAddress`.

Create User Segments

Next, we will plan the user segments. Please keep these things in mind when planning segments. First, you can only have one user in one segment. This rule is to avoid potential conflicts. Next, we use Azure Active Directory attributes for our segments. We won't use Exchange user profile attributes. Attributes are properties, such as department, job title, location, team name, and other job profile details. You can view a list of available attributes here: `https://erica.news/attributes`.

Please use one attribute only for all your information barriers. For example, if you decide to use the department attribute, you need to use this attribute for all your barrier policies. This method reduces the chance of someone being a member of multiple segments.

When choosing your attribute, please think about how you will maintain it. Continuing with our school example, would you want to update their profile attribute as the children advance in years? Another option is to use Active Directory groups to define your barriers. These groups can be either dynamic or static, and your organization may already be maintaining groups for other purposes. The right option will depend on your operational processes.

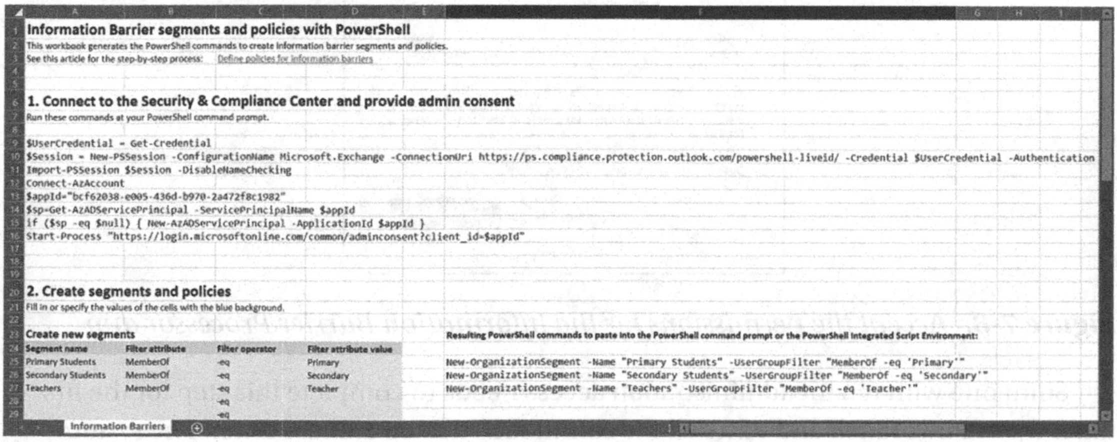

Figure 7-7. *Microsoft's Information Barrier planning spreadsheet*

Microsoft has provided an excellent information barrier planning spreadsheet, shown in Figure 7-7. This spreadsheet helps you to map out and plan your segments and generates the PowerShell commands that you can use to create these barriers. Even if you've never used PowerShell before, this planning tool makes the process easy. Access the planning spreadsheet here: `https://erica.news/IBSpreadsheet`.

The planning spreadsheet has two parts: first, the scripts you will need to enable your organization's information barriers and provide the permissions to configure them and, second, the scripts to set up the policies. I recommend that you complete the information in step 2 first, and then when you are ready to run the scripts, you can use the information in step 1.

We will spend the remainder of the chapter discussing how to configure the policies, so I will quickly explain step 1 in the spreadsheet. This section connects you to the Security and Compliance Center and asks you to grant permission to the Information Barriers Azure app to run in your environment.

Figure 7-8. *Accept the permissions for the Information Barrier Processor app*

Someone with tenant administration access needs to complete this step for the first time. Open PowerShell and paste all the commands in step 1. Press Enter. The system will ask you for your Microsoft 365 credentials. A browser window will appear asking you to grant permissions for the Information Barrier Processor, shown in Figure 7-8. This app is what configures your policies in the background. Click Accept and go back to the PowerShell window.

Next, you would paste the PowerShell commands from step 2 into the PowerShell window. I recommend running them one by one, so you can tell what line caused any errors.

Now let's look at how you generate the PowerShell scripts in step 2 and what options you have available. This step has four sections:

1. **Create new segments**: This segment is where you create groups of users, for example, where you define teachers as being in the Dynamic Azure AD group called Teachers.

2. **Create policies to block segments**: This allows you to prevent two segments from communicating with each other.

3. **Create policies to allow segments**: Use this option to allow two segments to communicate.

4. **Change status**: Microsoft recommends that you create each segment in an inactive state and activate all the information barrier policies simultaneously. This section is where you activate the policies.

Let's look at how to create new segments more in-depth. First, specify the segment names. We will use these names in the following sections where we block or allow communication. Next, select your attribute from this list: `https://erica.news/attributes`. Remember to use the same attribute for all your segments.

Create new segments				Resulting PowerShell commands to paste into the PowerShell command prompt or the PowerShell Integrated Script Environment:
Segment name	Filter attribute	Filter operator	Filter attribute value	
Primary Students	MemberOf	-eq	Primary	New-OrganizationSegment -Name "Primary Students" -UserGroupFilter "MemberOf -eq 'Primary'"
Secondary Students	MemberOf	-eq	Secondary	New-OrganizationSegment -Name "Secondary Students" -UserGroupFilter "MemberOf -eq 'Secondary'"
Teachers	MemberOf	-eq	Teacher	New-OrganizationSegment -Name "Teachers" -UserGroupFilter "MemberOf -eq 'Teacher'"
		-eq		
		-eq		

Figure 7-9. *Create a segment*

Now, choose your filter operator from the list. The spreadsheet includes all the valid operators on this list. Finally, enter the filter attribute value. This value is the property from the Azure Active Directory profile and is unique to your organization. In my example, in Figure 7-9, I'm creating a segment for primary students, secondary students, and teachers. I am using the MemberOf filter attribute because my organization already uses dynamic groups for each user group. The spreadsheet provides the resulting PowerShell command that I can copy and paste to create that segment.

Next, I will create policies to block segments because I want to prevent two groups from speaking or collaborating. First, enter the assigned segment for the policy. This field is the segment name from the previous section. Now, enter the segment name for the group with which they should not communicate. Again, that's the segment name from the preceding section.

Create policies to block segments					One command per direction
Assigned segment	Blocked segment	Direction	State		
Primary Students	Secondary Students	Two-way	Inactive		New-InformationBarrierPolicy -Name "Primary Students-to-Secondary Students" -AssignedSegment "Primary Students" -SegmentsBlocked "Secondary Students" -State Inactive New-InformationBarrierPolicy -Name "Secondary Students-to-Primary Students" -AssignedSegment "Secondary Students" -SegmentsBlocked "Primary Students" -State Inactive

Figure 7-10. *Create policies to block segments*

Then, I have the option to choose whether the block should be one way, where the assigned segment cannot talk to the blocked segment, or two-way, where neither segment can speak to each other. In this case, I'm going to choose two-way, and then I'll leave the policy as inactive.

Note   Blocking two segments from communicating requires you to run two PowerShell commands. You'll use one command for each direction.

In our example, shown in Figure 7-10, we will use primary students as the assigned segment and secondary students as the blocked segment. We want a two-way block, and we want to keep the policy inactive. Again, these choices create the PowerShell script that we will copy and paste into our PowerShell session to create the barrier. Note the highlighted names in Figure 7-10. We will use that in the final step to activate the policies.

You can also create policies to allow segments to communicate and collaborate. In this case, we will add teachers as our assigned segment, which then we let communicate with both primary and secondary students, shown in Figure 7-11. Again, we will leave the policy inactive. Copy and paste the PowerShell script as usual.

Create policies to allow segments				One command per allow policy
Assigned segment	Allowed segment	State		
Teachers	Primary Students	Inactive		New-InformationBarrierPolicy -Name "Teachers-to-Primary Students" -AssignedSegment "Teachers" -SegmentsAllowed "Primary Students" -State Inactive
Teachers	Secondary Students	Inactive		New-InformationBarrierPolicy -Name "Teachers-to-Secondary Students" -AssignedSegment "Teachers" -SegmentsAllowed "Secondary Students" -State Inactive

Figure 7-11. *Create policies to allow segments*

Finally, once we have built all our policies, we will want to activate them. You are going to want to change the policy's status to an active state, shown in Figure 7-12. Fill out the policy name under the Change status box.

Change status		
Policy name	Final state	One command per policy change
Primary Students-to-Secondary Students	Active	Set-InformationBarrierPolicy -Identity "Primary Students-to-Secondary Students" -State Active
Secondary Students-to-Primary Students	Active	Set-InformationBarrierPolicy -Identity "Secondary Students-to-Primary Students" -State Active
Teachers-to-Secondary Students	Active	Set-InformationBarrierPolicy -Identity "Teachers-to-Secondary Students" -State Active
Teachers-to-Primary Students	Active	Set-InformationBarrierPolicy -Identity "Teachers-to-Primary Students" -State Active

Figure 7-12. *Change the policy status*

The policy name can be difficult to find, so I highlighted it in the preceding screenshots. When you created the policies in the block and allow segments areas, the PowerShell script automatically generated a name for your policy. You can see it in the script after the -name but before the -assignment segment. In my example, my policy name is something like primary students-to-secondary students. Do not include the double quotation marks. Go ahead and paste the resulting PowerShell command into the window to activate the policies.

The system will start applying the policies within 30 minutes. The system applies policies per user. In general, the system processes about 5,000 user accounts per hour.

In this chapter, we went over information barriers. Here is a recap of the topics we covered:

1.   We defined what information barriers are and why you might use them.

2.   We discussed licensing and permissions.

3.   We discussed how information barriers work in Microsoft Teams, how they work in SharePoint, and how information barriers work in OneDrive.

4.   We went over how to set up information barriers, including accomplishing the prerequisites and using the Microsoft-provided Excel sheet to automatically generate the PowerShell script we'll need to build our barriers.

In the next chapter, we will go over information governance. We will discuss how we can use retention policies to keep the information we need in our organization and delete the content we do not need. We will also discuss importing archive content in PST files into Microsoft 365 and how archive mailboxes work, including the unlimited archive functionality.

CHAPTER 8

Information Governance

Information governance is a collection of solutions that help you manage your organization's life cycle of content. It allows you to keep what you need and delete what you do not need. Information governance includes tools for retention and deletion, importing PST files into Microsoft 365, and using the mailbox archive and unlimited archive to store large mailboxes. In the first part of this chapter, we will discuss the different retention methods available in Microsoft 365. We will then discuss how to import PST files into Microsoft 365 and, finally, how to enable archive and unlimited archive mailboxes.

An Introduction to Retention and Deletion Policies

Retention helps to reduce the risk of litigation present by keeping expired content. It helps reduce the risk of a security breach by deleting unneeded content. Retention also reduces the risk of regulatory fines that can be caused by deleting files too early. It also helps your organization be more productive by only having relevant content available in search and content repositories. Lastly, it supports all your security and compliance efforts because there is a smaller volume of content to manage.

Microsoft 365 can help you retain or delete content. This functionality ensures you cannot accidentally delete the content before you should delete it. It can also help you to remove content permanently at the end of the retention period. For example, Microsoft 365 could help you retain project documents three years after the project is complete. These policies can also help you automatically delete content. For example, many organizations do not want to keep Teams chat messages. A deletion policy can automatically delete Teams chats after 30 days to comply with your company policy not to store those chats.

213

E. Toelle, *Microsoft 365 Compliance*, https://doi.org/10.1007/978-1-4842-5778-4_8

There are two retention methods in Microsoft 365:

- Retention policies

- Retention labels

First, we will talk about retention policies. Then, we will move on to retention labels and deploying retention labels using retention label policies.

I have a quick note before we move on. Information Governance and Records Management are similar solutions. I would argue that the line between them is blurry and not well defined. One of the questions people frequently ask me is what solutions they can use with a specific license. To help answer that question, everything in this chapter requires an E3-type license, and everything in Chapter 9 requires an E5 license. Hopefully, this helps you understand the differences and make a case for purchasing E5 if you need that functionality.

What Are Retention Policies?

Retention policies apply general retention settings to broad areas of content. For example, you might want to retain all SharePoint content for three years or delete all Microsoft Teams conversations and chats after 30 days.

A benefit of retention policies is that they are easy to implement. You point a policy at sites or mailboxes, and that is it. Of course, you can configure the settings to make them more complex as needed. For example, if you want to follow a capstone approach for email, you will use retention policies. Have one broad retention policy for everyone in your obligation, and then target people with a more extended retention period with a different policy. You are not allowed to categorize individual documents with retention policies. You can only apply retention policies to all content in a location. You can use retention policies to keep or delete information, and it is also the best choice for email for reasons that I will explain later.

Here are some common business scenarios for retention policies. Retention policies are suitable for content sources with a high volume of content, such as Teams chats and conversations, Yammer content, Skype conversations, and email. You would never be able to classify each Teams chat or email, nor would you want to.

Retention policies are also excellent if you are not a government or highly regulated organization. If you want to eliminate redundant, obsolete, or trivial content in your environment, retention policies are for you. You can also use retention policies as a catch-all policy for content that is not covered by another type of retention.

Licensing and Permissions

To use retention policies, every user in the managed location, such as every user who is a member of a SharePoint site with a retention policy applied to it, needs to have one of the following licenses:

- Microsoft 365 E5
- Microsoft 365 E3
- Office 365 E5
- Office 365 E3

If you are only managing data stored in Exchange Online, you could use a Microsoft 365 Business Premium license or an Exchange Online Archiving license.

For permissions, you would need the Retention Management role to create and configure retention policies. Microsoft includes this role in the following default role groups:

- Compliance Administrator
- Compliance Data Administrator
- Organizational Management

Create a Retention Policy

To create a retention policy, visit the Microsoft 365 Compliance Center. In the left navigation, click "Information governance." Click the "Retention" tab.

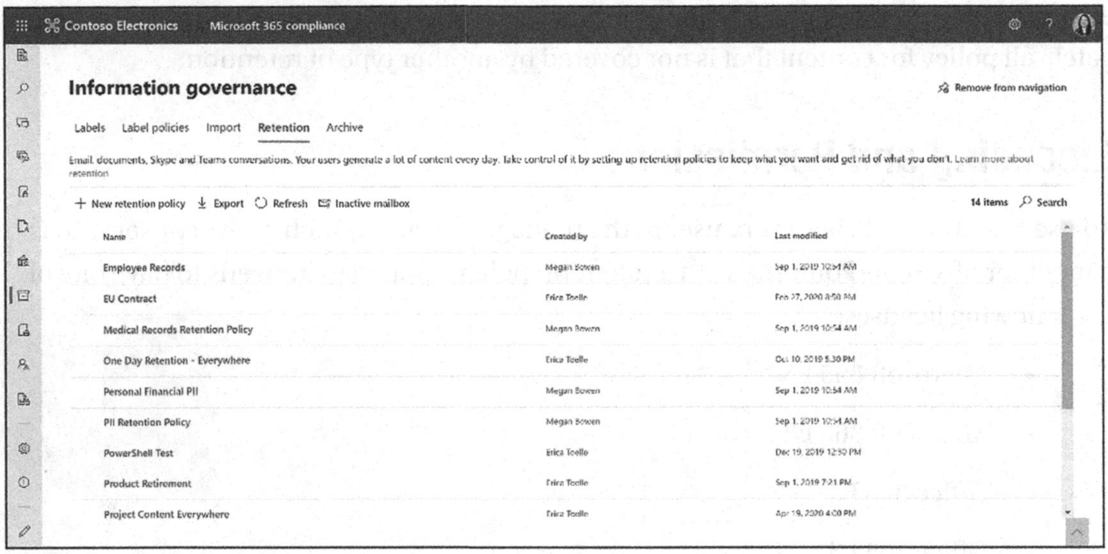

Figure 8-1. *The retention policy overview screen in the information governance solution*

This tab shows you an overview of all the retention policies currently in your organization, shown in Figure 8-1. It shows you who created the policy and when it was last modified. You can also click "Search" to search through your policies or export a list of retention policies.

To create a new retention policy, click "+ New retention policy." This click will bring us to a wizard that asks us to name our policy. Be sure to choose a specific name to help you understand what the policy does and what locations it covers. You can also enter a description that only is seen by administrators. Click "Next."

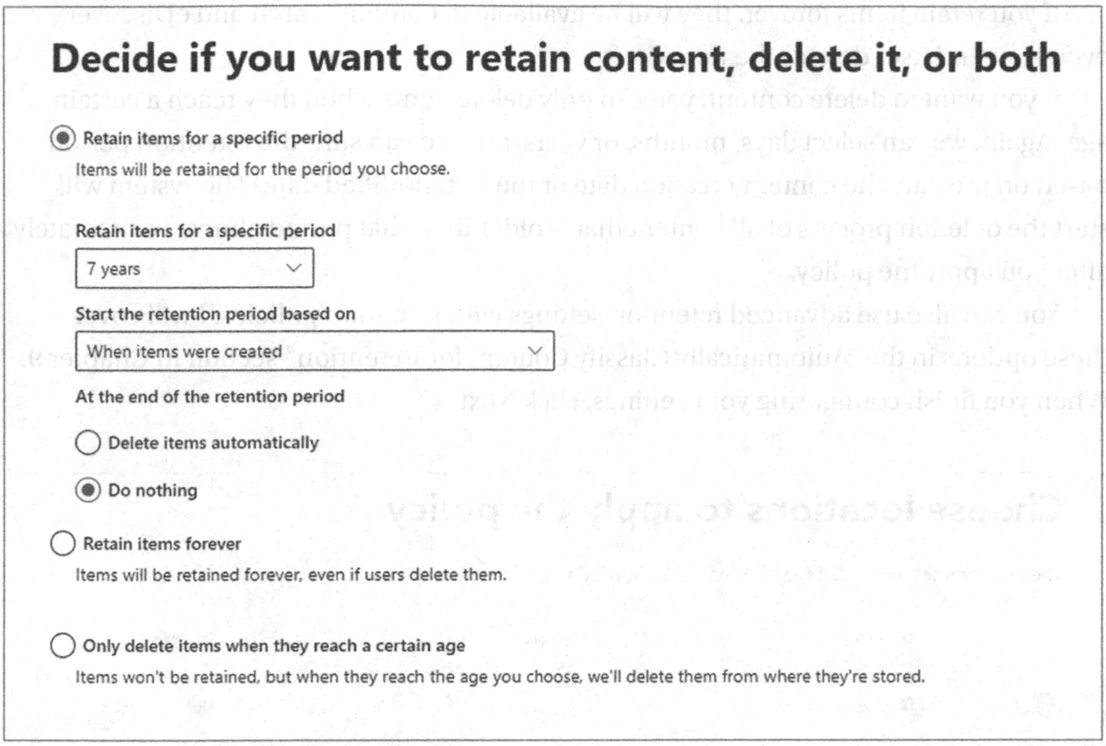

Decide if you want to retain content, delete it, or both

◉ Retain items for a specific period
Items will be retained for the period you choose.

Retain items for a specific period

| 7 years ⌄ |

Start the retention period based on

| When items were created ⌄ |

At the end of the retention period

○ Delete items automatically

◉ Do nothing

○ Retain items forever
Items will be retained forever, even if users delete them.

○ Only delete items when they reach a certain age
Items won't be retained, but when they reach the age you choose, we'll delete them from where they're stored.

Figure 8-2. Retention policy settings in the information governance solution

Now, we will configure the retention policy settings, shown in Figure 8-2. Our first decision is if we want to retain content. You can choose

- Retain items for a specific period

- Retain items forever

- Only delete items when they reach a certain age

If you want to retain content, you can choose to keep content for a certain number of days, months, years. By default, you can select 5, 7, or 10 years or custom to choose your duration. You can start the retention period based on the content creation date or the last modified date.

After the retention period is over, we can choose to delete the items automatically. In this case, the content will follow the process we discuss later in this chapter, in the section "How Deletion Works." Or we can do nothing and leave the content unprotected by a retention period. You can delete unprotected content by a user or an automated process.

If you retain items forever, they will be available to content search and eDiscovery even if an end user deletes the items.

If you want to delete content, you can only delete items when they reach a certain age. Again, we can select days, months, or years, and we can start the retention period based on the date the content creation date or the last modified date. The system will start the deletion process of all content that is older than that period almost immediately after you apply the policy.

You can also use advanced retention settings with retention policies. I will cover these options in the "Automatically Classify Content for Retention" section in Chapter 9. When you finish configuring your settings, click Next.

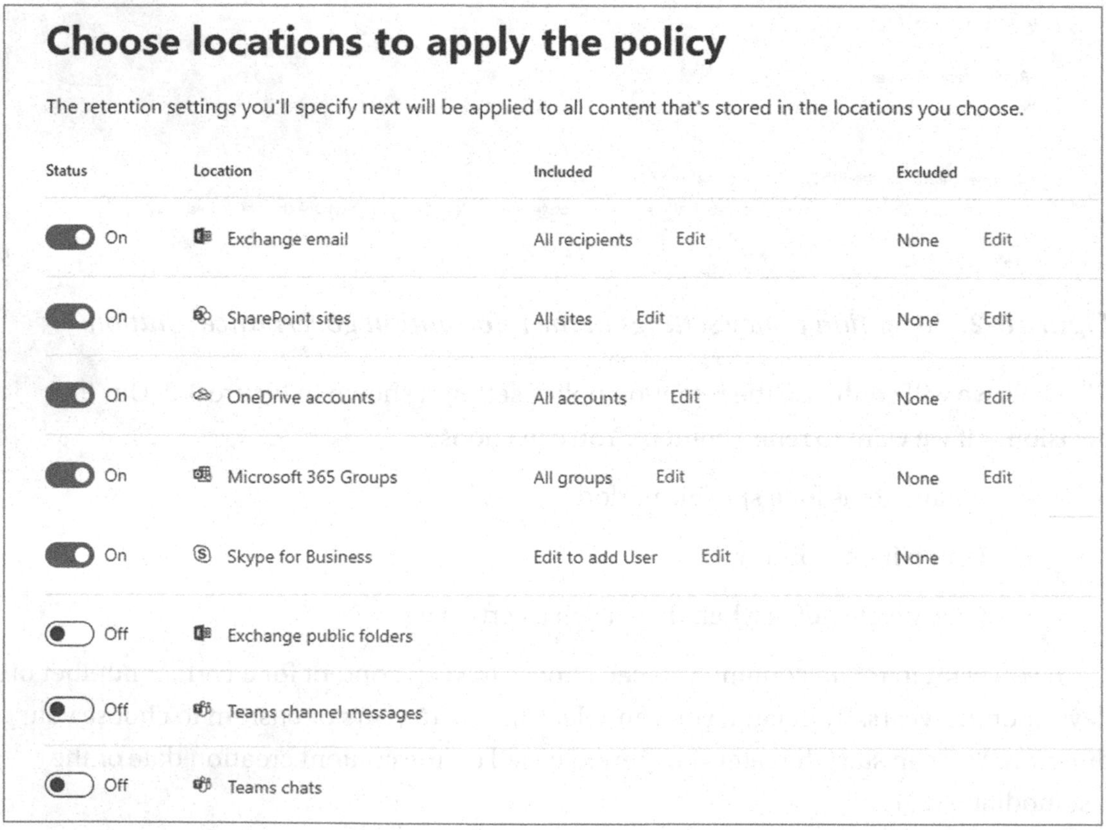

Choose locations to apply the policy

The retention settings you'll specify next will be applied to all content that's stored in the locations you choose.

Status	Location	Included		Excluded	
On	Exchange email	All recipients	Edit	None	Edit
On	SharePoint sites	All sites	Edit	None	Edit
On	OneDrive accounts	All accounts	Edit	None	Edit
On	Microsoft 365 Groups	All groups	Edit	None	Edit
On	Skype for Business	Edit to add User	Edit	None	
Off	Exchange public folders				
Off	Teams channel messages				
Off	Teams chats				

Figure 8-3. *Choose the locations to apply your retention policy*

The wizard will then ask us to choose locations where we want to apply the retention policy, shown in Figure 8-3. Your options are to select all locations, including Exchange email and public folders, SharePoint, OneDrive, and Microsoft 365 groups. I do not see many people using this option. Usually, they select one of the locations instead. These locations include Exchange email, SharePoint sites, OneDrive for Business, Microsoft 365 groups, Skype for Business, Exchange public folders, Teams channel messages, or Teams chats. Soon, you will also be able to choose Yammer groups or Yammer private messages as locations.

Please note that if you choose Teams channel messages or Teams chats as one of the location options, all the rest of the locations will be disabled. You would need to create a separate retention policy to manage content other than Teams.

You can also include or exclude certain locations, like specific sites or a particular person's email mailbox. To do this, click the Edit button under the Include or Exclude header in the location row you want to manage. Choose the specific locations you want to include or exclude. These policy exceptions are subject to the following limits:

- **Exchange mailboxes**: 1000

- **SharePoint sites**: 100

- **OneDrive for Business accounts**: 100

- **Microsoft 365 groups**: 1000

- **Skype for Business users**: 1000

- **Exchange public folders**: Unavailable

- **Teams channel messages**: 100

- **Teams chat users**: 1000

- **Yammer groups**: 1000

- **Yammer private message users**: 1000

Let us use an example to explain these further. Say 3,000 people in your organization have a different retention policy than everybody else. You would need to create three retention policies to cover all 3,000 of those accounts because you can only specify up to 1,000 recipients per policy.

If you go that route, I highly recommend that you look at PowerShell to automate this process. Otherwise, it is impossible to keep track of these policies and members manually. Also, note that you can have up to 10,000 retention policies per tenant. However, for Exchange Online, the maximum number is 1,800. These numbers include retention policies, retention label policies, and legal holds.

When you finish configuring your locations, click Done to create your retention policy. The system will apply this policy within 24 hours to all the content locations.

Retention Policies with Preservation Lock

Preservation Lock puts restrictions on how a retention policy or retention label policy can be modified. No one – including a global admin – can turn off the policy, delete the policy, or make it less restrictive. This configuration might be needed for regulatory requirements and can help safeguard against rogue administrators.

When a retention policy is locked

- No one can disable the policy or delete it.

- Locations can be added but not removed.

- You can extend the retention period but not decrease it.

To use a preservation lock, first, create the retention policy. You must use PowerShell if you need to use Preservation Lock. Because administrators can't disable or delete a policy for retention after this lock is applied, enabling this feature is not available in the UI to safeguard against accidental configuration.

For more information about this process, please see `http://erica.news/PreservationLock`.

Edit or Delete a Retention Policy

You cannot change some settings after you create a retention policy. These settings include

- The retention policy name

- The retention settings, except for the retention period

- When to start the retention period

If you edit a retention policy, all items governed by the policy will inherit the new settings.

This update can take several days. When the policy replication across your Microsoft 365 locations is complete, you'll see the retention policy's status change from On (Pending) to On (Success).

Inactive Mailboxes

Inactive mailboxes retain mailbox content after employees leave the organization. Inactive mailboxes allow you to remove their Microsoft 365 license and account but keep certain content. Without using an inactive mailbox, the system retains the employee's mailbox data for 30 days after removing the account.

A mailbox will automatically become inactive if the account's content is subject to a litigation hold or retention policy. The inactive mailbox will continue to exist as long as the content meets one of those two conditions.

You can view a list of inactive mailboxes by visiting the information governance solution and the Retention tab and clicking Inactive mailbox in the toolbar.

This section covered everything you need to know about retention policies. The next section will cover the other method to apply retention or deletion policies – retention labels.

Retention Labels

What are retention labels? Retention labels allow you to label individual files with specific retention or deletion period. They also allow you to leverage advanced retention options, such as a file plan, disposition review, or event-based retention. Retention labels are also useful for finalizing content as an immutable record. We will cover these advanced retention options in Chapter 9. In this chapter, we will cover how to create a label and apply it manually to content.

When you ask an end user to label content manually, you present them with a list of potential retention labels to apply to content. It is best to keep the number of labels provided to them to a minimum. There are numerous psychology studies, such as Miller (1956), on the amount of data that a human can keep in their short-term memory. While there is no agreement on the exact range, they all find between five and nine labels to be the maximum number. But of course, they are not testing the user's ability to remember and differentiate between records schedules. I have found that between two and three labels is best to ensure accuracy, such as asking users to label final content to declare it immutable manually. Three to four labels is okay. Suppose you give end users five to seven label choices. In that case, you are putting your accuracy level in danger unless you've already trained your organization to care about records management.

Licensing and Permissions

To use retention labels, each user needs one of the following licenses:

- Microsoft 365 F3.

- Business Premium.

- Office 365 E1/A1.

- Office 365 F3.

- Standalone Exchange plans provide the rights for a user to benefit from manually applying non-record retention labels to mailbox data.

- Standalone SharePoint plans provide the rights for a user to benefit from manually applying non-record retention labels to files in SharePoint or OneDrive.

For permissions, you would need the Retention Management role to create and configure retention labels. Microsoft includes this role in the following default role groups:

- Compliance Administrator

- Compliance Data Administrator

- Organizational Management

Create a Retention Label

To create a retention label, go to the Microsoft 365 Compliance Center. In the left-hand navigation, click "Information governance" and click the "Labels" tab, shown in Figure 8-4. Please note that you could also create a label through the Records Management solution from the File plan tab.

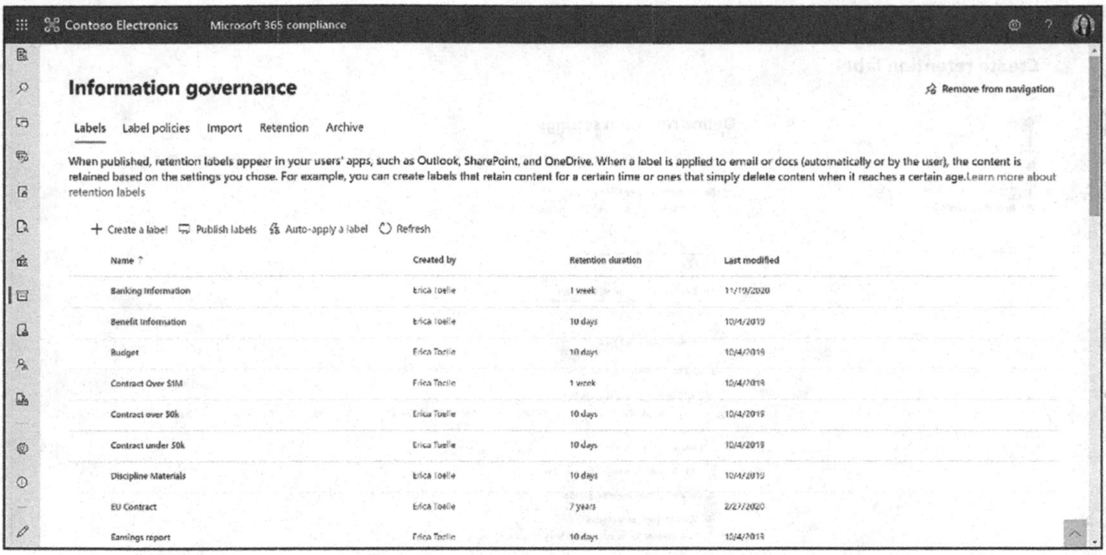

Figure 8-4. *Retention labels in the information governance solution*

To create a new retention label, click + Create a label. This click will bring up a wizard that will ask you to name your label. This label cannot be the same name as a retention policy or sensitivity label. Try to make the name specific and add a description for administrators. You can also add a description to help end users understand when to use this label. Once you complete these fields, click Next.

You may see a screen for the file plan descriptors. I will cover this screen in Chapter 9. Click Next.

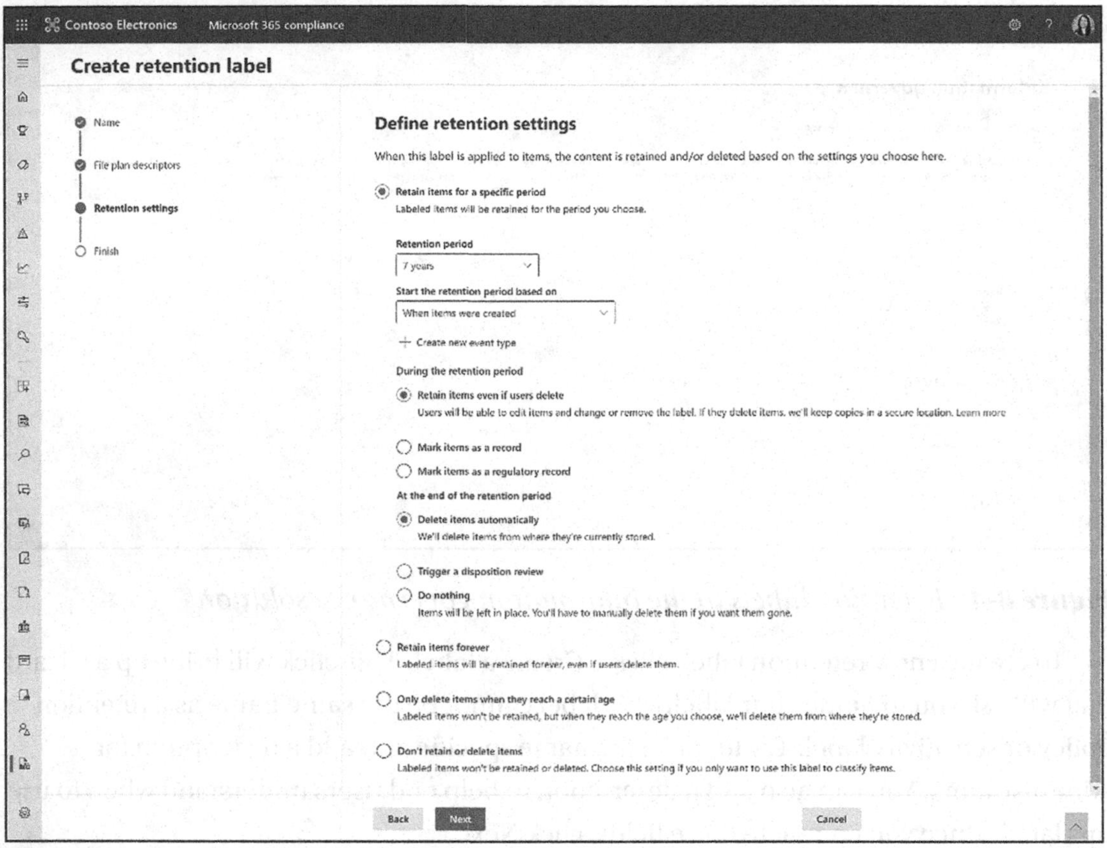

Figure 8-5. *Retention label settings in information governance*

The next screen shows the label settings, shown in Figure 8-5. The first decision is to choose one of the following:

- Retain items for a specific period

- Retain items forever

- Only delete items when they reach a certain age

- Don't retain or delete items

Let us start with the option to retain items for a specific period. When selecting this option, by default, you can choose 5, 7, or 10 years or custom to select your duration in days, months, or years. You can trigger retention based on the creation date, the last modified date, the date you label the content, or an event type. We will cover event types and event-based retention in Chapter 9.

Optionally, you can use the label to declare content as a record or a regulatory record. Again, we will cover these topics in Chapter 9.

At the end of the retention period, you can

- **Delete items automatically**: This choice will start the deletion process outlined in the "How Deletion Works section" of this chapter.

- **Trigger a disposition review**: This option is only available with advanced licenses. We will cover disposition in Chapter 9.

- **Do nothing**: Choosing this option means content will be left alone, without retention. A user or process can delete the file, or it will remain in its current location.

Our next option is to retain items forever. This option is self-explanatory.

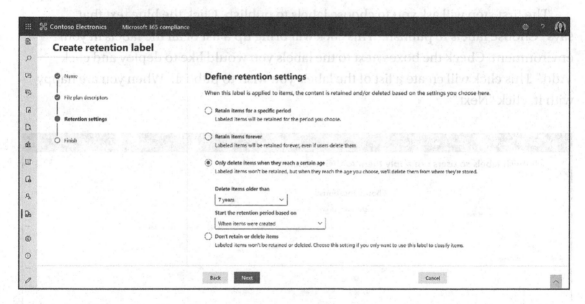

Figure 8-6. *Choices for a deletion label in information governance*

The next option is to only delete items when they reach a certain age. Use this option to enforce the deletion of content rather than retention. Selecting this option allows some additional fields to appear, shown in Figure 8-6. First, decide how old content should be when the system enforces deletion. You can specify the number of days, months, or years. Then, choose how to trigger the deletion period. You can begin based on the creation date, the date last modified, or the date you label the content.

The last option is Don't retain or delete items. This option is if you want only to label content but not enforce retention or deletion.

When you finish your selection, click Next. Here you can review your label settings and click Create label when you are happy.

Publish a Retention Label

For the label to appear to end users for manual labeling, you need to publish the label. You can publish one or many labels in the same policy. I recommend publishing all the labels for the target location in one policy. You can publish one label by checking the box next to it on the Labels tab and clicking Publish labels. Alternatively, you can publish many labels by clicking the "Label policies" tab and then "Publish labels." This click will bring up a wizard.

The first step will ask you to choose labels to publish. Click the blue text that says "Choose labels to publish." This click will bring up a list of all the labels in your environment. Check the boxes next to the labels you would like to deploy and click "Add." This click will create a list of the labels you wish to publish. When you are happy with it, click "Next."

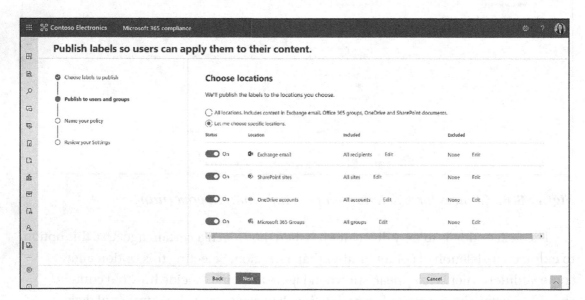

Figure 8-7. *Locations to publish a retention label in information governance*

Now, you will choose locations where you will publish the labels, shown in Figure 8-7. These will be the labels that are available to end users to label their content manually. You can target the labels to these locations:

- **All locations.** Includes content in Exchange email, Office 365 groups, OneDrive, and SharePoint documents

- Exchange email mailboxes

- SharePoint sites

- OneDrive accounts

- Microsoft 365 groups

You can include or exclude specific locations, such as a site or mailbox, within the preceding locations.

For example, let's say you have a list of retention labels you want to publish to finance SharePoint sites. In this case, I would turn off all the locations except for SharePoint, and then I would click "Edit" in the Included column next to "All sites." I would then paste in the URLs for each SharePoint site, one at a time. After going through the remaining publishing steps, within 24 hours, these labels will appear for manual labeling on the finance SharePoint sites.

Maintaining the list of finance sites and updating the policy could get quite tedious. Instead, you could automate managing the site list and policy using PowerShell. Another thing to note is that if you have connected your SharePoint sites to a Microsoft Team or their membership is managed with a Microsoft 365 group, you need to choose Microsoft 365 group as the location as opposed to SharePoint sites. The SharePoint site location will only work for sites that do not have their membership managed by a Microsoft 365 group.

Once you are happy with the locations, click "Next." Here you will enter a unique name for your policy and a description for admins. Click "Next," and then review your settings. Click "Submit" when you are happy.

Please note that it will take up to one day for the labels to appear to the end users. Labels will appear only in Outlook mailboxes with at least 10 megabytes of data. Sometimes this requirement confuses people when they are testing labels in a non-production environment. They have fake user mailboxes that do not have 10 megabytes of data in their accounts, and they wonder why their labels do not show up.

Manually Apply a Retention Label

What do these retention labels look like to the end users? Figure 8-8 shows what the end user sees when they apply a retention label to a SharePoint document library.

Figure 8-8. *Manually apply a retention label in SharePoint*

The labels appear as a dropdown, just like any metadata in the property pane of the file. You can also show the retention label as a document library column. Please note that for SharePoint and OneDrive, any user in the default members group, which has the edit permission level, can apply a label to content.

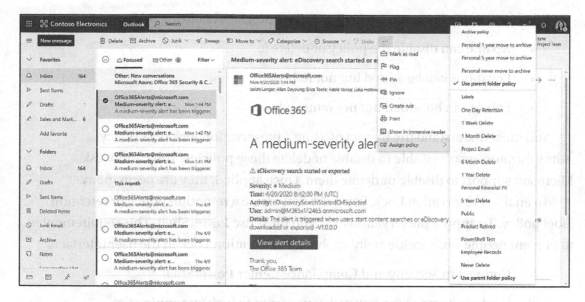

Figure 8-9. *Manually apply a retention label to an email*

In Outlook, users can label one email at a time, shown in Figure 8-9. To do this, right-click an email and choose "Assign policy." Then select the retention policy from the list that appears.

You can also manually apply labels in OneDrive. From OneDrive, select one or more documents. End users can choose the labels from the "Apply Retention Label" dropdown in the document property pane, similar to SharePoint.

Preservation Lock

Some regulatory requirements specify no one, including a global admin, can turn off the policy, delete the policy, or make it less restrictive. The Preservation Lock feature can fulfill this requirement. You can use Preservation Lock with both retention policies and retention label policies.

When you apply Preservation Lock to a retention policy

- No one can disable the policy or delete it.

- Locations can be added but not removed.

- Labels can be added but not removed.

When you apply Preservation Lock to a retention label policy

- No one can disable the policy or delete it.

- Locations can be added but not removed.

- Labels can be added but not removed.

You must understand the impact of using a preservation lock on a policy. Administrators won't be able to disable or delete these policies. You cannot ask Microsoft support to disable or delete them. Once applied, they are permanent.

To enable Preservation Lock, you must first create a retention policy or retention label policy. To apply a preservation lock, you must use PowerShell. This requirement is to prevent people from accidentally applying Preservation Lock in the user interface.

1. Connect to Security and Compliance Center PowerShell.

2. Find the name of the policy that you want to lock by running `Get-RetentionCompliancePolicy`. This command will output a list of your policies.

3. To place a preservation lock on your policy, run the following cmdlet. Replace <name of policy> with the exact name shown in the list from step #2. Keep the quotations:

   ```
   Set-RetentionCompliancePolicy -Identity "<Name of Policy>" -RestrictiveRetention $true
   ```

4. When prompted, read and acknowledge the restrictions that come with this configuration by entering Y:

5. Prompt to confirm that you want to lock a retention policy in PowerShell.

6. You now have a preservation lock on the policy. To confirm, run this command:

   ```
   Get-RetentionCompliancePolicy -Identity "<Name of Policy>" |Fl
   ```

7. You should see RestrictiveRetention set to True.

How Retention Works in Microsoft 365

To summarize, retention labels and retention policies are the two ways to apply retention in Microsoft 365. You can use one or both in the same environment. Now, let us go into how retention works once you have applied it to a document or location. We will discuss what happens if two retention periods could apply to the same document. We will also cover how Microsoft 365 deletes content once it reached the end of its retention period.

The Principles of Retention Policies

What if content qualifies for more than one retention policy? In that case, the system follows the principles of retention to decide what retention period and deletion action to apply to the content.

For information about how Microsoft resolves conflicts between two auto-apply retention labels, please see Chapter 9.

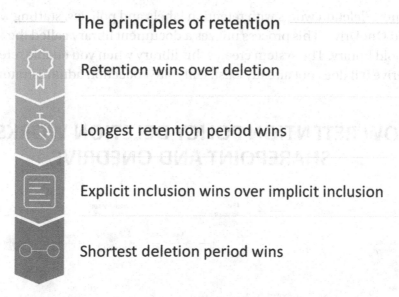

The principles of retention

Retention wins over deletion

Longest retention period wins

Explicit inclusion wins over implicit inclusion

Shortest deletion period wins

Figure 8-10. *The principles of retention policies in Microsoft 365*

We start at the top of the list, shown in Figure 8-10. If one of the principles resolves the conflict, we can stop, and we do not need to consider the rest of the principles. For example, the first principle states that retention wins over deletion. If you have one policy that retains content and one policy that deletes content, the former will be applied. The principles err on the side of caution.

If the first principle does not resolve the conflict, we go to the next principle: the longest retention period wins. If you have one policy that retains content for three years and one policy that retains content for seven years, the seven-year retention policy will apply.

The next principle states that explicit inclusion will always win over implicit inclusion. This principle means that the most specific policy will win. Because the previous principles have determined that the conflicting policies have the same retention period, this principle determines when to delete content. For example, let us say we have a retention policy of three years that applies to all content in all SharePoint sites. We also have a retention label of three years used on individual documents within sites. The retention period applied via the label will take precedence because it is more specific.

Finally, if none of the preceding principles resolve the conflict, the shortest deletion period would win. For example, let us say we have a policy that deletes Teams chats after 60 days. We have another policy that says to delete them after 30 days. The 30-day deletion policy will win.

How Deletion Works

Let us go into how deletion works with retention labels and policies, starting with SharePoint and OneDrive. This process utilizes a document library called the preservation hold library. The system creates this library when you enable retention on a site or OneDrive if it does not already exist. Only site collection administrators can see the library.

HOW RETENTION POLICY DELETION WORKS IN SHAREPOINT AND ONEDRIVE

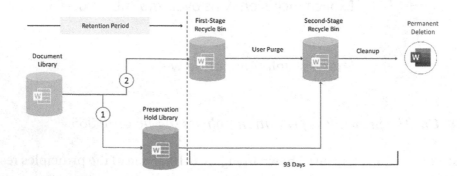

1. **If the content is modified or deleted** during the retention period
2. **If the content is not modified or deleted** during the retention period

Figure 8-11. *How retention policy deletion works in SharePoint and OneDrive*

Our first example uses a retention policy. Let us say that you have applied a retention policy to a SharePoint site. Here is what happens to the file, illustrated in Figure 8-11. The behavior of the document is different if the file already existed in the site when you applied retention vs. if it didn't:

1. If someone attempts to modify or delete the file, the system checks if the document has changed since you applied the retention settings.

    a. If the content already existed when you first applied the policy and if this is the first change since you applied retention, the system copies the content to the preservation hold library. This copy allows the person to change or delete the original content. It will stay here until the end of the retention period. At the end of the period, the system moves the file to the first-stage recycle bin, where it exists until it gets deleted permanently. The only exception is if an end user purges the first-stage recycle bin. In that case, the file moves to the second-stage recycle bin until deleted.

2. If the document is not modified or deleted by a user during the retention period, it stays in the document library. At the end of the retention period, the file moves to the second-stage recycle bin.

The system only retains the latest version of each file unless we preserve the file using records versioning, which we will discuss later in this chapter. The system names each file in this format: [Title GUID Version#]. If a document is not deleted or modified while in a document library, then a version of the file will not be kept in the preservation hold library, shown in Figure 8-12 below.

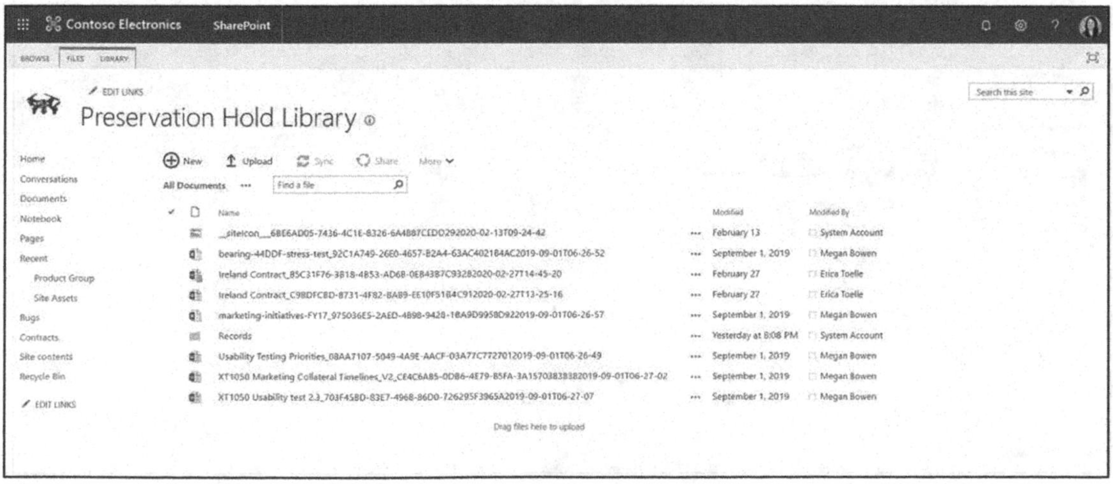

Figure 8-12. *The preservation hold library*

Remember that you cannot do a disposition review on content preserved using a retention policy. You can only do a review using a label. Therefore, once the retention period on the file has passed, one of two things will happen. The file in the preservation hold library will be moved to the second-stage recycle bin where it will stay for 93 days. The system permanently deletes the data after 93 days.

Note   Only site collection administrators can view and access the preservation hold library and the second-stage recycle bin.

Files that exist only in the document library will be moved to the first-stage recycle bin. They will stay there until an end user empties the first-stage recycle bin or for 93 days. When we empty the first-stage recycle bin, the files are moved to the second-stage recycle bin until the end of the 93 days. Also, note that files in either recycle bin are not indexed in search and therefore are not available for eDiscovery.

If you're using a retention label, the preservation and deletion process is more straightforward. If a document is retained in SharePoint or OneDrive using a retention label, the end user will get an error if they try to delete the document, shown in Figure 8-13 below. The error says, "The label that's applied to this item prevents it from being edited or deleted. Check the item's label for more details." Honestly, I hate this error and wish that record labels used the preservation hold library method instead. An end user isn't going to understand that message and can't look up any information about labels. They won't even know whether it's a sensitivity or retention label that's causing the error.

Figure 8-13. *The error when deleting a file with a retention label*

Once a label's retention period has passed, a few things can happen:

- If the label triggers a disposition review, then the file will follow the review process outlined in the preceding text. Once the review approves the disposal, the content is moved to the first-stage recycle bin and deleted after 93 days.

- If the label deletes the content automatically, it is moved to the first-stage recycle bin and kept for 93 days.

- If the label setting is Nothing, leave the content as is, and then the system does not act.

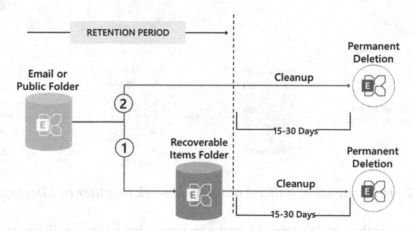

Figure 8-14. *How retention policies work in Exchange*

Now let us look at how deletion works in Exchange, illustrated by Figure 8-14 above:

1. If a user then tries to delete an item, the item will be moved to the hidden Recoverable Items folder in the user's Exchange mailbox. It will exist in that folder until the end of the retention period. At that point, there is a cleanup job that runs every 15–30 days, and then it will permanently delete that item.

2. If the content is not deleted or modified during that time, it will just exist in the user's mailbox or archive folder until the end of the retention period. Then, the same cleanup job will recognize the expired item and permanently delete it.

Now let's put the information about retention principles and the deletion information together into one scenario. This scenario is useful if you are concerned about the exact location of the file throughout this process. What if a retention label and a retention policy cover the same file? Where does the file physically live in the site? An excellent article covers these scenarios in detail authored by Stefanie Bier and the technical editor for this book, Ryan Sturm. I encourage you to check it out: `http://erica.news/LabelsAndPolicies`.

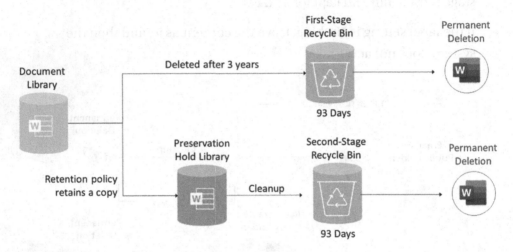

Figure 8-15. *How retention policies and labels work together in Microsoft 365*

To summarize the article's basic ideas, let us say we have three policies or labels that could apply to one file. This scenario is shown in Figure 8-15 above. These are

1. **Retention label**: Keep for three years and then delete.

2. **Deletion policy**: Delete after two years.

3. **Retention policy**: Retain for ten years and then delete.

Following the principles of retention tells us the following:

- It ignores the deletion policy.

- The retention label deletes the file after three years.

- The retention policy keeps a copy of the file for ten years and then deletes it.

The physical location of the file throughout this process is as follows:

1. While users collaborate, Microsoft 365 keeps the file in the SharePoint document library.

    a. If someone tries to delete the file before three years, the label will prevent the action. The file stays in the library.

    b. If a user deletes the file between three and ten years, the file moves to the preservation hold library.

2. After three years, the retention label moves the file to the first-stage recycle bin. Ninety-three days later, it deletes the file permanently.

    a. The system retains a copy of the file in the preservation hold library.

3. After ten years, the system moves the file to the second-stage recycle bin. After 93 days, the system permanently deletes the file.

This chapter has discussed retention policies, retention labels, and retention label policies. Additionally, we talked about how content is deleted from Microsoft 365 when it is subject to a retention policy and what happens when one document qualifies for two different retention periods. Next, we will switch gears to talk about how to import PST files into Microsoft 365 and how to enable an archive mailbox and unlimited archive.

How to Import Content into Microsoft 365

Import allows you to bulk-import PST files to Exchange Online mailboxes. People usually do this when they have old PST files sitting on a server. They may want to retain and dispose of the content or make the PST files available for eDiscovery.

There are two ways that you can import PST files to Microsoft 365. The first option uses network upload. The second option is to ship BitLocker encrypted hard drives to Microsoft. Each of these methods follows the same process.

First, we will want to collect the PST files. We need to discover where PST files exist in our organization and move them to one central location to upload them to Microsoft 365. We could also optionally prevent users from creating new PST files, so this is not an ongoing issue.

Second, we need to upload those PST files to a temporary Azure storage location. This upload is where the two options differ. If you have a reasonable amount of data, you could use the network upload option to get data into the Azure storage location yourself. However, if you have a lot of data and it would take too long to upload it yourself, you can ship the hard drives to Microsoft, and they will upload it for you.

It does not matter which method you use. Both approaches result in having your data in a temporary Azure storage location. After that, you will import the PSTs to the appropriate Microsoft 365 mailbox. We will talk about this process more in-depth in the rest of this section.

Permissions and Licensing

First, let us talk about permissions. You need to have something called the Mailbox Import Export role in Exchange Online to import PST files to Microsoft 365 mailboxes. By default, Microsoft 365 does not assign this role to any of the role groups in either Exchange Online or the Microsoft 365 Compliance Center. You will need to add that role to an existing group or create a new role group and add someone. Follow these steps to complete this assignment:

1. Visit the Exchange admin center here: `https://admin.exchange.microsoft.com/`.

2. In the left navigation, click Roles ä Admin roles.

3. Click Add role group.

4. Name the new role group. Click Next.

5. Scroll down until you find the Mailbox Import Export role. Check the box next to it. Click Next.

6. In the Members field, enter the user account that should have this role.

7. Click Next and Add role group.

8. Wait at least 15 minutes for the changes to propagate.

Additionally, to create an import job in the Compliance Center, you must have one of the following roles:

- Mail Recipients role in Exchange Online. By default, this role is assigned to the following role groups:

    - Organization Management

    - Recipient Management

- You could also be a global administrator.

To import PST files into Microsoft 365, you need one of the following licenses for each user to receive an import:

- Microsoft 365 E5

- Microsoft 365 E3

- Office E5

- Office 365 E3

- Office 365 E1

Also, note that to use the drive shipping option, you must have a Microsoft Enterprise Agreement. Drive shipping is not available through Microsoft Products and Services Agreement.

Using a network upload to import PST files is free, but drive shipping is not. We will get into the specific pricing structure for drive shipping in the "Drive Shipping" section later in this chapter.

Use Network Upload

Network upload is unfortunately not available everywhere. It is only available in the United States, Canada, Brazil, the United Kingdom, France, Germany, Switzerland, Norway, Europe, India, East Asia, Southeast Asia, Japan, Republic of Korea, Australia, and United Arab Emirates (UAE). Network upload will be available in more regions soon. You can import content into either an active or an inactive mailbox. If you are in an Exchange hybrid environment, you can import it into an online archive mailbox.

Before you begin, you must collect all the PST files for the import into one location. You must locate the PST files in a file share or file server in your organization.

There is some information to consider before we start. The speed of the upload depends on the capacity of your network. It typically takes several hours for each terabyte of data to be uploaded to the Azure storage area for your organization. If, for example, you are trying to upload 100 TB of data, that could take anywhere from 10 days to 100 days, depending on network capacity. This situation is where drive shipping might be a better option. After you copy the PST files to the Azure storage area, the system imports a PST file to a Microsoft 365 mailbox at a rate of at least 24 gigabytes per day. This rate is the same, whether you are using the network import or the drive shipping option.

If you import different PST files to different target mailboxes, the import process from Azure to the mailbox occurs in parallel, meaning it introduces each PST mailbox pair simultaneously. Likewise, if you import multiple PST files to the same mailbox, it will import them simultaneously. Each one of those different import threads has a rate of 24 gigabytes per day.

The Azure storage location keeps the data for 30 days, after which the system deletes the content. You can import up to 500 PST files per import job. Each PST file cannot be larger than 20 GB. The maximum message size is 35 MB. Watch the Exchange online mailbox size. You may need to turn on the archive functionality or auto-expanding archive if you import a large amount of data into already full mailboxes. You can import a maximum of 100 GB into one archive mailbox. We cover the archive mailbox functionality in the next section.

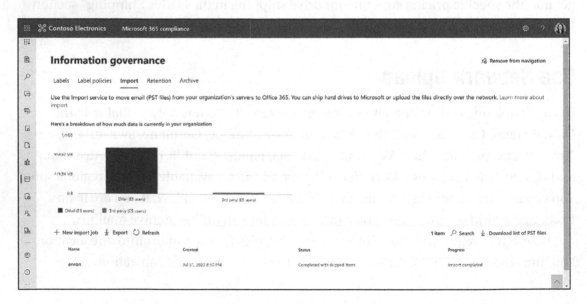

Figure 8-16. *The Import tab overview in the information governance solution*

To start an import PST process, visit the Microsoft 365 Compliance Center. In the left navigation, click Information governance. Then click the Import tab, shown in Figure 8-16. Here, you can see a breakdown of how much data is currently in your organization, including PST imports and third-party connectors. You can also see a list of previous PST imports, including the name, creation date, status, and progress information. You can also download a list of past import jobs or a list of the PST files contained in the import. Lastly, you can search for an import or refresh the list.

To start an import, click New import job. This click will bring you to a wizard where you first are asked to provide a name for your job. This name needs to be 2–64 lowercase letters, numbers, or hyphens. It must start with a letter and contain no spaces. Once you complete the Name field, click Next. Now, you will choose whether you want to upload or ship your data. In this example, we will choose to upload our data. Click Next.

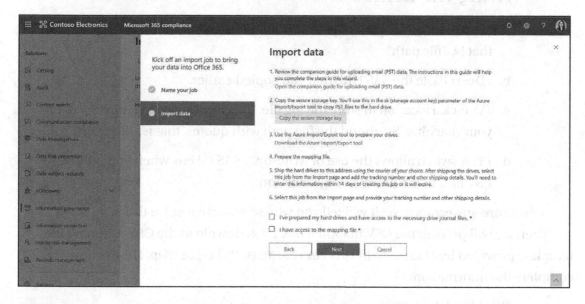

Figure 8-17. *Instructions to prepare for data upload*

The next screen has the steps you need to complete to import your data, shown in Figure 8-17. First, you will want to review the companion guide or Microsoft's instructions for uploading email PST data. You can click the first blue link to read that information.

Next, you will get your SAS URL key for the network upload. This SAS URL is the password that allows you access to your data, so please keep this confidential just as you would with any other password. Click Copy the secure storage key and then Copy to clipboard.

241

Now, you need to use the Azure AzCopy tool to upload your files. The link provided in the instructions is for AzCopy 8.1, but unfortunately, you need to use AzCopy version 10. You can download version 10 here: `http://erica.news/AzCopy10`.

Save the downloaded file in a location that is easy to access through a command prompt:

1. Open a command prompt on your local computer.

2. Navigate to the directory where you put the AzCopy.exe file.

3. Run this command. You will need to modify it to include your parameters:

   ```
   AzCopy.exe /Source:<Location of PST files> /Dest:<SAS URL>
   /V:<Log file location> /Y
   ```

   a. **/Source:** The file path of your PST files. Surround the file path with quotes, that is, "file path".

   b. **/Dest:** Paste the SAS URL that you copied earlier.

   c. **/V:** Pick a location to store the log file. This location can be anywhere on your machine. Surround the file path with quotes, that is, "file path".

   d. **/Y:** A switch allows the use of write-only SAS tokens when you upload the PST files to the Azure storage location.

If there are any errors here, it will tell you why so you can resolve them.

Then we will prepare the CSV mapping file. First, download the CSV mapping file template provided by Microsoft: `http://erica.news/PSTImportMap`. Here is how you complete the information:

- **Workload**: Exchange.

- **File path:** Leave that blank unless you uploaded the PST files into a subfolder. If you did, enter the subfolder name.

- **Name**: This is the name of your PST file. It is case sensitive, and you need to include the file extension (.pst).

- **Mailbox**: The email address for the mailbox where you put the data.

- If you want to use an inactive mailbox, put the mailbox GUID in this field. To get the GUID, run the following PowerShell command in Exchange Online:

```
Get-Mailbox <identity of inactive mailbox>
-InactiveMailboxOnly | FL Guid
```

- **IsArchive**: Use TRUE or FALSE. If TRUE, the process will import the data into the user's archive mailbox. If FALSE, it will import it into their primary mailbox. The user must have an archive already enabled to use the TRUE option. We go over the archive in the next section of this chapter.

- **TargetRootFolder**: Specifies where in the mailbox the process will place the data. For example, if you leave it blank, the import job will create a folder called "Imported" at the same level as the inbox.

    - Use /YourFolderName to change the folder name from "Imported" to what you specify.

    - Use /Inbox to merge the messages with what currently exists in the inbox.

    - Use /Inbox/YourFolderName to create a new folder under the inbox if it does not exist yet.

- **ContentCodePage**: We mostly use this field to import folder names in Chinese, Japanese, and Korean (double-byte characters) correctly.

    - Leave blank if you do not have any special characters.

    - If you have special characters, find the code on this page that matches the characters: http://erica.news/ CodePageIdentifiers.

- **SPFileContainer**: Leave blank.

- **SPManifestContainer**: Leave blank.

- **SPSiteUrl**: Leave blank.

When you finish, check the two boxes for "I'm done uploading my files" and "I have access to the mapping file."

The next screen will ask you to select the mapping file. Click Select Mapping File and browse to the file. Click the Validate button, which checks for common errors. It will turn green if there are no errors. Click Save. Now, you will see a screen that says, "Success! You have added an import job into Microsoft 365."

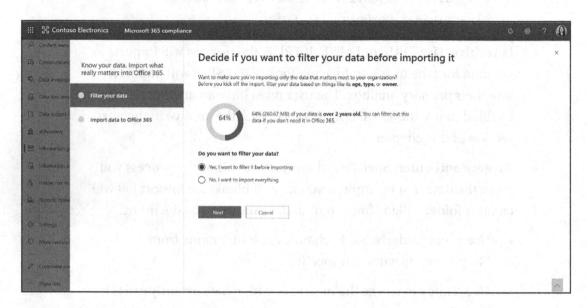

Figure 8-18. *Decide if you want to filter your data before importing it into Microsoft 365*

Now the process shows a screen that says status = analysis in process. You can walk away from the process and come back later. Click the import job name to check the status. When status = analysis complete, click the blue button that says Import into Office 365. This click will show you a screen with statistics about your data, asking you if you would like to filter it before importing it into Microsoft 365, shown in Figure 8-18. Select Yes or No and click Next.

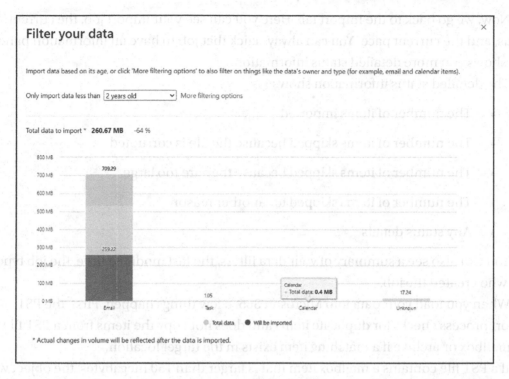

***Figure 8-19.** Filter the data from the PST files before import into Microsoft 365*

This screen allows you to filter the PST files' data before the actual import into Microsoft 365. The graph on this page changes as you select filters. The gray color represents the total data in the PST files. The blue color is what the system will import based on your current filters. There is a separate graph for Email, Task, Calendar, and Unknown, shown in Figure 8-19. You filter the data on

- **Age:** You can choose the age in year increments.

- **Type**.

- **Users listed in the From field**.

- **Users listed in the To field**.

- **Users listed in the Cc field**.

When you are happy, click Next. The next screen asks you to confirm your filter settings or your decision not to filter data. If you are happy, click Import data. The next screen tells you the job scheduled successfully, how much data it will import, and that you can check the progress column on the import page to see your import's progress. Go ahead and close this wizard.

Now, we go back to the Import tab. Here you can see your import job, the current status, and the current pace. You can always click that job to have an information panel that shows you more detailed status information.

The detailed status information shows

- The number of items imported

- The number of items skipped because the file is corrupted

- The number of items skipped because they are too large

- The number of items skipped for another reason

- Any status details

You can also see a summary of your data filters, the last modified time, the job type, and who created the job.

When you load your data into Microsoft 365, a few things happen. First, the PST import process checks for duplicate items and does not copy the items from a PST file to the mailbox or archive if a matching item exists in the target location.

If a PST file contains a mailbox item that is larger than 150 megabytes, the object will be skipped during the import process. The process does not change the original message metadata during the import process, and you cannot import a PST file that has 300 or more levels of nested folders.

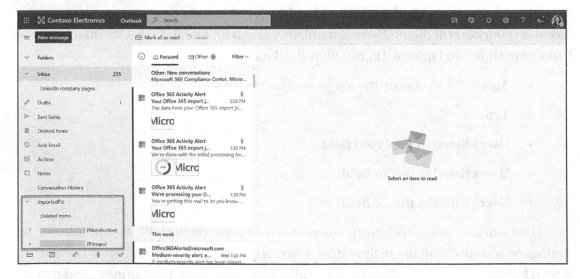

Figure 8-20. *The finished PST import in a user's mailbox*

Once the system completes the import, you can navigate to one of the mailboxes to view the files. Here I can see that I have my imported PST mailbox, shown in Figure 8-20.

The Microsoft 365 import service enables the retention hold setting for an indefinite duration after importing the PST files to a mailbox. The system does this hold, so the newly imported emails are not deleted right away by a retention policy. For example, let us say you have a retention policy on your mailbox that deletes emails older than three years. If you import emails older than three years and the system did not turn on the retention hold setting, it would delete all your newly imported emails.

If you're happy having this hold on the mailboxes, you can leave it on indefinitely. You can turn this setting on or off or set a different retention period using PowerShell. You can also configure the retention hold, so it turns off on some date in the future. You need to set the number of days in the future that you want it turned off. For example, take today's date, and if you wish to have it turned off in 120 days or four months, you will specify 120 days in the setting.

Drive Shipping

Now, let us talk about the drive shipping import option. Drive shipping is a way you can import PST files at scale to Microsoft 365. You must have an Enterprise Agreement with Microsoft to use this method. With drive shipping, you physically ship the hard drive to a Microsoft data center. When Microsoft receives the hard drive, data center personnel will upload the PST files on the hard drive to your organization's temporary Azure storage location. After your hard drive is received, it can take seven to ten business days to upload the PST files. Like the network upload process, Microsoft 365 would then analyze the data and the PST files and set filters to control what data gets imported. Subsequently, Microsoft would ship the hard drive back to you with the data intact.

The cost to use drive shipping to import PST files to Microsoft 365 is $2 USD per gigabyte of data. If you want to upload a terabyte of data, that would be $2,000. You can work with a partner to pay the import fee; you do not pay that directly to Microsoft. They only accept 2.5-inch solid-state drives or 2.5-inch or 3.5-inch SATA 2 or SATA 3 internal hard drives. They do not allow external hard drives. You can use hard disks up to 10 terabytes, and for import jobs, they will only process the first data volume on the hard drive. You must format your data volumes within NTFS, and you can ship a maximum of ten hard drives for a single import job, which equals an overall maximum of 100 terabytes for a single import job. You or your organization must have an account with FedEx or DHL because Microsoft will bill that account for the shipping cost when Microsoft returns it to you.

If you're going to use this option, there are a lot more details you should know. Check out the documentation here: `http://erica.news/DriveShipping`.

Lastly, I will mention that if you want to import files and documents to SharePoint sites or OneDrive accounts, you can do that. There are several methods available that do not involve the Compliance Center. Microsoft provides a free SharePoint migration tool. You can also migrate using PowerShell. Or you could always use a third-party migration tool to move that data.

In this section, we reviewed why you would want to import data into Microsoft 365. We went into details about how to do a network import job and briefly discussed drive shipping and file imports. Next, we will cover archive and unlimited mailboxes.

Archive Mailboxes and Unlimited Archive

Archive mailboxes provide additional email storage for people in your organization. Using Outlook or Outlook web app, people can view messages in their archive mailbox and move or copy messages between their primary and archive mailboxes. After an archive mailbox is enabled, messages older than two years are automatically moved to the archive mailbox by the default retention policy assigned to every mailbox in your organization. Of course, you can customize this policy for your needs. People mostly use archive mailboxes to free up storage in their primary mailbox. With archive mailboxes, you can also enable unlimited archive, allowing unlimited space in the archive mailbox folder.

Licensing and Permissions

A user must be assigned an Exchange Online Plan 2 license to enable the archive mailbox. Microsoft includes this license by default in all E3 and E5 plans. If a user is assigned an Exchange Online P1 license, you would need to assign them an additional separate Exchange Online Archive license to enable their archive mailbox. Auto-expanding or unlimited archiving also supports shared mailboxes. An Exchange Online P2 license or an Exchange Online P1 license with the Exchange Online Archiving license is required to enable the archive for a shared mailbox.

You must be a global administrator in your organization or a member of your Exchange Online Organization Management role group to enable auto-expanding archiving for your entire organization or specific users. Alternatively, you must be a member of a role group assigned the Mail Recipients role to enable auto-expanding archiving for particular groups.

Enable Archive Mailboxes

Now let us look at how to enable archive mailboxes. You can find archive mailboxes in the Microsoft 365 Compliance Center. In the left-hand navigation, click Information governance and then the Archive tab.

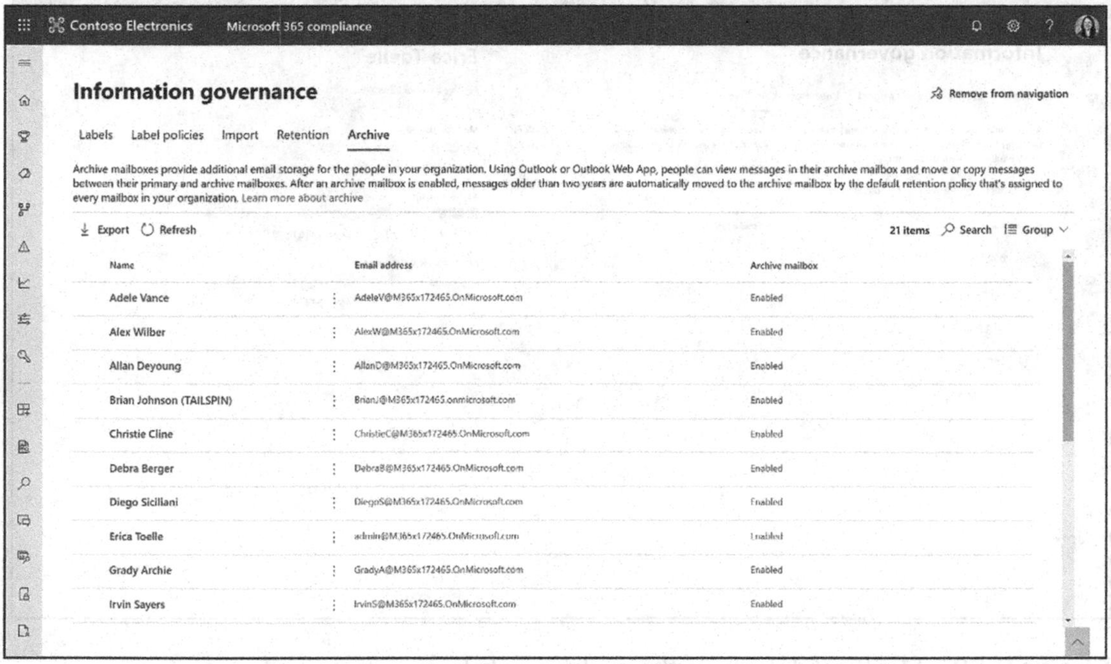

Figure 8-21. *The Archive tab in the information governance solution*

Here you see a list of the organization's users, their email address, and whether their archive mailbox is enabled or disabled, shown in Figure 8-21. The Export button downloads a report of all the users and whether their archive mailbox is enabled or disabled. You can refresh or search the list. Lastly, you can group the list by whether the archive mailbox is enabled or disabled.

If you would like to enable the archive mailbox, select one or more of the people in the list and click the toolbar's Enable archive text. A warning will appear saying, "If you enable this person's archive mailbox, items in their mailbox that are older than two years will be moved to the new archive. Are you sure you want to enable this archive mailbox?" Click Enable. You can also enable the archive through PowerShell.

You can disable archive mailboxes by selecting a user or multiple users and clicking Disable archive. In this case, Microsoft 365 will keep the archive for 30 days. If you reenable the archive within those 30 days, it will restore the archive to its prior state. After 30 days, the system deletes all content in the archive mailbox, and you cannot restore it. If you reenabled the archive after 30 days, it creates a new archive.

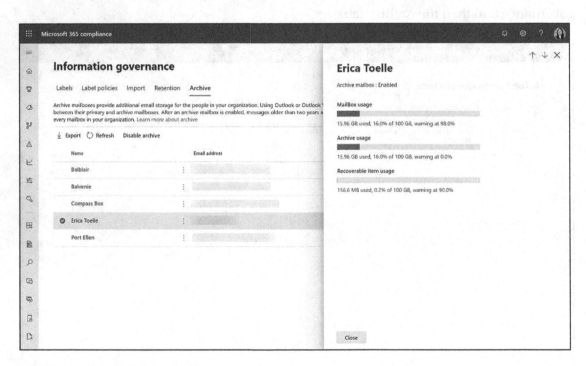

Figure 8-22. *Mailbox details in the archive solution*

You can also view mailbox information for each of the users to decide whether you should enable their archive. To do this, click a user from the archive location. A pane will open, shown in Figure 8-22. Here you can see their mailbox usage, including their quota information. If they already have an archive mailbox, you can see usage information for that too. Lastly, you can see their recoverable item usage.

Users can access the archive folder in Outlook client or web app. They cannot access the archive folder in the Outlook mobile client on a phone. Users can move content to and from the archive. When using content or eDiscovery search, it will automatically search both the archive and primary mailboxes for a user. The archive mailbox honors hold and retention policies.

There is a Default Exchange MRM Policy automatically assigned to the mailbox when the archive is enabled. This policy moves items older than two years to the archive. It also moves items in the Recoverable Items folder after 14 days to the archive Recoverable Items folder. You can replace this default policy with a custom MRM policy with any duration from the Exchange admin center.

Unlimited Archiving

After you enable archiving on a mailbox, the admin can also turn on an unlimited or auto-expanding archive. You will see the terms unlimited and auto-expanding used interchangeably in this section, Microsoft documentation, and other information, but they mean the same thing. Archive mailboxes start with a 100 GB quota, with a warning at 90 GB. Suppose a mailbox is placed on hold or assigned to a retention policy. In that case, the storage quota for the archive mailbox increases to 110 GB with a warning at 100 GB.

Once you have enabled unlimited archive, when the archive mailbox plus the Recoverable Items folder reaches 90 GB, it converts the mailbox to an unlimited archive. This conversion can take up to 30 days. Once that is achieved, the system automatically adds additional storage in 10 GB increments.

Sometimes the system moves folders and items in these folders to the auto-expanding archive. This move is so Microsoft can optimize storage. If it moves the whole folder, the folder name will remain the same. If it only moves a portion of the folder, the system will modify the folder name to be <folder name>_yyyy (Created on mmm dd, yyyy h_mm), for example, Project Falcon_2020 (Created on Dec 01, 2020 8_02).

Access the Unlimited Archive

You can access the unlimited archive using Outlook 2016, Outlook 2019 for Mac or Windows, or Outlook on the Web. You cannot access it from Outlook on mobile devices. If you want to search the unlimited archive, you need to search each folder separately. Do this by clicking the folder and choosing the current folder as the search scope. Item counts and read/unread counts might not be accurate. You can delete items in a folder, but not the folder itself. And you cannot use the Recover deleted items feature to recover an item that a user removed from an auto-expanded storage area.

Here are some warnings about the unlimited archive. Microsoft only supports the auto-expanding archive for mailboxes used for individual users or shared mailboxes with a growth rate that does not exceed 1 GB per day. A user's archive mailbox is intended just for that user. Using journaling transport rules or auto-forwarding rules to copy messages to an archive mailbox is not permitted. Microsoft reserves the right to deny unlimited archiving and instances where someone uses a user's archive mailbox to store archive data for other users or, in other cases, for inappropriate use.

Here is how the unlimited archive works with each of the significant compliance tools:

- **eDiscovery**: When you use an eDiscovery tool such as content search, it also searches the additional storage areas in an auto-expanded archive.

- **Retention**: When you manage the mailbox with a retention policy, it also manages the unlimited archive.

- **Messaging Records Management or MRM**: If you use MRM deletion policies in Exchange Online to permanently delete expired mailbox items, it also removes expired items in the auto-expanded archive.

- **Import service**: You can use the Microsoft 365 import service discussed in the previous section to import PST files to a user's auto-expanded archive. You can import up to 100 GB of data from PST files to the user's archive mailbox.

Enable Unlimited Archiving

To enable unlimited archiving, you need to use PowerShell. You can allow unlimited archive for the entire organization or just for specific people. After you turn it on, the system enables an auto-expanding archive for existing user mailboxes and newly created user mailboxes. When you create user mailboxes, be sure to allow the user's primary archive mailbox, so the auto-expanding archiving feature works for the new user mailbox. After you turn on auto-expanding archiving, you cannot turn it off. Instead of enabling auto-expanding archiving for every user in your organization, you might only allow it for specific users. You might do this because only some users require a large archive storage capacity.

To enable unlimited archiving

1. Connect to Exchange Online PowerShell.

2. To enable unlimited archive for everyone, run the following command:

    ```
    Set-OrganizationConfig -AutoExpandingArchive
    ```

3. To enable unlimited archive for specific users, run the following command:

    ```
    Enable-Mailbox <user mailbox> -AutoExpandingArchive
    ```

In this chapter, we covered the information governance solution. We started by discussing retention policies, including Preservation Lock and inactive mailboxes. Then we reviewed retention labels and how end users can manually apply them to emails and documents. We also covered the principles of retention and how retention deletion works in Exchange, SharePoint, and OneDrive.

Next, we discussed how to import PST files into Microsoft 365. You can either upload them through the browser or via drive shipping. Lastly, we covered archive mailboxes and the unlimited archive.

In the next chapter, we will discuss records management. This overview includes file plans, record labels, regulatory record labels, disposition approval, and event-based retention. I also include advanced compliance features such as the auto-application of retention labels and advanced records versioning.

CHAPTER 9

Records Management

Records management is not a new concept for many organizations. Most regulated and government organizations employ a records manager to ensure compliance with recordkeeping regulations, laws, and corporate policy. But, in the electronic age, records management and retention have become difficult due to the volume of data and proliferation of document management systems.

In this chapter, we will review the records management features that complement retention in the Compliance Center. These features include record labels, file plan manager, the ability to apply retention labels automatically, event-based retention, records versioning, and disposition review and approval. These features complement and extend the functionality we reviewed in Chapter 8. Be sure to also read that chapter to understand the complete records management solution.

But first, let's further define records management for people not familiar with recordkeeping.

What Is Records Management?

What does it mean to manage documents as records? We match a file to a records category, and the category tells us how long to keep the record, what starts the retention period, and what we should do with the file when the retention period ends. Here are some common records management terms and what they mean. In this chapter

- A **records or retention schedule** is an official and approved document that tells you how long to keep specific types of records and what should happen to those records. It contains this information:

© Erica Toelle 2021
E. Toelle, *Microsoft 365 Compliance*, https://doi.org/10.1007/978-1-4842-5778-4_9

- A **records series** is a category of records. It usually includes a title and description. The description helps you to identify how the records are used and what types of material might be included in a typical set of records.

- **Disposition** tells you what starts the retention and how long to retain the records. It also defines what to do with records once the retention period is over, such as destroy the file, approve it before it is deleted, or transfer it to an archive.

- A **file plan** is like a map for your retention schedule. It tells you where and how to store the records. This plan is helpful for new employees, eDiscovery teams, or employees who don't work with records often to understand where to find and store records. It is a less formal and smaller version of your retention schedule, usually scoped to a specific office or function.

- **Event-based retention** is when retention is triggered by an event, such as the end of a fiscal year or project or when an employee leaves the organization. Non-event retention is triggered by when a document is created, last modified, or some other editable date.

- Some records may be **immutable or finalized**, meaning people cannot edit or delete them. Most records start out in a draft or collaborative state and then become finalized at some point.

Microsoft 365 Records Management

Microsoft 365 provides a modern records management solution using the following features:

- Manage records in place.

- Microsoft 365 uses labels and label policies to assign retention periods and record settings to documents. These labels could be manual or automated.

- In Microsoft 365, records can have a built-in disposition review experience, including approval and a certificate of destruction.

- Microsoft 365 modern records management includes event-based retention, so you can trigger retention from the date when something happened rather than from the created or modified date of the document.

- You can use advanced data governance for automated label assignment, so you do not have to rely on end users for classification of content. Microsoft 365 provides label analytics, so you can see how you use labels throughout the organization.

- Additionally, you can use a complimentary feature called Microsoft Information Protection to identify sensitive content and automatically assign markings and protection policies to those documents. These documents containing sensitive content often have records management requirements.

You can access these records management features by visiting `https://compliance.microsoft.com`. In the left navigation, click Catalog and find the Information protection and governance category. Under the records management solution, click View. Next, click Open solution.

In this chapter, we are going to go over each area of the records management solution, including the overview dashboard, file plan, label policies, event-based retention, disposition, and records versioning.

When you open the records management solution (Figure 9-1), the first thing you will see is the overview page. This page provides a high-level overview of your retention labels. First, you can see a list of labels that have pending dispositions. You cannot click the individual items. But you can click View all pending dispositions, which will bring you to the Disposition tab.

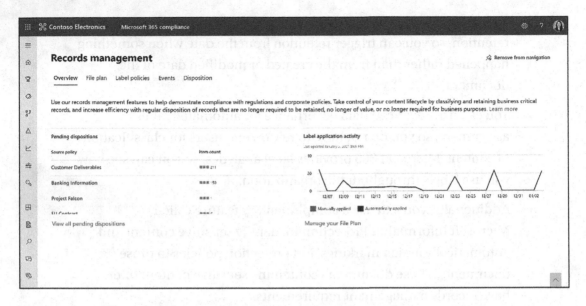

Figure 9-1. *The records management overview page*

Next, you can see a summary of label application activity, which shows manually and automatically applied label trends over the past month. You can click Manage your File Plan to go to the File plan tab.

Permissions and Licensing

The records management features described in this chapter require one of the following licenses:

- Office 365 E5

- Microsoft 365 E5/A5 Info Protection and Governance

- Microsoft 365 E5 Compliance

- Office 365 Advanced Compliance (retired)

Please note that I purposely covered the E3-level features in Chapter 8 and the E5 features in this chapter to help people understand what value you get with the license upgrade.

To use the records management solution, a user will need to have the following permission roles assigned:

- **RecordManagement**: View and edit the configuration of the records management feature.

- **Retention Management**: Manage retention policies, retention labels, and retention label policies.

- **View-Only Records Management**: View the configuration of the records management feature.

- **View-Only Retention Management**: View the configuration of retention policies, retention labels, and retention label policies.

These roles are included in the following default role groups:

- Compliance Administrator

- Compliance Data Administrator

- Organizational Management

The RecordManagement role is also included in the Records Management default role group.

Record and Regulatory Record Labels

We covered retention labels in Chapter 8. Record labels are a flavor of retention labels that applies additional restrictions on the content. Regulatory record labels are even more strict than a record label.

When content is declared a record

- Restrictions are placed on the items in terms of what actions are allowed or blocked.

- Additional activities about the item are logged.

- You have proof of disposition when the items are deleted at the end of their retention period.

Table 9-1 outlines the differences between the different types of record labels.

Table 9-1. *Types of retention labels in records management*

Action	Retention label	Record – locked	Record – unlocked	Regulatory record
Edit contents	Allowed	**Blocked**	Allowed	**Blocked**
Edit properties, including rename	Allowed	Allowed	Allowed	**Blocked**
Delete	Allowed [1]	**Blocked**	**Blocked**	**Blocked**
Copy	Allowed	Allowed	Allowed	Allowed
Move within container	Allowed	Allowed	Allowed	Allowed
Move across containers	Allowed	Allowed if never unlocked	Allowed	**Blocked**
Open/Read	Allowed	Allowed	Allowed	Allowed
Change label	Allowed	Allowed – container admin only	Allowed – container admin only	**Blocked**
Remove label	Allowed	Allowed – container admin only	Allowed – container admin only	**Blocked**

To create a record label or regulatory record label, follow the steps to create a retention label outlined in Chapter 8. On the retention settings page, select the option to mark items as a record or a regulatory record, shown in Figure 9-2.

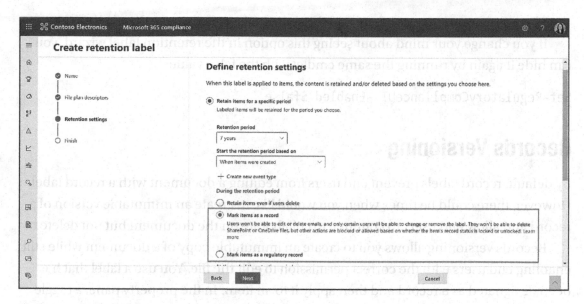

Figure 9-2. Create a record label

Regulatory Record Labels

The most crucial difference for a regulatory record is that nobody, not even a global administrator, can remove the label after applying it to content.

Also, retention labels configured for regulatory records have the following admin restrictions:

- You can't make the retention period shorter after you save the label.
  You can only extend the retention period.

- You can't use regulatory record labels with auto-labeling policies.
  You must apply them manually to content.

Because of these irreversible actions, make sure you need to use regulatory records before selecting this option for your retention labels. This option is not available by default to prevent accidental configuration. You must first enable it by using PowerShell as described in the following.

To display this option, you must first run a PowerShell command:

1. Connect to the Office 365 Security and Compliance Center PowerShell.

2. Run the following cmdlet:

```
Set-RegulatoryComplianceUI -Enabled $true
```

There is no prompt to confirm, and the setting takes effect immediately.

If you change your mind about seeing this option in the retention label wizard, you can hide it again by running the same cmdlet with the false value:

```
Set-RegulatoryComplianceUI -Enabled $false
```

Records Versioning

By default, record labels prevent end users from editing a document with a record label. However, there could be times when you would like to create an immutable version of a record and allow end users to continue to collaborate on the document but not delete it.

Records versioning allows you to create an immutable copy of a document while still enabling end users with the correct permission to edit the file. You use a label that has been designated as a record and then apply it to an item. In the property pane, a toggle switch appears to lock and unlock the item for editing.

This feature is available in SharePoint and OneDrive document libraries, but you cannot use it on OneNote folders. Records versioning is automatically available for any document with a retention label that declares the item as a record.

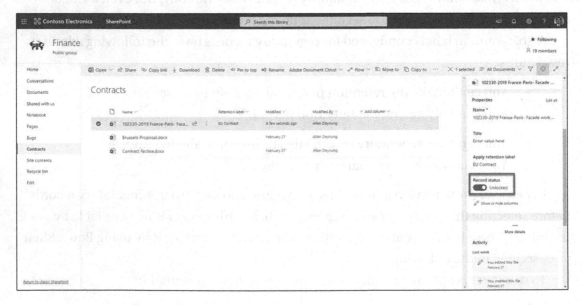

Figure 9-3. *Unlock a record to edit it*

Here is how you use records versioning, shown in Figure 9-3:

1.   Navigate to a document library where you are using a record label.

2.   Check the box next to the document and open the information pane.

3.   Scroll down until you see the field called Record status.

4.   Click the field to make it editable.

5.   Choose to lock or unlock the record. The field will automatically save.

The system saves document versions designated as an immutable record in the site collection's preservation hold library, in the records folder. The record will remain in this folder until the end of its retention period.

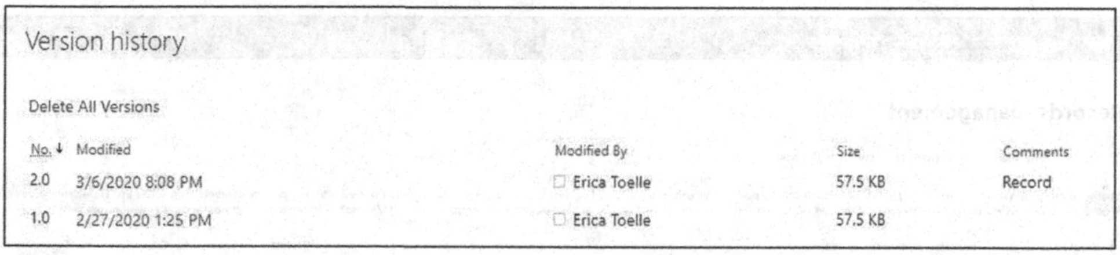

No. ↓	Modified		Modified By	Size	Comments
Version history					
Delete All Versions					
2.0	3/6/2020 8:08 PM		☐ Erica Toelle	57.5 KB	Record
1.0	2/27/2020 1:25 PM		☐ Erica Toelle	57.5 KB	

Figure 9-4.   *The version history of a file*

You can see the version history of a file. You can also see the versions designated as a record, shown in Figure 9-4. To access the version history of a document

1.   Mouse over the document. Three vertical dots will appear next to the file's name.

2.   Click the dots to view the action menu.

3.   Version history will be near the bottom of the menu. Click it to view the version history.

File versions designated as a record will have "Record" added to in the Comments column.

If you would like to audit when a record is locked or unlocked, you can view these actions in the Compliance Center audit log. To access the audit log, go to the Compliance Center. On the left side of the page, click Audit. Under Search, click View all activities. Under File and page activities, you will find two audit events: Changed record status to lock and Change record status to unlocked. To learn more about the audit log, see Chapter 16.

File Plan Manager

The file plan manager provides advanced management and organizational capabilities for retention labels and retention label policies. It does this by displaying the retention labels and policies in a grid-like format that mimics a traditional view of a file plan since we often keep file plans in Excel, shown in Figure 9-5.

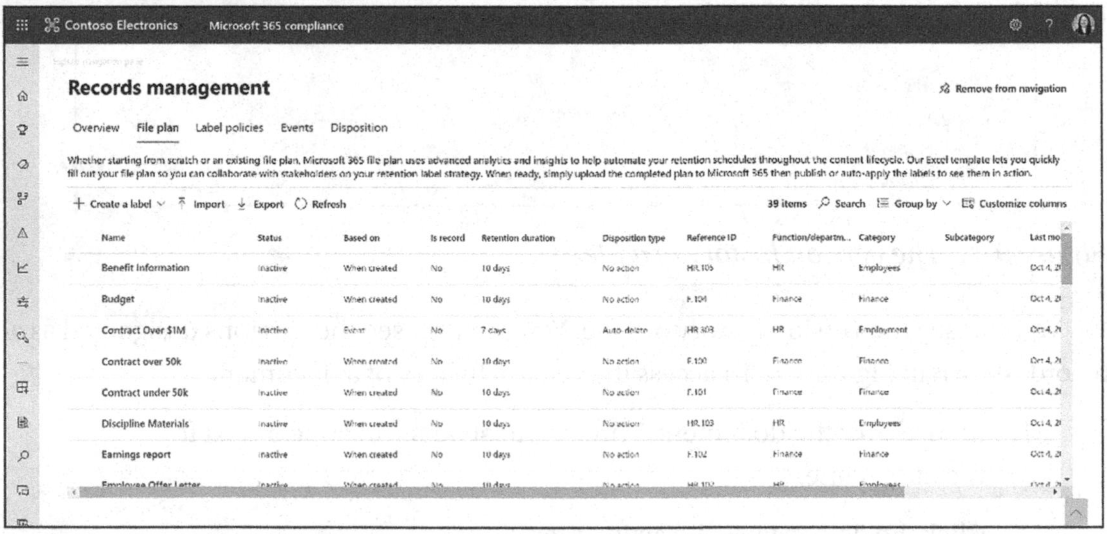

Figure 9-5. The file plan manager

You're able to view all the retention label descriptors that you created along with your retention label. For example, this could be the label category, the trigger for the retention period, the length of the retention period, and more. You are also able to sort the retention labels on any of these descriptors. You can customize the displayed columns to create a view that's most useful for you, shown in Figure 9-6. This view is customizable per person so that it won't affect other people's view of the file plan.

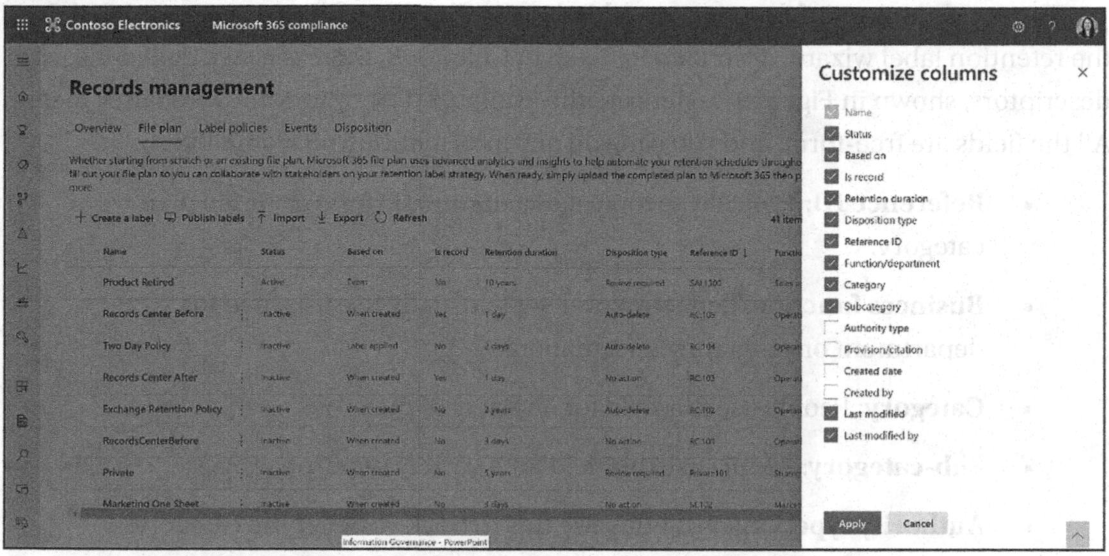

Figure 9-6. *Customize the file plan columns*

Click Customize columns, located in the upper right of the file plan. Here you're able to check the boxes of the columns that you would like to have displayed in the file plan view. Click Apply to change the view. Additional view options in the file plan include the ability to sort by any column, search the file plan, and group by function department, status, or category.

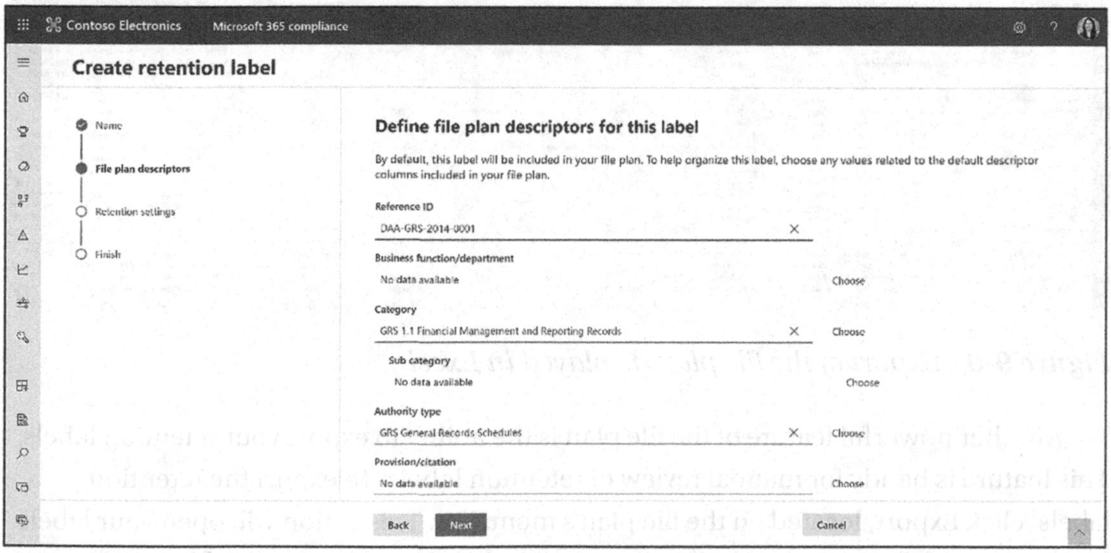

Figure 9-7. *File plan descriptors for a label*

These columns of information are added to the file plan when you create a label. In the retention label wizard, described in detail in Chapter 8, there is a step called file plan descriptors, shown in Figure 9-7. Here are the available descriptors and what they mean. All the fields are free-form, and you can add any information you would like:

- **Reference ID**: Typically, people add a unique ID from their file plan category.
- **Business function/department**: People usually use this field for department or geography information.
- **Category**: People use this field for a variety of purposes.
- **Sub-category**: People use this field for a variety of purposes.
- **Authority type**: Organizations use this to track whether the category is a regulation, law, or internal policy.
- **Provision/citation**: Add information about the specific citation or provision driving the need for the label.

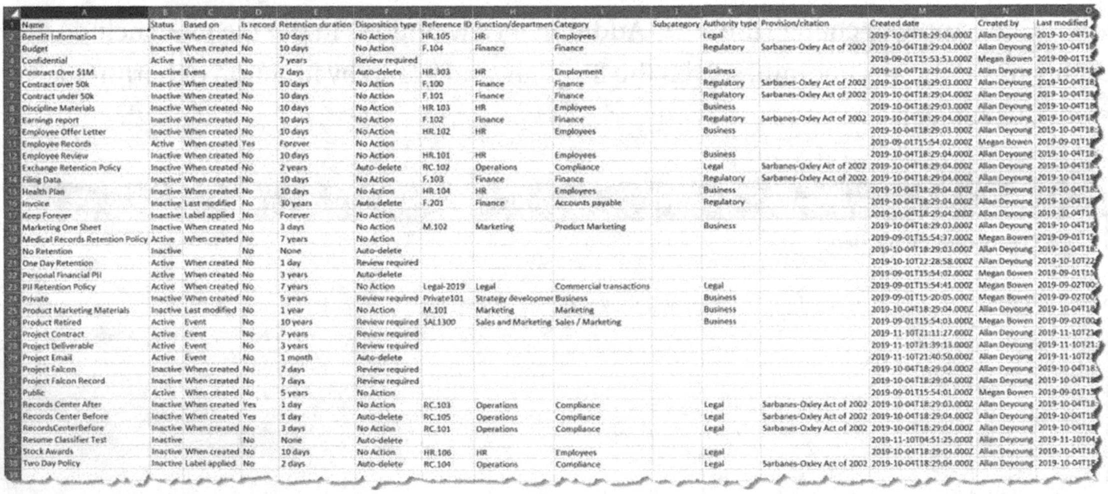

Name	Status	Based on	Is record	Retention duration	Disposition type	Reference ID	Function/departmen	Category	Subcategory	Authority type	Provision/citation	Created date	Created by	Last modified
Benefit Information	Inactive	When created	No	10 days	No Action	HR.105	HR	Employees		Legal		2019-10-04T18:29:04.000Z	Allan Deyoung	2019-10-04T1
Budget	Inactive	When created	No	10 days	No Action	F.104	Finance	Finance		Regulatory	Sarbanes-Oxley Act of 2002	2019-10-04T18:29:04.000Z	Allan Deyoung	2019-10-04T1
Confidential	Active	When created	No	7 years	Review required							2019-09-01T15:53:53.000Z	Megan Bowen	2019-09-01T1
Contract Over $1M	Inactive	Event	No	7 days	Auto-delete	HR.303	HR	Employment		Business		2019-10-04T18:29:04.000Z	Allan Deyoung	2019-10-04T1
Contract over 50k	Inactive	When created	No	10 days	No Action	F.100	Finance	Finance		Regulatory	Sarbanes-Oxley Act of 2002	2019-10-04T18:29:03.000Z	Allan Deyoung	2019-10-04T18
Contract under 50k	Inactive	When created	No	10 days	No Action	F.101	Finance	Finance		Regulatory	Sarbanes-Oxley Act of 2002	2019-10-04T18:29:04.000Z	Allan Deyoung	2019-10-04T1
Discipline Materials	Inactive	When created	No	10 days	No Action	HR.103	HR	Employees		Business		2019-10-04T18:29:03.000Z	Allan Deyoung	2019-10-04T18
Earnings report	Inactive	When created	No	10 days	No Action	F.102	Finance	Finance		Regulatory	Sarbanes-Oxley Act of 2002	2019-10-04T18:29:04.000Z	Allan Deyoung	2019-10-04T1
Employee Offer Letter	Inactive	When created	No	10 days	No Action	HR.102	HR	Employees		Business		2019-10-04T18:29:03.000Z	Allan Deyoung	2019-10-04T18
Employee Records	Active	When created	Yes	Forever	No Action							2019-09-01T15:54:02.000Z	Megan Bowen	2019-09-01T1
Employee Review	Inactive	When created	No	10 days	No Action	HR.101	HR	Employees		Business		2019-10-04T18:29:04.000Z	Allan Deyoung	2019-10-04T18
Exchange Retention Policy	Inactive	When created	No	2 years	Auto-delete	RC.102	Operations	Compliance		Legal	Sarbanes-Oxley Act of 2002	2019-10-04T18:29:04.000Z	Allan Deyoung	2019-10-04T1
Filing Data	Inactive	When created	No	10 days	No Action	F.103	Finance	Finance		Regulatory	Sarbanes-Oxley Act of 2002	2019-10-04T18:29:04.000Z	Allan Deyoung	2019-10-04T1
Health Plan	Inactive	When created	No	10 days	No Action	HR.104	HR	Employees		Business		2019-10-04T18:29:04.000Z	Allan Deyoung	2019-10-04T18
Invoice	Inactive	Last modified	No	30 years	Auto-delete	F.201	Finance	Accounts payable		Regulatory		2019-10-04T18:29:04.000Z	Allan Deyoung	2019-10-04T1
Keep Forever	Inactive	Label applied	No	Forever	No Action							2019-10-04T18:29:04.000Z	Allan Deyoung	2019-10-04T1
Marketing One Sheet	Inactive	When created	No	3 days	No Action	M.102	Marketing	Product Marketing		Business		2019-10-04T18:29:03.000Z	Allan Deyoung	2019-10-04T1
Medical Records Retention Policy	Active	When created	No	7 years	No Action							2019-09-01T15:54:37.000Z	Megan Bowen	2019-09-01T1
No Retention	Inactive		No	None	Auto-delete							2019-10-04T18:29:03.000Z	Allan Deyoung	2019-10-04T18
One Day Retention	Active	When created	No	1 day	Review required							2019-10-10T22:28:58.000Z	Allan Deyoung	2019-10-10T22
Personal Financial PII	Active	When created	No	3 years	Auto-delete							2019-09-01T15:54:02.000Z	Megan Bowen	2019-09-01T1
PII Retention Policy	Active	When created	No	7 years	No Action	Legal-2019	Legal	Commercial transactions		Legal		2019-09-01T15:54:41.000Z	Megan Bowen	2019-09-02T00
Private	Inactive	When created	No	5 years	Review required	Private101	Strategy developmer	Business		Business		2019-09-01T15:20:05.000Z	Megan Bowen	2019-09-02T00
Product Marketing Materials	Inactive	Last modified	No	1 year	No Action	M.101	Marketing	Marketing		Business		2019-10-04T18:29:04.000Z	Allan Deyoung	2019-10-04T18
Product Retired	Active	Event	No	10 years	Review required	SAL1300	Sales and Marketing	Sales / Marketing		Business		2019-09-01T15:54:03.000Z	Megan Bowen	2019-09-02T00
Project Contract	Active	Event	No	7 years	Review required							2019-11-10T21:11:27.000Z	Allan Deyoung	2019-11-10T2
Project Deliverable	Active	Event	No	3 years	Review required							2019-11-10T21:39:13.000Z	Allan Deyoung	2019-11-10T21:
Project Email	Active	Event	No	1 month	Auto-delete							2019-11-10T21:40:50.000Z	Allan Deyoung	2019-11-10T2
Project Falcon	Inactive	When created	No	7 days	Review required							2019-10-04T18:29:04.000Z	Allan Deyoung	2019-10-04T18
Project Falcon Record	Inactive	When created	No	7 days	Review required							2019-10-04T18:29:04.000Z	Allan Deyoung	2019-10-04T1
Public	Active	When created	No	5 years	No Action							2019-09-01T15:54:01.000Z	Megan Bowen	2019-09-01T1
Records Center After	Inactive	When created	Yes	1 day	No Action	RC.103	Operations	Compliance		Legal	Sarbanes-Oxley Act of 2002	2019-10-04T18:29:03.000Z	Allan Deyoung	2019-10-04T18
Records Center Before	Inactive	When created	Yes	1 day	Auto-delete	RC.105	Operations	Compliance		Legal	Sarbanes-Oxley Act of 2002	2019-10-04T18:29:04.000Z	Allan Deyoung	2019-10-04T1
RecordsCenterBefore	Inactive	When created	No	3 days	No Action	RC.101	Operations	Compliance		Legal	Sarbanes-Oxley Act of 2002	2019-10-04T18:29:04.000Z	Allan Deyoung	2019-10-04T1
Resume Classifier Test	Inactive		No	None	Auto-delete							2019-11-10T04:51:25.000Z	Allan Deyoung	2019-11-10T04
Stock Awards	Inactive	When created	No	10 days	No Action	HR.106	HR	Employees		Legal		2019-10-04T18:29:04.000Z	Allan Deyoung	2019-10-04T18
Two Day Policy	Inactive	Label applied	No	2 days	Auto-delete	RC.104	Operations	Compliance		Legal	Sarbanes-Oxley Act of 2002	2019-10-04T18:29:04.000Z	Allan Deyoung	2019-10-04T1

***Figure 9-8.** Export of the file plan displayed in Excel*

Another powerful feature of the file plan is the ability to export your retention labels. This feature is handy for manual review of retention labels. To export the retention labels, click Export, located on the file plan's menu bar. This action will open your labels and associated descriptors as a CSV file in Excel, shown in Figure 9-8. Table 9-2 shows the Excel sheet columns, the associated retention label fields, and the possible values.

To export your file plan, go to the File plan tab in the Records Management solution. Click Export. This click will download a CSV file containing all your file plan information.

Table 9-2. *File plan information from the CSV file*

CSV column name	Label descriptor	Possible values
Name	Retention label name	Any text
Status	Whether we have applied the label to content	Active or Inactive (automatic)
Based on	What triggers the retention period	When created, When modified, Event, When labeled
Is record	Is the label a record?	Yes or No
Retention	The duration of the retention period	Days, Months, Years, or Forever
Disposition type	What happens when the retention period is over	No action, Review required, Auto-delete
Reference	Label descriptor information	Any text
Function/department	Label descriptor information	Any text
Category	The category of the retention label	Any text
Sub-category	The sub-category of the retention label	Any text
Authority	Why you created the label	Any text, typically Business, Legal, or Regulatory
Provision/citation	The provision or citation associated with the label	Any text
Created date	The created date of the label	Cannot be edited (automatic)
Created by	The name of the person who created the label	Cannot be edited (automatic)
Modified date	The date the label was last modified	Cannot be edited (automatic)
Modified by	Who last modified the label	Cannot be edited (automatic)

You can also bulk-create labels using the file plan import functionality. This method also uses a CSV file, but the file requires different columns from the export.

Tip   I think it is much faster to create your labels using the export/import functionality. It is also easier to understand your labels when you see all of them next to each other in an Excel sheet.

To import a file plan, click Import on the File plan tab in the Records Management solution. On this page, there is a link to download a blank template. Do this and complete the information. Table 9-3 shows the columns in the template, what they mean, and what information you should include.

Table 9-3. *Column information for the file plan import CSV file*

Property	Type	Valid values
LabelName	String	This property specifies the name of the retention label
Comment	String	Use this property to add a description of the retention label for admins. This description appears only to admins who manage the retention label in the Compliance Center
Notes	String	Use this property to add a description of the retention label for users. This description appears when users hover over the label in apps like Outlook, SharePoint, and OneDrive. If you leave this property blank, a default description is displayed, explaining the label's retention settings
IsRecordLabel	String	This property specifies whether the label marks the content as a record. Valid values are **TRUE**: The label marks the item as a record, and as a result, you can't delete the item. **FALSE**: The label doesn't mark the content as a record. This value is the default.

(continued)

Table 9-3. (*continued*)

Property	Type	Valid values
RetentionAction	String	This property specifies what action to take after the value specified by the RetentionDuration property expires. Valid values are **Delete**: Items older than the value specified by the RetentionDuration property are deleted. **Keep**: Retain items for the duration specified by the RetentionDuration property and then do nothing when the duration period expires. **KeepAndDelete**: Retain items for the duration specified by the RetentionDuration property and then delete them when the duration period expires.
RetentionDuration	String	This property specifies the number of days to retain the content. Valid values are **Unlimited**: Items will be retained indefinitely. *n*: A positive integer, for example, **365**.
RetentionType	String	This property specifies whether the retention duration is calculated from the content creation date, event date, when labeled date, or last modified date. Valid values are **CreationAgeInDays** **EventAgeInDays** **TaggedAgeInDays** **ModificationAgeInDays**
ReviewerEmail	SmtpAddress	When this property is populated, a disposition review will be triggered when the retention duration expires. This property specifies the email address of a reviewer for the **KeepAndDelete** retention action. You can include the email address of individual users, distribution groups, or security groups. You can specify multiple email addresses separated by semicolons.
ReferenceId	String	This property specifies the value displayed in the **Reference ID** file plan descriptor, which you can use as a unique value to your organization.
DepartmentName	String	This property specifies the value that's displayed in the **Function/ department** file plan descriptor.

(*continued*)

Table 9-3. (*continued*)

Property	Type	Valid values
Category	String	This property specifies the value that's displayed in the **Category** file plan descriptor.
SubCategory	String	This property specifies the value that's displayed in the **Sub-category** file plan descriptor.
AuthorityType	String	This property specifies the value that's displayed in the **Authority type** file plan descriptor.
CitationName	String	This property specifies the name of the citation displayed in the **Provision/citation** file plan descriptor, for example, "Sarbanes-Oxley Act of 2002."
CitationUrl	String	This property specifies the URL that's displayed in the **Provision/citation** file plan descriptor.
CitationJurisdiction	String	This property specifies the jurisdiction or agency that's displayed in the **Provision/citation** file plan descriptor, for example, "US Securities and Exchange Commission (SEC)."
Regulatory	String	Leave blank. This property isn't used at this time.
EventType	String	This property specifies the retention rule that's associated with the label. You can use any value that uniquely identifies the rule, for example **Name** **Distinguished name (DN)** **GUID** You can use the Get-RetentionComplianceRule cmdlet to view the available retention rules. Note that because the EventType values are unique to an organization, if you export labels from one organization, you can't use the values for the EventType property from that organization to import labels into a different organization.

Once you complete the information about your labels in the CSV file, you can import them into the file plan. To do this, click Import on the file plan menu bar. This click will bring you to an import wizard where you can browse for the CSV file with your labels, shown in Figure 9-9. Click Upload, and then click Next to complete the upload. The wizard will now check for errors in the CSV file. If there are any errors, it will tell you why it occurred and the CSV cell that contains the error.

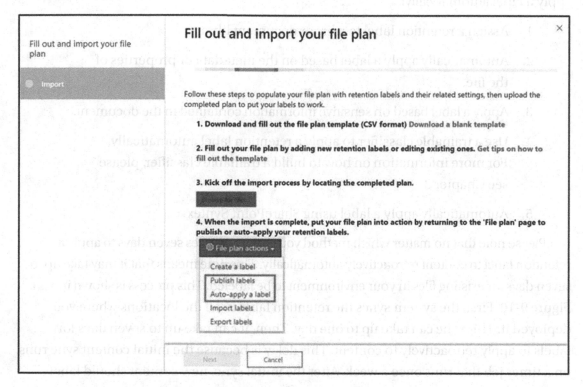

Figure 9-9. *Import a file plan from a .csv file*

If you would like to create labels or label policies at an even larger scale, you can use PowerShell to automate this process.

The last options on the File plan tab are Explore items and Explore activity. These links take you to the content explorer and activity explorer solutions to view information about how your labels get used. We cover these solutions in Chapter 3.

Automatically Classify Content for Retention

Chapter 8 discussed retention labels and how to allow end users to classify content using a label manually. The issue with manually labeling content is that end users don't always do it. They often don't care that much about retention and just want to get on with their work.

Auto-classification of content allows organizations to automatically apply a retention label to content without the end users having to take any action. There are five ways to apply a label automatically:

1. Assign a retention label to a list or document library.

2. Automatically apply a label based on the metadata or properties of the file.

3. Apply a label based on sensitive information contained in the document.

4. Use a trainable classifier to apply a retention label automatically. For more information on how to build a trainable classifier, please see Chapter 3.

5. Automatically apply a label using SharePoint Syntex.

Please note that no matter which method you choose, it takes seven days to apply a retention label to content retroactively automatically. This note means that it may take up to seven days for existing files in your environment to be labeled. This process is shown in Figure 9-10. First, the system syncs the retention label to all the locations where you deployed it. This sync can take up to one day. Then, it can take up to seven days for labels to apply retroactively to content. This delay is because the initial content sync runs on a timer job that runs once a week. After the initial sync, new content should label automatically within 15 minutes.

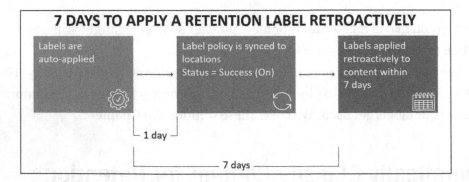

Figure 9-10. *Timeline for auto-application of retention labels*

I mention this timing mostly for when people are testing retention labels. They often get confused about why their labels are not showing up or are not applied to content as expected. You need to set up your test and then wait 1–7 days to see if the test was successful.

Auto-apply in a SharePoint Document Library

We can automatically apply a label by setting a default retention label for a document library. This way, any documents added to a library will inherit the correct retention label. If you are familiar with location-based metadata in SharePoint, this works in the same way.

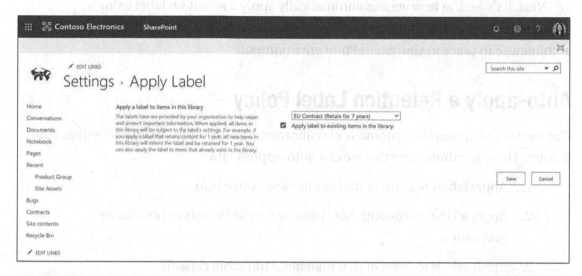

Figure 9-11. *Apply a retention label to items in a SharePoint document library*

Here is how you set a default retention label on a SharePoint document library, shown in Figure 9-11:

1. Navigate to a SharePoint document library or list.

2. In the upper-right corner of the screen, click the settings gear icon.

3. Click Library (or list) settings.

4. Under the Permissions and Management heading, click Apply label to items in this list or library.

5. Choose a label from the dropdown list. Only retention labels deployed to this location will show in the list.

6. Decide if you would like to Apply label to existing items in the library. If yes, check the box. If no, the label will only apply to new content added to the list or library.

7. Click Save.

You can also apply a default retention label in a list or library in bulk using PowerShell. This approach is useful if your organization has a consistent information architecture for SharePoint sites in place. The consistency allows you to feel confident that content placed in a location fits with a specific retention label. But keep in mind the principles of retention we discussed in Chapter 8.

Next, let's look at how we can automatically apply a retention label using a document's properties. This approach is useful when you have a less strict information architecture in place in your SharePoint environment.

Auto-apply a Retention Label Policy

Our next set of options for automatic classification uses the auto-apply a retention label feature. There are three ways that we can auto-apply a label:

1. Apply labels to content that contains sensitive info.

2. Apply a label to content that contains specific words or phrases or properties.

3. Apply labels to content that matches a trainable classifier.

To use any of the preceding options, we will start with the same steps. The options for locations to use with the auto-apply a policy feature are the same for all three methods, so I will only describe them in the first section:

1. First, navigate to the Records Management solution in the Compliance Center.

2. Next, click the Label policies tab. Then, click Auto-apply a label. A configuration wizard will appear that asks you to choose a label to auto-apply.

3. Click the blue text that says "Choose a label to auto-apply."

4. Check the boxes next to the labels you would like to auto-apply. Click Add and then Next.

5. On the next screen, the wizard asks you to choose one of the auto-apply options listed in the preceding text.

Note   In Exchange, the auto-application of retention labels for all three options is only to messages sent after deploying the policy. The label is only applied to items in transit. The label doesn't apply to all items currently in the mailbox, known as data at rest.

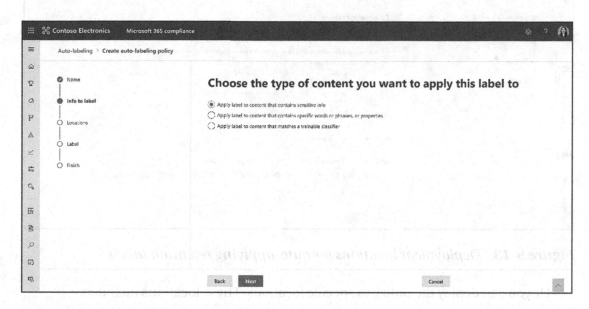

Figure 9-12. *Auto-apply options for retention labels*

Sensitive Information Types

First, let's look at the option to auto-apply a retention label based on sensitive information types. As we discussed in Chapter 3, there are several types of sensitive information, for example, a US Social Security number, an EU passport number, or a bank account number. Microsoft has over 130 pre-built templates for sensitive information types included with Microsoft 365. You could also build a custom sensitive information type.

To use this option, select the radio button next to "Apply label to content that contains sensitive info" shown in Figure 9-12. Click Next. On the next screen, select the sensitive information type template that you would like to use. Note that any custom templates you've created will be listed here. Click Next and adjust any settings, such as which specific information types you would like to detect, the accuracy, or the instance count. Click Next. In the Name field, enter a unique name for this policy. Click Next.

The next screen allows you to choose the locations where you will use your retention policy, shown in Figure 9-13. You can deploy it to all locations, including content in Exchange email, Microsoft 365 groups, OneDrive, and SharePoint.

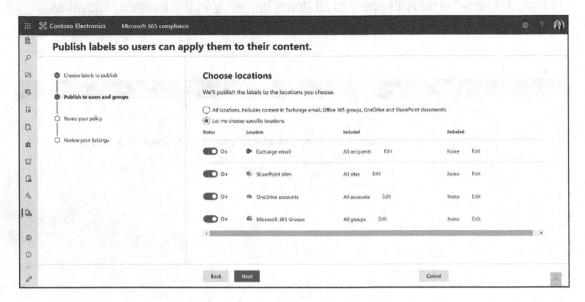

Figure 9-13. *Deployment locations for auto-applying retention labels*

Or you can deploy the policy to specific locations. These locations include

- **Exchange**: Apply to all Exchange mailboxes or include/exclude up to 1000 mailboxes.

- **SharePoint sites**: You can apply the policy to all SharePoint sites or include/exclude up to about 100 particular sites.

- **OneDrive accounts**: You can apply the policy to all OneDrive accounts, or you can include/exclude up to about 100 specific OneDrive accounts.

- **Microsoft 365 groups**: Apply to all Microsoft 365 groups or include/exclude up to 1000 groups.

As with all the include/exclude conditions, I recommend that you use PowerShell to manage these policies if you're going to build these policies at scale.

Click Next. Review your settings for the policy and click Auto-apply.

Keywords or Properties

Now let's look at the second option for auto-applying a retention policy. This option allows you to apply a label to content containing specific words or phrases or properties. This option is beneficial for organizations that have invested in information architecture in their SharePoint environments. You can automatically apply a label based on a content type, managed metadata field, or other metadata properties, for example. This method is also an excellent option for companies currently using a SharePoint records center to transition to Microsoft 365 retention.

I call this option "search auto-apply" as a shortcut when discussing this option with organizations. This name is because it uses a search query to locate the content for the policy. To find content, you can use the Keyword Query Language (KQL) syntax to design queries. You can refine your query by using search operators like "and," "or," or "not" to find the specific content you are after. Any document property, keyword, or phrase available in the Microsoft 365 search index can be used in the query. When using a custom SharePoint metadata property, first, add it to the search index as a managed property. Only then can we use it to apply a label.

Let's look at how to set up a search auto-apply policy. To use this option, select the radio button next to "Apply label to content that contains specific words or phrases, or properties." Click Next.

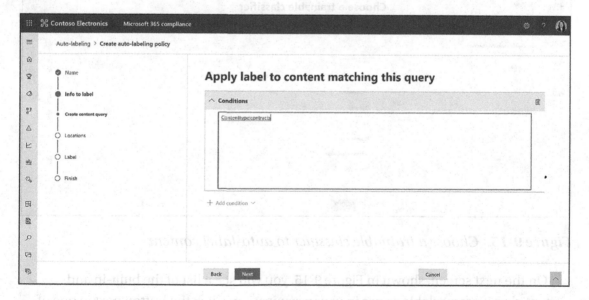

Figure 9-14. *Apply a label automatically to content with a specific property*

On the next screen, you see the keyword query editor box, shown in Figure 9-14. This box is where you put the KQL syntax for your content. For example, you might write Site:`http://contoso.sharepoint.com/sites/finance` AND contenttype:contract. This KQL syntax would find all documents in the finance site that also use the invoice content type. The system will apply a retention label to anything matching that condition.

Click Next and enter a name for your policy. Click Next and choose the locations where you will apply the policy. These locations are the same as described in the previous section.

Click Next, review your settings, and click Auto-apply.

Trainable Classifiers

Finally, let's look at the last option for auto-applying a retention label. This method uses one of the trainable classifiers we discussed in Chapter 3. The trainable classifier allows us to identify a document type located anywhere in SharePoint and OneDrive. When the system detects a document, it will automatically add a retention label to it.

To use this option, select the radio button next to "Apply label to content that matches a trainable classifier." Click Next.

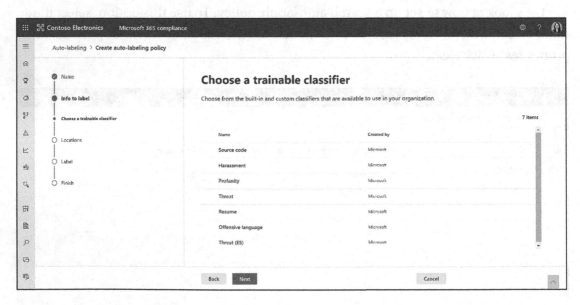

Figure 9-15. *Choose a trainable classifier to auto-label content*

On the next screen, shown in Figure 9-15, you will see a list of the built-in and custom classifiers available to use in your organization. Click the button next to one of the classifiers and click Next. Enter a name for your policy and click Next.

The location options are the same as in previous sections. Click Next, review your settings, and click Auto-apply.

Auto-apply Using SharePoint Syntex

SharePoint Syntex is an add-on license in Microsoft 365. One of the features allows you to create document understanding models. Document understanding uses artificial intelligence (AI) models to automate the classification of files and extraction of information. It works best with unstructured documents, such as letters or contracts. These documents must have text that can be identified based on phrases or patterns. The identified text designates both the type of file it is (its classification) and what you'd like to extract (its extractors). To learn more, see this article: `http://erica.news/DocUnderstanding`.

For records management, SharePoint Syntex allows you to create a custom model to identify common content types in your organization. Unlike trainable classifiers, Syntex models are applied at the document level rather than at the tenant level. You can also extract metadata from documents in support of other business processes. Finally, Syntex only requires five positive and one negative document examples to train a model.

You can specify a retention label to apply automatically when content matches a SharePoint Syntex document understanding model.

Event-Based Retention

First, let's cover what is an event and why do you need event-based retention. There are several types of events that could occur in your organization. Some common ones include an employee leaving an organization, a contract expiring, or a product reaching the end of life. Still, there are many, many types of events that could occur.

When the event occurs, retention policies on documents often change depending on the specific event's nature. For example, when an employee joins an organization, their employment contract's retention policy is permanent. Still, once they leave the organization, the retention policy would change to seven years from the date of departure. To accomplish the preceding scenario, we will use event-based retention.

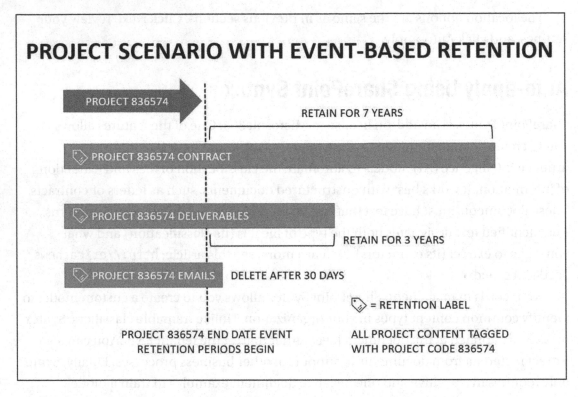

Figure 9-16. *An example scenario for event-based retention*

Let's look at a project scenario to explain event-based retention better, shown in Figure 9-16. Let's say that you have a project with a unique project code of 836574. As part of the project, you create several documents:

- **Project contracts**: Retain for seven years after the project ends.

- **Deliverables for customers**: Retain for three years after the project ends.

- **Project emails**: Delete 30 days after the project ends.

At some point, that project will end and have an official project end date. At that point, the retention period would begin for each type of project documents. As shown in the preceding text, each type of file has a different retention period.

You would need to create three retention labels for this scenario, one for project contracts, one for project deliverables, and one for project emails. You then tag all three types of content with the project code, which is 836574. The project code allows you to identify all the documents and emails that are part of the project.

How to Configure Event-Based Retention

There are four steps to enabling event-based retention:

1. Create a retention label for each of the document types.

2. Publish the retention label to the location where you will use it, such as SharePoint sites and Exchange mailboxes.

3. You would then add the unique project ID to each piece of content.

4. When the project is over, create an event and trigger it to start the retention period.

To create a retention label, we will follow the instructions in Chapter 5. On the label settings screen, select the dropdown next to "Retain or delete the content based on" and choose "an event" as shown in Figure 9-17. Next, click the blue text that reads "Choose an event type."

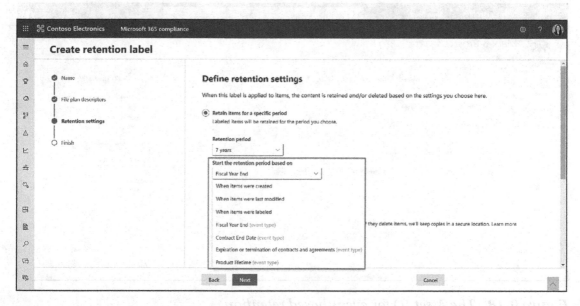

Figure 9-17. *The label settings for event-based retention*

This click will bring up a new screen. If you already have an event for "Project End Date," check the box next to the name. If not, click the blue text that says "Need a different event type? Create new event types." In the Name box, type Project End Date. Optionally, you can add a description for the event type. Click Finish. Check the box next to your new event type and click Add. Click Next and then Create this label.

Repeat these steps for each document type. In our example, you would create one retention label for the contract, one for a deliverable, and one for email. Set the appropriate retention period for each document type, as outlined in the preceding text.

Next, you would deploy the label using your preferred method. For example, end users could manually apply the retention label, or it could be automatically applied using one of the methods discussed earlier in this chapter. Be sure to await the appropriate amount of time for your labels to apply, depending on which way you choose. Then, either manually label the project content or check the label was automatically applied appropriately.

Once the content has an event retention label, we will add the unique project ID to all content. To do this in SharePoint, navigate to the document library where project content is stored. All content with an event label will have a metadata field called Asset ID on each document, shown in Figure 9-18. This field is where we put our unique project code of 836574.

Figure 9-18. *The Asset ID for event-based retention*

For Exchange emails, we would have to add the project code to every email manually. Some organizations do this by appending the project ID to each email subject. Others add it under the signature, where it is less conspicuous.

Those are all the steps we need to perform until the project is over. But once the project end date occurs, we will need to create an event in the Compliance Center. To do this, go to the Records Management solution. Click the Events tab and click Create. In the Name field, type something unique such as Project 836574 End Date. Click Next.

On the Event Settings screen, you have two options, shown in Figure 9-19:

1. **Use Event Types**: Use this option when you want to trigger retention on every label associated with the event type. To do this, click the blue text that says "Choose an event type." Check the box next to Project End Date and click Add.

2. **Use Existing Labels**: Choose this option when you want to trigger the retention period of a sub-set of labels. To do this, click the blue text that says "Choose labels." Click Add. A list of all the event-based retention labels will appear. Select the labels you wish to trigger. Click Add and Done.

Figure 9-19. Select the event settings

Tip   You do not have to use the Asset ID to identify SharePoint and OneDrive content. You could use any column with a unique value. Add this by using columnname:value.

Click Next to go to the Review your settings screen. On this screen, you will enter the unique project ID of 836574. Enter it as a keyword to identify Exchange content and as an Asset ID to identify SharePoint and OneDrive content. Finally, under "When did this event occur?" choose the event date. Click Next and then Create this event.

How to Automate Event-Based Retention

Depending on the volume of events in your organization, it may not be practical to perform the steps manually. Let's look at the ways that you can automate event-based retention.

We've discussed the options for automatically applying a retention label at length in this chapter. All the methods we reviewed will work for event-based retention labels.

There are a few options for automatically completing the unique project ID on each piece of content. First, you could use a Power Automate Flow to fill in the project ID. For example, let's say you have a site provisioning solution for projects. When they create a site, the user must fill out a field for the project ID. You could use a Power Automate Flow to grab that site-level project ID and then apply it to each document.

Another option for the project ID is to configure a custom column in a SharePoint list or library with a default value. You do this by visiting Library settings and Column default value settings, clicking the column name, and setting the project ID as the default. Please note that this would need to be a new custom column. You cannot use this method to complete the Asset ID column.

To automate event creation, there are REST APIs available. You can use this to create new events with either a Power Automate Flow, PowerShell, or another HTTP client to call the REST APIs to create the event. You can trigger event creation from data in a system outside of Microsoft 365, such as an HR system. Microsoft has a great example in their documentation here: `http://erica.news/AutoEvent-Based`.

Now that we've reviewed all the options for using retention labels and retention policies, let's talk about what happens when it is time to delete or dispose of content.

Retention Disposition

What is retention disposition? Retention disposition is the process of deleting content after the retention period is over. It often requires an approval process before we delete the content. It also may require proof of deletion, which we refer to as a certificate of destruction. Regulations often require retention approval and disposition, and timely disposition of content reduces risk of litigation.

First, let's look at how to create a retention label with a disposition review. Please note that disposition reviews are only available with an advanced compliance license. We covered how to create a retention label in Chapter 8 in the "Retention Labels" section. The following process is the same, with one exception. The only difference is that with this label, you will choose to trigger a disposition review, shown in Figure 9-20.

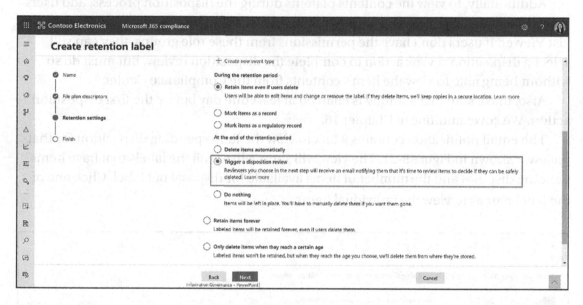

Figure 9-20. *Trigger a disposition review for a retention label*

When you choose to trigger a disposition review, you will also need to designate a reviewer. You can enter an individual's name or a security group. These people will be notified by email when an item is ready for review and will complete the review. The email to the reviewers is sent once per week per label.

Tip   It is best to use a security group to designate the reviewer and not an individual's name. This way, you can update the membership of the group as needed rather than modify the label.

To successfully access the Disposition tab in the Microsoft 365 Compliance Center, users must have the Disposition Management admin role. This role is included in the Records Management default admin role group. By default, a global admin isn't granted the Disposition Management role.

To grant users only the permissions they need for disposition reviews without granting them permission to view and configure other features for retention and records management, create a custom role group (named "Disposition Reviewers") with the Disposition Management role.

Additionally, to view the contents of items during the disposition process, add users to the following two role groups: Content Explorer Content Viewer and Content Explorer List Viewer. If users don't have the permissions from these role groups, they can still select a disposition review action to complete the disposition review, but must do so without being able to view the item's contents from the Compliance Center.

Also, make sure that auditing is enabled at least one day before the first disposition action. We cover auditing in Chapter 16.

The email notification contains a link to view the items pending disposition for that reviewer shown in Figure 9-21. The view will show a list of all the labels that have items pending disposal and the number of items available for disposal per label. Click one of the label names to view the individual items.

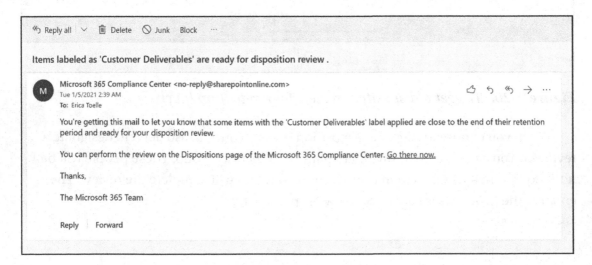

Figure 9-21. *The email notifying a reviewer of pending disposition review items*

Here you will see the list of all the items pending disposition for the label. There are a few options for customizing this view. First, you can filter the items by type, and the choices are a document or email. You can also search across all the items for a keyword. Next, you can select a start date or an end date, which is based on the date when the item is ready for review.

Then, once you select an item, a panel will pop up on the right that asks you to finalize your decision shown in Figure 9-22. You can add a comment, and you can click Approve disposal, extend retention, or relabel it with a different label.

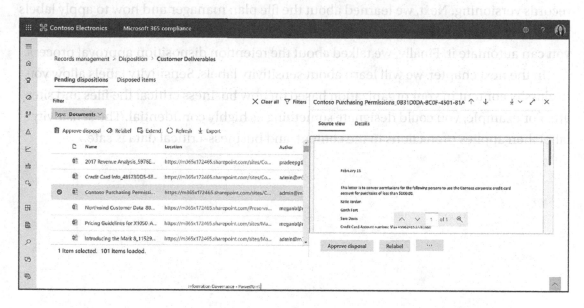

Figure 9-22. The Pending dispositions screen in records management

Also, keep in mind that only one person needs to approve the disposal of a document. There is no option to customize the approval process or require that multiple people approve the content disposition. The ability to customize the disposition process is a popular request, so I hope Microsoft adds this ability soon!

Additionally, you also have the option to export a list of all the items ready for disposition to a CSV file. Some people prefer to use an Excel sheet to review their items, which allows you to do that. However, you would still need to go back to this screen to act. Unfortunately, you cannot mark them in the CSV file and then reimport them.

Next, you're able to view the disposed items. Any item that has been disposed of and deleted will show up in this view. Once you approve the document's disposal, it will take 93 days for the file to appear in the Disposed items view and 15–30 days for Exchange content. We covered why it takes this amount of time to delete content in the previous chapter.

In this chapter, we reviewed the features of records management in the Microsoft 365 Compliance Center. This chapter included an overview of records management and everyday business scenarios. We also covered record labels, regulatory record labels, and records versioning. Next, we learned about the file plan manager and how to apply labels to content automatically. Then, we looked at how event-based retention works and how you can automate it. Finally, we talked about the retention disposition approval process.

In the next chapter, we will learn about sensitivity labels. Sensitivity labels allow you to classify content in your organization based on how business critical the files and sites are. For example, you could designate something as highly confidential. The sensitivity label then applies protections to the content, and business-critical data is safe.

CHAPTER 10

Insider Risk Management

The world of the modern workplace offers innovative technology that employees love. It empowers them to communicate, collaborate, and produce with agility. In this world, trusting your employees is the key to creating a dynamic, inclusive workspace and increasing productivity. But with trust also comes risk, a risk that an employee may negligently breach that trust by inadvertently leaking confidential information and corporate communications. Or an employee maliciously violates that trust by stealing intellectual property.

We know from our own experience that it is hard to maintain trust without the right visibility, processes, and control. However, the effort required to identify these risks and violations is not trivial. Think about the number of people accessing resources and communicating with each other and the natural cycle of entering and leaving the company. How do you quickly determine the risk that is intentional vs. unintentional at scale? How do you achieve visibility while aligning to your environment's cultural, legal, and privacy requirements?

For example, genuinely malicious insiders do things such as intentionally stealing your intellectual property, turning off security controls, or harassing others at work. Still, there are many more situations in which an insider might not even know they are causing a risk to the organization or violating your policies, for example, when they are excited about something new and send files or photos to tell others about it.

Ultimately, it is essential to see the activities and communications that occurred to take the correct course of action. The only way to do this efficiently and at scale is by leveraging intelligence and machine learning. Human-driven processes cannot keep up and are not always that accurate. Furthermore, a holistic solution to this problem requires effective collaboration across security, HR, legal, and compliance departments and a balanced approach across privacy and risk management.

© Erica Toelle 2021
E. Toelle, *Microsoft 365 Compliance*, https://doi.org/10.1007/978-1-4842-5778-4_10

Identifying indicators across phases of the critical path can help to enable higher-fidelity detections:

1. **Predisposition**: Fifty-one percent of employees involved in an insider threat incident had a history of violating IT security policies leading up to that incident.

2. **Stressor**: Ninety-two percent of insider threat cases were preceded by a negative work event, such as a termination, demotion, or dispute with a supervisor. Unmet expectations were identified in 21.6% of sabotage incidents, such as a promotion, financial reward, or recognition.

3. **Concerning behavior**: Ninety-seven percent of insider threat cases studied by Stanford University involved an employee whose behavior a supervisor had flagged, but the organization failed to follow up.

4. **Risk**: Fifty-nine percent of employees who leave an organization voluntarily or involuntarily say they take sensitive data with them.

What Is Insider Risk Management?

Microsoft's answer to these common problems is the Insider Risk Management (IR) solution. It allows you to identify and act on critical insider risks. IR has built-in privacy and anonymity controls to ensure you share data about risks appropriately within your organization. There are tailored playbooks that intelligently correlate native and third-party signals to identify insider risks with high fidelity. You can conduct end-to-end investigations with integrated investigation workflows that allow for collaboration across IT, HR, and legal departments.

Microsoft incubated this solution in its internal digital security and risk engineering organization and then brought it to scale with the Microsoft 365 engineering team. IR provides the ability to quickly identify insider risks, which are employees or contractors with corporate access. It allows you to collaborate with HR and legal departments to minimize the negative impact on corporate policy compliance, competitive business position, and brand reputation.

Licensing and Permissions

To use insider risk management, each monitored user needs one of the following licenses assigned to them:

- Microsoft 365 E5

- Microsoft 365 E5 Compliance

- Microsoft 365 E5 Insider Risk Management

To administer and use insider risk management, we have the following roles:

- **Insider Risk Management Admin**: Create, edit, delete, and control access to the Insider Risk Management feature.

- **Insider Risk Management Analysis**: Provides access to all insider risk management alerts, cases, and notice templates.

- **Insider Risk Management Investigation**: Access all insider risk management alerts, cases, and notice templates and the content explorer for all cases.

- **Insider Risk Management Permanent Contribution**: This role group is visible but used by background services only. Do not use.

- **Insider Risk Management Temporary Contribution**: This role group is visible but used by background services only. Do not use.

If you do not need to use the least permissions model, you can add users to this role group to manage all cases:

- **Insider Risk Management**: This role group contains all the insider risk management permission roles listed in the preceding text.

Additionally, you can add individual users as contributors to specific cases.

How Insider Risk Management Works

We can access insider risk management by going to the Microsoft Compliance Center. In the left navigation, click Insider risk management. This click takes you to the Insider Risk Management dashboard shown in Figure 10-1.

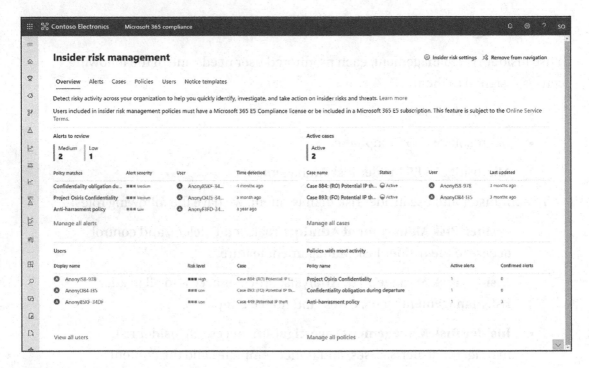

Figure 10-1. *The Insider Risk Management overview dashboard*

The Insider Risk Management dashboard displays an overview of alerts needing review, active cases, users, and policies with the most activity. You can also see these tabs: Alerts, Cases, Policies, Users, and Notice templates. The display names for users can be pseudo-anonymized to prevent conflicts of interest, maintain privacy, and enable bias control. This anonymity ensures that no one purposely overlooks a relative, friend, or your boss on the list. While the solution anonymizes user information in the UI, the original user information is stored on the back end to investigate further when it finds an issue.

Here is an overview of the tabs in insider risk management:

- **Alerts**: After a triggering event occurs for a user, policies assign risk scores to detected activity. If the risk score is high enough, the system generates an alert. Confirm alerts if you want to investigate further or dismiss them if they do not require additional investigation.

- **Cases**: Insider risk cases are created from policy alerts and are used to investigate a user's activities detected by the related policy. Review related content and collaborators, add contributors to the case, and act if needed.

- **Policies**: We base insider risk policies on predefined templates that contain the risk activities you want to detect and investigate, such as data theft or data leaks.

- **Users**: Users appear here if they have an active alert or a triggering event (like a DLP policy match) or when you add them temporarily to a policy.

- **Notice templates**: These templates will be available to use when you need to send an email notification to users in an insider risk case.

We will review each one of these areas in depth later in the chapter. But first, we need to understand the global settings for IR. You need to configure these before you create your first policy.

Global Settings

Figure 10-2 shows the global settings area. You can access the settings by clicking Insider risk settings from the top-right corner of any page. Settings cover solution areas such as how you can configure policies, how the detection of risk activities is processed, Power Automate and Microsoft Teams integration, and more. Let us look at each one of these areas.

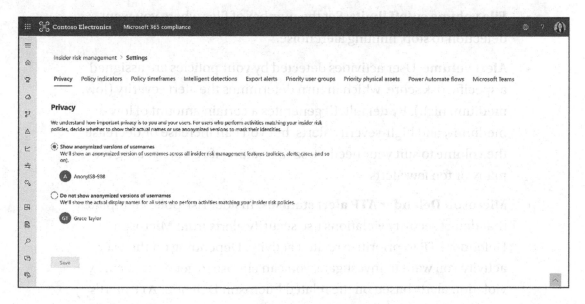

Figure 10-2. Insider Risk Management global settings

The Privacy tab allows you to decide whether to show actual names or use anonymized versions to mask people's identities. Select the radio button next to your choice.

Policy indicators define what to include in your policy templates. They are things like sharing files with people outside your organization, copying files to a USB device, and more. Indicators define the risky behavior for which you are looking. Check the boxes next to the indicators you want to enable for your policies. The system will gray out the indicators you do not select during the policy creation process, so you cannot use them.

Policy timeframes go into effect for a user when they trigger a match for an insider risk policy. For example, suppose you set the activation window to 30 days and past activity detection to 60 days. A user triggers a policy match on December 1. In that case, that policy will retrieve user activity from 60 days ago (October 1). It will continue to record new activity for 30 more days (December 31). You can set the activation window from 1 to 30 days. You can set past activity detection from 1 to 180 days.

The next tab is Intelligent detections. This setting allows you to define how the solution processes the detection of risk activities for insider risk alerts. This area contains the following settings:

- **File type exclusions**: List the file types you want to exclude from insider risk detection.

- **File volume cutoff limits**: Set the number of files where you want detection to stop, limiting alert noise.

- **Alert volume**: User activities detected by your policies are assigned a specific risk score, which in turn determines the alert severity (low, medium, high). By default, IR generates a certain amount of low-, medium-, and high-severity alerts, but you can increase or decrease the volume to suit your needs. Use this setting if you are getting too many or too few alerts.

- **Microsoft Defender ATP alert statuses**: Insider risk policy templates that detect security violations use security alerts from Microsoft Defender ATP to prioritize related activity. Depending on the user activity you want to investigate, you can choose to generate security violation alerts based on the related Microsoft Defender ATP alert's investigation status. Select Unknown, New, In progress, and/or Resolved.

- **Unallowed domains**: The system will assign activity related to these domains a higher risk score.

- **Allowed domains**: The system will assign these domains a lower risk score.

- **Third-party domains:** If your organization uses third-party domains for business purposes (such as cloud storage), include them here so you can receive alerts for related activity.

Next is the tab for Export alerts. This setting allows you to export IR alerts and details to other applications your organization may use to manage or aggregate insider risks. For example, many companies use a security information and event management (SIEM) service such as Azure Sentinel. We transfer this information using the Office 365 Management Activity API.

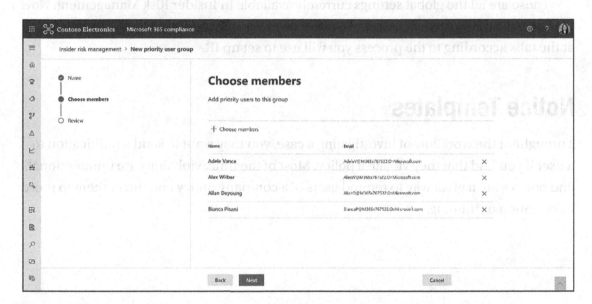

Figure 10-3. *Designate priority users in insider risk management*

Now let us move on to the Priority user groups tab. Here you can define users or groups whose activity requires closer inspection based on factors such as their position, level of access to sensitive information, or risk history. You can include these groups in some of the policy templates to make it easier to prioritize alerts for these users. To add members, click New priority user group, name the group, and choose the members, shown in Figure 10-3.

Next is the Priority physical assets tab. This setting leverages the Physical Badging Systems Data Connector to get signals about badge scans in IR. We cover Data Connectors in detail in Chapter 4. These assets represent priority locations in your organization, such as company buildings or server rooms.

The next tab is Power Automate flows. You can use Power Automate flows to manage insider risk management processes and tasks automatically. You can create flows using built-in insider risk management templates or use the Power Automate console to create custom flows.

The last tab is for Microsoft Teams. When you enable this feature, IR will automatically create a Microsoft Team for each IR case. This Team allows people to investigate the case using chat and files collaboratively. By default, Teams will automatically include members assigned the Insider Risk Management, Insider Risk Management Analysts, and Insider Risk Management Investigators role groups.

Those are all the global settings currently available in Insider Risk Management. Now that we have configured these, we can move on to the other solution areas. We will look at the tabs according to the process you will use to set up IR.

Notice Templates

Throughout the workflow of investigating a case, you may want to send a notification to a user if you find that they violate a policy. Most of the time, violations are unintentional, and notices are a great way to remind users of a company policy and direct them to more information or training.

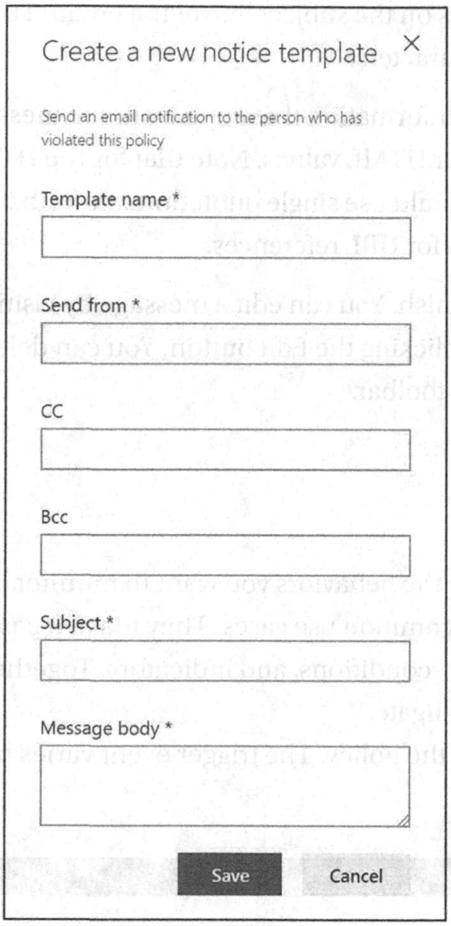

Figure 10-4. *Create a new notice template*

To access your existing notices, click the Notice templates tab in IR. Here you can see a list of any existing notices, including the notice names. To create a new notice, click Create notice template. Here are the fields you need to complete, shown in Figure 10-4:

1. **Template name**: Enter a name for the template.

2. **Send from**: The address from which you want to send the notice. If the user replies to the message, the reply will send to this address.

3. **CC**: Email accounts to CC on the notice.

4. **Bcc**: Email accounts to Bcc on the notice.

5. **Subject**: Appears on the subject line of the email. This field supports text characters.

6. **Message body**: Information that appears in the message body. It supports text or HTML values. Note that for the HTML href attribute, you should use single quotation marks instead of double quotation marks for URL references.

Click Save when you finish. You can edit a message by visiting the Notice templates tab, clicking a policy, and clicking the Edit button. You can delete a policy by selecting it and clicking Delete on the toolbar.

Policies

Insider risk policies define the behaviors you want to monitor. Microsoft provides eight policy playbooks to cover common use cases. They make it easy to set up your policies. IR policies contain triggers, conditions, and indicators. Together, these detect the risk activities you want to investigate.

First, an event triggers the policy. The trigger event varies based on the policy template.

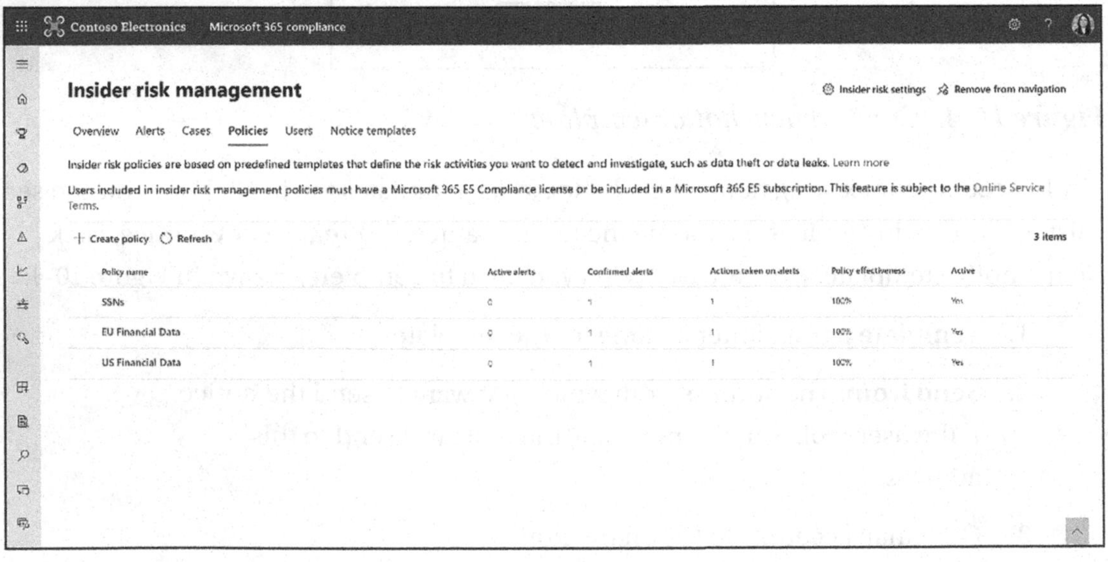

Figure 10-5. Insider risk management policies

In the Policies tab, you can see a list of all the current policies in the solution, shown in Figure 10-5. In this view, you can see the policy name, the number of active alerts, and the total confirmed alerts. You can also see the total actions taken on alerts, the percentage of policy effectiveness (determined by total confirmed alerts divided by total actions taken on alerts), and whether the policy is currently active.

Now let us create an internal risk management policy. Click Create policy. This click opens a wizard to walk you through the creation process. Start by naming your policy and input a description. Scroll down the page to see the list of available policy templates, shown in Figure 10-6.

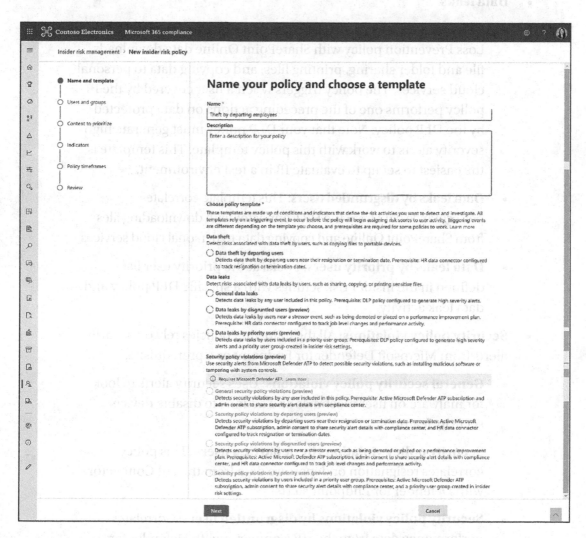

Figure 10-6. *Available policy templates in insider risk management*

Available policy templates include the following. You can have up to five active policies per template:

- **Data theft**

  - **Data theft by departing users**: Looks for users downloading files from SharePoint Online, printing files, and copying data to personal cloud locations. This template leverages the HR Data Connector we covered in Chapter 4 to correlate these activities with resignation or termination.

- **Data leaks**

  - **General data leaks**: Correlate data protected by a specific Data Loss Prevention policy with SharePoint Online data downloads, file and folder sharing, printing files, and copying data to personal cloud services. The policy triggers when a user covered by the IR policy performs one of the preceding actions on data protected by the DLP policy. Note that your DLP policy must generate high-severity alerts to work with this policy template. This template is the easiest to set up to evaluate IR in a test environment.

  - **Data leaks by disgruntled users**: This template correlates performance data from the HR Connector with downloading files from SharePoint Online and copying data to personal cloud services.

  - **Data leaks by priority users**: Looks at the priority user list defined in the insider risk settings with a specific DLP policy and data leak activity.

- **Security policy violations:** All the following policies rely on security alerts from Microsoft Defender for Endpoint as a prerequisite.

  - **General security policy violations**: Uses security alerts to look for malware on user machines and actions to disable device security features.

  - **Security policy violations by departing users**: This policy correlates resignation or departure data from the HR Connector with Defender for Endpoint alerts.

  - **Security policy violations by disgruntled users**: Correlates performance data from the HR Connector with Defender for Endpoint alerts.

- **Security policy violations by priority users**: Looks at Defender for Endpoint alerts for the priority users you defined in insider risk settings.

Select the radio button next to one of the templates and click Next.

The following settings apply to all policies. First, you will choose users and groups to which the policy applies. Click "Choose users" or "Choose groups" and search for the entity you want to add. Check the box next to the user or group and click Add. Alternatively, check the box next to All users and mail-enabled groups to apply the policy to everyone. Click Next.

Optionally, you can specify up to 15 SharePoint sites, sensitive info types, or sensitivity labels to prioritize with the policy. Setting content as a priority increases the risk score for any associated activity, which increases the chance of generating a high-severity alert. Click Next.

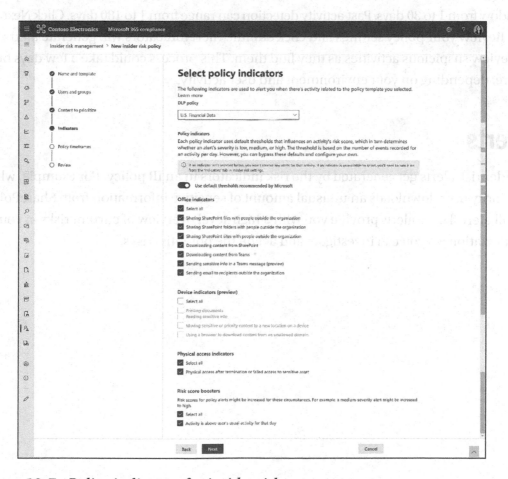

Figure 10-7. *Policy indicators for insider risk management*

Next is the policy indicators page shown in Figure 10-7. If your template involves a DLP policy, you will first select it from a dropdown list here. Each policy indicator uses default thresholds that influence an activity's risk score, which in turn determines whether an alert's severity is low, medium, or high. The system bases the threshold on the number of events recorded for an activity per day. However, you can bypass these defaults and configure your own.

To set your own thresholds, toggle off the switch for "Use default thresholds recommended by Microsoft." Each selected indicator will then have fields where you can put specific numbers for a low, medium, or high number of events per day. Check or uncheck the indicators you want to use in the policy. If an indicator is grayed out, it means you need to enable it in the insider risk settings. When you finish, click Next.

The next screen asks you to set policy timeframes. If you set timeframes in the insider risk settings area, then you cannot modify them here. As a reminder, you can select the activation window from 1 to 30 days. Past activity detection can range from 1 to 180 days. Click Next.

Review your policy settings and click Submit. Alert indicators will generate alerts to review suspicious activities as they find them. This process could take a few days or more, depending on your environment and user activity.

Alerts

Insider risk alerts get generated by the risk indicators in an IR policy. For example, when a priority user downloads an unusual amount of sensitive information from SharePoint, it will alert. These alerts provide you with a high-level overview of current risks in your organization, so you can investigate and act on the potential risks.

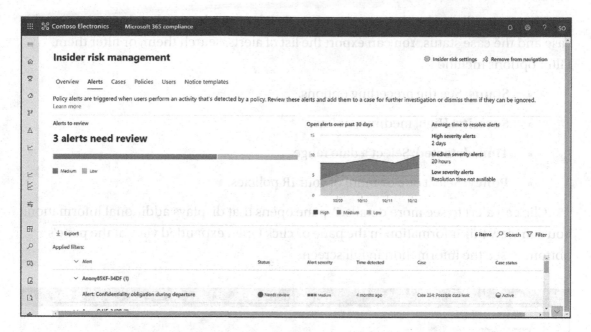

Figure 10-8. *The Alerts tab in the insider risk management solution*

To access alerts, open the insider risk management solution. Click the Alerts tab. Here you will see two graphs, shown in Figure 10-8. One graph is a stacked column chart of the number and severity of alerts waiting for review. The other graph shows the number of low-, medium-, and high-severity alerts over the past 30 days across all policies.

To the right of the Open alerts over past 30 days graph are some statistics about how long, on average, it takes your organization to resolve different alert severities. Below the graphs, you can see a list of all your alerts.

The alert list shows the username or anonymized information. Then it has the name of the triggered policy. The options for alert statuses are

- **Confirmed**: An alert confirmed and assigned to a new or existing case.

- **Dismissed**: An alert dismissed as benign in the triage process.

- **Needs review**: A new alert where no one has taken triage actions.

- **Resolved**: An alert that is part of a closed and resolved case.

Then you will see the alert severity when the alert was detected and any associated case and the case status. You can export the list of alerts, search them, or filter them. Filter options include

- **Status**: See the preceding options.

- **Severity**: High, medium, or low.

- **Time detected**: Select a date range.

- **Policy**: Select one or more of your IR policies.

Click an alert to see more details. A pane opens that displays additional information. You can view this information in the pane or click Open expanded view at the pane's bottom to see the information in full screen.

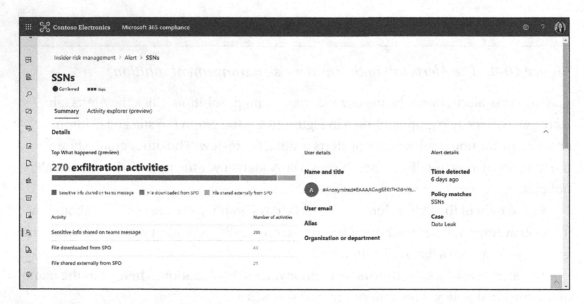

Figure 10-9. *Expanded alert activity*

In the alert details screen, we can see a summary of what triggered the alert. In Figure 10-9, we can see there were 270 exfiltration activities, including sharing sensitive information in Teams, downloading files from SharePoint Online, and sharing data externally from SharePoint Online. Individually these activities may not cause concern, but taken together in context, it represents a potential risk.

Additionally, if anonymized data is disabled, you could see the user's name and title, email address, alias, and department. You can also see alert details such as the time detected, policy matches, and the case name if you have already created one.

If you want to view more detailed information about the activities that created the alert, click the Activity explorer tab.

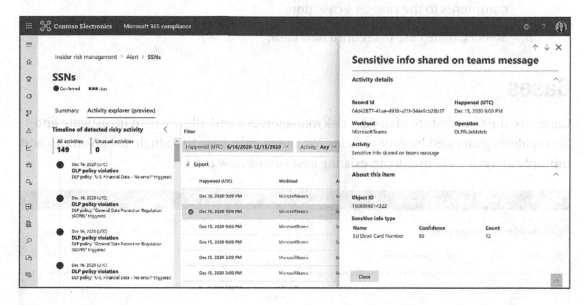

Figure 10-10. *Expanded alert activity – the Activity explorer tab*

Activity explorer in IR shows a timeline of the detected risky activity. Here you can see the count of all activities and unusual activities. You can also see a list of the activities, shown in Figure 10-10, including the workload and the activity when it happened. You can also see the item type, object ID, and file name. You can filter the activities on 30 different fields by clicking the filter button. You can also customize the view to show any of the 30 columns by clicking Customize columns. Finally, you can export a list of activities.

Click an activity to show the details for that activity. Details include the record ID, the date it happened, what sensitive data it matched (if applicable), and more.

If you would like to add this alert to a case for further investigation, do the following:

1. Click the Alerts tab.

2. Click the alert you want to add.

3. On the alert details pane, select Actions ➤ Confirm alert and create case.

4. On the Confirm alert and create insider risk case dialog, enter a name for the case, select users to add as contributors, and add comments as applicable. The system automatically adds comments to the case as a case note.

5. Select Create case to create a new case.

Cases

Cases are the core feature of insider risk management and allow you to investigate and act on alerts generated by your policies. We scope each case to a single user. You can add multiple alerts for the user to an existing case or to a new case.

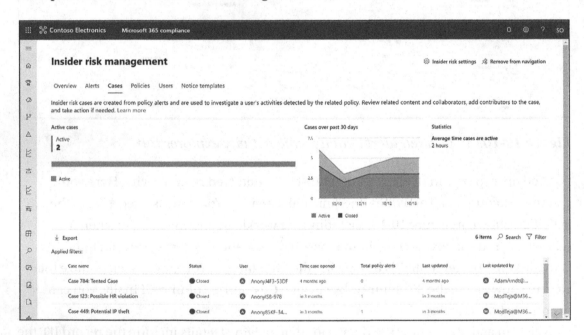

Figure 10-11. *The Cases tab in insider risk management*

To access your case, click the Cases tab in IR. The Cases tab shows an overview of all the active cases in your organization, shown in Figure 10-11. You can see the case's name, the status, the user, the time that the case opened, the total number of policy violation alerts, when the case was last updated, and who last updated the case. You can also filter this information by the case status, the case opened date, and the date updated. Finally, you can export a list of cases.

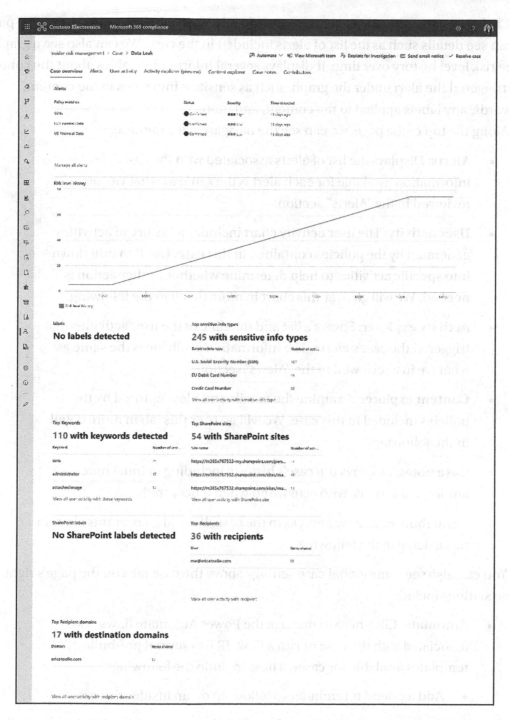

Figure 10-12. *The case overview page in insider risk management*

Click the name of a case to view the case details, shown in Figure 10-12. On this page, we can see details such as the list of alerts included in the case. We can also see a graph of the risk level history over time. It displays several information tables about the content that triggered the alert under the graph, such as sensitive info types in the content, keywords, any labels applied to the content, and more.

Along the top of the page, we can see the navigation for the case:

- **Alerts**: Displays the list of alerts associated with the case. The information available for each alert is the same as what we just reviewed in the "Alerts" section.

- **User activity**: The user activity chart includes a history of activities generated by the policies contained in this case. Use it to drill down into specific activities to help determine whether further action is needed. We will go over this chart in more detail in the following.

- **Activity explorer**: Shows a list and timeline of the user activities that triggered the case's alerts. The information available is the same as what we just reviewed in the "Alerts" section.

- **Content explorer**: Examine the emails and files captured by the policies included in this case. We will go over this tab in more detail in the following.

- **Case notes**: Displays the case's history, including manual notes, automated actions, who acted, and when it occurred.

- **Contributors**: Manage access to the case. We will go over this chart in more detail in the following.

You can also see some global case settings above the case tabs on the page's right. These settings include

- **Automate**: Click here to manage the Power Automate flows associated with the case or run a flow. IR has several pre-built templates available for cases. These include the following:

  - Add a calendar reminder to follow up on an insider risk case

  - Request info from HR or a business about a user in an insider risk case

- Notify manager of insider risk alerts for the user

  Additionally, you can build a custom flow using the compliance connector. Here is the information about the actions and triggers available in the connector: `http://erica.news/ComplianceConnector`.

- **View Microsoft Teams**: Opens the Microsoft Team associated with the case, so contributors can collaborate using chat and files.

- **Escalate for investigation**: Creates an Advanced eDiscovery case for this user and notifies any admins who have the eDiscovery Manager and eDiscovery Administrators roles assigned.

- **Send email notice**: This option allows you to choose a notice template we created in the "Notice Templates" section.

- **Resolve case**: Closes the case and the associated alerts.

  - You can choose to resolve the case as benign or a confirmed policy violation.

  - There is a required field to note actions taken in the case.

  - The Team associated with the case is archived.

There is also a panel on the right side of the page that you can show or hide in case. The panel displays case details such as the case name, status, and overall risk score. It lists the confirmed alerts and has a link to the associated Microsoft Team. It also shows the specific SharePoint and OneDrive sites involved in the case. If available, you can see the user data.

Let us look at the User activity tab in the insider risk case.

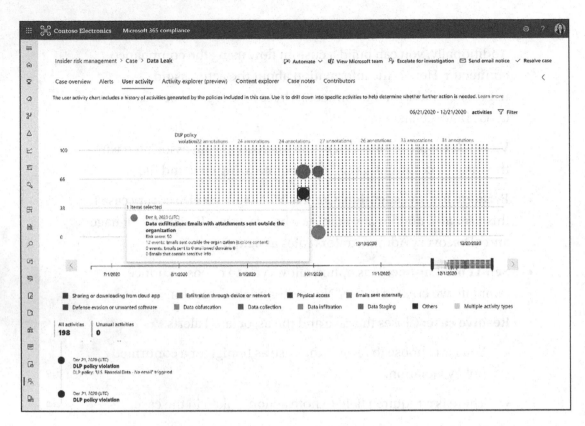

Figure 10-13. *The User activity tab in an insider risk case*

You can see a curated timeline of activity or insights for the user under investigation in the User activity tab, shown in Figure 10-13. This view is a historical view of the events starting with the most recent activity and going back to older events. On the graph, each circle corresponds to one or more sets of insights. We also see annotations on the chart that show HR Connector information, such as if the user resigned and when they will leave the company. This macro exploration of user activity is critical to making timely and informed risk management decisions. An important issue in security is the ability to track repeat offenders. We always assume positive intent, and if we see a policy violation, we may drive education or training, maybe even more than once. But if there is a pattern of behavior, you might increase the course of action you take for remediation in severity.

Across the X-axis is time, and across the Y-axis is risk level. You can use the slides to zoom in on a specific time. The bubbles are color-coded to correspond to a particular type of user activity. You can see the color key below the timeline. The size of the bubble indicates the volume of activity. The vertical dotted lines indicate DLP policy matches for the user. You can click a bubble to view the activity details. Click an annotation above the graph to get details on the DLP policy matches. Below the graph is the full list of activities.

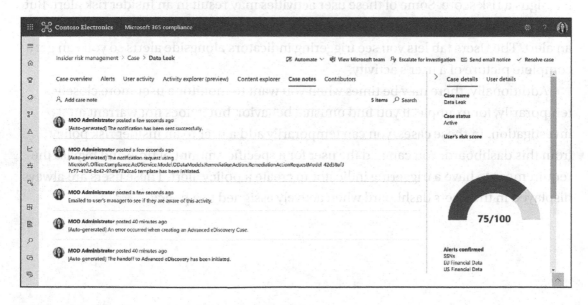

Figure 10-14. *The Content explorer tab in an insider risk case*

The next tab we want to dive into is Content explorer, shown in Figure 10-14. This tab allows us to view the specific documents and emails involved in the case. Here you can search using conditions. The conditions work as they do in content search, so please see Chapter 12 for more details about conditions. Or open a document to see the contents. You are also able to customize the view by editing the displayed columns.

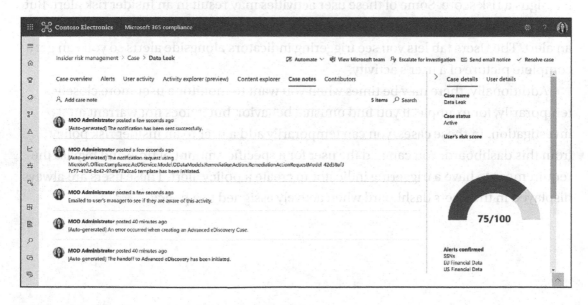

Figure 10-15. *Case notes in an insider risk case*

The Case notes tab, shown in Figure 10-15, displays information about actions taken in the case. Notes are auto-generated when you perform activities such as sending a notification or escalating the case for investigation. Your team can also add manual notes to the case. These notes are beneficial when the case is still open. But they can be more valuable for repeat offenders when you need to understand what actions people took in previous cases.

Our last tab is Contributors. This tab is where we manage who can access the case. By default, it lists all users assigned the Insider Risk Management Analysts and Insider Risk Management Investigators roles as contributors for each active and closed case. To add someone to only this case, click Add contributor. Type their name or email to provide contributor access to the case. You can also copy a case link from this page.

That is all the functionality available in an insider risk management case. Lastly, let us look at the Users tab at the insider risk solution level, not inside a case.

Users

The Users tab in insider risk management shows any user with an active alert, a triggering event, or people whom you have temporarily added to a policy. When you add a user to an insider risk management policy, background processes are automatically evaluating user activities for triggering indicators. When the process finds an indicator, it assigns a risk score. Some of these user activities may result in an insider risk alert. But some activities may not meet a minimum risk score level, and the solution will not create an alert. The Users tab lets you see triggering indicators alongside alerts so you can get a complete picture of a user's activity.

Additionally, there may be times when you want to monitor a user more closely temporarily, for example, if you find unusual behavior, but it does not warrant an investigation. In these cases, you can temporarily add a user to an insider risk policy from this dashboard. You can add the user for a specific amount of time and bypass the requirement to have a triggering indicator to create a policy alert. These users are always displayed in the Users dashboard when actively assigned to a policy.

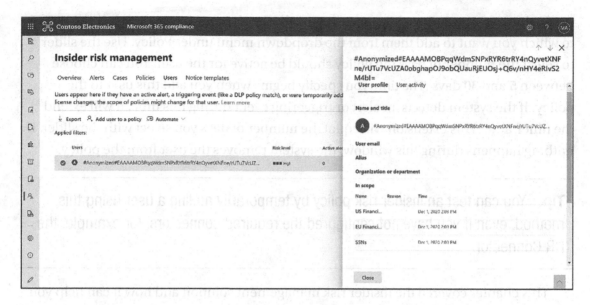

Figure 10-16. *The Users tab in insider risk management*

To access the Users tab, open the insider risk management solution. Click the Users tab. Here you can see a list of the users who match one of the preceding criteria, shown in Figure 10-16. You can see the user's anonymous name or their real name if you have permission. You can also see the risk severity, how many alerts the user has currently, how many confirmed violations they had over the last year, and any open and active cases.

You can also filter this view by severity or search for a specific case or a particular user. Additionally, you can export the list of users or start a Power Automate Flow. You can also manually add a user to a policy, which we will cover in just a moment.

To view the details for a user, click their name. This click brings up a pane showing the user's information to see it or their anonymized details. Under the In scope heading, it lists the policies of which they are a member. Click the User activity tab in the details pane to see a list of all the user's activities. It highlights unusual activities in a different color, and you can click the text to show only those activities. Click Close when done.

To add a user to a policy temporarily, click Add user to a policy. If you temporarily add a user to a policy, the system immediately assigns risk scores to their activity from that point forward. This action bypasses the requirement for the system to detect a triggering event first. It might take a few hours for this user to appear in the list of users for the policy.

In the pop-up window that appears, type the user's name or email. Select the policy to which you want to add them from the dropdown menu under Policy. Use the slider to select the number of days the policy should be active for the user. You can choose between 5 and 30 days. The time you specify begins when you add this user to the policy. If the system detects an alert or triggering event during this time, it will extend the timeframe. This extension will equal the number of days you select with the slider. If nothing happens during this window, the system removes the user from the policy.

Tip   You can test an insider risk policy by temporarily adding a user using this method, even if you have not configured the required connectors, for example, the HR Connector.

This chapter covered the insider risk management solution and how it can help you monitor and detect risky user behavior. We configured global settings for the solution and built a notice template. Then we created an insider risk policy and monitored policy alerts. We opened a case for some of the alerts to see a timeline of the user's behavior and act on any violations. Finally, we monitored users to see if we should add them to a high-risk policy.

In the next chapter, we will look at how Communication Compliance can help manage insider risk from communication content, such as email and Teams messages.

CHAPTER 11

Communication Compliance

Organizations face a broad range of risks from insiders. These risks could be everything from workplace harassment, IP theft, violence, insider trading, accidental data spillage, other types of data handling violations, fraud, conflicts of interest, or sensitive data leaks.

Typically, these types of insider risks fall into three types of policy violations:

1. **Corporate policies**: Policies that employees must comply with in all their business-related communications, such as acceptable use, ethical standards, or other corporate policies.

2. **Risk management**: Organizations are responsible for all communications throughout their infrastructure and corporate network systems. Identifying and managing potential legal exposure and risk from sensitive data can help prevent damage to corporate operations.

3. **Regulatory compliance**: Many organizations must comply with some regulatory compliance standards as a part of their routine operating procedures. These regulations often require organizations to implement some oversight process for messaging that applies to their industry.

In my experience, monitoring for these types of insider risks typically brings up some common pain points.

The first pain point is the proliferation of channels. There are many different communication channels used in organizations today, from traditional email to new chat apps. People are collaborating more than ever. It is difficult to monitor all these channels for insider risk.

© Erica Toelle 2021
E. Toelle, *Microsoft 365 Compliance*, https://doi.org/10.1007/978-1-4842-5778-4_11

The second is the increasing volume of data. As you probably know, data is exploding. The volume of data created every day is increasing and is not showing any signs of stopping. Your insider risk solution needs to be able to contend with an increasing volume of data.

Third, most communication compliance processes are labor-intensive. They are manual processes, and it takes a lot of time to review all the communications and keep up with the volume of data. It can also be challenging to find subject matter experts who understand the policy and have the time to review potential violations.

The fourth pain point is the cross-department collaboration that is required to resolve policy violations. This resolution often requires collaboration, especially between IT, HR, compliance, and legal departments.

The fifth pain point is the rise of regulatory enforcement. There is an increasing number of regulations that require an organization to monitor communication channels for insider risk.

Lastly, the summary of all these pain points results in violations slipping through the cracks, putting your organization at risk.

What Is Communication Compliance?

Microsoft Communication Compliance is the solution to manage insider risk from communications. Communication Compliance allows you to identify and remediate the corporate code of conduct policy violations. It can also monitor for sensitive information share in communications and monitor messages for regulatory compliance purposes. It does this through intelligent, customizable templates.

Communication Compliance leverages machine learning to detect potential policy violations across Microsoft Teams, Exchange, Yammer, Skype for Business, and third-party content. It can monitor a massive volume of content across all the communication tools in Microsoft 365, as well as some third-party tools.

Communication Compliance also has flexible remediation workflows that allow for cross-department collaboration. Remediation workflows act quickly on violations and enable you to bring in the right people to deal with the issue. The machine learning capabilities make the review process less labor-intensive by de-duplicating communications and threading Teams and Exchange conversations.

Lastly, Communication Compliance has actionable insights. There is an interactive dashboard to show policy violations, actions, and trends. The solution also has full auditing capabilities for both review actions and policy changes.

Communication Channels Monitored

Communication Compliance works across a variety of content sources. First, it can monitor Microsoft Teams conversations and associated attachments in public and private Microsoft Teams channels and individual chats. Matching Communication Compliance policy conditions are processed every 24 hours and then are available in Communication Compliance reports.

Exchange email mailboxes hosted on Exchange Online are all eligible for message scanning. Emails and attachments matching Communication Compliance policy conditions are instantly available in Communication Compliance reports.

Chat communications and associated attachments in Skype for Business Online can be monitored using Communication Compliance. Skype for Business Online chats matching Communication Compliance policy conditions are processed once every 24 hours and are then available in Communication Compliance reports.

You can monitor Yammer group messages and private chats if your Yammer network is in native mode. All Yammer networks are in native mode by default if you create them after January 2020. Policy conditions are processed once every 24 hours and are then available in Communication Compliance reports.

You can also scan communications from third-party sources for data imported into mailboxes into your Microsoft 365 organization. To use this functionality, you must first set up a data connector, as described in Chapter 4. You can see a full list of the available connectors there. Once you set up your connectors, they will appear as a location for a Communication Compliance policy.

Communication Compliance Licensing and Permissions

To use Communication Compliance, each monitored user must have one of the following licenses assigned to them. This licensing means that every user with a monitored mailbox or member of a monitored Microsoft Team or Yammer group must have a license:

- Microsoft 365 E5

- Microsoft 365 E5 Compliance

- Office 365 E5

- Microsoft 365 E5 Insider Risk Management

- Office 365 Advanced Compliance (retired)

For permissions, these are the roles related to Communication Compliance:

- **Communication Compliance Admin**: Used to manage policies in the Communication Compliance feature.

- **Communication Compliance Analysis**: Used to perform an investigation and remediation of the message violations in the Communication Compliance feature. Can only view message metadata.

- **Communication Compliance Case Management**: Used to access Communication Compliance cases.

- **Communication Compliance Investigation**: Used to perform investigation, remediation, and review of message violations in the Communication Compliance feature. Can view message metadata and messages.

- **Communication Compliance Viewer**: Used to access reports and widgets in the Communication Compliance feature.

- **View-Only Case**: Allows people to access communication compliance cases. Use this in conjunction with the preceding roles if you create a custom role group.

These are the default role groups for communication compliance. As a reminder, you can create a custom role group, as described in Chapter 1. I find that the default role groups work well for the least permissions model:

- **Communication Compliance Administrators**: Administrators of communication compliance can create/edit policies and define global settings.

- **Communication Compliance Analysts**: Analysts of communication compliance can investigate policy matches, view message metadata, and take remediation actions.

- **Communication Compliance Investigators**: Investigators of communication compliance can investigate policy matches, view message content, and take remediation actions.

- **Communication Compliance Viewers**: Viewers of communication compliance can access the available reports and widgets.

An Overview of the Communication Compliance Solution

There are three steps to use Communication Compliance, shown in Figure 11-1:

1. **Configure**: In this step, you will create and tune the policies, using either the templates or a custom policy. You will need to monitor alerts, productivity reports, and audits.

2. **Investigate**: This step identifies violations. You can then review potential violations, tag them, add comments, conduct document reviews, and see a user's history of violations.

3. **Remediate**: In this step, you resolve violations. You can notify parties about their violation and provide them additional training on the policy. You could also escalate the violation to another reviewer, such as the HR or legal department, or you could hand it off to a different compliance solution for further investigation, such as the Advanced eDiscovery solution or the internal investigation tool.

We will review these steps in more detail in this section.

HOW TO USE COMMUNICATION COMPLIANCE

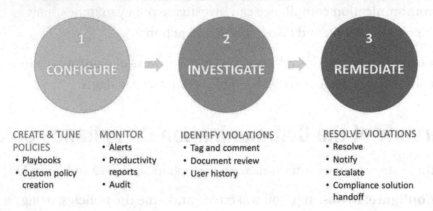

CREATE & TUNE POLICIES
- Playbooks
- Custom policy creation

MONITOR
- Alerts
- Productivity reports
- Audit

IDENTIFY VIOLATIONS
- Tag and comment
- Document review
- User history

RESOLVE VIOLATIONS
- Resolve
- Notify
- Escalate
- Compliance solution handoff

Figure 11-1. *The three steps to use the Microsoft 365 Communication Compliance solution*

Before you create your first Communication Compliance policy, you will want to plan the supervised users and groups. Here is my recommended approach for planning supervised users.

First, plan out the policies you want to enforce. Look at the three types of standard policies: corporate policies, risk management, and regulatory compliance. Ask yourself which policies you want to implement.

Once you have decided on the policies, you will need to determine which users or groups you would like to supervise within each policy type. You will want to determine whether existing Microsoft 365 groups or distribution lists include the members you want to monitor. If they do not, you will need to create a new Microsoft 365 group or distribution list for this purpose.

Once you have planned the supervised users and groups, you can start by making your first policy. To access Communication Compliance, visit the Compliance Center, located at https://compliance.microsoft.com. On the left-hand side of the page, click Communication compliance.

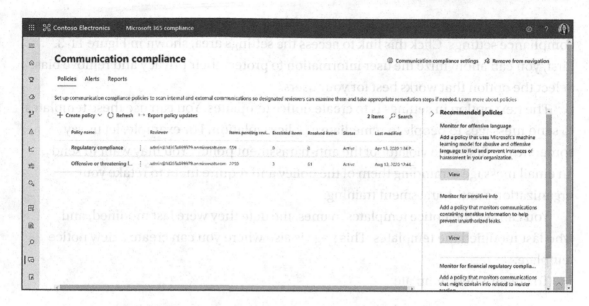

Figure 11-2. *The Communication Compliance policy page*

This click brings you to the Communication Compliance policy page shown in Figure 11-2. On this page, you can view all the Communication Compliance policies in your organization. Each policy listed includes additional information, such as the policy reviewers, the date the policy was last modified, a count of the items that need review, the number of escalated items, and the number of resolved items. You can create or edit a policy from this page, which we will review in the next section.

Figure 11-3. *The Communication Compliance settings page*

Additionally, in the upper-right corner of the page, you can see the communication compliance settings. Click this link to access the settings area, shown in Figure 11-3. First, you can anonymize the user information to protect their privacy and remove bias. Select the option that works best for your users.

The next option in settings is to create notice templates. You can use these templates to send messages to people to remediate a policy violation. For example, let us say someone is a first-time violator of the anti-harassment policy. You may want to send an email message reminding them of the policy and require them to retake your organization's anti-harassment training.

You can see the notice templates' names, the date they were last modified, and who last modified the templates. This page is also where you can create a new notice template.

To create a new template

1. First, enter a template name.

2. Second, select an email address to use to send the notice.

3. Third, enter any name, group, or distribution list that should be Cc'd or Bcc'd on the notice.

4. Fourth, enter a subject for the message. Then, enter the message body. In the message body, you can use HTML to format the message. Please note that the HTML href attribute implementation in the Communication Compliance notice template only supports a single quotation mark instead of the standard double quotation mark for URL references as of this book's writing, for example, href='URL'>text<a>.

5. Lastly, click Create to finish your notice template.

Now your template will be available in the policy review section of the solution.

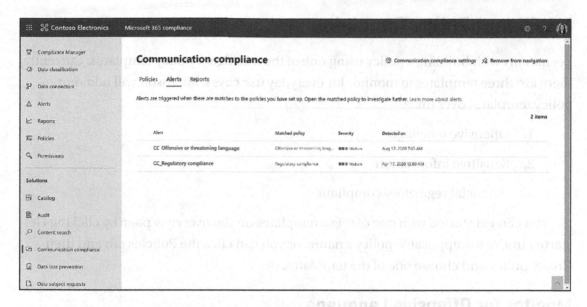

Figure 11-4. *The Communication Compliance Alerts tab*

Now let us look at the Alerts tab, shown in Figure 11-4. Here you can see the alerts for matches to the policy. You can also see these alerts alongside all Compliance Center alerts by clicking Alerts in the left navigation.

The last tab is Reports. We will review this tab near the end of the chapter.

Create a Communication Compliance Policy

Now, let us get started on our first Communication Compliance policy. There are two ways to create a Communication Compliance policy:

1. **Intelligent templates**: These templates leverage machine learning to reduce false positives. They are pre-configured to address common communication risks.

2. **Custom policy creation**: Custom policies allow you to create your Communication Compliance policy from scratch. You can configure the settings in a way that makes the most sense for your organization and your situation. You can also leverage the pre-built machine learning models in custom policies or even build your machine learning model to detect violations unique to your organization. For information on how to build a custom machine learning model, please see Chapter 3.

Intelligent Policy Templates

Let us start with building a policy using one of the intelligent policy templates. Currently, there are three templates to monitor for everyday use cases. Microsoft will add more policy templates over time:

1. Offensive language

2. Sensitive information

3. Financial regulatory compliance

You can get started with one of these templates on the overview page by clicking Get started under the applicable policy's name, or you can click the Policies tab and then Create policy and choose one of the templates.

Monitor for Offensive Language

This policy monitors for language that could be considered offensive, harassing, or threatening. It looks for the context of the language and individual keywords to have more accurate policy matches. Please note that Microsoft will probably adjust this model over time to improve its effectiveness.

This template has a combination of settings that Microsoft has filled out for you and settings you need to complete, shown in Figure 11-5.

Monitor communications for offensive or threatening language

×

About this template   ∧

Creates a policy that uses built-in trainable classifiers to detect content containing profanity or language that might be considered threatening or harassment.

Settings we need from you   ∧

Policy name *

Offensive or threatening language

Users or groups to supervise *

Start typing to find users or groups

Reviewers *

Start typing to find users

Settings we've filled in for you   ∧

You can change these later. Click 'Customize policy' if you want to configure different settings now.

Communications to monitor

Monitored locations

Exchange, Teams, Skype for Business, Yammer

Conditions and percentage

Communication direction

Inbound, Outbound, Internal

Percentage to review

100

Detect content matching these trainable classifiers ⓘ

- Harassment
- Profanity
- Threat
- Threat (ES)
- Adult images
- Racy images
- Gory images

| Create policy | Customize policy | Cancel |

Figure 11-5. *The offensive or threatening language policy template*

Microsoft has completed the following settings:

- The policy name, which is set to Offensive or threatening language. You're welcome to change the policy name.

- Communications to monitor have been set to Exchange, Teams, Skype, and Yammer.

- It will monitor all communication directions.

- For review conditions, the policy will send 100% of matches for review.

You will need to complete the following settings. First, choose the users or groups to supervise. For example, if you want to monitor everyone in the company for offensive language, select all users.

Next, select the reviewers. These will be the people who will review potential violations for this specific policy. Then click Create policy to finish the policy creation.

Monitor for Sensitive Information

Now, let us look at the settings to monitor for sensitive information. As we reviewed in Chapter 3 in the section "Sensitive Information Types," this can include data such as personally identifiable information (PII), financial information such as bank or credit card numbers, or a type of sensitive information unique to your organization.

Microsoft has completed the following settings for this policy template:

- The policy name is Sensitive information. Again, you can change this name if you would like.

- Communications to monitor have been set to Exchange, Teams, Skype, and Yammer.

- It will monitor all communication directions.

- For review conditions, the policy will send 100% of matches for review.

The settings you will complete include the users or groups to supervise and the reviewers. You will also need to choose a sensitive information type or a custom dictionary that will provide the information for which the policy should monitor.

Monitor for Regulatory Compliance

Many organizations have a regulatory standard they must follow. These regulations often require organizations to implement supervisory or oversight processes for messaging appropriate for their industry. This policy template allows you to scan and report on communications to meet this requirement.

Microsoft has completed the following settings for this policy template:

- The policy name, which is Regulatory compliance. Again, you can modify this name.

- Communications to monitor will include all inbound and outbound communications across all channels.

- For review conditions, the policy will select a random sample of 10% of emails that contain standard leak terms or where the attachment is larger than 1 megabyte.

You will need to complete the following information. First, choose the users or groups to supervise and the reviewers. Next, choose the dictionary or lexicon of regulatory compliance terms for which you want to monitor.

If one of these templates does not meet your needs, you can create a custom template instead. Next, let us look at how to build a custom compliance policy for Communication Compliance.

Create a Custom Communication Compliance Policy

To create a custom policy, go to the Policies tab, click Create policy, and then click Custom policy. A window will pop up that will take you through the steps to create the policy.

The first step is to name and describe your policy. I recommend that you choose a unique name that is descriptive of the policy. Only the policy name will show on alerts, so a descriptive name will allow you to understand what the policy does without checking the policy settings.

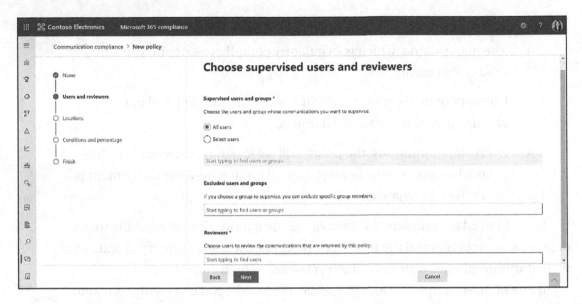

Figure 11-6. *Choose supervised users and reviewers for your custom policy*

Next, you will need to choose supervised users, enter optional excluded users, and select reviewers, shown in Figure 11-6. I recommend that you avoid using individual usernames in Communication Compliance policies. This way, you can avoid editing the policy every time a user starts employment or leaves your organization. It is more manageable to edit a Microsoft 365 group, distribution list, or Microsoft Team membership.

Add Supervised Users, Excluded Users, and Reviewers to a Policy

Let us look at an example of how you might set up supervised and excluded users and groups. In this example, you want to create a Communication Compliance policy that monitors everyone's email in the sales department. To do this, you would enter the sales distribution list in the supervised users and groups field.

To continue the example, let us say the sales distribution list includes sales managers, but you want to exclude them from this policy. You would enter the sales manager distribution list in the excluded users and groups field. This setting prevents emails from being monitored.

To complete our example, you will need to choose people to review potential policy violations. The reviewer information can be entered as individual usernames. You cannot add reviewers by using a distribution group or a dynamic distribution group. Again, I recommend using a mail-enabled security group rather than an individual's name. Even if there are only a few names in the group, it is easier to manage membership there rather than remembering to edit the policy if the reviewer leaves your organization.

Now let us review the different ways you can add supervised and excluded users and communication channels to a policy. Please see Figure 11-7 for a summary of this information.

TYPES OF MONITORING	ADD TO POLICY USING...			
	INDIVIDUAL USER	OFFICE 365 GROUP	DISTRIBUTION LIST	MICROSOFT TEAM
Individual User's Email	✓	✗	✓	✗
Shared Mailbox	✗	✓	✗	✗
Teams Channels	✗	✓	✗	✓
1:1 Teams/Skype Chats	✓	✗	✓	✗

Figure 11-7. *How to add supervised users and communication channels to a custom policy*

If you want to monitor an individual user's email, you will need to add them to the policy using either an individual username or distribution list.

To supervise a shared mailbox, you will need to add the Microsoft 365 group associated with the shared mailbox to the supervised users and groups field in the policy.

To scan Microsoft Teams channel messages, you will need to add either the Microsoft 365 group associated with the Microsoft Team or the Microsoft Team itself to the supervised users and groups field.

Note   You will need to explicitly add new Microsoft Teams to your Communication Compliance policy if you would like the messages monitored. As of the writing of this book, there is no way to automate this using PowerShell.

If you would like to monitor Teams chats, which are messages sent between individuals, not to a Team, then add them to the Communication Compliance policy using either an individual username or distribution group.

Please note that supervised users and reviewers must have an Exchange Online mailbox for Communication Compliance policies to work.

Choose Locations to Monitor in the Policy

Now let us move on to the next step in the custom policy wizard. In this step, you will need to choose locations or communication channels to monitor in your Communication Compliance policy, shown in Figure 11-8.

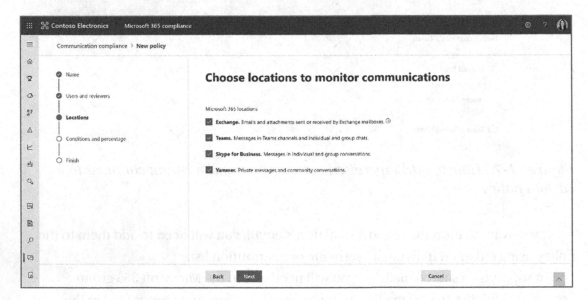

Figure 11-8. *Communication channels to monitor in a custom policy*

Available locations include

- Exchange emails and attachments
- Microsoft Teams messages and attachments in both channels and chats
- Skype for Business Online individual or group conversations
- Yammer messages in individual or group conversations
- Third-party sources, such as Bloomberg or other connectors

Note   For third-party sources to appear in this view, you will need to have added them as a connector in Microsoft 365. Please see Chapter 4 for instructions on setting these up.

Check the boxes of the locations you want to monitor and click Next.

Choose Conditions and Review Percentage

The policy wizard asks you to choose policy conditions and the policy review percentage on the next screen, shown in Figure 11-9. First, you will need to select the communication direction, which can be inbound, outbound, or internal. Then you will need to choose the conditions to trigger the policy. Finally, you will select the review percentage of communications. Let us look at these options in more detail.

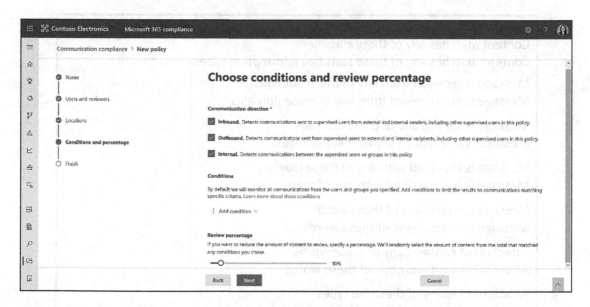

Figure 11-9. *Choose conditions and the review percentage for a custom policy*

The review percentage specifies how many communications that match the policy conditions are sent for review. If you want to reduce the amount of content to review or only see a random sample, you can specify a lower review percentage. A review percentage of less than 100 selects a real-time, random sample of content from the total percentage of content matching the chosen policy conditions. If you want reviewers to see all the items that match a policy, you can set the review percentage to 100%.

Next, let us look at the communication direction options. Your choices are

- Inbound, which covers communications sent to a supervised person.

- Outbound, which monitors communication sent from a supervised person.

- Internal, which supervises the communication sent between two supervised people.

Now, let us look at the conditions to trigger the Communication Compliance policy. The dropdown will allow you to select from many different communications options. Figure 11-10 lists the available conditions.

CONDITION
Content matches any of these classifiers
Content matches any of these sensitive information types
Message is received from any of these domains
Message is not received from any of these domains
Message is sent to any of these domains
Message is not sent to any of these domains
Message is classified with any of these labels
Message is not classified with any of these labels
Message contains any of these words
Message contains none of these words
Attachment contains any of these words
Attachment contains none of these words
Attachment is any of these file types
Attachment is none of these file types
Message size is larger than
Message size is not larger than
Attachment is larger than
Attachment is not larger than

Figure 11-10. *Available conditions in a custom policy*

For example, if you are concerned about data leaks, you might scan communications for attachments above a specific size. Or you can monitor communications for a message that contains a word from a list you specify.

Tip   Work with your legal, IT, and HR departments to determine how to configure your communication policies and conditions for your organization. They will also help you decide which action to take when you find a policy violation.

Please note that they will be treated as "and" statements and not "or" statements if you use multiple conditions. The communication must meet the criteria of all conditions to trigger the policy. For example, if your policy uses the condition "Message contains any of these words" and the condition "Attachment contains any of these words," one of the words must appear in the message *and* the attachment.

I also want to be sure you notice that you can use a classifier from your custom policy's communication compliance templates. The condition is called "Content matches any of these classifiers." In addition to the classifiers mentioned earlier in this chapter, you can use any of the pre-built classifiers we discussed in Chapter 3. Of course, you can also use a custom classifier built by your organization in your custom communication compliance policy.

Next, let us look at what happens once your communication compliance policies are used and locating policy matches. When we find a policy violation, we can review and act.

Review Potential Policy Violations

First, let us see where and how we can view messages that have matched a policy as a potential violation. From the Communication Compliance overview page, click the Policies tab. Here you can see a list of all your active policies, the number of items pending review, the number of escalated items, and the number of resolved items.

Click the name of the policy that you want to review. This click takes you to a page that provides an overview of that policy. The overview page will show you all the alerts for that policy, the age of the pending items, and the users with the most policy matches.

Next, we will look at the items that are ready for review. Click the Pending tab. The pending view shows all the communications that are pending review. This page is also where you can act on the items.

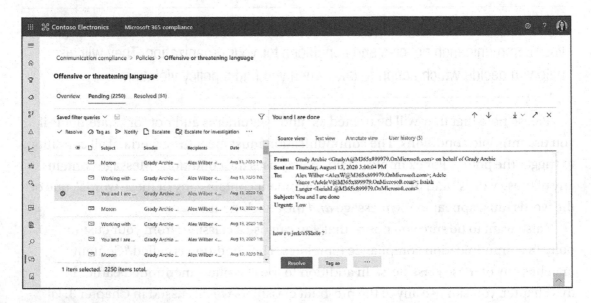

Figure 11-11.   Pending items are available for review

Check the box next to one of the communications to see the content of the message. Select the text view of the message. Here you can see a summary view of the message, highlighting the concerning text in yellow. Note that the highlight does not appear when using a classifier to find information. It works well when using a lexicon to trigger the policy. You can also see a text-only view or an annotate view if you want to add notes to the message. You can also view the user's history of violations.

Figure 11-11 shows a view of communications across multiple channels. You can view messages from all channels together or filter the view to show only one channel. To reduce the number of items that need to be reviewed, Communication Compliance uses artificial intelligence to show related messages together. For example, Microsoft Teams chat will show the context of the entire chat thread. Exchange emails will group emails from the same conversation.

Additionally, you can customize this view by grouping and filtering the items. You can save this view as a custom query for later reference. The solution stores view changes per reviewer, and customization of the view does not affect other reviewers.

Available filters include

- **FilterDetailsDate:** The date the message was sent or received by a user in your organization.

- **File class:** The class of the message based on the message type, either *message* or *attachment*.

- **Has attachment:** The attachment presence in the message.

- **Item class:** The source of the message based on the message type, email, Microsoft Teams chat, Bloomberg, and so on.

- **Recipient domains:** The domain to which the message was sent. This is normally your Microsoft 365 subscription domain by default.

- **Recipient:** The user to which the message was sent.

- **Sender:** The person who sent the message.

- **Sender domain:** The domain that sent the message.

- **Size:** The size of the message in KB.

- **Subject/Title:** The message subject or chat title.

- **Tags:** The tags assigned to a message, either *Questionable*, *Compliant*, or *Non-compliant*.

- **Escalated To:** The username of the person included as part of a message escalation action.

Next, let us look at the actions we can take on the pending messages.

Review Actions

The pending view also has a variety of review actions that you can take on each message. We will dive into each one individually in the following sections, but here are all the actions you can take on a message:

- Resolve the item when you want it archived.

- Tag the item as compliant, not compliant, or questionable.

- Send a notice to the user who violated the policy.

- Escalate the message to another reviewer.

- See near duplicates.

- View exact duplicates.

- Resolve as a false positive if you used a pre-built classifier.

- Start a Power Automate Flow.

- View message details.

- Improve classification.

- View item history.

- Group by family or conversation.

Resolve archives an item when you have finished acting on the message. This step could be when you have completed your investigation or process. It could also be when you find the message to be compliant, so no further action is needed. The solution retains resolved messages for seven years.

You can also tag content as either being questionable, compliant, or non-compliant. These tags allow you to sort on items and find what needs further action. For example, you may need to escalate questionable items to another reviewer for their opinion. Non-compliant items may need to have a notice sent to the violator.

Next, you can notify the user who violated the policy, letting them know about the violation and optionally asking them to take further action, such as training. The notice can use the notice templates that we reviewed at the beginning of the chapter, or you can create a new notice if needed. If you click Send notice, a wizard will pop up that allows you to choose a notice template, shown in Figure 11-12. The template will either pre-populate the sender, Cc, and Bcc information, or you can customize this information. You will have a pre-populated subject and message body.

Figure 11-12. *Send a notice to a user*

You could also escalate the message to another reviewer. The escalation allows you to send the message for further review or action from the reviewer. You can select from all available reviewers and write a note about the reason for the escalation.

You can also resolve the message as a false positive. This option appears when you are using one of the pre-built classifiers, and it allows you to anonymously notify the machine learning algorithm that incorrectly identified a violation.

Next, you can review near duplicates of the message. As mentioned earlier, viewing duplicate messages is extremely helpful when reviewing email and Microsoft Teams messages. This option also allows you to view message details, which is the complete metadata of all the messages.

Then, you can also download items to keep them in a different location or take offline action.

Resolved Items

The last tab in the policy view is for resolved items. This view shows the archive of items that no longer require action. Like pending items, you can sort, filter, and save a custom query of resolved items. Actions include viewing message details, viewing the history of the items, or downloading the item.

Figure 11-13. *View the history of remediation actions*

The history of each item is especially helpful when working with a group of people to review and remediate Communication Compliance violations. The history of remediation actions shows you a list of all remediation actions that reviewers performed on this item before resolution, shown in Figure 11-13. For example, it will show you the date of the action, the person who acted, and any comments or metadata, such as a tag they added to the item.

Here you can view user history, so you can see the specifics of how previous violations for a user were resolved. You can see the previous remediation actions, such as notifications or escalations, the date on which they occurred, and the person who acted. This information can help further inform your decisions about the next step to take on a current violation.

View Reports

Communication compliance has a tab to view reports. These reports include data from all the policies.

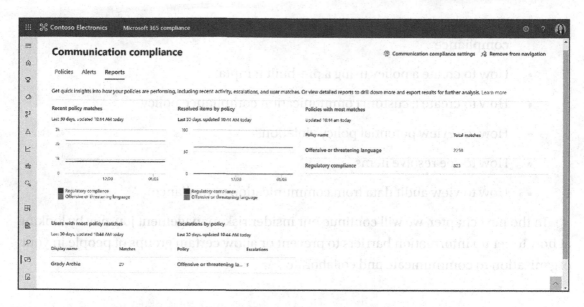

Figure 11-14. *View reports for communication compliance*

These reports include the following, shown in Figure 11-14:

- **Recent policy matches**: Shows trends for policy matches.

- **Resolved items by policy**: Shows trends for how items are resolved per policy.

- **Policies with most matches**: Shows the policies and the number of matches.

- **Users with most policy matches**: Lists the users and the number of matches.

- **Escalations by policy**: Shows the policy name and the number of escalations.

In this chapter, we covered the Microsoft 365 Communication Compliance policies. This chapter included

- The business problem for which you need Communication Compliance in your organization

- An overview of Microsoft's solution of the communication compliance problem

- The monitored communication channels in Microsoft's solution

- The licensing and permissions required for communication compliance

- How to create a policy using a pre-built template

- How to create a custom communication compliance policy

- How to review potential policy violations

- How to see resolve items

- How to view audit data from communication compliance

In the next chapter, we will continue our insider risk management journey by looking at how to set up information barriers to prevent or allow certain groups of people in your organization to communicate and collaborate.

CHAPTER 12

Content Search

Content search allows you to find any content in Microsoft 365 without needing permissions for each location. You can search for content using locations and keywords and then use search conditions to narrow down your results. Content search is leveraged by all the discover and respond tools, such as Core and Advanced eDiscovery and Data Investigations. Content search is easy to use but very powerful. This chapter will teach you about the specifics of content search so that you can better use the tool across all these Microsoft 365 compliance solutions.

For example, we will cover what locations content search can and cannot search. We will also review how to build a search query and how to handle partially indexed items. Search statistics, estimations, and previews help you understand if you have searched for the right items. They can help you modify your search, if necessary, to be more targeted toward what you are looking to find. We will also cover how to export content.

When would you use content search? Content search is excellent if you want to view all content in a specific location, such as a SharePoint site. It can also help you see all emails where the user was the sender or receiver, Cc'd, Bcc'd, or included in a distribution list message. You can also use content search to see all content that has a retention label applied. Another example is to see all Teams meetings that occurred in the past week. Finally, you could use content search to export content, or a summary report of content, outside of Microsoft 365.

Just a note, there are two content search topics that we will not cover in this chapter, but I want you to be aware they exist. First, you can automate searches using PowerShell. Additionally, you can limit what locations a person can search by using compliance boundaries. Compliance boundaries are a common way people limit search locations based on geography or department, so users can only see content in the compliance boundary areas.

© Erica Toelle 2021

E. Toelle, *Microsoft 365 Compliance*, https://doi.org/10.1007/978-1-4842-5778-4_12

Content search indexes the following solutions, and they will appear in search results:

- Bookings

- Calendar

- Excel

- Microsoft Lists

- Microsoft 365 Group Email

- Office Lens

- OneDrive for Business

- OneNote

- Exchange email and group mailboxes

- Exchange public folders

- Forms

- People

- PowerPoint

- SharePoint

- Skype for Business chats

- Sway

- Tasks

- Teams chats and Conversations

- To Do

- Video

- Visio

- Word

- Yammer (if in native mode)

Locations that cannot be searched by content search include

- Access

- Flow

- Kaizala

- Planner

- Power Apps

- Power BI

- Project

- Publisher

- Stream

- Whiteboard

Licensing and Permissions

To use content search, you need to be assigned one of the following licenses:

- Microsoft 365 E5

- Microsoft 365 E3

- Microsoft 365 F3

- Microsoft 365 F1

- Microsoft 365 Business Premium

- Office 365 E5

- Office 365 E3

- Office 365 E1

- Office 365 F3

A few permissions are needed to search, view the search results, export data, and search and purge data. You could give someone all these roles or just one of the roles, depending on how much access they need:

- **Compliance Search role**: Allows people to search mailboxes and public folders, SharePoint Online sites, OneDrive for Business sites, Skype for Business conversations, Microsoft 365 groups, Microsoft Teams, and Yammer groups.

- **Preview role**: This role will enable you to view a list of items returned from a content search and open each item from the list to view its contents.

- **Export role**: This role allows you to export mailbox and site content returned from searches.

- **Search and Purge role**: This role lets people bulk-remove data that match the criteria of a content search.

Create a Content Search

Now, let us create a content search. To do this, we visit the Microsoft 365 Compliance Center. In the left navigation, click Content search. This click will bring you to the content search overview page.

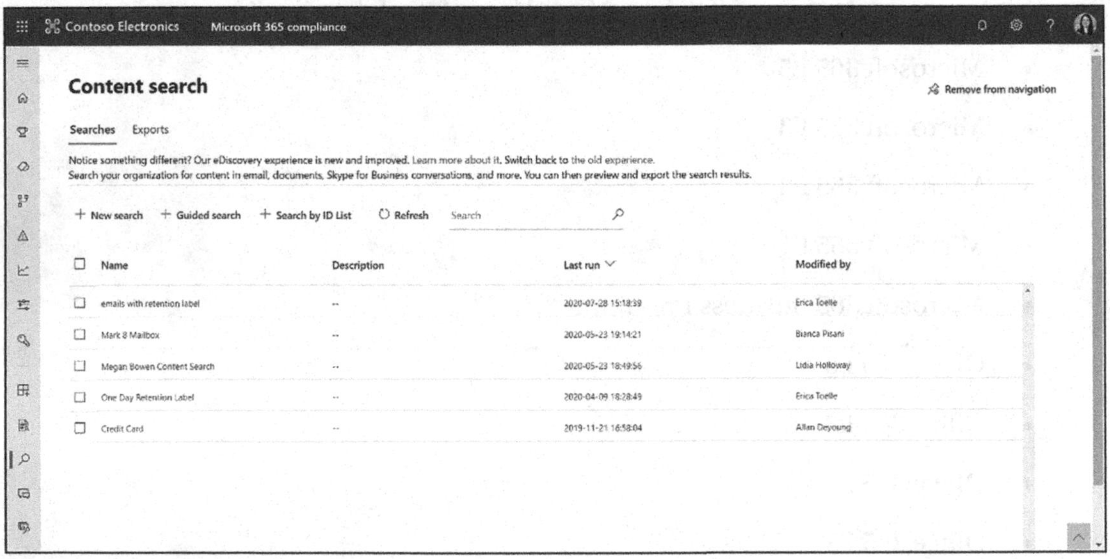

Figure 12-1. *The content search overview page*

On this page, shown in Figure 12-1, you can see a list of existing searches that people have saved. The information displayed includes the search's name, a description, the last time someone ran the search, and the last person to modify it. Additionally, you can see buttons to create a new search, create a guided search, or search by an ID list. You also have a field to refresh the search list or an area to search for a specific search. We can also see a tab for exports on this page, which we will discuss later in this chapter.

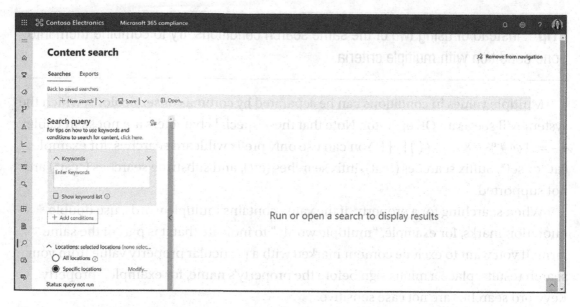

Figure 12-2. *Create a new search page*

For now, let us go ahead and click New search to go through the steps to create a search. Clicking New search will bring you to the details for that search query, shown in Figure 12-2. On the left-hand side is the area where you will build your query, and the right side is where your search results will display after you run the query. To start the query, enter keywords or conditions. For a full list of properties, conditions, and search operators, please see this page: `https://erica.news/SeachProperties`.

Search Keywords and Conditions

Conditions are the most common properties of items. You can select a condition and then add your criteria, and the system will automatically build out your search query for you. However, you could also use any of the conditions listed on the preceding documentation page. To do that, you would enter the property in the keyword field by using this syntax: property name:"value". You could use Boolean search operators such as AND, OR, and NOT to refine your search results.

You will need to capitalize the Boolean search operators for them to work. Conditions are connected to keywords by an AND operator. If you use two or more unique conditions, the system will join them with an AND operator. If you use two or more of the same conditions added to a search query, it will see it as an OR operator.

Tip   Instead of using two of the same search conditions, try to combine them into one condition with multiple criteria.

Multiple values in conditions can be separated by commas or semicolons, which the system will see as an OR operator. Note that these special characters are not searchable: + – = : ! @ # % ^ & ; _ / ? ( ) [ ] { }. You can use only prefix wildcard searches, for example, cat* or set*. Suffix searches (*cat), infix searches (c*t), and substring searches (*cat*) are not supported.

When searching for a property, if the value contains multiple words, use double quotation marks, for example, "multiple words," to indicate that it is part of the same term. If you want to exclude content marked with a particular property value from your search results, place a minus sign before the property's name, for example, -property. Keyword searches are not case sensitive.

Search Locations

Now, let us look at the search locations. The next part of the query tells the search where to look for content. You can choose to search for all areas, meaning across all the previously mentioned content locations in Microsoft 365. You can either search all email inboxes or all SharePoint and OneDrive sites or all Exchange public folders, shown in Figure 12-3.

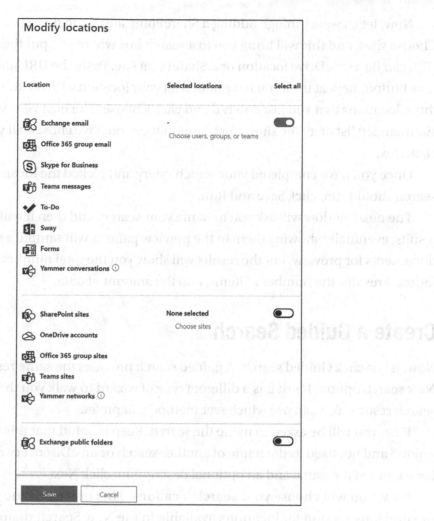

Figure 12-3. *Available search locations*

Additionally, you can select specific locations within these groups. For example, you could choose to search only a single user's email inbox or a particular SharePoint site.

Let us click Choose users, groups, or teams. This click will bring up an option to edit Exchange email locations. Click Choose users, groups, or teams again. Now, it will bring up a search box.

Enter at least three letters of the name of a user group or team and click Enter. A list of values that match your search will appear. Check the boxes next to the items that you want to include in the search and click Choose. This click will bring you to a screen that shows you a list of all the items you chose. Click Choose again. This screen shows you a summary of everything you selected. Click Done. You can see under Selected locations the number of users, groups, or teams you picked.

Now, let us walk through adding a SharePoint site. To do this, click Add site. Click Choose sites, and this will bring you to a search box where you put the site URL. This URL can be a OneDrive location or a SharePoint site. Paste the URL and click the plus button. Repeat until you have added all your locations. Check the boxes next to those locations that you just entered and click Choose. The next view will show you a summarized list of all the sites. Click Done. Once you have chosen all your locations, click Next.

Once you have completed your search query and picked the locations where the search should run, click Save and Run.

The next window will ask you to name your search, and then it will run the search results, eventually showing them in the preview pane. It will sample a subset of the documents for preview, but the results will show you the total number of estimated indexed results, the number of items, and the amount of data.

Create a Guided Search

Now, let us click Guided search. A guided search provides the same results as using the New search option. It just has a different type of wizard to walk you through creating the search results. You can use whichever method you prefer.

First, you will be asked to name the search. Keep in mind that this name must be unique and not used as the name of another search or an eDiscovery case. Once you have entered the name and an optional description, click Next.

Now, you will choose your search locations. This process is the same as that of the previous section for locations available in the New Search dialogue, so I will not repeat it here.

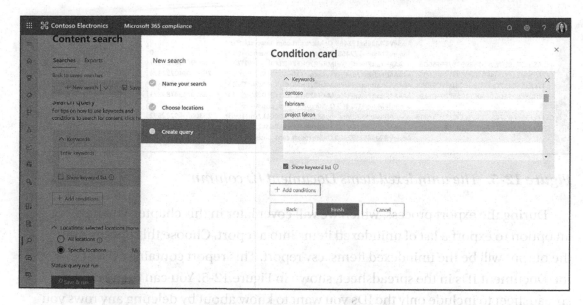

Figure 12-4. *The guided search wizard with a keyword list*

Now, it will ask you to build your query. This process is the same as we described in the previous section. Additionally, you can create a keyword list, shown in Figure 12-4. A keyword list allows you to enter up to 20 keywords or key phrases on each line. The system will build your query for you, putting an OR statement between each one of these keywords. It will represent this as an OR statement in your search query, written as (c:s).

Once you have built your keywords and configured your conditions, click Finish. Suppose any of your conditions are incompatible with the locations chosen previously, such as wanting to use the participant's condition but selecting a SharePoint site. In that case, it will display a warning that you have used filters that will not apply to the specific workload that you specified earlier. Either go back and fix your query or click Continue. Once your search runs, it will show you a list of all your search results, just the same as we described previously.

Search by ID List

The last option is to search by ID list. This option lets you search for specific email messages and other mailbox items using a list of Exchange IDs. To create an ID list search, you submit a comma-separated value or CSV file that identifies the specific mailbox items for which to search. The ID list searches only support mailbox items. We usually use this search option to find messages for follow-up or further investigation. For example, let us say that you want to see specific unindexed items in a search.

	A	B	C	D	E	F	G
1	ExportItem Id	Item Identity	Document ID	Selected	Duplicate	Original Pa	Locati
2		AdeleV@M365x172465.OnMicrosoft.com_unsearchable	0				
3		admin@M365x172465.OnMicrosoft.com_unsearchable	0				
4	482A5B40719D764FD18899997E9F56D5	AAAAAFttaJtPmcdPI/YeJMRHB20HAKHITbCH7V9KvZTK1a:	88197154781877			admin@M	admin
5	482A5B40719D764FD18899997E9F56D5	AAAAADIvdgf5K7dMIy0mvA8cMMMHAG0GSk2/mexEvzi:	253600640232994			AdeleV@N	AdeleV
6	C647CF36A0417CF7DDD3CCBD31C570BB	AAAAAFttaJtPmcdPI/YeJMRHB20HAKHITbCH7V9KvZTK1a:	88197154781874			admin@M	admin
7	FE9B9D9EB898DCC640F72C69CB2F0AEO	AAAAAFttaJtPmcdPI/YeJMRHB20HAKHITbCH7V9KvZTK1a:	88197154781871			admin@M	admin
8		admin@M365x172465.OnMicrosoft.com_unsearchable	0				
9	C647CF36A0417CF7DDD3CCBD31C570BB	AAAAADIvdgf5K7dMIy0mvA8cMMMHAG0GSk2/mexEvzi:	253600640232992			AdeleV@N	AdeleV
10	FE9B9D9EB898DCC640F72C69CB2F0AEO	AAAAADIvdgf5K7dMIy0mvA8cMMMHAG0GSk2/mexEvzi:	253600640232990			AdeleV@N	AdeleV
11		AdeleV@M365x172465.OnMicrosoft.com_unsearchable	0				
12							

Figure 12-5. *The unindexed items Document ID column*

During the export process, which we will cover later in this chapter, you have
an option to export a list of unindexed items into a report. Choose this option, and
the output will be the unindexed items .csv report. This report contains a list of
the Document IDs in the spreadsheet, shown in Figure 12-5. You can then edit the
spreadsheet to include only the IDs you want to know about by deleting any rows you
do not need. Then you can use the search by ID list option to search for those specific
messages and examine them to figure out why they were unindexed items and if they are
relevant to your case.

View Search Results

Now that we have run our search, let us go through the details of how we can view our
search results. To do this, start on the content search page and double-click one of
your saved searches. In just a moment, this will bring up a list of your previewed search
results. You can click an item in the search results to view it or the metadata. You can also
download a copy of the original file.

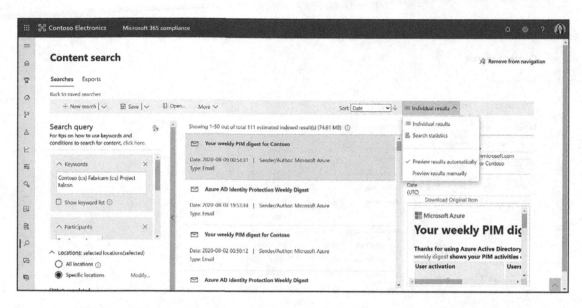

Figure 12-6. *Search results page*

The top gray bar lists other actions you can take from this screen, shown in Figure 12-6. These actions include creating a new search. Click the +New search dropdown to choose either Guided search, New search, or Search by ID List. You could also save the current search if you have modified the search criteria or save it as a new search. You can click Open to open a saved search, which brings up a list of searches from the main page, or you can click More to either export a summary report of the search or export the search results. We will discuss exports in the next section. You can sort the search results by date, type, sender, author, and subject or title in either ascending or descending order. Then, you can stay in the Individual results view or choose Search statistics. Search statistics are beneficial for refining your search, so let us click that.

In the Search statistics view, you can first see a summary of your indexed search results. The overview shows you the different types of locations, such as Exchange mailboxes and SharePoint sites. Within those groups, it shows you how many of these places have hits in your search results. It also shows how many items it found and the size of the results in the locations. For any of these search statistics reports, you can print the item or download the report to a CSV file by clicking the associated icons. Click the Type dropdown and choose Queries.

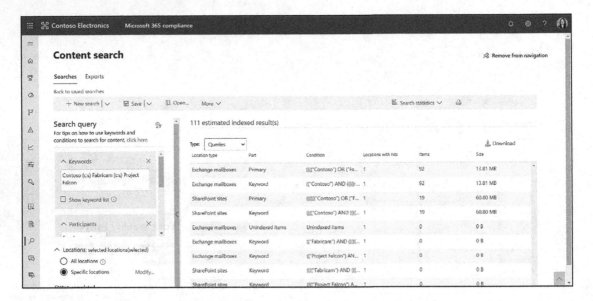

Figure 12-7. *Search query statistics*

This view shows you the exact queries that the system built to search each of the locations, as demonstrated in Figure 12-7. For example, you can see that it searched Exchange mailboxes, and you can see the exact search query used to perform the search. You can see for that search query how many locations had hits, how many items it found, and the size.

If you used any keywords, you could see a line in this report per keyword. Each row shows the query constructed per keyword, so you can see which keywords were most effective. This information helps you decide if you want to remove some keywords or add different keywords. This information also enables you to see if you need to modify your search query to get the results you want.

Now, let us click the Type dropdown and choose Top Locations. This report shows you the estimated search results for different locations. It lists each mailbox and each site as a location. Again, this helps you understand your search results and see if you need to modify your search query to include an entire location rather than searching by keyword or refine it further. Now, let us look at how we can export search results.

Export Search Results

To export search results, click one of your saved searches from the Searches tab. This click opens a pane displaying the details for your search. From this pane, you can click Export results or Export report. Alternatively, you can go to the search results view, click More, and choose either Export report or Export results.

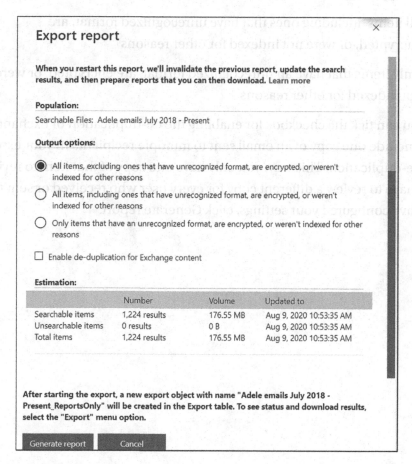

Export report   ×

When you restart this report, we'll invalidate the previous report, update the search results, and then prepare reports that you can then download. Learn more

Population:

Searchable Files: Adele emails July 2018 - Present

Output options:

◉ All items, excluding ones that have unrecognized format, are encrypted, or weren't indexed for other reasons

○ All items, including ones that have unrecognized format, are encrypted, or weren't indexed for other reasons

○ Only items that have an unrecognized format, are encrypted, or weren't indexed for other reasons

☐ Enable de-duplication for Exchange content

Estimation:

	Number	Volume	Updated to
Searchable items	1,224 results	176.55 MB	Aug 9, 2020 10:53:35 AM
Unsearchable items	0 results	0 B	Aug 9, 2020 10:53:35 AM
Total items	1,224 results	176.55 MB	Aug 9, 2020 10:53:35 AM

After starting the export, a new export object with name "Adele emails July 2018 - Present_ReportsOnly" will be created in the Export table. To see status and download results, select the "Export" menu option.

Generate report   Cancel

Figure 12-8. *Export report options*

Let us start by selecting Export report. This selection will bring up a screen of options. The first choice is the Output options, shown in Figure 12-8. Under this heading, you can choose from the following options. Please see the section "Unindexed or Partially Indexed Items" later in this chapter for more information about these items:

- All items, excluding ones that have unrecognized format, are encrypted, or were not indexed for other reasons

- All items, including ones that have unrecognized format, are encrypted, or were not indexed for other reasons

- Only items that have an unrecognized format, are encrypted, or were not indexed for other reasons

Next, you can tick the checkbox for enabling the de-duplication of Exchange content. It will only include one copy of an email sent to multiple recipients in your export when you allow de-duplication. This way, you only have one copy of that item to review, and you do not have to review a different copy for every user who received or sent the email. Once you have configured your settings, click Generate report.

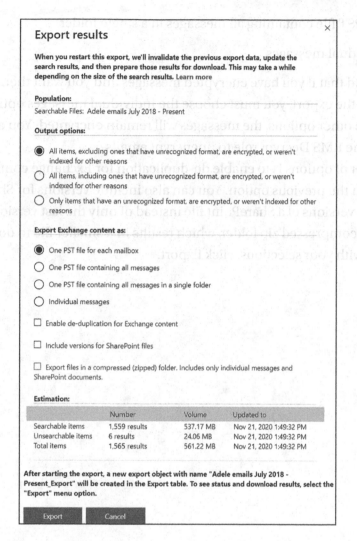

Figure 12-9. *Export results options*

The other export option in our More dropdown menu is Export results. When you export results, you have some additional options to configure your export, shown in Figure 12-9. In addition to Output options, you have options for how to export Exchange content. You can export it as

- One PST file for each mailbox

- One PST file containing all messages

- One PST file containing all messages in a single folder

- Individual messages

Keep in mind that if you have encrypted messages and you want them to be unencrypted in the export, you must choose the Individual messages option. If you select any of the other options, the messages will remain encrypted. You also must have permission to the RMS Decrypt role to unencrypt emails.

Your next set of options is to enable de-duplication for Exchange content, which we just explained in the previous option. You can also include versions for SharePoint files, consisting of all versions of a SharePoint file instead of only the last version. You can also export files in a compressed zip folder, which results in a smaller file to download. Once you are happy with your selections, click Export.

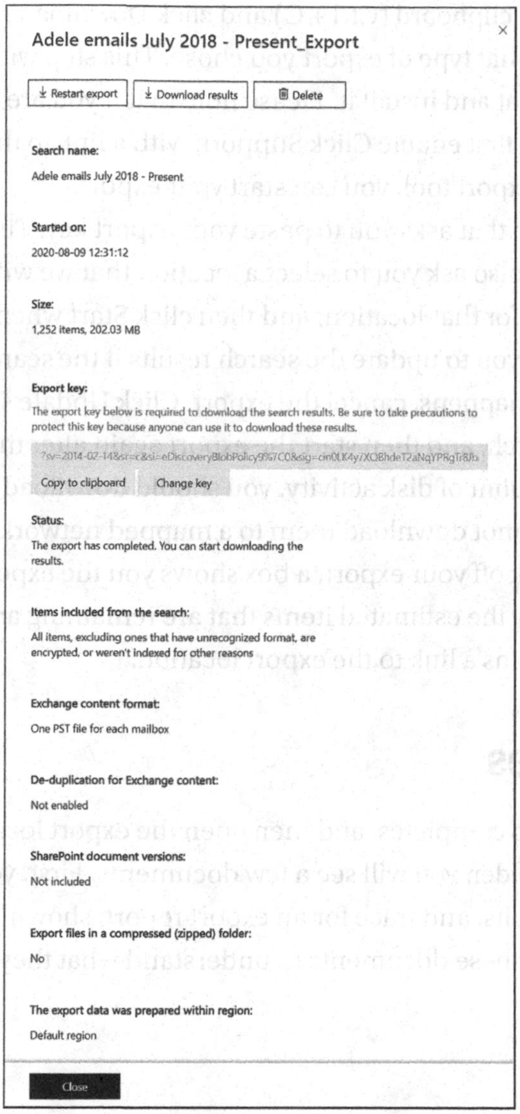

Figure 12-10. *Download export details*

You can now go to the Exports tab in the content search solution and see a list of all the exports that you created through one of those two methods. Go ahead and click one of the exports to view the export details, shown in Figure 12-10. The export details will include summary information about your export and the settings you chose and an export key. This export key is like a password to the temporary Azure location, where your export is stored. Anybody who has this key can download the information, so keep it safe.

Copy that key to the clipboard (Ctrl + C) and click Download report or Download results, depending on what type of export you chose. This step will prompt you to install the export tool, so do that and install it. Please note that if you are using Microsoft Edge, you receive a prompt to first enable Click Support, with a link to the instructions. Once you have installed the export tool, you can start your export.

A screen will pop up that asks you to paste your export key. That is the key that we have just copied. It will also ask you to select a location that we will use to store the download files. Browse for that location, and then click Start when you are ready. Please note that it will prompt you to update the search results if the search results are older than seven days. If this happens, cancel the export. Click Update search results in the details pane for the search, and then start the export again after the results are updated.

Due to the high amount of disk activity, you should download search results to a local disk drive. You cannot download them to a mapped network drive or other network locations. Once you kick off your export, a box shows you the export's progress. This progress bar will display the estimated items that are remaining and the estimated time remaining. It also contains a link to the export location.

View Export Files

Wait until the export job completes, and then open the export location on your computer. Inside this folder, you will see a few documents. First, you will see an export summary, manifest results, and trace for an export report, shown in Figure 12-11. Let us go through each one of these documents to understand what they do.

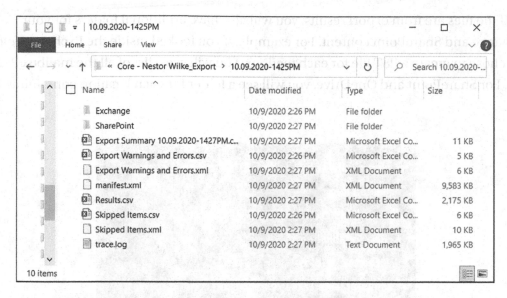

Figure 12-11. Files included in an export download

The export summary is an Excel document that contains an overview of the export. This overview includes information such as the number of searched content sources. It also consists of the number of search results from each content location, the estimated number of items, the actual number of exported items, and the estimated and actual sizes of exported items.

Export warnings and errors will only appear if there was a problem with the download. It contains the error messages and provides the information you need to resolve them.

The export manifest is a file in XML format that contains information about each item included in the search results.

The Results Excel document contains a row with information about each item included in the search results. For email, the results log contains information about each message. For documents in SharePoint and OneDrive for Business, the results log includes information on each file. It also includes the metadata for each file in the export.

The Skipped Items file would have a list of unindexed and partially indexed items if you chose that option when creating the export.

The trace log file has information about the export, including errors. This log is where you will see the details about that error to figure out how to fix it.

If the files are from export results, you will also have additional folders for your Exchange and SharePoint content. For example, if you looked inside the Exchange folder and chose to create a PST file for each mailbox, you will see a list of all the mailbox PST files. For SharePoint and OneDrive, you will see a folder for each location containing the files.

Figure 12-12. *A PST file exported from content search and then imported into Outlook*

If you import one of the exported PST files into Outlook, you can see each PST file's structure. I get asked a lot by business users what the folder structure means, so here is an explanation of each folder. Note that this mailbox has archive enabled, so you see a (MainArchive) and (Primary) mailbox. Users without archive enabled will only have a (Primary) folder that will contain the three following categories:

1. **Recoverable Items**: Litigation Hold and In-Place Hold use the Recoverable Items folder to preserve Exchange content. The system hides the Recoverable Items folder from the default view of Outlook, Outlook on the Web, and other email clients.

2. **Top of Information Store**: This folder contains user mailbox folders. This folder is what end users see when they use Outlook.

3. **Search Folders**: A search folder is a virtual folder that provides a view of all email items that match specific search criteria. For example, the Unread Mail Search Folder enables you to view all unread messages in one folder, even though someone might keep the emails in different folders across their mailbox. This folder will only contain information if the user utilizes the Search Folders feature. If they do, you will see a list of all their saved searches.

Next, let us examine the Recoverable Items folder. Administrators use the Recoverable Items folder, and the end user does not see it. By default, when a user deletes a message from a folder other than the Deleted Items folder, the message is moved to the Deleted Items folder. When a user soft deletes an item (by pressing Shift + Delete) or deletes an item from the Deleted Items folder, the message is moved to the Recoverable Items folder, thereby disappearing from the user's view.

The system retains items in the Recoverable Items folder for the deleted item retention period configured on the user's mailbox database. By default, the system sets the deleted item retention period to 14 days for mailbox databases, but this can be increased to 30 days by the Exchange admin.

The Recoverable Items folder contains the following subfolders used to store deleted items in various states and facilitate Litigation Hold and In-Place Hold. The export PST will only contain folders that have objects. So your export might not show every one of these folders:

- **Deletions**: Items removed from the Deleted Items folder or soft-deleted from other folders are moved to the Deletions subfolder and are visible to the user when using the Recover Deleted Items feature in Outlook and Outlook on the Web. By default, items reside in this folder until the deleted item retention period passes or the mailbox expires.

- **Purges**: When a user deletes an item from the Recoverable Items folder using the Recover Deleted Items tool in Outlook and Outlook on the Web, the item is moved to the Purges folder. Items that exceed the deleted item retention period configured on the mailbox also

move to the Purges folder. Items in this folder are not visible to
users if they use the Recover Deleted Items tool. When the mailbox
assistant processes the mailbox, it removes items in the Purges folder
from the mailbox database. When you place the mailbox user on legal
hold, the mailbox assistant does not purge items in this folder.

- **Versions**: When you put a user on legal hold, mailbox items must be
  protected from tampering or modification by the user or a process.
  This system accomplishes this task by using a copy-on-write method.
  When a user or a process changes specific properties of a mailbox
  item, it saves a copy of the original item in the Versions folder
  before it commits the change. The system repeats this process for
  subsequent changes. After you remove the hold, it terminates copies
  in the Versions folder.

The Top of Information Store contains the folders that end users see and use every
day. The following folders could be listed in this location:

- **Archive**: A feature to keep your Inbox clear of messages you have
  already answered or acted upon. If you use the "Archive" button in
  Outlook, it moves items to this location.

- **Deleted Items**: The system moves items that you delete to the
  Deleted Items folder. The system does not delete these items until a
  person or process empties this folder.

- **Drafts**: Outlook automatically saves all unfinished messages for you.
  By default, it saves incomplete messages to your Drafts folder every
  three minutes.

- **Inbox**: The location where Outlook sends new emails.

- **Journal**: This folder will not appear unless the user utilizes this
  feature. Journal automatically records actions that you choose related
  to specific contacts and puts the Timeline view's activities.

- **Notes**: This folder will not appear unless the user utilizes this feature.
  Microsoft Outlook provides small digital notes that visually resemble
  traditional sticky notes.

- **Outbox**: This folder rarely appears in exports. The Microsoft Outlook Outbox is a temporary holding folder for outgoing messages composed within the program.

- **RSS Feeds**: This folder will not appear unless the user utilizes this feature. RSS Feeds are an easy way to stay up to date with your favorite websites, such as blogs or online magazines.

- **Sent Items**: The Sent Items folder contains copies of all the messages the user has sent to others.

Now that we have covered the happy path of content search, let us investigate how we remediate unindexed or partially indexed items.

Unindexed or Partially Indexed Items

Customers frequently ask me why they have unindexed or partially indexed items appearing in their searches. There are some common reasons why an item could be unindexed or partially indexed.

First, the file type is unrecognized or unsupported for indexing; second, messages have an attached file without a valid handler, such as an image or a video file. This reason is by far the most common cause of partially indexed items because people share images all the time in emails. Other reasons include

- An indexing error occurred for a specific file.

- Too many files are attached to the email message.

- A file attached to an email message is too large.

- A file is encrypted with non-Microsoft technologies.

- A file is password protected.

If you want to understand how many unindexed items you might have in your organization or understand your exposure, here is a process you can follow. Partially indexed items are Exchange mailbox items and documents in SharePoint and OneDrive for Business sites that, for some reason, were not wholly indexed for search.

Run a search and prepare an export by choosing Export ➤ Results. Select the option Only items that have an unrecognized format, are encrypted, or were not indexed for other reasons. Run that export and download the content.

This download will consist of the unindexed items .csv file. This CSV file contains fields called error tags and error properties. The error tags and error properties fields will give you the information you need to know about the error, and it will help you narrow down why it is happening. Also, remember there are fields in the CSV file called error type and error message. Those are legacy fields, so you can just ignore them. Investigate error tags and error properties instead.

Many times, these errors are going to be images or videos attached to an email. The body, the subject, and the email properties are still indexed and viewable in your search. The error indicates that it does not know what is in that image file, so it is partially indexed.

You can examine each row to determine if the item is worth remediation. You can use this spreadsheet to run a search by ID list, which will return the items for further investigation.

Please consider using the Advanced eDiscovery solution, which conducts additional processing on items to resolve some of these errors if you are concerned about the number of unindexed or partially indexed items.

In this chapter, we learned how to use the content search solution in the Compliance Center. We covered how to create a new search using three different methods, how to view search results, and how to export content. We also learned the locations you can search and how to remediate partially indexed items.

In the next chapter, we will discuss how to use Core eDiscovery for litigation and internal investigations. Core eDiscovery builds on the content search functionality and adds additional features.

CHAPTER 13

Core eDiscovery

Organizations use eDiscovery for many purposes. One is for litigation, when you need to gather information or evidence for a legal case. People also use eDiscovery for internal investigations, such as employee misconduct or another matter where you need content to understand what happened. You might need to understand the scope and impact of data leaks, such as when someone shares a confidential document accidentally and you need to locate all the copies. Finally, another purpose is to find customer data for a data subject request or similar privacy request.

There are two versions of eDiscovery available in Microsoft 365. The first is Core eDiscovery. This tool allows you to accomplish the basic requirements of the scenarios listed in the preceding text. You can put custodians on hold, which will prevent their information from being modified or deleted for the duration of the case until you release them from the hold. Next, you can collect case data by performing a search across all Microsoft 365 data. This search functionality is the same content search functionality that we discussed in Chapter 12. Finally, you can export that content in various ways into a different eDiscovery system either for review and analysis or some other purpose.

The second tool in Microsoft 365 is Advanced eDiscovery. Advanced eDiscovery builds on the capabilities available in Core eDiscovery, but adds more powerful tools around processing data, searching, running pre-case analysis and analytics, using machine learning to determine relevancy, and more. These tools reduce the cost and time needed to review the information in a case. If you have access to Advanced eDiscovery through your licensing, I recommend looking at that tool instead of Core eDiscovery. We cover Advanced eDiscovery in Chapter 14.

© Erica Toelle 2021

E. Toelle, *Microsoft 365 Compliance*, https://doi.org/10.1007/978-1-4842-5778-4_13

Licensing and Permissions

Core eDiscovery is available with the following licenses:

- Office 365 E3

- Office 365 E5

- Microsoft 365 E3

- Microsoft 365 E5

- Exchange Online Archiving (for Exchange data only)

To use Core eDiscovery, you will need to be a member of either the eDiscovery Administrator or eDiscovery Manager compliance role group. eDiscovery managers can view and manage the Core eDiscovery cases they create or those that include them as a member. If another eDiscovery manager makes a case but does not add a second eDiscovery manager as a member of that case, the second eDiscovery manager will not be able to view or open the case from the Core eDiscovery page in the Compliance Center.

eDiscovery administrators can perform all case management tasks that an eDiscovery manager can do. Additionally, an eDiscovery administrator can view all the cases listed on the Core eDiscovery page, manage any case in the organization after they add themselves as a member of the case, and access and export case data for any case in the organization.

In general, you can add most people in your organization to the eDiscovery Manager role group. Because of the broad scope of access, an organization should have a limited number of eDiscovery administrators. I also recommend creating custom role groups if you have more than a few eDiscovery managers. For example, if you have different eDiscovery managers for the United States vs. Canada, create a custom role group for each geography. We covered how to create custom role groups in Chapter 1.

Create a Case

To access Core eDiscovery, you will need to be a member of one of the role groups mentioned in the preceding text before it appears in your view of the Microsoft 365 Compliance Center. In the left-hand navigation, expand eDiscovery and click Core eDiscovery. This click will bring you to the Core eDiscovery landing page shown in Figure 13-1.

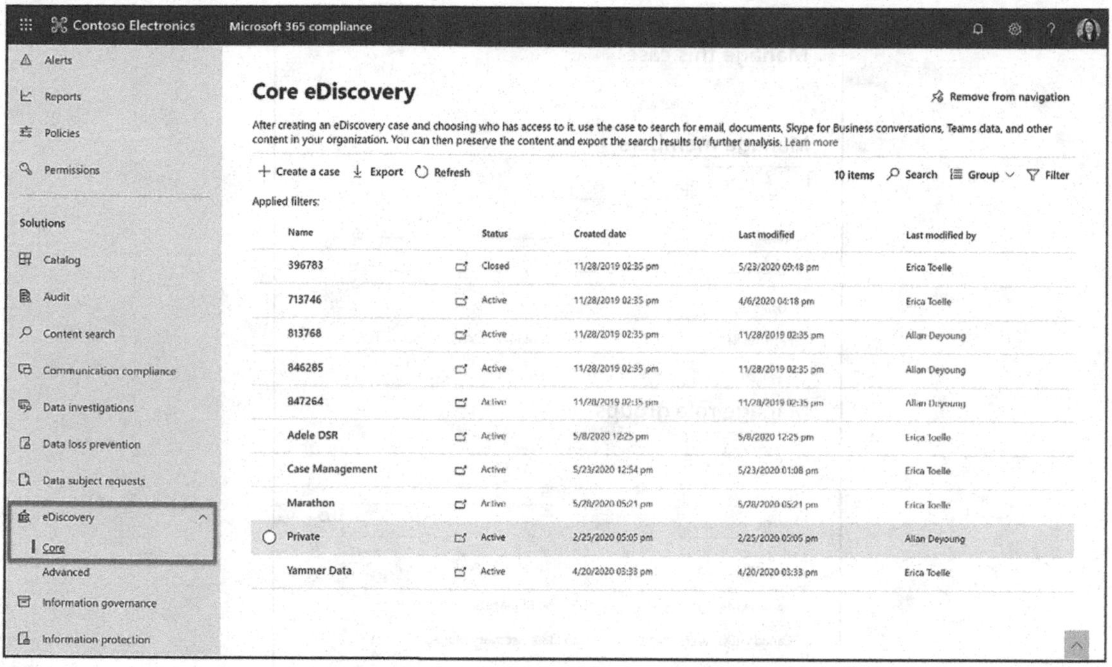

Figure 13-1. *Core eDiscovery case list*

Here you can see a list of all of the cases in your organization; the status, whether they are active or closed; the case creation date; the date they were last modified; and then who last modified the cases. Remember that eDiscovery administrators will see all the organization's cases, while eDiscovery managers will only see the cases where they are a member.

To create a new case, click Create a case. A dialogue box will appear where you can add a case name and a case description. Keep in mind that the case name must be unique and cannot be the same as any saved content search, Advanced eDiscovery case, Data Investigation case, or Data Subject Request. Click Save to create the case.

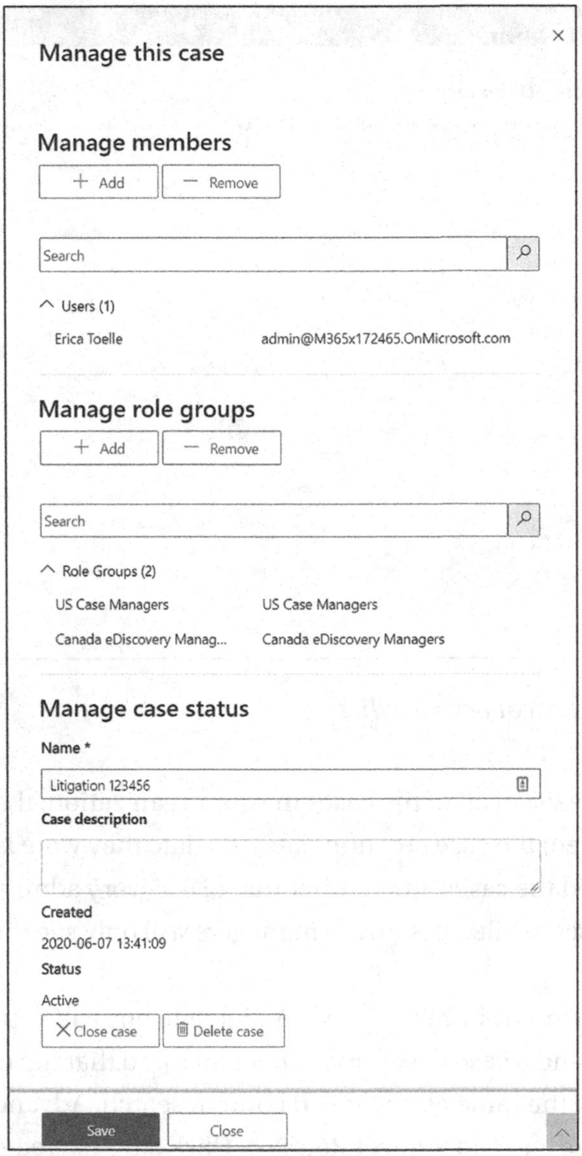

Figure 13-2. *Manage this case screen*

This click will bring you back to the list of all cases. To access the area to manage case settings, click the case name. Manage this case options will appear in a sidebar, shown in Figure 13-2. Here you can manage case members or manage role groups for the case. You can change the name or the description, and you can close or delete the case. Once you have made your changes, click Save.

Again, it brings you back to the list of all cases. To access the case details, click the Open case button, which looks like a square with the arrow to the case name's right. The case will open in a new tab.

When you open a specific Core eDiscovery case, it will bring you to the Home tab. The Home tab displays some basic information about the case. This information includes the case name; the case creation date; the status, whether it is active or closed; and a description.

In the next section, we will investigate how to apply a legal hold on custodians and locations to ensure content related to the case cannot be deleted or modified.

Place Custodians and Locations on Hold

Now, let us look at legal holds. Holds allow you to preserve data related to the Core eDiscovery case. When you place data on hold, it cannot be modified or deleted. You might put data on hold to preserve it for a legal case or an internal investigation. Please do not use legal holds to retain information as a part of a normal business process. Instead, use retention labels and policies, which we cover in Chapter 8.

You can put custodian information on hold, such as an individual's email mailbox, OneDrive, and Microsoft Teams chats. You can also put locations on hold, such as a SharePoint site, a group mailbox, or an entire Microsoft Team.

To create a hold, click the Holds tab. Here you will see a list of any existing case holds and the date they were last modified. Click the Create button. This click will bring you to a wizard where it will ask you to name your hold. Enter a descriptive name and a friendly description. Click Next.

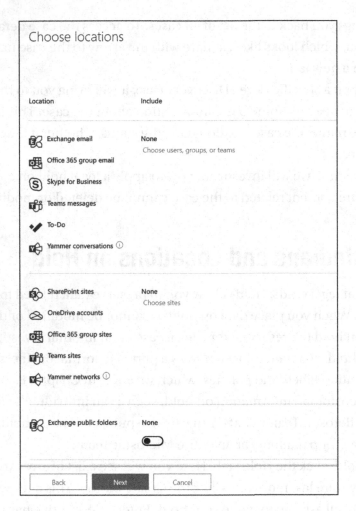

Figure 13-3. *Choose locations for the hold*

Now you can choose users and locations to place on hold (Figure 13-3). If you have not already, please look at Chapter 1, in the section titled "Where Microsoft 365 Stores Content." It is essential to understand this information to select the correct options in the following. You have three groups of options:

1. **Users, groups, or teams**: This option is where you select Exchange email locations. Remember that Microsoft 365 stores a copy of Teams chats for compliance purposes in Exchange.

2. **Sites**: This option is where you select SharePoint locations. Microsoft stores all files in Microsoft 365 in SharePoint. Remember that under the covers, OneDrive is a SharePoint site.

3. **Exchange public folders**: You can only choose to put all Exchange public folders on hold.

First, let us choose a user, group, or team to add to the hold. To do this, we will click Choose users, groups, or teams. This click will open a dialogue box that says Exchange email. Click Choose users, groups, or teams again. Here you will need to type a minimum of three characters to get a mailbox list.

You can add people using a distribution list or a mail-enabled security group, and it will expand so that it creates an in-place hold for the mailboxes in the list or group. It will only include the mailboxes that are currently members of the list or group in the hold. Mailboxes added to or removed from the group or list later will not be added or removed to or from this hold.

Check the boxes next to the individual users, distribution lists, or Microsoft 365 group mailboxes that you want to include. Click Choose. You will see a list of all users, groups, or teams that you added on the next screen. Click Done.

Next, let's add some SharePoint site locations. Click Choose sites. Click Choose sites again. On the screen that appears, you will enter the URL for the SharePoint site or OneDrive account that you would like to add, one by one. You will need to get this URL from some other source, such as browsing to the SharePoint site to copy the URL or by running a PowerShell script to generate this list. Enter the URL for one site, click the plus button, and repeat until you have added all the sites and OneDrive accounts. Click Choose and then Done.

You also have the option to put all Exchange public folders on hold. You cannot choose specific public folders to put on hold. You must put them all on hold or nothing. This situation is the same for Yammer networks. You can set your entire Yammer network on legal hold, but you cannot put individual Yammer groups on hold.

Note   When users add new documents and emails to the hold locations, the system will put them on hold.

When you have chosen all the locations, click Next. On the next screen, you can create a query to narrow down the items in your hold. As an example, you could search for specific keywords that occur in those locations. Or you could limit the hold to a particular date range. Think of the locations as deciding what areas you are going to search in your environment, and the query and conditions narrow down the items within those locations that you want to put on hold. If you are going to put everything in all those locations on hold, you can leave this query blank and click Next.

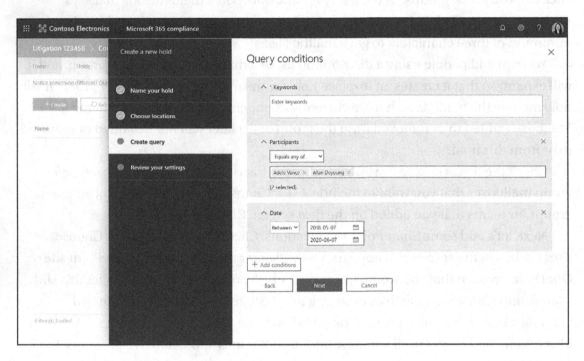

Figure 13-4. *Query conditions for a hold*

However, if you want to narrow the hold's scope, you can do that by either entering keywords to search for or conditions. The conditions available are the same as the ones we went over in Chapter 12. Let us use this example as a reminder. We want only to find emails where the participants are Adele or Allen, which were sent or received between May of 2018 and June of 2020, shown in Figure 13-4. We accomplish this query by using the participants condition and selecting Adele and Allen. We would then add the date condition and set a date range of May 2018 to June 2020. Once you complete the query, click Next. Now review the hold settings and click Create this hold.

The system sends you back to the Holds tab. You can see the details of your hold by double-clicking the hold name. The details help you check that the hold results are what you expected and the hold was applied successfully. The details include the following information:

- The hold description

- How many mailboxes and sites are in the hold

- Hold statistics, including the number of items and the volume of data, and when the statistics were last run

- The date the hold was last modified

- Who last modified the hold

- Whether the hold is on or off

You could also edit or delete the hold from the details screen. When you finish with the information, click Close.

In the next section, we will search for content related to the case to export it for a relevancy review or other purposes.

Search for Case Content

Holds preserve content while a search discovers content relevant to your use case. A search provides the evidence or content you will later use to investigate or export out of Microsoft 365.

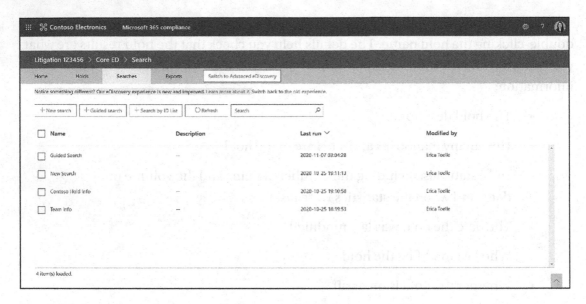

Figure 13-5. *A list of searches in a Core eDiscovery case*

To run a search, click the Searches tab in your eDiscovery case. This click brings you to a screen that shows you all the saved searches for the case, their descriptions, the date they were last run, and who last modified them, shown in Figure 13-5.

This search UI and features are the same as the content search solution. Please see Chapter 12 for an in-depth discussion on performing a search. I am only going to review the basics in this section quickly.

There are three types of searches available, listed in the following. We will go through each one of these to explain how they work:

1. New search

2. Guided search

3. Search by ID list

First, we will create a new search. To do that, click the New search button. This click will bring you to a screen where you can create a new search query. This functionality works exactly like the search queries that we just did in the previous section and queries in the content search solution. In this case, we can add keywords, a list of keywords, and our usual list of conditions.

Additionally, we can select locations for the search. We can search for the following:

- **All locations**: Searches everything in our Microsoft 365 environment.
- **Only search locations we put on hold**: Scopes the search to only locations on hold in our case.
- **Specific locations**: Choose the locations to search.

For example, I often see people creating one search query for email mailboxes and a different, second search query for SharePoint and OneDrive files. This method is because you usually use other conditions and search queries for different types of data. Separating locations with different queries allows you to get more specific, making it easier to see how to refine your queries.

People will also often create a broader search than the hold locations. This decision is because they want to err on including too much information in the investigation. Including extra information reduces the risk of missing content in discovery.

Once you set up your query, click Save and Run. It will ask you to name your search query, and then the search will appear in the list on the Searches tab.

Now let us create a new guided search. To create a guided search, click the Guided search button. A wizard will pop up that asks you to name your search and provide a description. Next, you will choose the locations. You can choose to apply the search to all areas or only places on hold or select specific locations. Choose your options and locations and click Next.

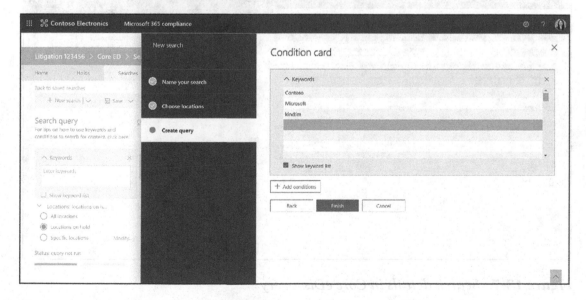

Figure 13-6. *Use a keyword list in a Core eDiscovery guided search*

Now we are going to create our search query for the guided search. Here we have the option to use a keyword list, shown in Figure 13-6. A keyword list allows you to enter one keyword or keyword phrase on each line. Core eDiscovery will build out the query where each line is an "OR" statement. The result of placing one keyword per line would be a query like keyword one OR keyword two OR keyword phrase three. In addition to adding keywords or a keyword list, you can add conditions as usual. When you complete the query, click Finish.

Lastly, we can use search by ID list. We covered this option in depth in Chapter 12, so we will not repeat the instructions here.

You can also perform bulk actions on your searches. To do this, select the checkbox next to multiple searches. A box will appear with the following options:

- Delete selected searches

- Edit locations

- Edit conditions

- Search statistics

- Export results

- Export report

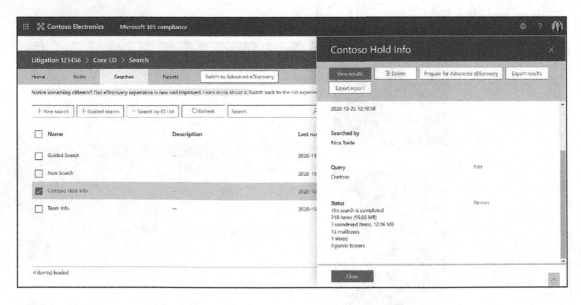

Figure 13-7. *Search details in Core eDiscovery*

Now that we have reviewed all the options to create a new search, let us talk about the search results preview. From the list of searches, click the name of a search. A window appears that contains information about the search, shown in Figure 13-7. The status details give us an idea if our search results returned what we expected. You can see the search description and the date the search was last run. You can also view the name of the person who ran the search and the search query. Under Search statistics, you can see whether the search is complete or in progress, the number of items and volume of information, and the number of mailboxes, sites, and public folders in the search.

Along the top of the box, you see buttons for the following:

- **View results**: Brings you to a page displaying the search results.

- **Delete**: Delete the search.

- **Prepare for Advanced eDiscovery**: This button does not do anything. It is a legacy feature that they should remove from the UI.

- **Export results**: Create an export of all search results.

- **Export report**: Create a summary report of the search results.

We will cover the last two export options in the next section of this chapter.

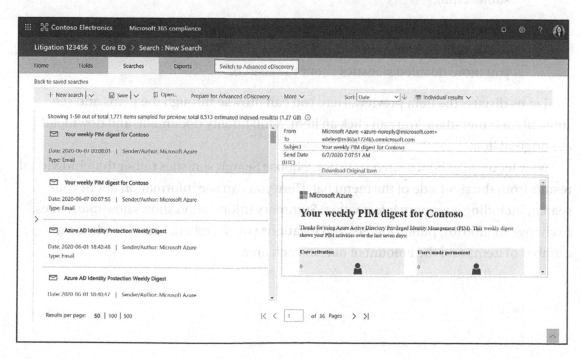

Figure 13-8. *View search results in Core eDiscovery*

Click the View results button. The next screen shows a random sample of the preview items, shown in Figure 13-8. On the left side, you will see your search query. You can choose to modify the query here if the search preview results are not what you expect. Click the "<" symbol to collapse this pane. Along the top, you have some options:

- **New search**: Choose from the three search options described in the preceding text.

- **Save or Save as**: Allows you to save the current search or save any changes as a new search.

- **Open**: Open a different saved search.

- **Prepare for Advanced eDiscovery**: Ignore this option; it does not do anything.

- **More ➤ Export report**: Create a summary report of the search results.

- **More ➤ Export results**: Create an export of all search results.

- **Sort** the results by date, document type, sender author, or subject title.

- **View individual results or search statistics**. Individual results are the default view and show the individual files. Search statistics show you more detailed statistics about the search.

Let us discuss the item preview. Here you can browse through the items and see some of their metadata. You can click an item, a full fidelity document, and download the original item.

Now let us talk about search statistics. Choose Search statistics rather than Individual results from the right side of the menu bar. Here you can see information about your search, including summary information. Summary information shows how many sites, Exchange mailboxes, public folders, and locations you searched. It also displays the number of items and the amount of data in each area.

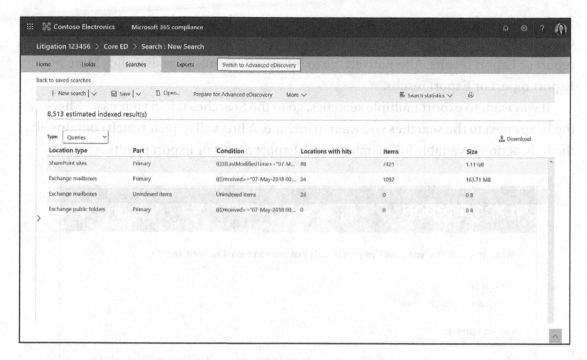

Figure 13-9. *Search statistics for each query*

By choosing the Type dropdown, you can also see the queries you used and the individual hits, items, and size for each query. This view, shown in Figure 13-9, is beneficial for refining your queries to get the search results that you want.

Finally, you can see the individual sites and mailboxes with the most items in the top locations. This view displays how many items are in each location and the total size or volume. You can also download any of these search statistics reports to a CSV file for further analysis.

Finally, when you are happy with your search results, click More. Here you have two export options. First, you can export a report of the results, which is a summary. Second, you can export all your results. We will cover both these options in the next section.

Export Core eDiscovery Data

Core eDiscovery allows you to get content out of Microsoft 365 through an export. These are two types of exports available in Core eDiscovery. First, you can export content from a single search. Second, you use one export for multiple searches in your case at the same time. You can export all the content or a summary report about the content for both export types.

Let us start by exporting content from a single search. Go to the Searches tab in your Core eDiscovery case. Click the case name. From the hold details screen, click Export report or Export results. Alternatively, go to the search results page and click More ➤ Export report or Export results.

If you want to export multiple searches, go to the Searches tab in your case. Check the boxes next to the searches you want to include. A box will appear which contains all the bulk actions available for searches. Click Export report or Export results.

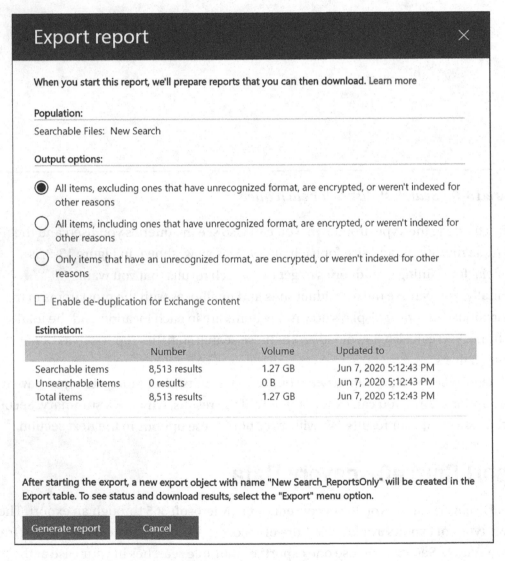

Figure 13-10. *Export a report in Core eDiscovery*

Let us start by choosing Export report from one of the preceding options. A window pops up that allows you to configure your report options, shown in Figure 13-10. First, under the Population heading, we can see the searches that we included in the export. Next, we have three choices for what information to include in our export report under Output options:

1. All items, excluding ones that have unrecognized format, are encrypted, or were not indexed for other reasons

2. All items, including ones that have unrecognized format, are encrypted, or were not indexed for other reasons

3. Only items that have an unrecognized format, are encrypted, or weren't indexed for other reasons

As you can see, the main difference between these options is how we handle files with an unrecognized format, are encrypted, or were not indexed for other reasons. We cover these items in depth in Chapter 12, in the "Unindexed or Partially Indexed Items" section. As a reminder, the system could not index these items for some reason, so the system cannot read the file contents.

You will need to decide if you are concerned about unindexed items for your scenario. If you are unsure if they matter, I recommend choosing the preceding option #3 to get a list of the files and their metadata. You can then examine the list to see if the items are related to your case.

Our last option is to enable the de-duplication of Exchange content. This option will remove duplicate emails, such as when there are multiple people on an email thread. If you do not check this box, each participant in the thread will have a copy of every email in their mailbox. If you check it, the system will include only one copy of that email in the export.

The last section on the page is an estimation of information included in the export report. This information includes searchable items, unsearchable items, and total items, including the number, the volume, and the date of the search results. When you are happy with your settings, click Generate report.

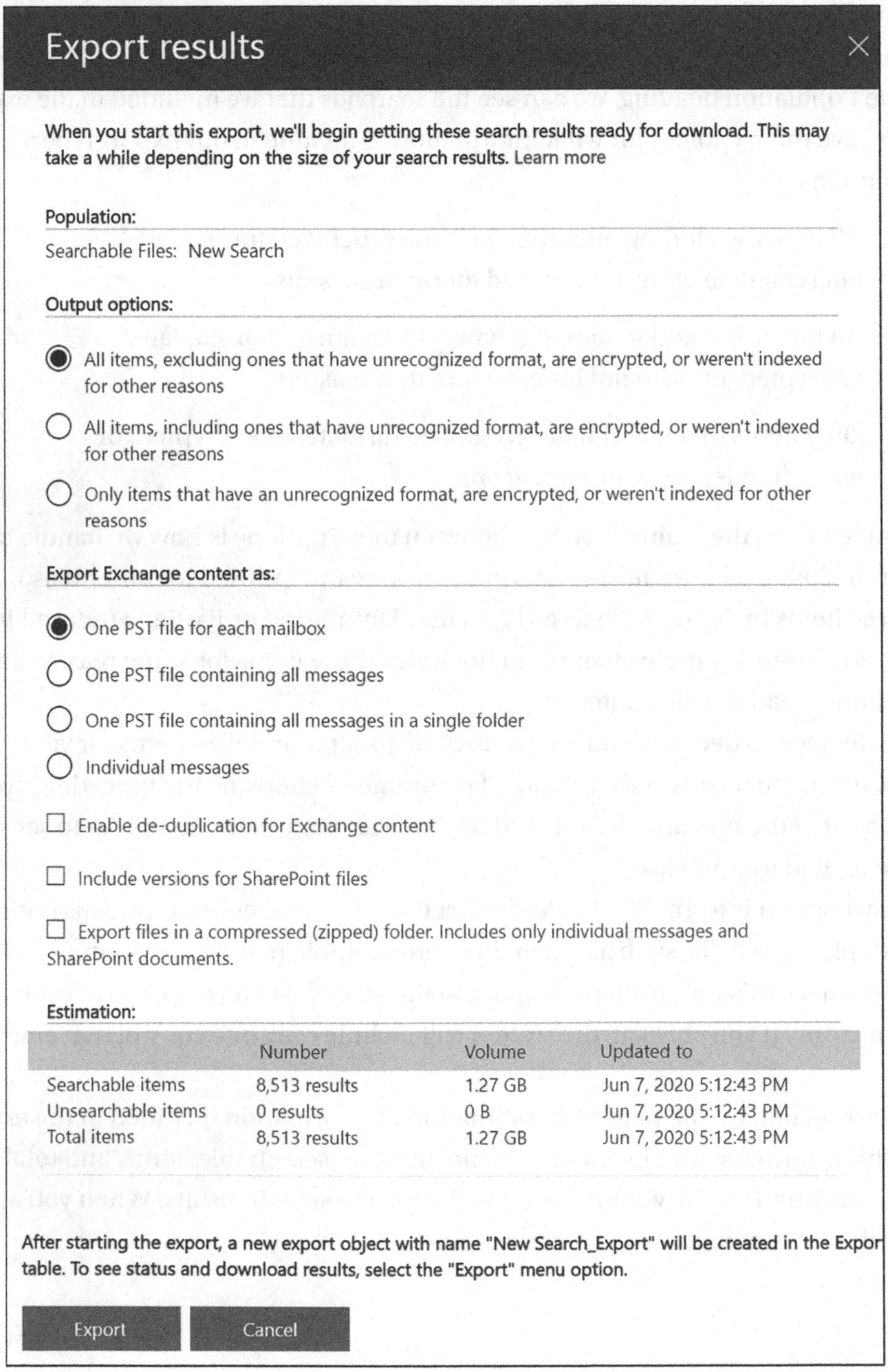

Export results   ✕

When you start this export, we'll begin getting these search results ready for download. This may take a while depending on the size of your search results. Learn more

Population:

Searchable Files: New Search

Output options:

◉ All items, excluding ones that have unrecognized format, are encrypted, or weren't indexed for other reasons

○ All items, including ones that have unrecognized format, are encrypted, or weren't indexed for other reasons

○ Only items that have an unrecognized format, are encrypted, or weren't indexed for other reasons

Export Exchange content as:

◉ One PST file for each mailbox

○ One PST file containing all messages

○ One PST file containing all messages in a single folder

○ Individual messages

☐ Enable de-duplication for Exchange content

☐ Include versions for SharePoint files

☐ Export files in a compressed (zipped) folder. Includes only individual messages and SharePoint documents.

Estimation:

	Number	Volume	Updated to
Searchable items	8,513 results	1.27 GB	Jun 7, 2020 5:12:43 PM
Unsearchable items	0 results	0 B	Jun 7, 2020 5:12:43 PM
Total items	8,513 results	1.27 GB	Jun 7, 2020 5:12:43 PM

After starting the export, a new export object with name "New Search_Export" will be created in the Expor table. To see status and download results, select the "Export" menu option.

    Export   Cancel

Figure 13-11. Export results options in Core eDiscovery

Our other option is Export results, which exports all the files included in the search. Figure 13-11 shows this screen. The information under Population and Output options is the same as described in the preceding text. There is a new section called Export Exchange content as. Under this heading, we have a few options:

1. One PST file for each mailbox

2. One PST file containing all messages

3. One PST file containing all messages in a single folder

Usually, this option will depend on how you will use the files after export, especially if you are going to import them into another system. They will usually be a format that you need to use to get the content into the other eDiscovery system successfully.

Next, you can enable or disable de-duplication for Exchange content. This option is the same as described in the preceding text. You also can choose whether to include versions for SharePoint files. Otherwise, it will only include the latest version. Lastly, you can choose to export data into a compressed zipped folder. This option reduces the download size but will only have individual messages and SharePoint documents, not PST files. Finally, the estimation statistics are the same as in the preceding text. When you are happy with these settings, click Export.

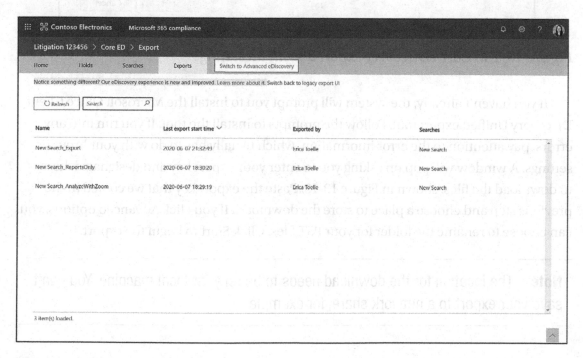

Figure 13-12. *The list of exports in Core eDiscovery*

You can view your list of exports in the Exports tab of your Core eDiscovery case, shown in Figure 13-12. These exports will work for 14 days, after which it will ask you to update the search and restart the export to make sure you have the latest information included.

To download the export, click the name of one of the exports. This click will open a window that helps you to start the export. This window will include information about your export, like the search name, when you started the export, the size of the export, and the export key, which you're going to need in the next step. Copy that to your clipboard. It'll show you the status as well as any error details. And it'll remind you of a summary of the settings you chose for the export. Click Download results.

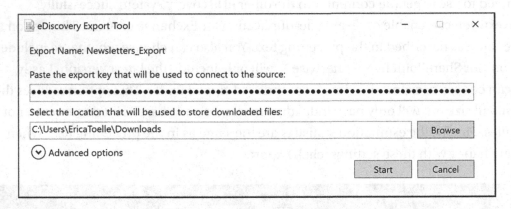

Figure 13-13. *Core eDiscovery export download settings*

If you haven't already, the system will prompt you to install the Microsoft Office Client Discovery Unified export tool. Follow the prompts to install the tool. If you run into any errors, pay attention to the error information, which usually has to do with your browser settings. A window will pop up asking you to enter your export key and designate where to download the files, shown in Figure 13-13. Paste the export key that we copied in the previous step and choose a place to store the download. If you click Advanced options, you can choose to rename the folder for your PST files. Click Start to begin the export.

Note   The location for the download needs to be on your local machine. You can't save your export to a network share, for example.

The export tool opens a window that shows you the status of your export. This status includes how many items are in the export and how many items remain. It also has an estimate of the time remaining and the speed. Let the process run until it's complete. Once the export completes, open the export folder to view the files. The next section reviews the contents of this folder.

Export Results

Remember that we have two types of exports: the results export and a summary report. If you download a summary report only, you would see

- The export summary

- A manifest

- The results

- A trace file

If you ran a results export, in addition to those files, you'd see folders for Exchange and SharePoint, which contain your data. Let us look at each one of these files and see what they include. An example export is shown in Figure 13-14.

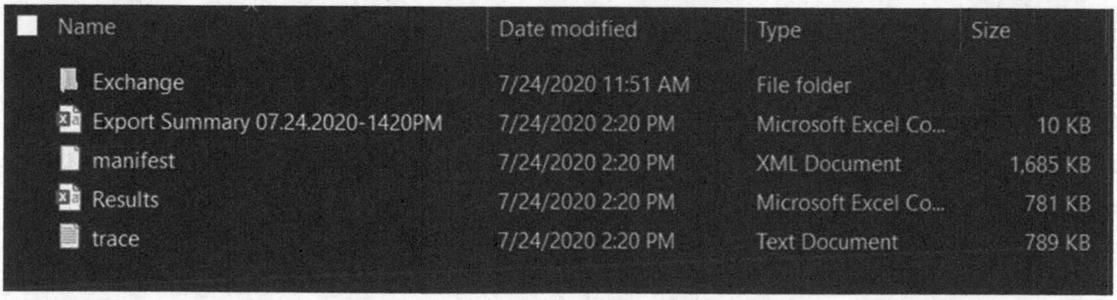

Name	Date modified	Type	Size
Exchange	7/24/2020 11:51 AM	File folder	
Export Summary 07.24.2020-1420PM	7/24/2020 2:20 PM	Microsoft Excel Co...	10 KB
manifest	7/24/2020 2:20 PM	XML Document	1,685 KB
Results	7/24/2020 2:20 PM	Microsoft Excel Co...	781 KB
trace	7/24/2020 2:20 PM	Text Document	789 KB

Figure 13-14. The file and folder structure of a results export

First is the export summary. This summary will show you essential information about your export, including the number of locations, estimated items from the locations and size, folders, list items, and then a manifest of every place included in the export, the number of items, the size, and so on. This report can be useful if you want to get more detailed statistics about your export before spending the time to download all the individual items.

Next, we have the manifest. The manifest is an XML representation of your data, and you can use it to import files into another eDiscovery system.

Then, we have a results spreadsheet. It contains information about each item, including the item's unique identifier, whether it is a duplicate, and all the file's metadata about the item. This inventory can help you double-check your export and make sure it contains what you would like.

Finally, we have the trace file. This file is a log for your export. If you get any errors or anything unusual, you can look here in the trace file to figure out what is going on and solve it.

Next, if you export the results, you will have a folder for Exchange and another for SharePoint. If you click into the Exchange folder, you will see a list of your files. These may be structured as one PST for each mailbox, one PST file for all emails, or all PST files in one folder, depending on your export settings.

If you look at the SharePoint folder, it will have one subfolder for each site and additional site subfolders for each library.

This chapter discussed why you would want to use the Core eDiscovery functionality instead of other discover and respond tools in the Compliance Center. Then we talked about creating a new case, putting items and locations on legal hold, searching for information to add it to a case, and then exporting the results of those searches.

In the next chapter, we will dive into Advanced eDiscovery, which has many useful tools for reviewing your search results to cull the data. You are only exporting data relevant to your case, and you have additional tools to add locations more efficiently, such as viewing a list of teams where the custodian is a member. We can also use machine learning to search for themes in our case, as a part of early case analysis or to develop a relevancy model.

CHAPTER 14

Advanced eDiscovery

Advanced eDiscovery can help your organization in a few ways. First is to respond to litigation, meaning there is a legal matter, for example, a civil action or dispute. These suits require an evidence and information discovery process. The second is freedom of information requests when a citizen requests information from a government organization. Another reason is to comply with the European General Data Protection Regulation (GDPR) or California Consumer Privacy Act (CCPA) data subject requests (DSRs) from people outside your organization. These requests require you to let these people know what personal data you have about them. Advanced eDiscovery can also help with other types of internal investigations or any situation where you want to search for information in Microsoft 365, review it for relevancy to your situation, and export the results. It is a much more powerful tool than Core eDiscovery or content search.

This chapter will focus on litigation because it covers all the available features in Advanced eDiscovery. The other scenarios mentioned in the preceding text utilize only some of the features. For example, to respond to a data subject request, you would not use the legal hold and custodian communication features but would rely heavily on search, review sets, and exports. Table 14-1 explains which sections of this chapter you should read to accomplish your scenario.

© Erica Toelle 2021
E. Toelle, *Microsoft 365 Compliance*, https://doi.org/10.1007/978-1-4842-5778-4_14

Table 14-1. *Which chapter sections you should read to accomplish each scenario*

Chapter section	Litigation	Information requests	Data Subject Requests	Investigation
Create an Advanced eDiscovery Case	X	X	X	X
Manage Custodians and Holds	X			X
Custodian Communications	X			
Processing and Error Remediation	X	X	X	X
Advanced eDiscovery Searches	X	X	X	X
Manage Review Sets	X	X	X	X
Relevancy	X			
Export	X	X	X	X

The Litigation Process

Please remember that I am not a lawyer and this chapter is not legal advice about running a case. The process I describe is used as an example and is for illustrative purposes only. Let us start by reviewing the litigation process, so we all have a common understanding of how eDiscovery fits into the litigation process. I have mapped out a generic example of the litigation process in Figure 14-1.

Figure 14-1. *The litigation process*

First, someone will initiate a suit, meaning somebody informs a party that they intend to sue or take civil action against them. The receiving party then answers the lawsuit and files a motion to dismiss the suit or agrees to proceed.

Next, both parties move into the discovery phase, where we look for potential evidence or documents related to the case. This discovery process is where we focus in this chapter on Advanced eDiscovery.

When discovery is complete, there will be a motion process, where the legal council will move to either proceed or dismiss the case. At this point, if the parties have not settled the lawsuit, it will move to a trial. Cases rarely get to a trial and usually settle before they go to trial.

There could be an appeal process after the trial until finally, there is a final disposition and the case is closed. You do not have to go through all the steps in the cycle. You can complete some of them and skip to the final disposition at any point.

Litigation and discovery focus mostly on organizations in the United States. Still, there are equivalent processes worldwide, such as the United Kingdom's common law system or the civil law system in France. Litigation in these locations is not subject to the same rules but involves mostly the same process. There is a beginning, a middle, and an end to the case. The initiation is always when someone files a complaint in court, and this begins the life of the suit.

What Is eDiscovery?

As mentioned in the preceding text, discovery is the middle part of the litigation process. We find out about the underlying evidence, the issue regarding the complaint, or the response. During the discovery process, we could demonstrate that the opposition is blaming the wrong person or that the defense is grounded in evidence. We could also move to dismiss the case because the opposition sued the wrong person.

Discovery also includes exchanging information between the parties in the suit. It is focused on evidence and what evidence and witnesses they will present at trial. The discovery process is to identify, locate, preserve, secure, collect, prepare, review, and produce facts, information, and materials. Its purpose is to fulfill a request to produce documents. There is no rule for when discovery begins or ends, and it is an ongoing obligation. If at any time you come across relevant information, you need to give it to your adversary.

eDiscovery is the electronic aspect of identifying, collecting, and producing electronically stored information in response to discovery requests in a lawsuit or investigation. We refer to the content we are dealing with throughout the discovery process as electronically stored information (ESI). The goal of eDiscovery is to produce a core volume of evidence for litigation in a defensible manner.

The initial phase of litigation requires the parties in a dispute to provide each other relevant information and records, along with all other evidence related to a case. eDiscovery and legal hold obligations run from when a lawsuit is foreseeable to the time they present digital evidence in court. Attorneys do work upfront to agree with the opposition about what they will and will not include in discovery. For example, are you going to have document versions? How much effort, time, and expense will you go through to discover relevant documents? Since you are only required to produce what is reasonable, how do we define what is warranted in this situation?

Why do we have discovery? It enables the parties to know what evidence the opposition will present during the trial before it begins. It gives each side an understanding of the strengths and weaknesses of the case. And most importantly, the process is meant to be reasonable and not burdensome, meaning you only must produce what is not going to be a burdensome cost or a substantial time investment. This caveat is something I see people running the technical aspects of eDiscovery forget. If something is difficult to produce, talk to your legal team for advice.

There are several challenges with eDiscovery, especially when working with electronic files. First is the volume of information; there is just a lot of information produced in organizations today, and the rate at which we create data is not slowing down. Second, electronic data and metadata are dynamic, and electronic data is typically in an intangible form. Third, there are many different stakeholders involved, so it can be tough to coordinate with them about storing data. Fourth, the export of data can be time-consuming and sometimes takes days if not culled before export. Fifth, the explosion of social media applications adds complexity to the problem. There's also widespread adoption of third-party apps and cloud computing, which scatters information across multiple platforms. Sixth, there's further dispersal of this electronic information to mobile devices, employee-owned devices, and the Internet of things. Finally, there are increased concerns for privacy and data security that go along with all the preceding points.

The great news is that Advanced eDiscovery in Microsoft 365 can help you solve all these challenges. Let us discuss how, in the next section.

The Electronic Discovery Reference Model

To best explain how Advanced eDiscovery can help us solve these challenges, let us use the Electronic Discovery Reference Model (EDRM), an open source model explaining the discovery process shown in Figure 14-2. Think of the EDRM as the detailed subprocess for the discovery box in Figure 14-1 covering the litigation process.

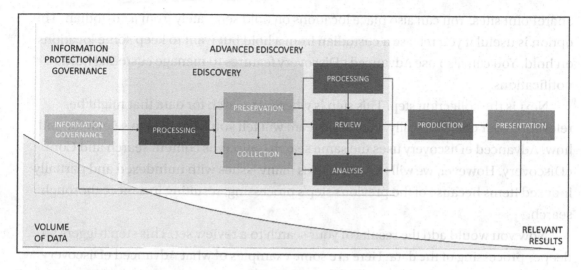

Figure 14-2. The Electronic Discovery Reference Model

Before we even get into eDiscovery, you want to manage your organization's data volume through excellent information protection and governance practices. Implementing processes like managing retention and deletion of your content reduces risk in the discovery process. Retention ensures people do not delete content prematurely, which would result in fines. Deletion reduces risk because if you can find it and it is relevant, you must produce it in discovery. It would not be enjoyable to lose a case based on information that you could have legally deleted. Deletion also reduces the volume of discoverable information, which reduces costs in the review process. We covered information governance in Chapter 8.

The next step in the EDRM is the processing stage. In the processing stage, we try to convert electronically stored information into forms suitable for reviewing and analyzing the data for this case. For example, in Microsoft 365, Advanced eDiscovery breaks apart emails into the message and any attachments. This way, we can search for each of them. Processing also conducts more in-depth indexing of locations on hold to search on all the metadata. Finally, Microsoft 365 Advanced eDiscovery will attempt to process and reindex any partially indexed or unindexed items and provides a report for anything unsuccessful in the Processing tab.

Now let us look at the preservation step. You might also call this step a legal hold. In this step, we identify the data related to our case to preserve it, meaning that people cannot delete it or modify it. Advanced eDiscovery allows you to put custodians on hold and customize the specific locations. For example, you could select their email, OneDrive, Teams of which they are a member, Yammer private messages, and

SharePoint sites. You can also place locations on hold separately from a custodian. This option is useful if you release a custodian from a hold but want to keep some locations on hold. You can also use Advanced eDiscovery features to manage custodial hold notifications.

Next is the collection step. This step is where we search for data that might be relevant to our case. Typically, your legal team will tell you what data to search for and how. Advanced eDiscovery uses the same search options as content search and Core eDiscovery. However, we will not run into as many issues with unindexed and partially indexed items because of the previous step's processing, resulting in a more thorough search.

Now you would add the results of your search to a review set. This step triggers a deeper processing of the data. Here are some examples of what Advanced eDiscovery does in this processing step:

- The system reruns the search so we can work with the most up-to-date data.

- The system copies all search results from the original data source in the live services to a secure Azure storage location. The system also adds additional metadata to the content specific to the discovery process.

- Content and metadata are reindexed so that all data in the review set is fully and quickly searchable during the review of the case data.

- If you have enabled optical character recognition (OCR), text from images is extracted and included with the data.

- The system can reconstruct emails and Teams and Yammer chats and conversations into threads for a faster and more accurate review.

Our next step is to review the data for relevance and privilege. This review step is the point in the process where the attorneys decide what content to produce for the opposition. This step can be manual and costly. Here are some ways that Advanced eDiscovery helps us to reduce time and cost:

- The system groups duplicate and near-duplicate content, including email threads and files, so you only must review and tag them once.

- It automatically identifies potentially privileged content.

- The system enables us to import files from outside of Microsoft 365 into the review set.

- For large cases, we can use a predictive coding relevancy module to train a machine learning module that can predict which content is relevant in a case.

Throughout the search and review process, your team may perform early case analysis to ensure you are on the right track with your discovery. This analysis finds critical patterns, topics, people, and discussion items in the data. Advanced eDiscovery supports early case analysis in almost every step of the EDRM process, even though the model shows it as a separate step. This analysis can include statistics about your holds and searches. It also includes charts and graphs showing content metadata, using artificial intelligence to identify themes in your dataset, and detailed reports and statistics. This analysis can help you refine search queries, identify other custodians, and more.

Next, you will reach a point where the discovery process is complete and you are ready to export your data. Some organizations may export the content and go directly to producing it to the opposing counsel. Other organizations may export Microsoft 365 data into another eDiscovery tool, where they combine data from all the electronic content sources in their company. Advanced eDiscovery can handle both scenarios and has many options for how to configure the export. It can even create load files with tagging information that you can use for your import into the other system. The export process is the last step in the EDR model involving Microsoft 365.

The next step is to produce the discovery to the opposing counsel. Advanced eDiscovery does not help with this step. There are specialized tools that the legal team uses for production.

The final step in the EDRM process is to produce your evidence in court. Again, there are specialized tools for this step, and you would not use Microsoft 365 for this purpose.

Now that you understand the overall process for discovery, the rest of the chapter will review complete details for each step and how Advanced eDiscovery works. With that, let us start by discussing how we create a new case.

Licensing and Permissions

Each custodian in an Advanced eDiscovery case needs one of the following licenses:

- Microsoft 365 E5 Compliance

- Microsoft 365 E5 eDiscovery and Audit

- Office 365 E5

There are two ways to manage permissions in Advanced eDiscovery. First, you can add people to the default role groups. This method is useful if you want a simple permissions model. The second way to manage permissions is to create custom role groups. This way is great if you will utilize the least permissions model and only permit people to perform the tasks required by their role.

To utilize the default role groups, visit the permissions page in the Security and Compliance Center. Scroll until you find the eDiscovery Manager role group. Click the name to open the details pane and then click Edit role group. Click the Choose eDiscovery Manager or Choose eDiscovery Administrator tab, depending on which one you want to edit. The details of each of the role groups are in the following. Click Save when you finish:

- **eDiscovery Manager**: Can perform all functions within a case. eDiscovery managers can only access and manage the cases they create. They cannot access or manage cases made by other eDiscovery managers.

- **eDiscovery Administrator**: An eDiscovery administrator is a member of the eDiscovery Manager role group and can perform all functions in a case. Additionally, an eDiscovery administrator can

  - Access all cases in both Core and Advanced eDiscovery in the Compliance Center.

  - Access case data in Advanced eDiscovery for any case in the organization.

  - Manage any eDiscovery case after they add themselves as a member of the case.

To use the custom role groups, go to the Security and Compliance permissions area. Click Create. Choose a name for your group and click Next. Click Choose roles and then Add. Check the boxes next to the roles you want and click Add. Choose any of the following roles or a combination of roles. Note that you always need to include either the Case Management or Review role in your custom group so the person can access the case itself. I recommend using the Review role because the Case Management role allows people to manage permissions, defeating the purpose:

- **Case Management**: Create, edit, delete, and control access to eDiscovery cases.

- **Communication**: Manage all communications with the custodians.

- **Compliance Search**: Perform searches across mailboxes and get an estimate of the results.

- **Custodian**: Identify and manage custodians for Advanced eDiscovery cases.

- **Export**: Export mailbox and site content returned from searches.

- **Hold**: Place content in mailboxes, sites, and public folders on hold.

- **Preview**: View a list of items returned from content searches and open each item from the list to view its contents.

- **Review**: Use Advanced eDiscovery to track, tag, and analyze documents.

- **RMS Decrypt**: Decrypt RMS-protected content when exporting search results.

- **Search and Purge**: Lets people bulk-remove data that match the criteria of a content search.

To finish creating your role group, click Done and Next. Click Choose members and then Add, and check the boxes next to the people you want to add to the custom role group. Click Add, Done, and Next. Review your settings and click Create role group. You will need to add the custom role group to each case separately.

Create an Advanced eDiscovery Case

From the Microsoft 365 Compliance Center, in the left-hand navigation, click eDiscovery and then Advanced.

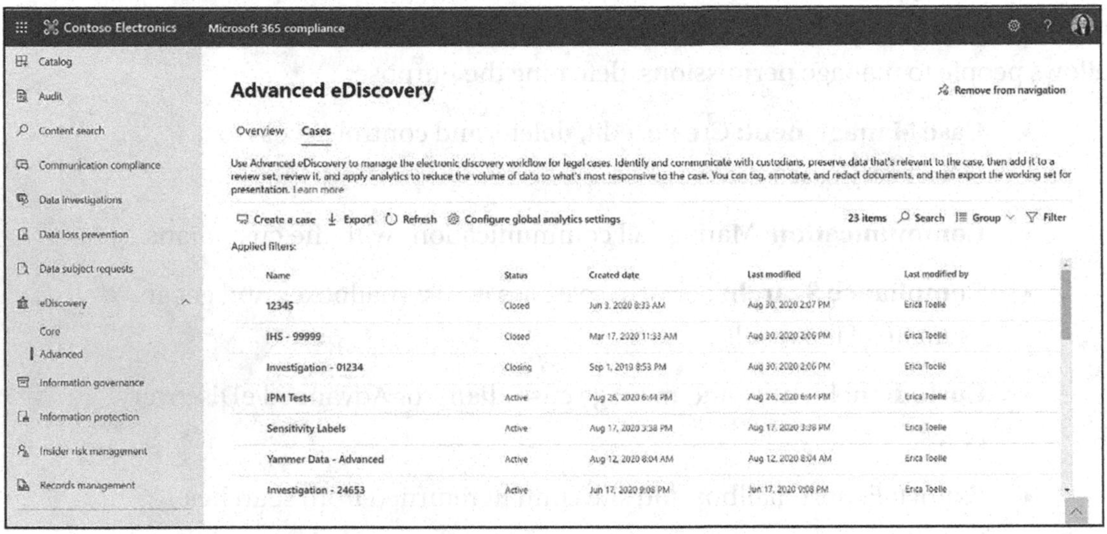

Figure 14-3. *The Advanced eDiscovery Cases page in the Compliance Center*

Click the Cases tab. Here you can see a list of all your cases, as shown in Figure 14-3. This list shows both active and closed cases but not deleted cases. You can view the case name, the status, the created date, last modified date, and the person who last modified the case. You can also export a list of the cases, search for a case, group the cases by status, and filter the list by case status.

Also, on the Cases page is the option to configure global analytics settings. At the time of writing, the only option is to manage the attorney-client privilege setting. This feature helps us when we get to the point where we are reviewing content for privilege in a review set. If you have an attorney-client privilege detection setting on, Advanced eDiscovery runs an attorney-client privilege model on your data and flag documents that are likely to be privileged. This flag is based on content analysis and by comparing participants against a user-provided attorney list, which you can upload on this page. This feature does not replace the need for privilege review. It helps you to get started and save time.

From the Cases page, click Create a case. This click brings up a page where you can enter a case name. This case name needs to be unique and not used in any solutions such as Advanced eDiscovery, Core eDiscovery, and Data Subject Requests. You can also enter an optional case number. The case description is also optional. Then you choose whether you want to configure additional settings for this case. Your choices are "Yes, I want to add members or configure the analytics settings" or "No, go to the homepage." I recommend that you say yes to configure the case analytics settings, which we will review shortly. Click Save to create the case.

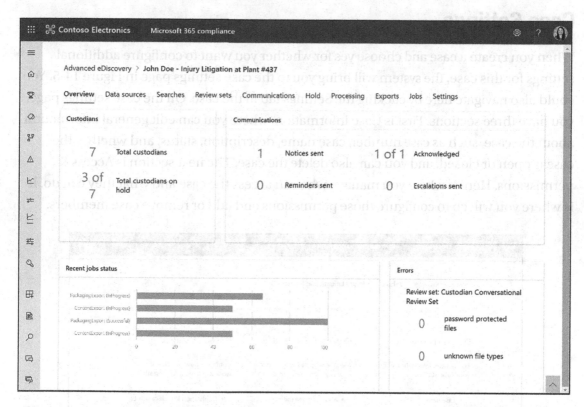

Figure 14-4. *The case overview page*

If you select no, the system will bring you to the case homepage in Figure 14-4, where you can see several widgets and information about your case. First, you can see the custodian information, including how many total custodians there are in the case and how many custodians are on hold. Next, you can see the communications widget, which shows you how many custodian notices you have sent. This widget also provides how many custodians have acknowledged the notice. You can also see how many reminders you sent and how many escalations you sent. You can then see recent job status. This view shows you recent jobs that you have ran in the eDiscovery case across different types of jobs and how complete they are. Lastly, you can see any errors for the specific review set. These are unprocessed content, such as how many files are password protected or how many have unknown data types.

You will see the following tabs: Overview, Data sources, Searches, Review sets, Communications, Hold, Processing, Exports, Jobs, and Settings. In the rest of the chapter, we will go through each one of these tabs. For now, let us look at case settings.

Case Settings

When you create a case and choose yes for whether you want to configure additional settings for this case, the system will bring you to the case settings page in Figure 14-5. You could also navigate here by clicking the Settings tab in the case. On the case settings page, you have three sections. First is Case information, where you can edit general information about the case, such as case number, case name, description, status, and whether the case is open or closed, and you can also delete the case. The next section is Access & permissions. Here is where you manage who can access the case and what they can do. It is where you will go to configure those permissions and add or remove case members.

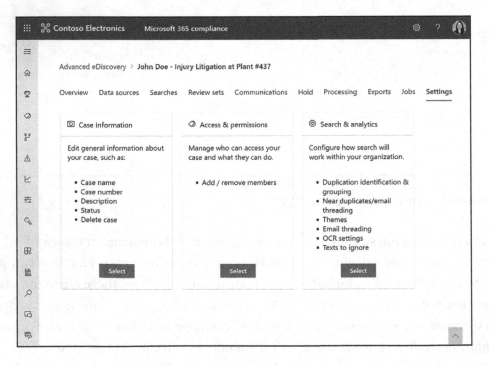

Figure 14-5. *Advanced eDiscovery case settings*

Lastly is Search & analytics. The search and analytics section is where you configure the processing options for the case. It is where you can set analytics settings such as identifying duplicate information. You can also thread emails and Microsoft Teams conversations. There are settings for machine learning and artificial intelligence capabilities such as theming and OCR. You can also specify text that you would like to ignore in the case.

Click Case information. Here you will see the unique case ID. You are also able to edit the case name, case number, and case description. You can also see that the case type is Advanced eDiscovery. You can see whether the case is active or closed and the date the case was created. If you would like to close the case, this is where you would come to perform that action. You could also choose to delete the case entirely. Click Settings to exit.

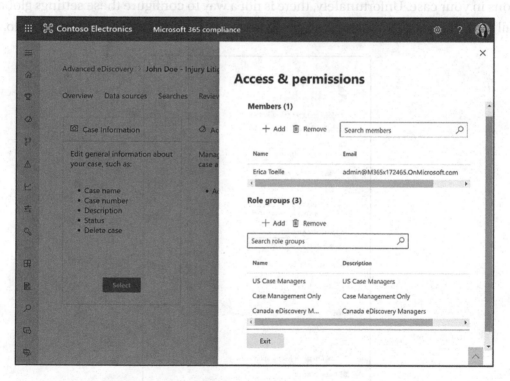

Figure 14-6. *Members and role groups for the case*

The next section in settings is Access & permissions. Click Select to access the options. Here you will see individual members of the case and role groups that you have added to the case, shown in Figure 14-6. For example, if you have designated role groups based on geography for Advanced eDiscovery, instead of adding individual members to the case, you could add that geography's role group to grant everyone in that geography access. See the "Licensing and Permissions" section earlier in this chapter to learn more about role groups and Advanced eDiscovery permissions.

If you would like to change case permissions, click Add under either the Members or Role groups heading. Here, you will see a list of all users or compliance role groups in your organization. If you would like to narrow down the list, you can use the search functionality to show a subset of role groups. Check the box next to a name and click Add. Once you have added your users and your role groups, click Exit.

The next section on the settings page is Search & analytics. On this page, we configure our settings related to analytics and optical character recognition. The system will use these settings to process the case data when you add a search to a review set. I highly recommend that you configure these settings before you perform any other actions in your case. Unfortunately, there is not a way to configure these settings globally for all cases. Let us go through each one of these settings and talk about what they do.

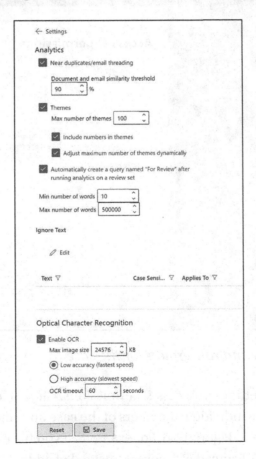

Figure 14-7. *Search & analytics settings*

First is the checkbox in Figure 14-7 for near-duplicate/email threading. This checkbox allows artificial intelligence (AI) in Advanced eDiscovery to process what emails, Microsoft Teams chats and conversations, and Yammer messages are a part of a thread or conversation. Threading helps to decrease the time required for manual review. The idea is that it is easier for someone to review a conversation thread than individual messages. It is also easier to review all near-duplicates at one time, highlighting the documents' differences.

For Teams conversations in a channel and Yammer messages in a group, a thread is a post and its replies. For Teams chats, it groups threads by the time stamp. The system groups discussions that occurred around the same time. Emails are grouped in conversations by threads. Near-duplicate detection parses every document with text. It compares every document to determine whether the similarity is greater than the set threshold. If it is, the system groups the documents. You set the threshold using the document and email similarity threshold percentage under the checkbox.

Next are themes. Themes use AI to help you find topics related to your dataset, of which you were not aware. For example, a theme might be a project, customer, or keyword. You can then modify your search to include discovered topics. You can set the max number of themes that you would like the AI to find. Another choice is whether to include numbers as themes. For example, you might have the fiscal year of 2020 that the system would represent as a theme number. Next, you can choose whether to adjust the maximum number of themes dynamically. If you check this box, the artificial intelligence module will decide the number of appropriate themes for your dataset. If unchecked, it will find the number of themes from the Max number of themes box.

There is a checkbox to automatically create a query named "For Review" after running analytics on a review set. This query filters out duplicate items from the review set, so you only review unique items. You will need to run analytics on the review set, covered in the "Review Set Settings" section of this chapter, for this view to work.

Then, you have options to set a min number of words and a max number of words. These fields are related to the near-duplicate and email threading. They ensure that near-duplicate and email threading analyses are performed only on documents that have at least the minimum number of words and, at most, the maximum number of words.

Finally, we can ignore text. This feature is useful for things like an email disclaimer footer, which can throw off your searches and near-duplicate detection. If you add this disclaimer to ignore a text, the system will not use it in search and analysis in your dataset.

The last set of options is for optical character recognition (OCR). OCR allows us to extract text from images. To make this feature performant, we can set a maximum image size that should be analyzed. Large images can increase the processing time and slow down your results. Images with sizes above the set size will not have their text extracted.

Similarly, you could set whether you want a low or a high accuracy for the text extraction. This accuracy setting will affect your processing times. Finally, you can select your timeout for OCR, meaning that if the system cannot extract the text from an image in this number of seconds, it will stop and move on. If this happens, the system will list that image as a processing error that you can remediate later. We will discuss processing and error remediation in a later section of this chapter.

Once you are happy with your settings, click Save. Now that we have configured all the case settings, we can either put people and content on hold or perform a search if you do not need the hold functionality.

Manage Custodians and Holds

What is a custodian? A custodian is a person of interest in your eDiscovery case. You usually want to put a custodian on hold to ensure that no one deletes or modifies relevant case information. When you add a custodian to a case, a hold is placed on all the associated data sources that you have chosen for that custodian.

The other option is to put non-custodial data sources on hold. We recommend this method when you have a data location, such as a project site, related to a case but not necessarily tied to a custodian. Holds placed on these types of areas separate from a custodian are not affected when you release the custodian from the hold. You can also use a search query to narrow down content within the chosen locations to place on hold, referred to as a query-based hold.

In Microsoft 365, holds are in place, meaning the system places one copy of the information on hold. It protects the original email or documents from deletion or modification by maintaining a copy of that information if the users attempt either action.

To manage custodians, visit the Microsoft 365 Compliance Center. In the left-hand navigation, click eDiscovery ➤ Advanced. Click the Cases tab. Double-click the case that you would like to open. Click the Data sources tab. On this tab, you have two sections: Custodians and Data locations. Custodians is where you can place a person on hold, and Data locations is where you put a location on hold.

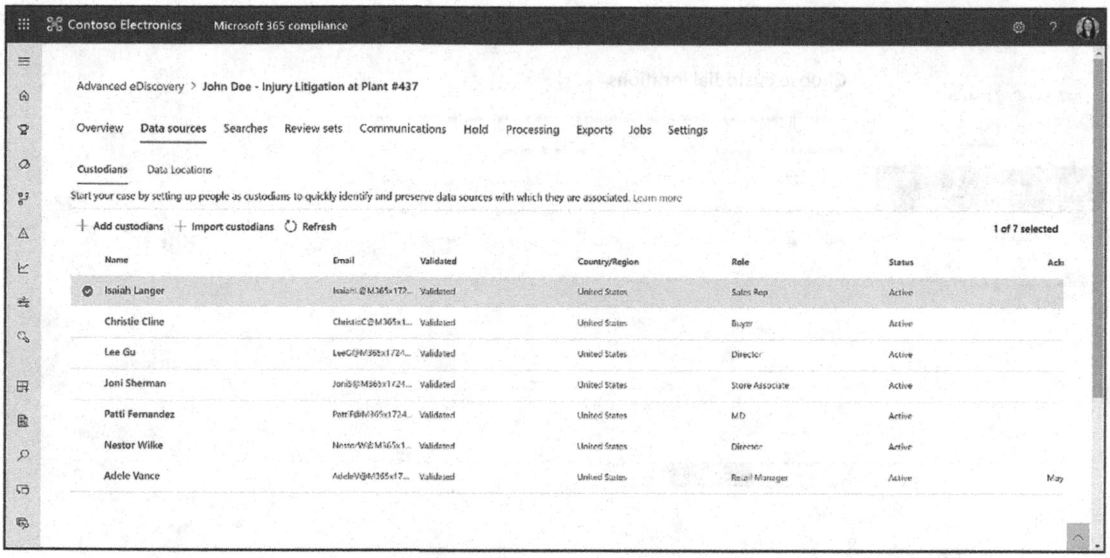

Figure 14-8. *The Data sources tab in Advanced eDiscovery*

Starting with custodians, you can see each custodian's name and their email address, seen in Figure 14-8. The Validated column confirms the custodians and their corresponding data sources are valid. The information on each custodian also includes their country/region, their role, and the status of the hold, which is active or inactive. Then you can see the date the custodian acknowledged their hold if you use the custodian communications module. Finally, you can see the custodian indexing status and the date the index was last updated.

There are two ways to add a custodian to a case. You can add them in bulk using a spreadsheet or add them a few at a time. Please note that there is currently a limit of 100 custodians per case. If your case has more than 100 custodians, you will need to create a separate case to manage them. We will cover adding bulk custodians in the next section. Let us start with adding one or a few custodians.

Add Custodians to the Case

To add one or a few custodians, click Add custodians. The first screen will ask you to choose custodians. You need to type at least three letters of the custodian's name for the search to start. It will then bring up the custodian names that match the search. You can click their name to add them to the hold. Click Next when there are no more custodians to add.

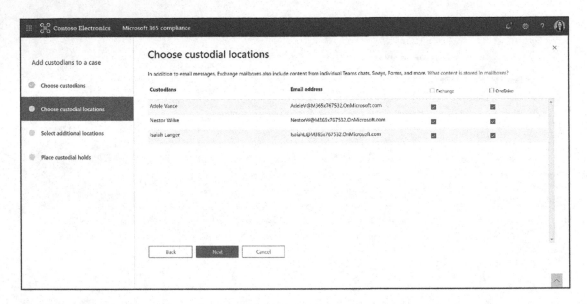

Figure 14-9. *Choose custodial locations in Advanced eDiscovery*

On the next screen, shown in Figure 14-9, you will need to choose the custodian locations. By default, the system will check both the Exchange and OneDrive locations, which will add the Exchange mailboxes and OneDrive accounts to the hold. Go ahead and check and uncheck the boxes as needed to make the hold. Click Next.

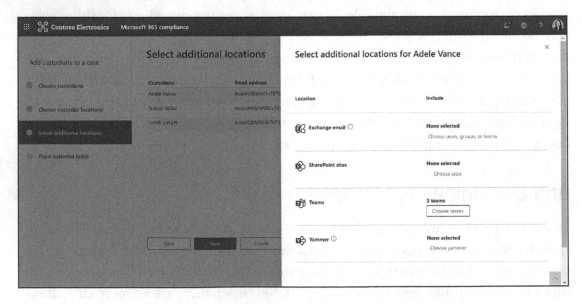

Figure 14-10. *Addition locations you can add to the custodian hold*

On the next screen, you can set additional locations for each custodian, shown in Figure 14-10. We associate these locations with the custodian. When we release a custodian from a hold, it will include associated locations. You can add additional locations for each custodian, such as Exchange mail accounts, including user mailboxes, group email accounts, or Microsoft Teams chats. You can also add SharePoint sites, Microsoft Teams, and Yammer groups.

Let us start by adding additional Exchange email locations. Click Choose users, groups, or teams. This click will bring you to a screen to choose which user or group mailboxes to add to the hold. Type a minimum of three characters to get the list of mailboxes that match that search. Check the boxes next to the group mailboxes or individual users that you would like to add to the hold. When done, click Choose and then Add.

Next, let us add a SharePoint site to the custodian hold. Click Choose sites and then Choose sites again. Here, the system will bring you to a screen to paste the entire URL for the SharePoint site. If you want to add an additional OneDrive account, you could do that as well by pasting the URL of that person's OneDrive here. Check the boxes next to the sites; click Choose and then Done.

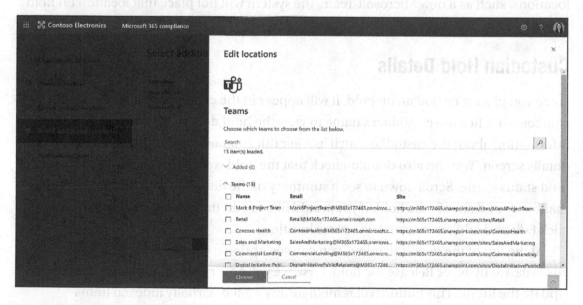

Figure 14-11. Add additional Teams locations to the hold

To add a Microsoft Team, click Choose Teams and then Choose Teams again. Here, it will show you a list of all the Teams where the custodian is a member or owner, shown in Figure 14-11. This filter is helpful because you do not have to use a different process to find Teams where the custodian interacts. Check the boxes next to any Microsoft Teams you would like to add to the hold. Click Choose and then Add. Please note that if you add a custodian to a new Team, it will not automatically place that Team on hold. You will need to update the hold locations on an ongoing basis to account for new team memberships.

Now let us add a Yammer location. Click Choose Yammer and Choose Yammer again. Again, the system will show you a list of all the Yammer group memberships for that individual user. Check the boxes next to the groups you want to add; click Choose and then Done.

When you finish adding locations, click Save. The screen will summarize the additional locations for the users, and you can click Next. The next page is where you place the hold. Uncheck the boxes if you are not ready to put the person on hold to save the configuration. Click Complete. Please note the system will put new content items, such as emails, within a location on hold. But as a reminder, for entirely new locations, such as a new Microsoft Team, the system will not place that location on hold automatically.

Custodian Hold Details

Once you place a custodian on hold, it will appear in the custodian list on the Data sources tab. Click the custodian's name to view the hold details. You will see summary information about the custodian, such as their title, manager, location, and more, on the details screen. You can also double-check that the hold went through correctly by seeing hold status = true. Scroll down to see a summary of the data sources, like the number of mailboxes and sites in the hold. If you would like to edit the custodian's data sources, click Edit and add or remove data source locations.

At the top of the details window, you can see options: Update the index, View custodian activity, or Release the hold. First, we will cover Update the index. Click Update the index. This button will remediate any added partially indexed items since you last ran the last index. This click will also update the case information and information about the data sources. Please do not update the index more than once a day as it is a long-running process.

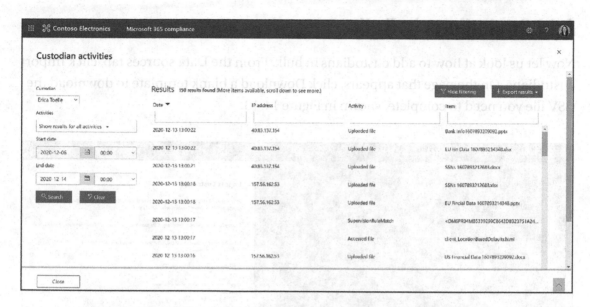

Figure 14-12. *Custodian activities in Advanced eDiscovery*

To view custodian activity, make sure the person viewing the activity has View-Only Audit Logs or Audit Logs permissions. The audit log also must be enabled in your tenant. Click View custodian activity to see a screen showing you the custodian's audit log activities, shown in Figure 14-12. Here you can filter options by date, IP address, activity, or item name. You can also show results for all activities in the audit log, or you can show specific audit log activities. You can also export the audit log. If you are interested in this feature, please see Chapter 16.

The last action on the custodian details page is Release custodians. When you click this button, it will give you a warning that asks if you are sure you want to remove the custodian from the hold. You can choose yes or no. If you release this custodian from the case, all holds placed on the custodian's data sources will be removed. Any holds placed on the custodian's data sources in other cases will still apply. You can also release custodians from their holds in bulk. To do this action, select multiple custodians and click the Release source button that appears on the Custodians toolbar when you select multiple people. You can also update the index for those custodians or view their activities.

Add Custodians in Bulk

Now let us look at how to add custodians in bulk. From the Data sources tab, click Import custodians. On the page that appears, click Download a blank template to download the CSV file you need to complete, shown in Figure 14-13.

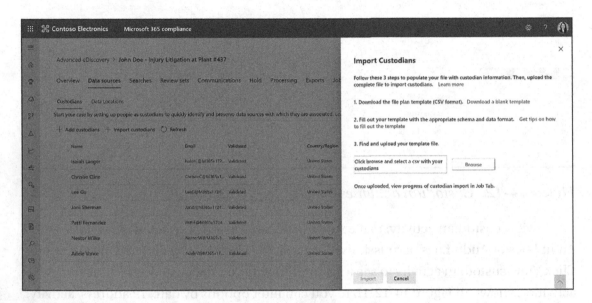

Figure 14-13. *Import custodians in bulk to Advanced eDiscovery*

Add the custodial information to the CSV file and save it on your local computer. See the next section for information about the properties in the CSV file. On the Data sources tab, click Import custodians again. On the page that appears, click Browse and upload your CSV file.

After the CSV file is uploaded, the system creates a BulkAddCustodian job, which you can find on the Jobs tab. The job validates the custodians and their corresponding data sources and then adds them to the Custodians tab on the case's Sources page.

Here is how to complete the CSV file:

- **Custodian ContactEmail**: Enter the UPN email of the custodian, for example, etoelle@contoso.com.

- **Exchange Enabled**: Enter TRUE to put their mailbox on hold and FALSE if not.

- **OneDrive Enabled**: Enter TRUE to put their OneDrive on hold and FALSE if not.

- **Is OnHold**: Enter TRUE to put the custodian on hold and FALSE if not.

- **Workload1 Type**: Enter ExchangeMailbox, SharePointSite, TeamsMailbox, TeamsSite, YammerMailbox, or YammerSite. This functionality is to add additional locations to the custodian's hold, described in the previous section.

- **Workload1 Location**: Depending on your workload type, this would be the data location of your workload (e.g., the email address of an Exchange mailbox or the URL of a SharePoint site).

Currently, you can only import custodians who are in Azure Active Directory (AAD). The system validates and finds custodians using the UPN value in the Custodian ContactEmail column in the CSV file. If it cannot validate a custodian, it will show them as Not validated in the Validated column on the Data sources ➤ Custodians tab.

Put Data Locations on Hold

If you would like to put content on hold that is not associated with a custodian, you can use Data locations. From within the case, click the Data sources tab and then Data locations. Click Add data locations.

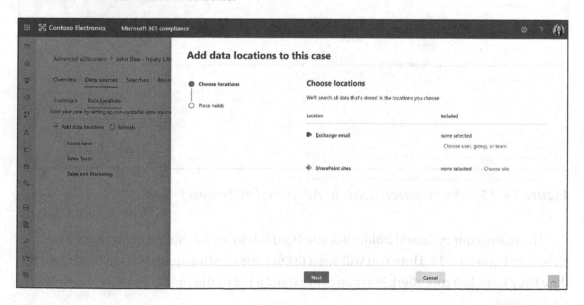

Figure 14-14. Add data locations to the case

This click will bring you to a pop-out window that asks you to choose locations, shown in Figure 14-14. For example, you can select specific users, groups, or teams based on Exchange mailboxes to include in the hold. Or you can add URLs to SharePoint sites or OneDrive accounts. Once you are happy with your location, click Next. The final screen asks you to place the hold. You can uncheck the box if you want to save the configuration but not activate the hold. Click Submit.

The hold will now appear in the data locations list. Click the name of the hold to view the hold details. Here you can see the information about the hold, update the index, or release the hold.

Create a Query-Based Hold

Query-based holds are a bit different than the other types of holds. For one, you create them from a separate tab. Second, only they put the items on hold that match the search query rather than the entire location.

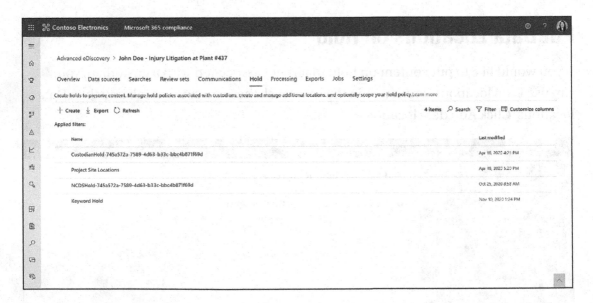

Figure 14-15. *Query-based holds in Advanced eDiscovery*

To create a query-based hold, click the Hold tab in an Advanced eDiscovery case, shown in Figure 14-15. Here you will see a list of your existing query-based holds and the date they were last modified. You can also export a list of the holds. To make a new hold, click Create.

A window will appear and ask you to name and optionally describe the hold. Click Next. The next screen asks you to choose locations. These locations will scope your search query. For example, if you later choose a date range when you create your query, it will only find the items within that date range for the locations you choose here – let us say Exchange. Choosing only Exchange returns mailbox items that fall within the date range.

These locations are the same as in content search. We review them in depth in Chapter 12, in the "Create a Content Search" section. As a reminder, the first location group corresponds to Exchange mailboxes. You can click Choose users, groups, or teams to select individual or group mailboxes. If you choose an individual mailbox, it captures that person's emails, other mailbox items, Teams chats, Yammer private messages, and To Do tasks. Selecting a group mailbox covers any group emails and other mailbox items and Teams conversations if the mailbox is associated with a Team. However, it does not include Yammer group messages.

The next group of locations covers site locations, such as SharePoint and OneDrive accounts. You can add these items by using the site's URL. You can also put an entire Yammer network on hold by adding the URL of your Yammer network.

Let us pause for a moment and discuss Yammer group holds. Suppose you want only to put individual Yammer groups on hold and not the entire network. You can do that by associating a Yammer group with a custodian as described in the "Add Custodians to the Case" section. If you want to place your Yammer network on hold permanently, I recommend creating a separate query-based hold only for that purpose, so you can easily understand how to disable the hold later.

The last section in the Choose locations screen is for Exchange public folders. You can either place all public folders on hold or none of them. My advice is like Yammer networks. If you want to put public folders on hold, do that in a separate query-based hold. When you finish selecting locations, click Next.

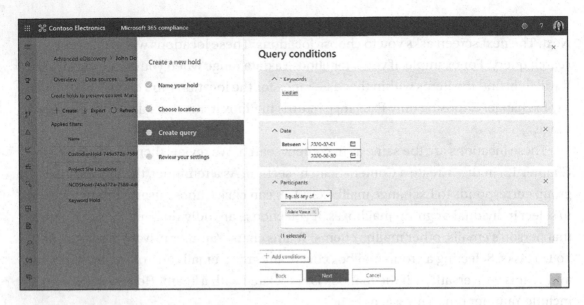

Figure 14-16. *A query for a hold in Advanced eDiscovery*

The Create query screen is where you create the search conditions for what content you place on hold. Figure 14-16 shows an example of a query. This query looks for Teams chat messages (keyword =kind:im) created between February 1, 2020, and June 30, 2020, sent or received by Adele Vance. In the location step, I choose Adele's Exchange mailbox as the location. Again, for more details on creating a search query, see Chapter 12. Click Next when you are finished. On the next screen, you can review your settings for the hold. Click Create this hold when you are happy.

Once you add a hold, you can see it in the list on the Hold tab. If you would like to see more details about the hold, double-click its name. The details screen will pop up. Here you can edit or delete the hold. You can also see hold details such as the locations, statistics, last modified information, and any errors.

Additional Hold Details

What happens to the content we have put on hold? Let us start with Exchange Online. When we put content on hold in Exchange Online, if someone edits a message or attachment, the modified version will stay in the mailbox, and the custodian can view it. The original message is moved to the Versions subfolder and is kept intact in an immutable state. If someone deletes an email message, it is moved to the Deletions subfolder in the Recoverable Items partition. If the item is also under a retention policy, then the hold will always override the retention policy, meaning that we cannot delete content prematurely if it is on hold, and then once the hold is released, the retention policy would then take over as to whether the item is kept or deleted.

When a custodian's email content is on hold, if a custodian tries to delete an item in the Deletions folder, the item will be moved into the Purges subfolder. The system preserves it according to the hold settings.

The system purges a message that is on targeted hold. When a targeted hold has been placed on specific messages or attachments, rather than on the entire mailbox, a cleanup process runs roughly every week, which acts on items that exceed the single item recovery limit. The cleanup process moves the items that matched the targeted query criteria to the Discovery Hold folder for ongoing preservation. The system also moves items with any index errors to Discovery Hold for continued preservation. The cleanup process then expunges the rest of the items that do not match the criteria and have no index errors.

If your organization uses Exchange Online archiving, which we covered in Chapter 8, the system moves mailbox items to an Archive folder after two years by default. When you place a custodian's Exchange mailbox on hold, the hold takes effect for this archive, the same as for the primary mailbox. If the custodian tries to delete archive content on hold, the system preserves the content in the Recoverable Items folder of their Exchange Online mailbox. Microsoft 365 eDiscovery searches include the Exchange Online archive, so you do not have to include it as a secondary source location. Every time you search a custodian's mailbox, it also searches the archive.

Now let us cover how holds work in SharePoint Online and OneDrive for Business. These locations use a preservation hold library to store content on hold, which is viewable by site collection admins, SharePoint admins, and tenant admins. When a custodian's content is on hold, the system stores deleted content in the preservation hold library. Here is what happens under different scenarios when you place SharePoint Online and OneDrive for Business content on hold:

1. **On hold content is due to expire under a retention policy**:
   If you apply a retention policy to SharePoint Online or OneDrive content, if content expires under a retention policy while it is on hold, the system preserves the content in the preservation hold library. When you remove the hold, the system deletes the content.

2. **Someone deletes the content**: The system preserves deleted content in the preservation hold library. When you remove the hold, the system permanently deletes the content.

3. **Document versioning is enabled**: Document versioning is enabled in SharePoint Online by default. When a custodian creates a new version of a document, the system preserves the previous version in the site's Versions directory.

The last thing I want to mention in this section is that it is possible to use PowerShell to script eDiscovery holds. You can also use the Microsoft Graph API to create and manage custodian holds. Microsoft will release more APIs in the future, so please check the documentation for the latest information.

Custodian Communications

What are custodian communications? Often there is a legal requirement or organization policy to notify custodians when you place them on hold. You may want to simplify the process of issuing and tracking notifications. Sending communications instructs custodians to preserve electronically stored information and any content relevant to an active or impending legal matter. Legal teams must know that each custodian has received, read, understood, and agreed to comply with the given instructions. As mentioned in the preceding text, there are also sometimes laws around notifying custodians that they are on hold.

There are four types of communications in Advanced eDiscovery:

1. **The issuance notice**: The issuance notice is a legal hold notice issued or initiated by a notification from the legal department to custodians who may have relevant information about the case matter. This notice instructs the custodians to preserve any information that you may need for discovery.

2. **The reissuance notice**: You may require custodians to preserve additional content or less content than was previously requested during the case. For this scenario, you can update the existing hold notice and reissue it to custodians.

3. **The release notice**: Once a matter is resolved and the custodian is no longer subject to a preservation requirement, you can release the custodian from the case. Additionally, you can notify the custodian that they are no longer required to preserve content and provide instructions about how to resume their regular work activity concerning their data.

4. **Reminders and escalations**: In some instances, just issuing a notice is not enough to satisfy legal discovery requirements. With each notification, legal teams can schedule a set of reminders and escalation workflows to follow up with unresponsive custodians automatically. First is the reminder workflow. After a legal hold notice has been issued or reissued to a set of custodians, an organization can set up reminders to alert unresponsive custodians. Second are escalations. In some cases, if a custodian remains unresponsive even after a set of reminders over some time, the legal team can set up an escalation workflow to notify the unresponsive custodian and their manager.

Set Up Custodian Communications

To use custodian communications, open an Advanced eDiscovery case. Click the Communications tab. Here you will see a list of any previous communications that you sent to custodians, shown in Figure 14-17. You can see the name of the communication, the status (draft or published), the date it was last modified, the number of custodians associated with the communication, and the number of people who acknowledged the notice. Additionally, you can export a list of communications.

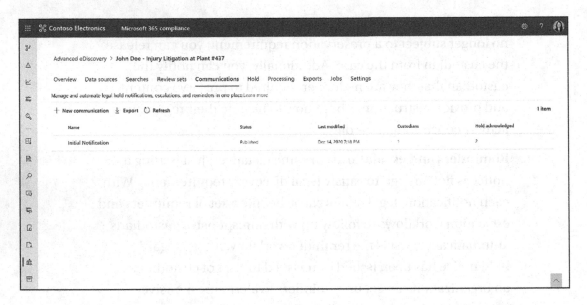

Figure 14-17. *The custodian communications overview page in Advanced eDiscovery*

To create a new communication, click the New communication button. In the wizard that appears, name your communication – for example, initial notification. You will also choose your issuing officer. Any member of the case or an eDiscovery administrator assigned to the case can be the issuing officer. Click Next.

Note   People added to the case through a role group cannot be an issuing officer. You must add a person individually to a case to show in the Issuing officer dropdown.

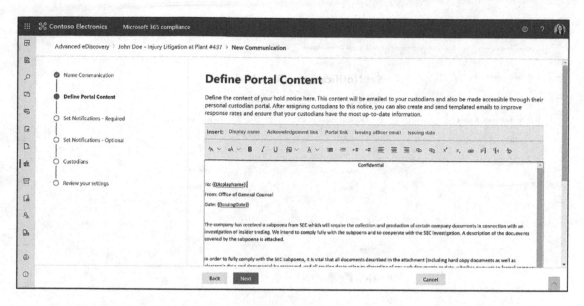

Figure 14-18. *Add content for the hold notice to custodians*

You will define the portal content on the next screen, shown in Figure 14-18. The portal content is your hold notice that you send to custodians. You will usually get the language for this notice from your legal department. You can insert dynamic fields, such as display name, the acknowledgment link for the custodians, the portal link, the issuing officer's email address, and the issuing date. You can also use formatting options to use different fonts and settings like you would when editing a Word document. These dynamic fields will update with the relevant information when you send the notice to custodians. Click Next when done.

Figure 14-19. *Set custodian notifications for communications*

On the next page, you set notifications for the custodians, shown in Figure 14-19. The notifications contain the details we need to send emails to the custodians. For example, you select who to Cc and Bcc on the communication, the email subject, and any additional text you want to appear above the portal content. Click Edit next to the notification name to edit it.

Table 14-2. *What triggers notifications*

Type of communication	Trigger
Issuance notices	The initial creation of the notification. You can also manually resend a hold notification
Reissuance notices	Updating the portal content on the Define Portal Content page in the Edit communication wizard
Release notices	Releasing the custodian from the case.
Reminders	The interval and number of reminders configured for the reminder.
Escalations	The interval and number of reminders configured for the escalation.

There are several types of notices, explained in Table 14-2 above. First, we configure the required issuance notification. The issuance notification tells the custodian that they are on hold. The email sender is the issuing officer we designated in the first step. You can add additional people in the Cc or Bcc line. Enter a subject and the body. Again, you have full formatting capabilities as well as dynamic content fields that you can add. Click Save.

Next is the reissue notification. The system will automatically trigger this notification if the portal content changes. Now we configure the release notification. The system automatically sends this notification when you release a custodian from hold. It has the same options as previous notices.

Once you have configured these notices, click Next.

Next, you can set optional notifications, shown in Figure 14-20. These optional notifications remind the custodian to acknowledge the notice and send an escalation to the custodian's manager if they have not acknowledged it. The system starts the escalation workflow when it runs out of reminders to send to the custodian.

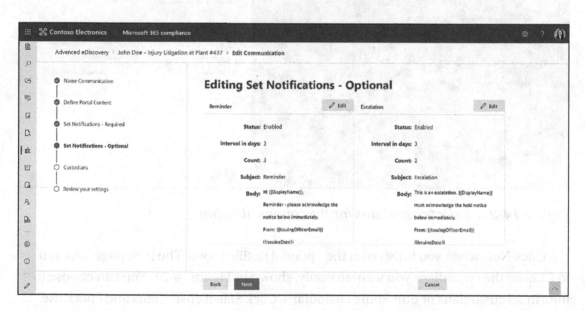

Figure 14-20. *Optional notices for custodian communications*

First, let us configure the reminder notification. On the configuration screen, you can toggle the reminder on or off. You can set the reminder interval, which is the number of days between each reminder, and the count, which is the number of reminders. For example, suppose you set the reminder interval for three days and the count to three. In that case, it will send the first reminder email three days after the initial notice if the custodian does not acknowledge the notice. Then, it will wait three days and send another reminder for three total cycles. You have the usual notice configuration fields for the subject and body. Click Save.

Now let us configure the escalation notice. The system sends the escalation to the person's manager as defined in Azure Active Directory. Click Edit next to Escalation. The options are the same as reminders. Toggle escalations on or off and set the escalation interval and the number of escalations. Configure the text for the subject and body.

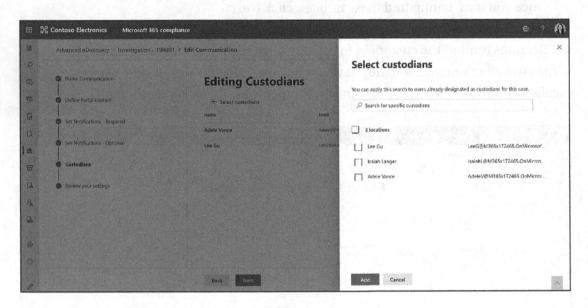

Figure 14-21. *Select custodians for the communication*

Click Next when you finish with the optional notifications. The next page asks you to Choose the custodians you want to notify, shown in Figure 14-21. You can choose to inform all custodians or only some custodians. Click Select custodians and check the boxes next to the names you want to add. Click Next.

The last page asks you to review the settings for your communication. When you are happy, click Submit. The system will immediately send the notification to all the selected custodians.

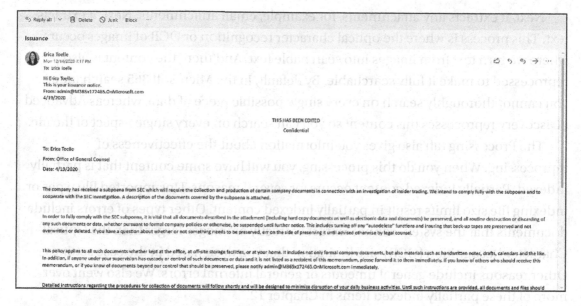

Figure 14-22. *The custodian view of the issuance notice*

The custodians will receive the issuance email asking them to acknowledge the hold, shown in Figure 14-22 above. Once they click the acknowledgment, it will bring them to a page that says, "Thank you. Your acknowledgment has been recorded." The system records their acknowledgment, and you can see it counted on the Communications tab and in Data sources ➤ Custodians.

You can also view details about each communication on the Communications tab. Click the name of the notice to open the details pane. Here you can see how many people have acknowledged the hold notice and how many are awaiting acknowledgment. You can also see the list of custodians and their responses. You can also edit or delete the communication from the details pane or resend the notice.

Finally, you can download the complete text and configuration of the communication for your records.

Processing and Error Remediation

What is processing? Processing provides visibility into advanced custodian indexing. It is where you can address processing errors with file identification, expansion of embedded documents and attachments, and text extraction. When you place content on hold, a reprocessing of this content occurs. First, it identifies the files that need to be processed. Next, it expands embedded documents. For example, if you have a Word document with an embedded PowerPoint presentation, it will expand those into two separate files.

Next, it extracts any attachments, for example, email attachments. Next, it extracts text. This process is where the optical character recognition or OCR of images occurs, where we turn text from images into searchable text. And then, the content is also reprocessed to make it fully searchable. By default, in the Microsoft 365 search index, you cannot thoroughly search on every single possible piece of data, whereas Advanced eDiscovery reprocesses this content so you can search on every single aspect of the file.

The Processing tab also gives you information about the effectiveness of reprocessing. When you do this processing, you will have some content that is partially indexed. Partially indexed content occurs for several reasons. Unsupported file types or indexing file size limits result in partially indexed content. Other types of errors include documents that the system cannot extract correctly or images larger than the Optical Character Recognition (OCR) size limitation that you designated in the case settings. Other reasons include general timeouts or general internal errors. We also went over more of these partially indexed items in Chapter 12.

This partially indexed item list is compelling because Microsoft Advanced eDiscovery is one of the only eDiscovery tools that will show you this partially indexed content upfront so that you can remediate it at the beginning of your discovery process. This timing allows us to include those files as a part of the case review and analysis. Other tools will not tell you about partially indexed files until the export phase.

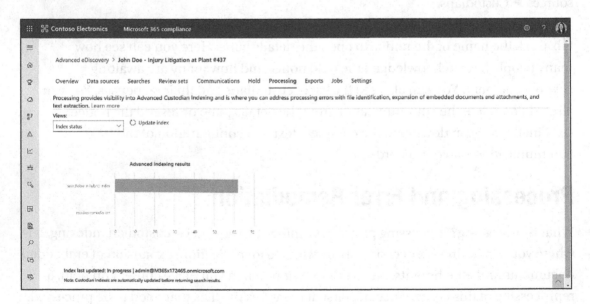

Figure 14-23. *The processing overview screen in Advanced eDiscovery*

Now, let us go through the Processing tab and the options that are available there. To access processing, click the Processing tab in an Advanced eDiscovery case. You see the processing overview page in Figure 14-23. Here you can select your view and see either index status, processing errors, or remediations. Looking at the index status page first, we can see that it gives you information about the hybrid index. The hybrid index is where Advanced eDiscovery stores the reprocessed content. It is a separate search index just for this eDiscovery case, and it is stored separately from the usual Microsoft 365 search index in Azure.

On another note, if the case is long-running, meaning you have the case open for months or years, you will need to update the custodian index to reprocess partially indexed items. If things are not partially indexed, meaning they went through the processing just fine, it will automatically update those on an ongoing basis. However, it is very typical that your custodians might have partially indexed content, and for that, you will need to reprocess the index. Only after you do the reprocessing will the new partially indexed items show up in this Processing tab. We cover this topic in the section of this chapter titled "Add Custodians to the Case."

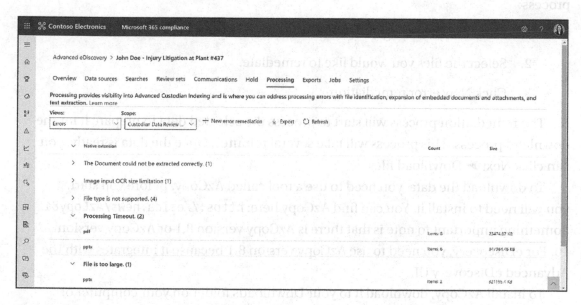

Figure 14-24. *The processing errors view in Advanced eDiscovery*

The next view contains errors, which are processing errors. This view is where you will see a list of all the processing errors that the system encountered, shown in Figure 14-24 above. You can scope this view by the entire case or by review set. The view shows the errors grouped by error type, and you can expand or collapse those groups. Each line item displays a file extension within the groups, and then the count and size of the files with that extension and type. You can also export a list of errors.

There are two ways that you can remediate processing errors:

1. Bulk remediation

2. Single file error remediation

The individual item error remediation is useful because you can view the file's metadata to decide if it is worth your time to do error remediation. The error remediation process for both options is manual, meaning you will need to download the file, open it up, fix the error, and reupload it to the eDiscovery case. Because this process is time-consuming, it may not be required to do that for every single file.

Bulk Remediation

The first way we will look at remediating the errors is through the bulk remediation process:

1. From the errors page, click New error remediation.

2. Select the files you would like to remediate.

3. Click New error remediation.

The remediation process will start to process the selected data to prepare it for the download process. This process will take several minutes. Once the data is ready, you can click Next ➤ Download files.

To download the data, you need to use a tool called AzCopy. Before you start, you will need to install it. You can find AzCopy here: `https://erica.news/AzCopy81`. Something important to note is that there is AzCopy version 8.1 or AzCopy version 10. For eDiscovery, you need to use AzCopy version 8.1 because it integrates with the Advanced eDiscovery UI.

To install AzCopy, download it to your Downloads folder on your computer or similar. Double-click the executable. This click will bring you to an install screen. Click Next and go through the install process.

When installed, start AzCopy by searching for it in Windows. Click the name to open and run it. AzCopy will open in a window that looks like a command prompt. It will be blue and text only.

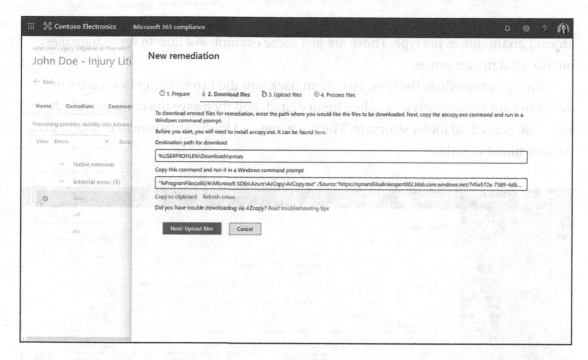

Figure 14-25. *Build the download command prompt for remediation files*

Go back to Advanced eDiscovery to the screen where we left off. Fill out the destination path for the download, shown in Figure 14-25. This path is where you want your downloaded remediation files to go. By default, files will be downloaded to your Downloads folder on your local machine in a folder called Errors. Filling out the destination path for download is going to populate the next field automatically.

Under the heading Copy this command and run it in a Windows command prompt, click Copy to clipboard, go back to AzCopy, paste it, and press Enter. This step is why we want to use AzCopy 8.1. With AzCopy version 10, you cannot easily copy and paste that command. With 8.1, you can paste the tool's information, and you do not have to know how to write PowerShell.

Then, the files will download to the destination you specified, and you can go to Downloads ➤ Errors on your computer to view the files.

Now you need to remediate each item. The exact steps will depend on the error. For example, if the error is a password-protected file, like when someone puts a personal password on their Excel sheet, you will need to get the person's password or run a password cracking tool to break into the file. If it was an unrecognized file type, you need to save it as a file type that eDiscovery can process. Or, if it is a text-based file, you could copy and paste it into something like Notepad, so at least the text is discoverable to get around an unknown file type. Those are just some examples of how to remediate files, but do what makes sense.

Once you remediate the files, save them back into the Errors folder or create a new folder in your Downloads area called Remediated, and then save the content with the same file name and folder structure. The file name and folder structure needs to match the download exactly.

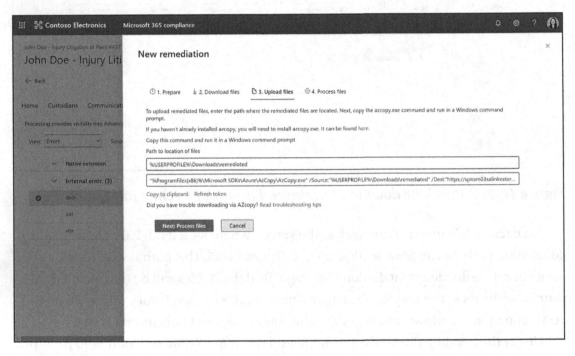

Figure 14-26. *Upload the remediated files back into Advanced eDiscovery*

Go back to eDiscovery and click Next on the upload file screen. You will put the path to the remediated files' location in the first field, shown in Figure 14-26. Again, copy the resulting command to the clipboard, go back to AzCopy, paste it, and press Enter to upload your remediated files. Then Advanced eDiscovery will process the files. This process may take several minutes, depending on the amount of data. When the processing completes, the remediated files will now be available in the search index.

Here is a note about what happens in file remediation. When you remediate files, all the metadata on the data will remain the same. The exception is for the following fields:

- Extracted text size

- Has text

- Is error remediate

- Load ID

- Processing error message

- Processing status

- Text

- Word count

- Working set ID

These fields are all related to Advanced eDiscovery and do not change the files themselves.

Single File Error Remediation

The second way to remediate files is through single file error remediation. We will first need to add search results to a review set, which we will go over in the next two sections of this chapter. Once you have added your data to a review set, you can filter your view or search the review set to show only files with processing errors. To do that, open your review set. Click New query and create a name for the query. Add the condition called "processing status," and then choose the errors that interest you. I like to use the "equals any of" conditions to check the boxes for multiple error types. Leave "Success" unchecked because that option corresponds to successfully processed items. Save the query. Now, you can click that saved query anytime to view files with processing errors. Click one of the files to view its metadata to help decide if you want to remediate it.

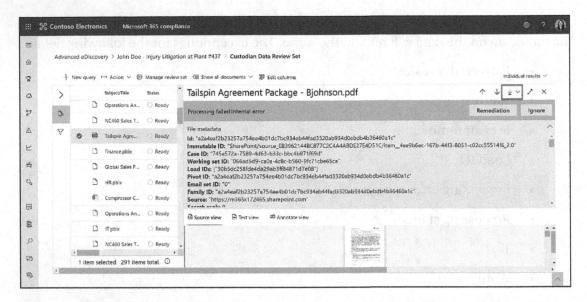

Figure 14-27. *The document metadata and processing error for a partially indexed file*

Above the file metadata, you will see a red box that says "Processing failed: [error type]", shown in Figure 14-27. Here I have two choices. First, I can ignore the file, which removes it from the bulk remediation list, and I will not see it again in this view. Second, I can click Remediation. When I click that, it allows me to upload a remediated file. First, download the individual file by clicking the downward-facing arrow with the line under it, located in the document pane's upper-right corner. I added a box around it in Figure 14-27. You then perform the file remediation and click the Remediation button to upload the new file. When the upload is complete, the system reprocesses it and lets you know when processing is complete.

Another usual review set query related to processing remediation is a query to view remediated files. To set this up, click New query and name the query. Add the condition "was remediated." Choose equals true. This query shows a list of all the files that you have remediated through either the single item remediation or bulk remediation method.

After performing file remediation using either option, you now have a fully searchable set of files for either your custodial or search data. The files are fully indexed and ready for the full discovery process. In the next section, we will examine how to perform an eDiscovery search to gather files for review, analysis, and export.

Jobs

Advanced eDiscovery has several long-running processes. These processes can include running a search, indexing custodian data, adding content to a review set, and more. You can track the status of these long-running processes in the Jobs tab in your case.

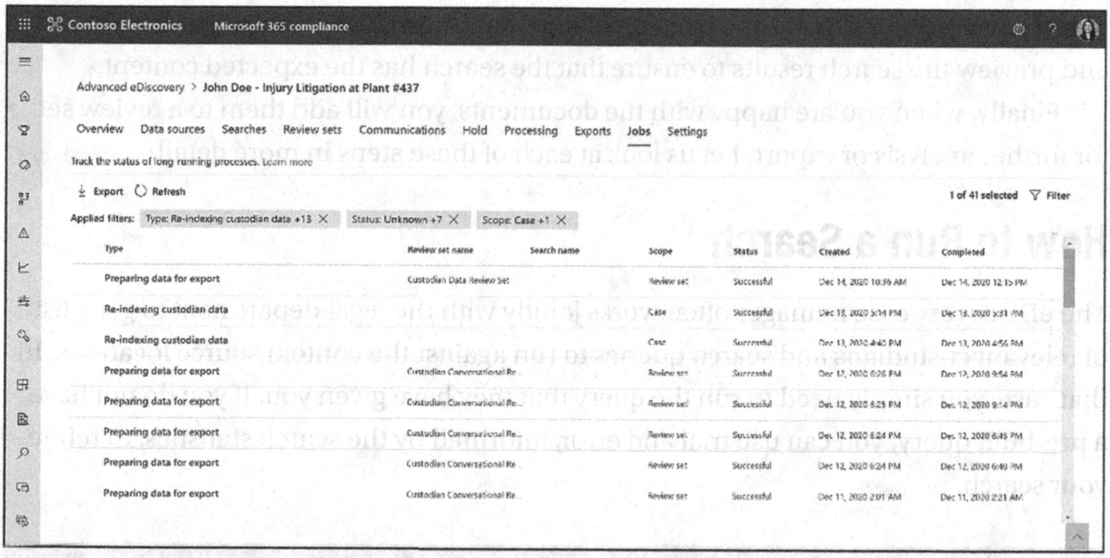

Figure 14-28. *The Jobs tab in an Advanced eDiscovery case*

The Jobs tab shows each of the processes in your case, shown in Figure 14-28 above. You can see the job type, review set name (if applicable), search name (if applicable), scope, status, date created, and date completed. You can export a list of jobs or refresh the view.

You can filter the jobs view to see a subset of information. To do this, click the filter button. Here you can filter by job type, status, or scope.

Click a job to view the job details. Here you can see the job type, job status, progress, and subtasks of the process and their status. You can also get support information from the job details. This screen is useful if you want a more detailed status on the process. It is also helpful if there is an error, so you can see why the error occurred. If you contact Microsoft support because of a processing error, they will need the support information in this details pane.

Advanced eDiscovery Searches

We use searches in Advanced eDiscovery to identify the content for your case or investigation. This identified content is what you will review and/or export.

Advanced eDiscovery has two steps. First, you will build the search query and run the search. This step uses the content search functionality we went over in Chapter 12. Please review that chapter for a deep dive on search. Next, review the search statistics and preview the search results to ensure that the search has the expected content.

Finally, when you are happy with the documents, you will add them to a review set for further analysis or export. Let us look at each of these steps in more detail.

How to Run a Search

The eDiscovery case manager often works jointly with the legal department to get a list of relevant custodians and search queries to run against the content source locations. In that case, you simply need to run the query that they have given you. If you do not have a pre-built query, you can use trial and error, informed by the search statistics, to refine your search.

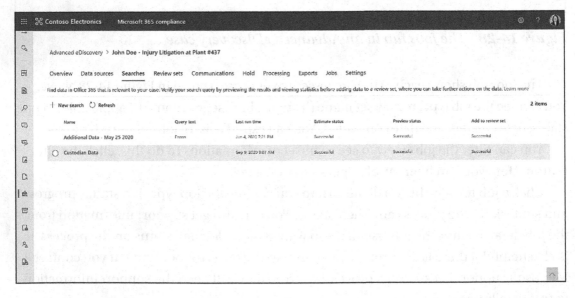

Figure 14-29.   The search overview page in Advanced eDiscovery

To create a search, go to the Searches tab in the Advanced eDiscovery case, shown in Figure 14-29 above. You can see a list of your searches, any query text, and the last time someone ran the search. You can also see the search estimate status, the preview status, and the add to the review set process.

To create a new search, click New search. The first screen asks for a name and a description. Click Next. If you would like to run the search against custodian data locations, select a custodian here. You also have the option to choose all custodians. Selecting a custodian will run a search against all the data sources mapped to that custodian. You do not have to add a custodian. This step is optional. Click Next.

Now you are asked to add non-custodian locations to the search. Again, you can select some or all locations. This step is also optional. Click Next.

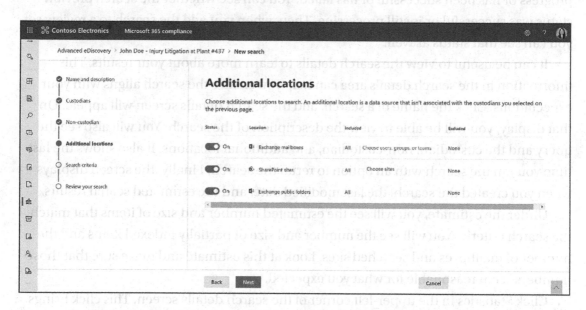

Figure 14-30. *Search additional locations in Advanced eDiscovery*

Next, the wizard asks if you would like to add additional locations to the search, shown in Figure 14-30 above. This step allows you to search locations that are unrelated to the custodian or non-custodian data sources. You can choose to search all Exchange email mailboxes and SharePoint sites or specific locations. You can also search all Exchange public folders. Click Next.

The next screen asks for the search criteria. This search criterion is the same as in content search. You can add keywords, a keyword list, KQL, or no keywords. You can also add conditions to the search, such as a date range or participants in an email. Click Next. Review your search settings and click Submit. There are some limits that affect search. Microsoft increases these limits frequently, so please see the latest information here: `http://erica.news/AeDLimits`.

Search Statistics

Searches are a long-running process. You can view the status of your search from the Searches tab. For example, this page's information will tell you if the search is still in progress or has been successful or has failed. You can see whether the search preview status was successful or is still processing. Then, when you add the search to a review set, you can see that status as well.

It can be useful to view the search details to learn more about your results. This information in the search details area can help you ensure the search aligns with your expectations. Click the name of a search, and the search details screen will appear. On that display, you will be able to view the description of the search. You will also see the query and the custodian, non-custodian, and additional locations. It also shows the last time you ran the search with an option to rerun the search. Finally, the screen displays when you created the search, the last modified date, and the estimated search results.

Under the estimate, you will see the estimated number and size of items that match the search criteria. You will see the number and size of partially indexed items and the number of mailboxes and searched sites. Look at this estimate and make sure that those numbers seem reasonable for what you expected.

Click Statistics in the upper-left corner of the search details screen. This click brings you to a page that provides information about the search. It includes a summary, top locations, and detailed statistics about the search query. First, in the summary view, you can see the search results broken down by a location type, such as Exchange or SharePoint, and then see the following information displayed for each location type. It will show you the number of locations with items that matched the search query, the total number of items from each location type that matched the search criteria, and the overall size of items from each location type that matched the search criteria. You can also download a report of this data.

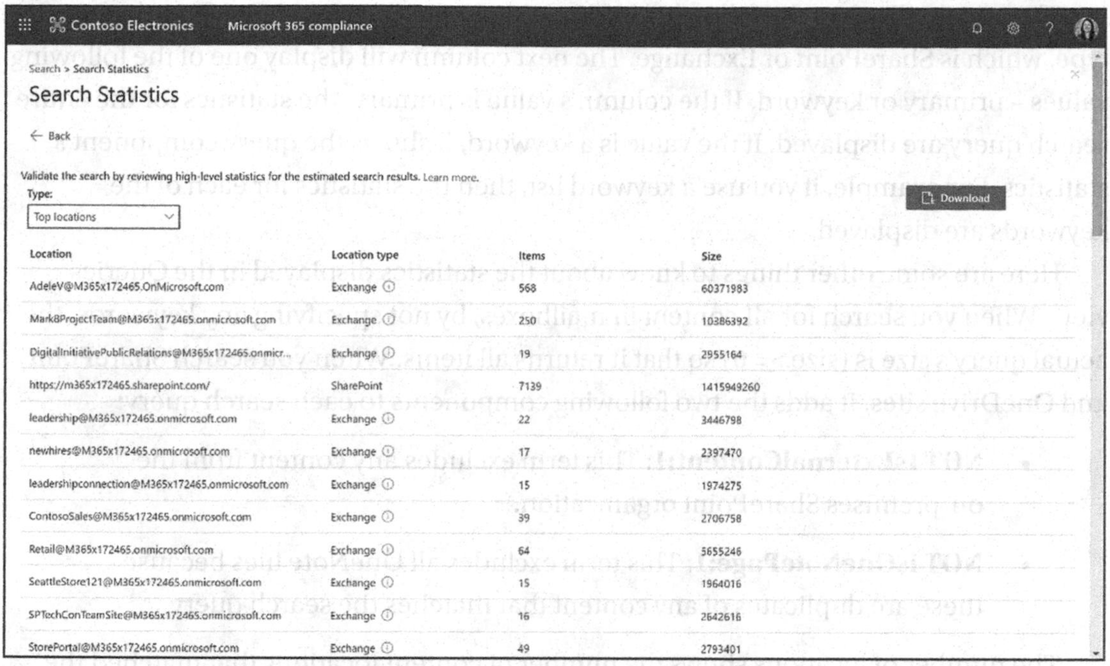

Figure 14-31. *The Search Statistics Top locations view*

Next, for Type, choose Top locations. In this view, shown in Figure 14-31 above, you see the individual content locations with the most items that matched the search query. For each content location, it displays the following information. First, it shows the name of the location. This name could be the email address for mailboxes or the URL for SharePoint sites. Next, it shows the location type, which is Exchange or SharePoint. Then, the number of items that matched the search criteria for that location is displayed. Lastly, the total size of all items that met the search criteria for that location is shown. You can click Download to get a report on this view. This report can be useful because if your search is hitting any search limitations, you can use it to see what locations have the most significant size in your search. You can use that information to break the locations out into multiple searches.

Lastly, for Type, choose Queries. You can see the detailed search statistics for each component of the search query in the Queries view. For example, if you used the keyword list in the search query, you could see enhanced statistics in the Queries view, showing how many items matched each keyword or keyword phrase. This view helps you identify which parts of the query are the most and least significant. You can then use that information to modify your query as needed.

The system displays the following information in the Queries view – first, the location type, which is SharePoint or Exchange. The next column will display one of the following values – primary or keyword. If the column's value is primary, the statistics for the entire search query are displayed. If the value is a keyword, it shows the query component's statistics. For example, if you use a keyword list, then the statistics for each of the keywords are displayed.

Here are some other things to know about the statistics displayed in the Queries view. When you search for all content in mailboxes, by not specifying any keywords, the actual query's size is (size >= 0) so that it returns all items. When you search SharePoint and OneDrive sites, it adds the two following components to each search query:

- **NOT IsExternalContent:1**: This term excludes any content from the on-premises SharePoint organization.

- **NOT isOneNotePage:1**: This term excludes all OneNote files because these are duplicates of any content that matches the search query.

The number of locations shows the number of content locations that matched the search query for the part or condition displayed in the row. Note that archive mailboxes are counted as a separate location if they contain items that match the search query:

- **Items**: Displays the total number of things that matched the search criteria for the part or condition in the row.

- **Size**: Shows the total number of items that matched the search query for the part or condition in this row.

Click the back arrow to return to the search details screen.

Next, let us click Preview in the search details window. This option allows us to see a sample of our search results. You can click an item to view the file's contents in full fidelity or the file metadata. Click the back arrow to return to the search details pane.

The next option is to add results to a review set. We will review this option in the next section. The Edit option allows you to modify the search query. You can change anything except the name of the search. Click More to see further options. Here you can delete or copy the search. You can also sample the search.

The sample option allows you to add a statistically significant sample of the search to a review set for a more detailed analysis. When you click Sample, the system will bring you to a wizard that asks you to select the sampling parameters. You can specify a confidence level and confidence interval or take a random sample of the data and specify a percentage for how much data to include. Select which option you would like and click Next.

You can then choose the review set where you would like to add the data. If you have existing review sets, they will show up as options. You can also create a new review set. Then you can choose the collection options. We will discuss these options in the next section about creating a review set. When you finish your selections, click Next and then Submit. Now you can use the options we discuss in the next section to analyze the sample.

Now let us go over the options for adding a search or sample to a review set.

Manage Review Sets

First, what are review sets? Review sets are a static set of documents where you can analyze, query, filter, view, tag, and export data in a case. When you add the results of a search to a review set, the following things occur:

1. The search is rerun. This action means the actual search results copied to the review set may differ from the estimated results returned when the search previously ran. This change mostly happens if there was a gap when you initially ran the search and when you add it to the review set. It adds the most up-to-date search results to the review set.

2. The system copies all search results from the original data source in the live services to a secure Azure storage location. This copy means that you have a separate copy of the items from where they live in the live services.

3. It reindexes all items, including the content and metadata, so that all data in the review set is fully searchable during the review of the case data. Reindexing the data results in thorough and fast searches when searching the data in a review set during the case investigation.

4. If OCR is enabled, text from the image is extracted and included with the data. OCR is supported for loose files, email attachments, and embedded images. Remember that you need to enable this option in the case settings before you add the content to a review set.

5. A file encrypted with Microsoft encryption technology and is attached to an email message returned in the search results is decrypted when you add the email message and attached file to the review set. You can review and query the decrypted file in the review set. You must be assigned the RMS Decrypt role to add decrypted email attachments to a review set.

6. Conversation threading. Advanced eDiscovery reconstructs Teams and Yammer conversations into threads so that you can review the entire conversation. Please note you need to choose the option Collect contextual Teams and Yammer messages around your search results when you add your search to the review set to see the entire thread. Otherwise, you will only see messages that match your search query. This process preserves unique message-level metadata across all your messages within a conversation.

Please note that there is currently a limit of 20 review sets per case, and you cannot delete review sets from a case.

Create a Review Set

There are two ways to create a review set:

1. Create an empty review set.

2. Add a search to a review set.

To create a new empty review set, click the Review sets tab in an Advanced eDiscovery case. Click Add review set. In the window that appears, create a name and optional description.

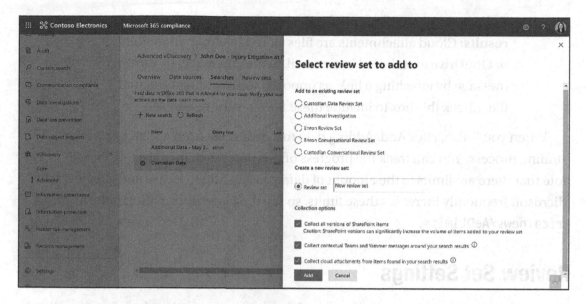

Figure 14-32. *Add search results to a review set in Advanced eDiscovery*

To create a review set by adding search results, visit the Searches tab. Click the search name. In the search details pane that appears, shown in Figure 14-32 above, click Add results to review set. You then have a few options to configure.

First, choose the review set where you want to put the search results. If you have existing review sets, you can see them here and select one. You also have the option to create a new review set.

Second, you have three collection options:

1. **Collect all versions of SharePoint items**: This option includes all versions of a SharePoint file instead of only the most recent version. Keep in mind this can significantly increase the amount of content. By default, SharePoint Online keeps 500 major versions of a file. Your admin can increase or decrease this number or can set the number of versions to unlimited.

2. **Collect contextual Teams and Yammer messages around your search results**: If you check this box, it will bring all messages in the conversation if one message meets the search criteria. For Teams chat and Yammer private messages, it will include messages from about four hours before and after the message that met the search criteria. For Teams conversations and Yammer groups, it will consist of the original post and any replies.

3. **Collect cloud attachments from items found in your search results:** Cloud attachments are files stored in either SharePoint or OneDrive and shared in an email, Teams message, or Yammer message by attaching a link, as opposed to attaching the actual file. Check this box to include these files in your review set.

When you finish, click Add. Adding data to a review set from a search is a long-running process. You can track the progress of this process in the Jobs tab. Please note that there are limits to the amount of data you can add to a case and a review set. Microsoft frequently increases these limits, so see the latest information here: `http://erica.news/AeDLimits`.

Review Set Settings

Like the case settings, you may want to configure review set settings before proceeding with the data review. These settings allow you to create additional analytics and reports, add non–Office 365 data to the case, configure your review tags, and use machine learning to predict document relevance.

To access the review set settings, go to the Review sets tab in your Advanced eDiscovery case. Click Manage review set in the top navigation, which brings you to the settings screen. There are a few options available on this screen:

1. **Analytics**: This option allows you to analyze documents in the review set for more efficient reviews.

2. **Summary report**: View a summary of the documents in this review set.

3. **Load sets**: View load set statistics, compare load sets, or download a load set report.

4. **Tags**: Manage the review tags for your case.

5. **Non–Office 365 data**: This section allows you to load data into a review set from sources other than Office 365.

6. **Relevance**: This module allows you to train the system to identify responsive documents automatically. The relevance module is most useful for large cases involving outside counsel, where you outsource some of the reviews of your data to low-cost resources. We will cover relevance in a later section of this chapter.

Now let us look at the details for the review set settings. First, let us start with analytics. Before you can view analytics for the review set, you need to run an additional process. Click Run analytics for the review set. A warning will pop up that says, "This will take some time. Are you sure?" That is because running analytics is a long-running job that can take from several minutes to several hours.

When the system runs the analytics, it does a few things:

1. **Near-duplicate detection**: Remember that we set our document and email similarity threshold in the case settings near the chapter's beginning. For example, if we put this threshold to 80%, any documents that have text that is at least 80% similar will be considered a near-duplicate. If they are 100% similar, the system regards it is as a duplicate. This way, we can review all the near-duplicates in bulk, highlighting only the differences, to speed up our manual review.

2. **Threads emails**: The system looks at each email individually and compares it to other emails. It categorizes each email into one of the following buckets:

   a. **Inclusive**: The last message in the email has unique content, and the email has all the attachments included in other emails. Because it is the last message in the thread, it contains all the previous messages. You can review only this email and see all the thread's content.

   b. **Inclusive minus**: The email's last message has unique content, but the email does not contain some of the attachments included in other emails.

   c. **Inclusive copy**: An exact copy of an inclusive/inclusive minus email.

    d. **None**: This email's content is in at least one email marked as inclusive/inclusive minus, so you do not need to review it.

3. **Find themes in your review set**: The themes functionality in Advanced eDiscovery attempts to mimic how humans reason about documents. Themes identify the dominant document theme as the one that appears the most often in the document. It then shows you the most prevalent themes in your review set. Themes can help you find patterns in your data you were not aware of, so you can further investigate the interesting ones. Please see the section "Query and Filter Data in a Review Set" to view the resulting themes.

Running analytics also reindexes the data with the near-duplicates considered. The system will rerun the search index, taking the email threads into account. It will also look for document themes, which we will talk about in just a second, and then it will run another index after it finds the themes to include that in the search results. After you run analytics, a query called "For Review" will appear. You can use this to only review unique information in your review set.

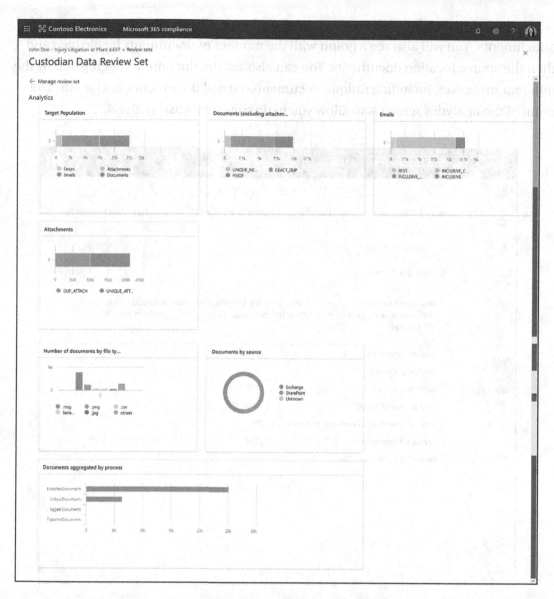

Figure 14-33. *Review set analytics in Advanced eDiscovery*

Once you run the analytics, you can click View report under the Analytics heading in the review set settings. The report will give you additional data about your review set, shown in Figure 14-33. For example, it will tell you the target population, including the number of errors, emails, attachments, and documents. It will also show you documents, excluding attachments, and how many are unique vs. exact duplicates. Other useful information includes statistics about the emails and how many are inclusive vs. other types.

For attachments, it will show you how many are duplicate attachments vs. unique attachments. You will also see a graph with the number of documents by file type and then the source location documents. You can also see the documents aggregated by the different processes, including unique documents, tagged documents, and so on. The point of the analytics screen is to allow you to do some pre-case analysis.

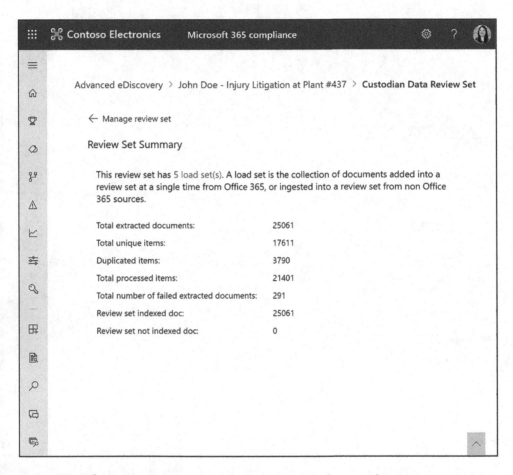

Figure 14-34. *The review set summary report in Advanced eDiscovery*

Now's let us talk about the summary report, shown in Figure 14-34 above. Go back to the settings screen. Under the Summary report heading, click View summary. The review set summary will give you some additional summary data about your review set. It will show you how many load sets are in the case. We will talk about load sets in the next paragraph. The statistics show you things like the total extracted documents, total unique items, duplicate items, total processed items, the total number of failed extracted documents, review set indexed documents, and review set not indexed documents. Again, this information lets you see an overview of what content is in your review set to help with pre-case analysis.

Next, let us cover load sets. Go back to the settings screen. Under Load sets setting, click Manage load sets. A load set is a collection of documents that you added to a review set at a single time from Microsoft 365 or ingested into a review set from non–Office 365 sources. For example, every time you run a search and click Add results to review set, that would be considered one load set. If you then later added another search, the system would view that as a second load set. This area will show you all the load sets added to the review set. If you like, you can download a report, and that report will show you the same information you see on the screen. Each load set has a unique load ID, and it will show you some information about the source and from where it came.

Suppose I double-click one of these load sets. I can see even more detailed statistics about the load set, such as total errors to skipped items, data processing information, and search index information. It is a good idea to look at this report to ensure that there are no errors that you need to remediate and that everything looks reasonable.

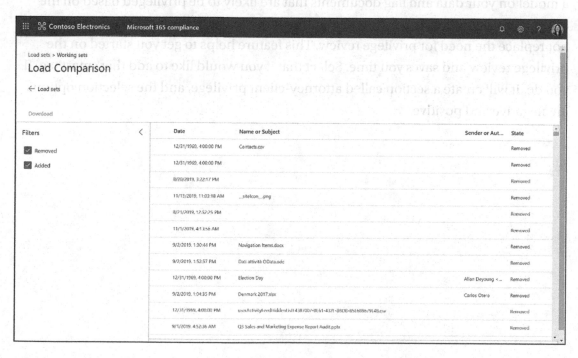

Figure 14-35. *The load set comparison tool in review set settings*

I can also select two load sets and compare them, shown in Figure 14-35 above. This view allows you to understand what files are added or removed from load set to load set. This information can be useful if you have a long-running case and you reran the search to get new search results and then added them to the review set. It might be useful to see how many new files you added need to be reviewed and processed.

Now let us manage tags. The tags are what you will use to tag the documents during the actual review process. These tags are completely customizable based on your business needs. Go back to the settings screen and under the Tags heading, click Manage tags.

Here you will see a blank screen where we can add groupings and tags. First, click Add section and select Add smart tag group. This area is where some of the cool artificial intelligence features of Advanced eDiscovery come into play. When we include a smart tag, we will eventually have several models from which to choose. As of the writing of this book, the available one is the attorney-client privilege smart tag.

Suppose you have the attorney-client privilege detection setting on. Remember that we configured this tool at the beginning of the chapter. In that case, the system will run a model on your data and flag documents that are likely to be privileged based on the content and compare participants against the provided attorney list. This feature does not replace the need for privilege review. This feature helps to get you started on the privilege review and saves you time. Select that if you would like to add that smart tag. If you do, it will create a section called attorney-client privilege, and the selection options are negative and positive.

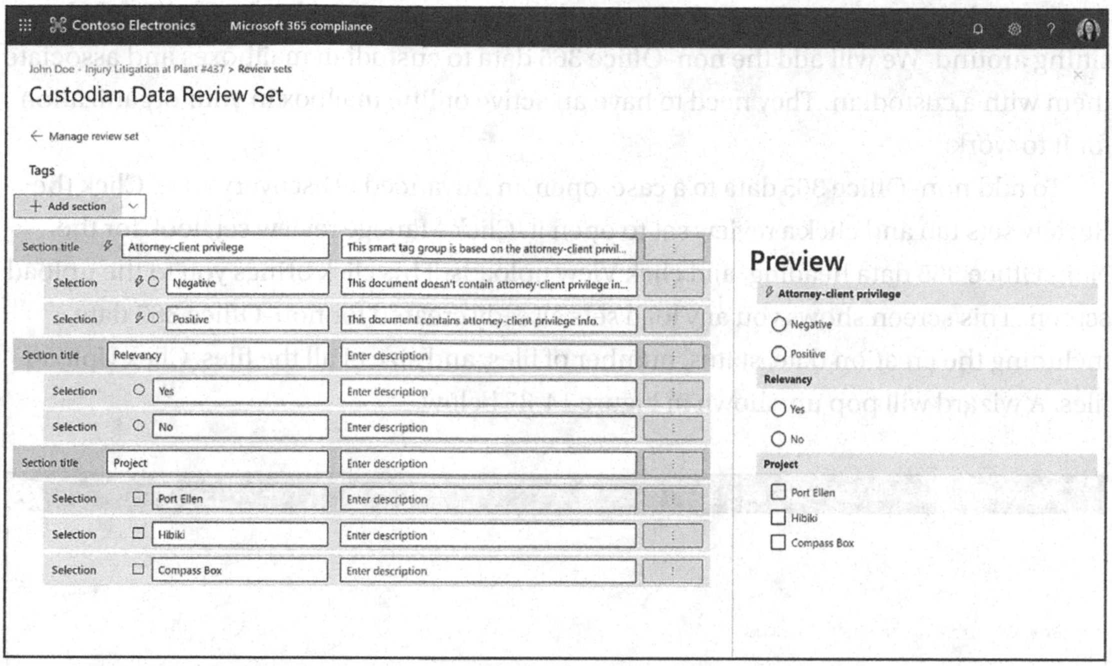

Figure 14-36. *An example of a tagging panel for a review set*

Now let us add more tags to the review set. Click Add section. Here you will be able to add a section title and click Save. Then, from there, you can click the ellipsis that is to the right of the description for the section title, and you have the option to add a button if you need to have mutually exclusive tags. You can add a checkbox if people can select more than one option. You can move the section up so it is above other sections, or you can delete the section. You can also see a live preview on the right side of the screen that shows you these changes and additions in real time. Add your sections and tags as needed. An example of a complete tagging panel is shown in Figure 14-36 above.

If you go back to the review set settings screen, we have gone over all the options except for the non–Office 365 data import, which we will go over in the next section, and the relevance model we will go through near the end of this chapter.

How to Add Non–Office 365 Data into a Case

You may want to add non–Office 365 data to a review set for a couple of reasons. First, if you have old PST files that you are keeping for discovery purposes, your organization may sometimes store those in a file share or other locations. You can add those to your discovery by uploading the PST files to your case.

Second, this process also works for any documents or other files that you might have sitting around. We will add the non–Office 365 data to custodian mailboxes and associate them with a custodian. They need to have an active online mailbox in your organization for it to work.

To add non–Office 365 data to a case, open an Advanced eDiscovery case. Click the Review sets tab and click a review set to open it. Click Manage review set, look for the Non–Office 365 data heading, and click View uploads. This click brings you to the upload screen. This screen shows you any load sets already created for non–Office 365 data, including the creation date, status, number of files, and size of all the files. Click Upload files. A wizard will pop up, shown in Figure 14-37 below.

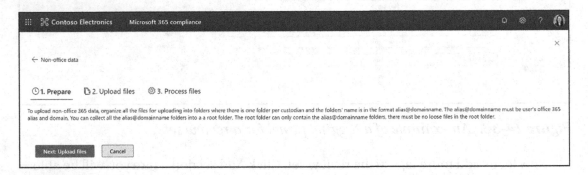

Figure 14-37. *Instructions to prepare non–Office 365 data for upload*

The first step is to prepare the non–Office 365 data for upload. Organize all the files you will upload into folders, naming each folder as a custodian email address. The format for the folder needs to be alias@domainname.com or alias@domainname without .com. You can put all those folders into a root folder, but the root folder can only contain these custodian folders and not any loose files. Otherwise, this process will error out. As of March 2021 you cannot import more than 300 GB at one time. Microsoft is working to increase these limits, so view the latest information here: `http://erica.news/AeDLimits`. If you have more than 300 GB of data, please divide the custodian folders into more than one root file and import them in multiple batches.

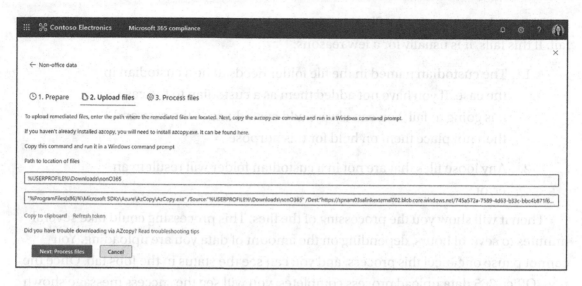

Figure 14-38. *Instructions for uploading files using the AzCopy tool*

Once you have prepared all these files, click Next ➤ Upload files. The resulting screen is shown in Figure 14-38 above. We will upload the files using AzCopy.exe. If you have not yet installed it, you can find the instructions for installing AzCopy in the "Processing and Error Remediation" section of this chapter. For the path to the files' location, put in the path of the root folder containing the custodian folders you prepared in the preceding text. This process will then auto-generate the script you can run in AzCopy. Copy the script to the clipboard, paste it into AzCopy, and press Enter.

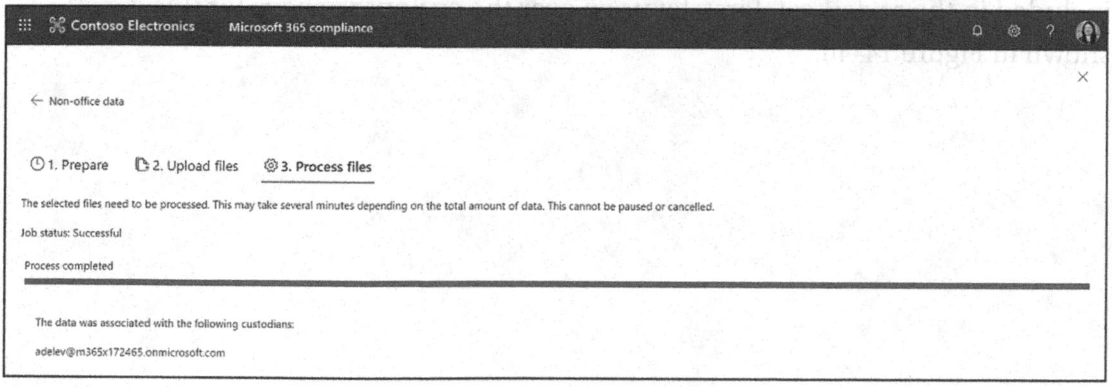

Figure 14-39. *A successful upload of non–Office 365 data*

This click will transfer the files into the case. You might get some errors, or this might fail. If this fails, it is usually for a few reasons:

1. The custodian named in the file folder needs to be a custodian in the case. If you have not added them as a custodian to the case, it is going to fail. You can always add custodians to the case and then not place them on hold for this purpose.

2. Any loose files that are not in a custodian folder will result in an error.

Then it will show you the processing of the files. This processing could take several minutes to several hours, depending on the amount of data you are uploading. You cannot pause or cancel this process, and you can see the status in the Jobs tab. Once the non–Office 365 data upload process completes, you will see the success message shown in Figure 14-39 above. The import will appear in the list of non–Office 365 data load sets.

When you search against the review set, you can search the files by the individual custodian location, which is their Exchange mailbox.

Reviewing Data in a Review Set

Now that you have all your data in your review set and have analyzed it, let's discuss how we will review the data. From your Advanced eDiscovery case, click the Review sets tab and then click the name of your review set. Here, it shows you all the files included in the review set. First, let us go over the options we have for this view, shown in Figure 14-40.

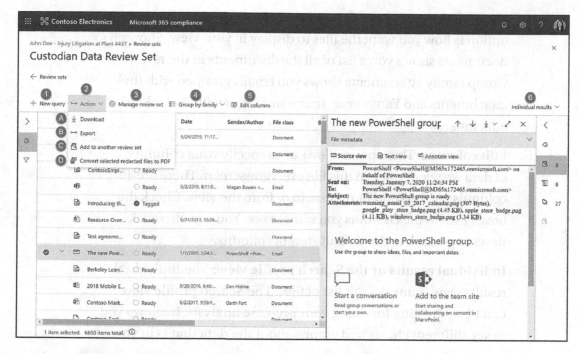

Figure 14-40. *Review set options in Advanced eDiscovery*

1. **New query**: This option will allow you to search within the review set. We will go over how to do this in the next section.

2. **Action**: This has a few sub-options.

    a. If one or many files are selected, you can download those individual files.

    b. Export data outside of Microsoft 365. We will review that option in detail in the last section of this chapter.

    c. Add the data to another review set, which could be useful if you want to analyze a subset of documents separately.

    d. Convert all redacted files to PDF. We will show you how to redact files later in this section. You must convert the redacted files to PDF before an export to preserve the redactions.

3. **Manage review set**: This will take you to the review set settings described earlier in this section.

4. **Show all documents or Group family attachments**: The next option is how you want the files to display in your view. Show all documents shows you a list of all the documents in the review set. Group family attachments shows you emails grouped with their attachments and Yammer or Teams messages with their cloud attachments.

5. **Edit columns**: This option allows us to specify what columns of data we want to see in this file overview screen. There are 49 columns you can add or remove to or from the view. Check the boxes next to the columns you want to see. You can also click Reset to go back to the default view of columns.

6. **Individual results or the Search profile view**: The Individual results view is our default list of files. The Search profile view can be interesting for doing your pre-case analysis. It allows you to see different charts and graphs about the data that is in your review set.

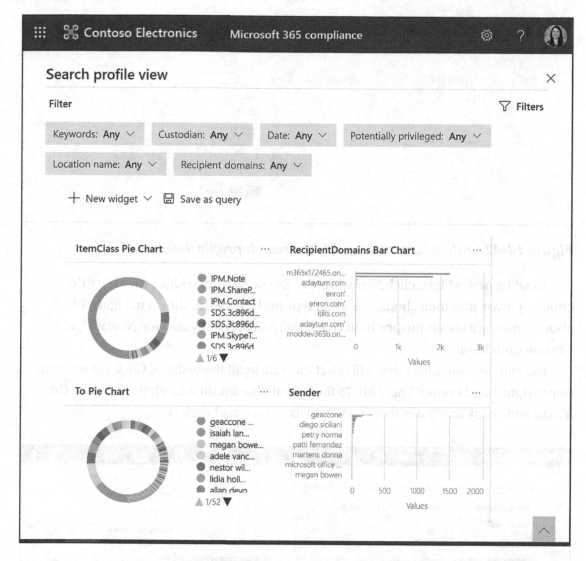

Figure 14-41. *The search profile dashboard for your review set*

In the Search profile view, run the review set analytics first, described in the section "Review Set Settings." If you click Search profile view, it will bring you to a new screen that allows you to filter all the charts on the page based on different criteria, shown in Figure 14-41. You can also either add new filters or add new chart widgets to the page.

First, let us look at the widgets. We can see things like the custodian column chart, which shows you the different number of files available for each custodian. We could see the file class pie chart, which will show you how many emails, documents, or attachments are in the review set. We could look at a recipient bar chart, which will show us the number of files per email recipient.

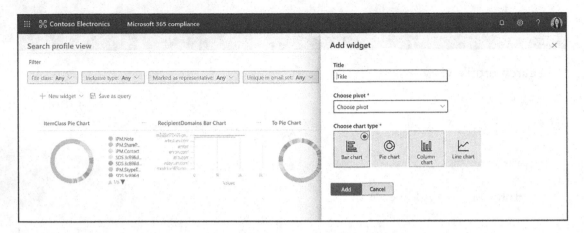

Figure 14-42. *Add a custom widget to the search profile dashboard*

To add a new widget, click New widget ➤ Create custom widget. Create a title, choose a pivot, and then choose the chart type and click Add, shown in Figure 14-42 above. There are also some pre-built charts you can access by clicking New widget ➤ Choose from library.

You can also add filters that will affect the data in all the widgets. Click Filters in the upper right-hand corner. There are 75 filters available for the Search profile view. Go ahead and check any boxes that you would like to see and click OK.

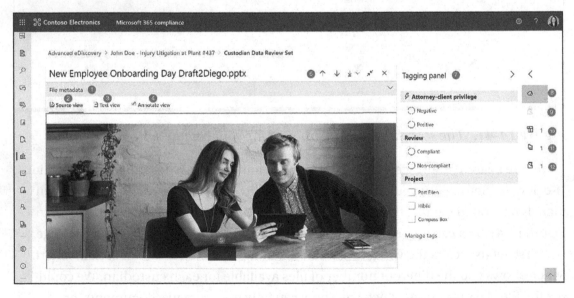

Figure 14-43. *The document review options in Advanced eDiscovery*

Click the X in the upper right-hand corner of the screen to go back to the view of documents to review content.

Now we will review the content. Click the name of a file to view the contents. Click the diagonal arrows on the upper-right side of the document to make the document full screen.

Here is an overview of each of the features on this screen, shown in Figure 14-43. We will go over each of them in detail in this section:

1. **File metadata**: Expand this panel to see every piece of metadata associated with the file. This metadata includes the original file data and the metadata added by Advanced eDiscovery. We will go over this in detail in the following.

2. **Source view**: Allows us to view the file as any end user would see it.

3. **Text view**: Shows only text and no formatting. On the right side of the text view, you will also see a highlighting of where terms that matched the query are present in the document.

4. **Annotate view**: Redact or write on the content. We will go over this in detail in the following.

5. **Zoom and rotate**: Make the document larger/smaller or rotate it on the screen.

6. **Navigation**: The up and down navigation arrows move us to the next document. The downward arrow with a line lets us download the original document or download it as a PDF. The two arrows pointing toward each other decrease the document's size to go back to our standard view. The X closes the document that we are viewing to go back to the list view.

7. **Tagging panel**: Displays the tags we configured in the review set settings. This location is where we tag the documents.

8. **Tagging panel display**: Click this button to show or hide the tagging panel.

9. **Document family display**: Shows previously grouped items, such as an email and its attachments.

10. **Conversation display**: This shows us emails in a thread, Teams chats, conversation threads, or Yammer threads. We will go over this in detail in the following.

11. **Near-duplicate display**: Shows similar documents based on the threshold you designated in the case settings. We will go over this in detail in the following.

12. **Exact duplicate display**: This shows us exact duplicates of the file so that you can tag them in bulk instead of each file. We will go over this in detail in the following.

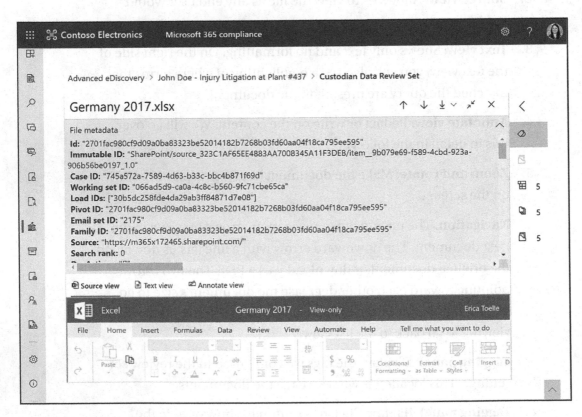

Figure 14-44. *The file metadata view in an Advanced eDiscovery review set*

You can view a file's metadata by expanding the gray bar above the file viewer, shown in Figure 14-44 above. Here you can see all the metadata for the file, including information added by Advanced eDiscovery. To see a full list of the metadata fields and their meaning, visit this link: `http://erica.news/AeDFileProperties`.

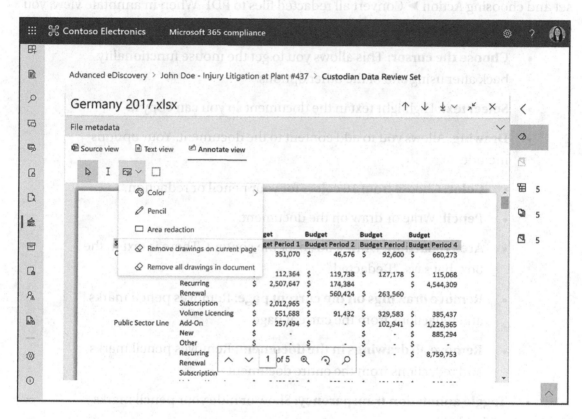

Figure 14-45. *Annotate view in an Advanced eDiscovery review set*

The annotate view lets you write on a document or redact it, shown in Figure 14-45 above. Any drawings you make will only affect the document within the eDiscovery case and will not modify the original document. Be sure to save redacted files as PDFs before export to preserve your drawings. You can do this by opening the review set and choosing Action ➤ Convert all redacted files to PDF. When in annotate view, you can see the following options:

- **Choose the cursor**: This allows you to get the mouse functionality back after using one of the other options.

- **Select text**: Highlight text in the document so you can copy it.

- **Drawing**: Allows you to add content to the document. Your options include

  - **Color**: Choose from 16 colors for your pencil or redaction.

  - **Pencil**: Write or draw on the document.

  - **Area redaction**: Draw a box over the content. There is text in the box that says, "Redacted."

  - **Remove drawings on the current page**: Removes pencil marks and redactions from the current page.

  - **Remove all drawings in the document**: Removes pencil marks and redactions from the entire document.

- **Toggle annotation transparency**: Show or hide your pencil marks and redactions.

Document family includes an email and the email's attachments, shown in Figure 14-46. It can also include an Office document and any embedded files. Viewing content as a document family allows you to see all the files in one another's context. It also allows you to bulk tag all the files in the family. To do this, select all the documents and click Tag documents.

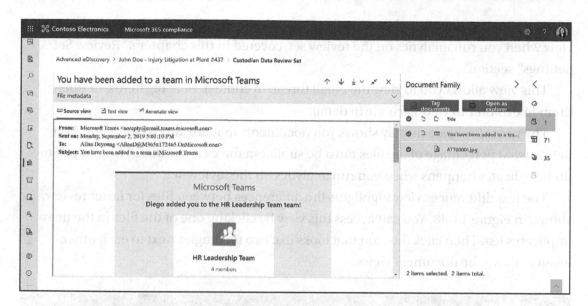

Figure 14-46. *A document family in an Advanced eDiscovery review set*

You can also open the documents in explorer view. This view will open a new window with a list of the documents, shown in Figure 14-47.

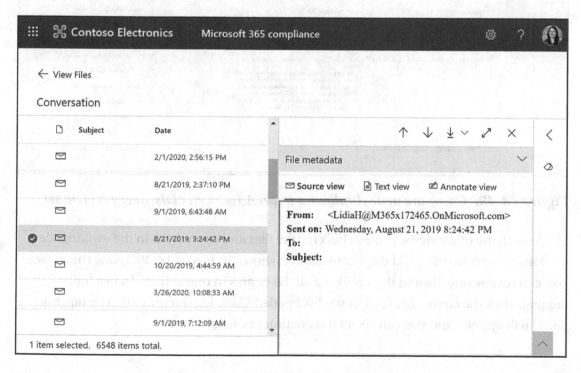

Figure 14-47. *Email conversation view in an Advanced eDiscovery review set*

The conversation view shows an email thread conversation. The system creates this view when you run analytics on the review set, covered in this chapter's "Review Set Settings" section.

This view allows you to view the email thread in context, bulk tag items, or open them in explorer to view each file in detail.

The near-duplicate display shows you documents that are almost the same. You define what percentage of the files must be similar in the case settings. The analysis to find duplicates happens when you run analytics on the review set.

The text differences view highlights the differences between files for faster review, shown in Figure 14-48. You can access this view by clicking one of the files in the near-duplicates list. Then click the icon that looks like two rectangles next to each other, located above the document viewer.

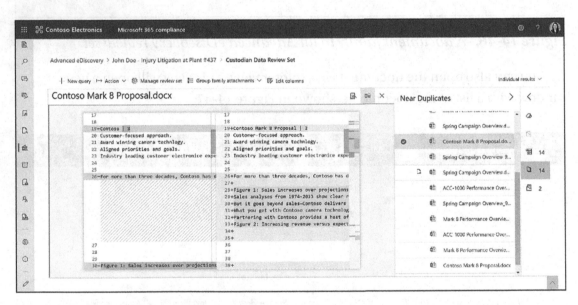

Figure 14-48. *Compare near-duplicates in an Advanced eDiscovery review set*

As with the other views, you can bulk tag the files and open them in the explorer view.

Lastly, we have the exact duplicate display, shown in Figure 14-49. Using this view, you can review one file and then bulk tag all the copies in one action. To use bulk tagging, click the circle checkbox in the list header. Click Tag documents. The tagging panel will appear, and you can select the documents. Click Done.

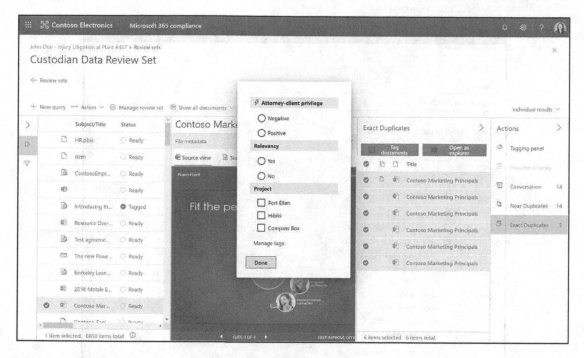

Figure 14-49. *Bulk tag exact duplicates in an Advanced eDiscovery review set*

Query and Filter Data in a Review Set

When working with documents in a review set, you might need to filter or refine the search to work with the files. To do this, you can use the search and filter functions within the review set.

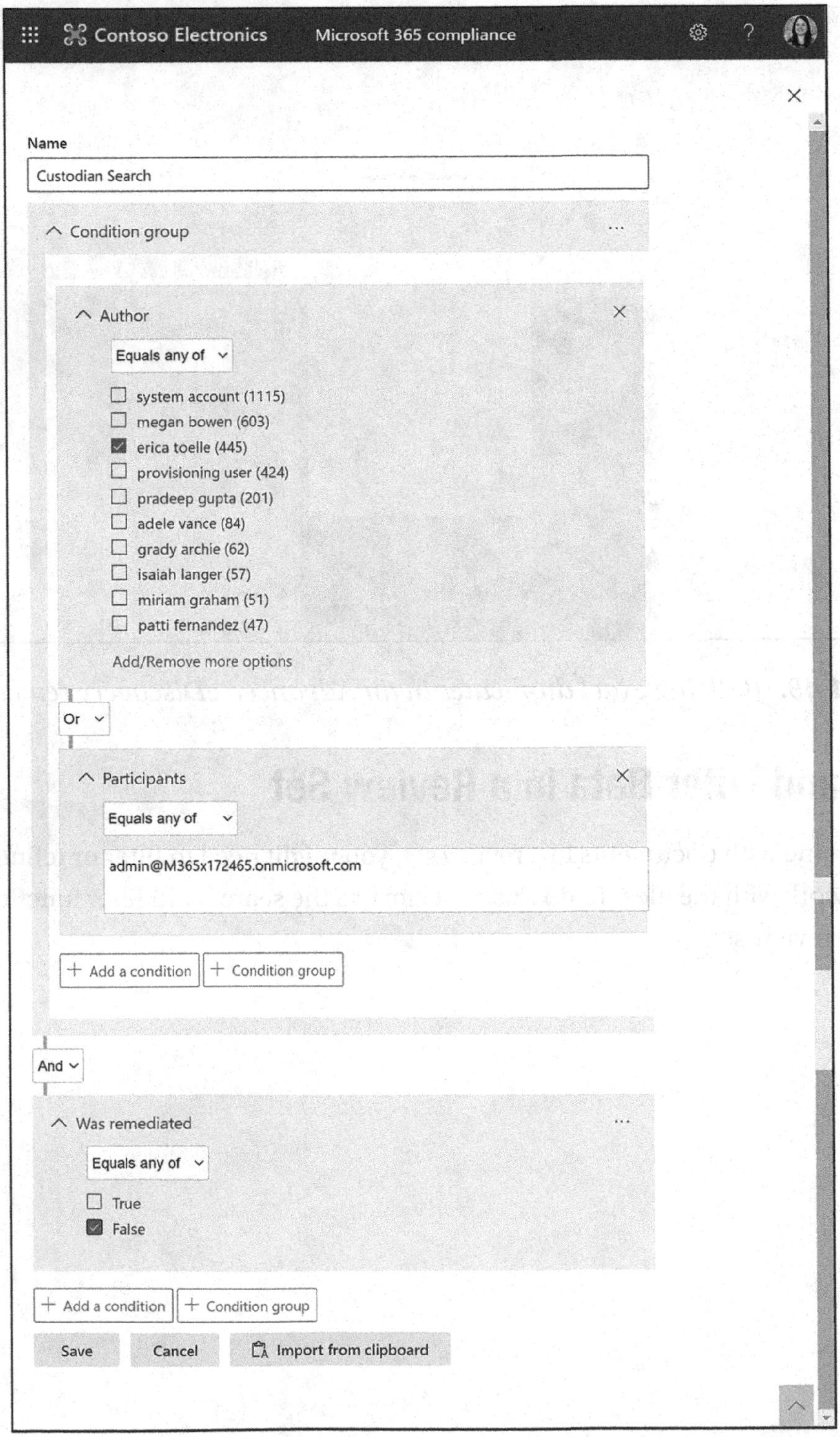

Figure 14-50. *Example of a search query in a review set*

To create a new search, click New query from within the review set. This click will bring you to the query wizard, where you can add conditions and condition groups, shown in Figure 14-50 above.

Click Add condition group. The condition group evaluates the conditions, with AND or OR statements connecting the group's conditions. You then add conditions to the group.

Click Add condition. Adding a condition allows you to choose from many different metadata fields in Microsoft 365 and Advanced eDiscovery. There are over 50 fields from which to choose. For example, if we want to search for documents authored by a specific individual or email that they participated in, we will do the following. First, choose the condition "author" and select "equals any of," and check the box next to the custodian's name. Then we will create a second condition and choose the "participants" condition. We will select "contains all" and put the individual's email address in the box below. We will connect these two statements with an "OR" operator. If we are only interested in finding documents and emails within a specific date range, we would add a new condition group, select date, and choose the date range we want to search.

We will connect the two condition groups with the AND operator. Our query says that if the author or the participant on the email is Adele Vance and the date range is within the last year, return the result. We would then save the search query so that we can use it later.

Next, let us talk about filters. Filters are useful when you want to query data temporarily. They are an addition to the search query, meaning you are filtering the data within the query view. You also do not have the flexibility to group conditions with AND and OR statements with a filter. If you click a different search query, you will lose the filter. In comparison, the system saves searches for reuse, and you can build complexity in the query with multiple conditions in groups, using AND and OR.

To create a filter, click Filters ➤ Add condition. This click will bring up the same list of conditions that were available for a search. Check the boxes next to the conditions you want to use and click Add. Add the values to the conditions and click Search.

Remember, back at the beginning when we created the case, we set up the case settings. Well, one of the things that we configured was case themes. Now, you may be wondering, "What are those themes, and how can I use them?" The answer is that the theme has been added to files as a piece of metadata. Therefore, we can use them as a condition in our search and filter queries inside a review set. I show an example of using themes as a filter in Figure 14-51.

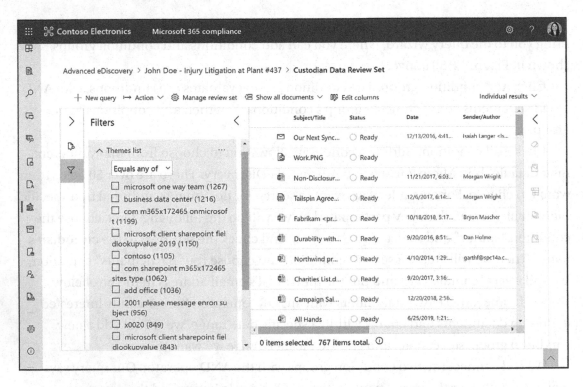

Figure 14-51. *Create a filter within a review set search query*

First, go ahead and create a new filter. Add a condition and scroll down until you see the condition called themes list. Click Add. Now you are going to see the list of themes that the analytics engine created for your case. You can browse through the list of themes and check the boxes next to ones that seem interesting to explore them further.

Relevancy

The relevancy module in Advanced eDiscovery is a technology-assisted review (TAR) solution. TAR has been prominent in the last few years and has significantly impacted how firms do high-volume review work. TAR uses machine learning to identify responsive content without a manual review by utilizing predictive coding. The predictive coding process is as follows:

- The attorney from an outside counsel looks at 200 to a few thousand random samples of documents.

- They code these documents as either responsive or nonresponsive.

- The predictive coding module looks at how these documents have been marked and learns from this information.

- It gives the remaining documents a 0–100 score predicting responsiveness, where 100 is responsive and 0 is nonresponsive.

The relevancy module is excellent for data investigations, where accuracy is not essential. It is also great to reduce costs where accuracy is necessary. We are looking for a statistically significant model where we can make a call, such as "We'll only review documents that have a score of 35 and above that are most likely to be relevant, and then we'll ignore all the documents that are 35 and below."

We will then take an illusion sample, which is a statistically significant random sample of everything below 35, to make sure that we can prove that these documents are not responsive. An attorney will then do a privileged review and pass off everything else to the government or opposing counsel.

People have done studies that show the Microsoft algorithm is slightly more accurate than if a human manually marked all the content as responsive or nonresponsive. The risk is that this process will produce nonrelevant content to the opposing counsel. Remember, we are trying to find most of the responsive documents while having a reasonable discovery cost. Through predictive coding, we can prove that we statistically found 95% of responsive documents in the organization and that the cost to find the remaining 5% would be too great. Everyone involved in the case would typically agree that this percentage is reasonable.

Specifically, the Advanced eDiscovery relevancy module will produce the best culling of data and prioritize relevant results when your collection of documents has more than 10,000 items. At a minimum, your control set, called the assessment, will need to contain 500 documents but usually will need to have a lot more. And then, if you include that plus 50 training iterations to reach stability to apply the classifier, you are looking at an attorney tagging 2,500 documents at a minimum. Because of this time investment in tagging documents, the relevancy module is an excellent tool for service providers with lower-cost attorneys on staff to process and review huge matters. The relevancy module is usually not as useful for issues that remain in house because they are not big enough and the cost of the attorney's time is too much.

The Relevancy Process

There are three steps + settings and configuration in the Advanced eDiscovery relevancy module process, shown in Figure 14-52:

1. **Prepare**: Actions to set up our case and issues correctly.

2. **Train and apply**: Tagging documents and validating the model.

3. **Validate and test**

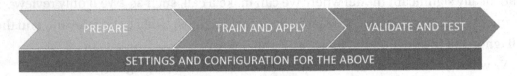

Figure 14-52. *The relevancy process in Advanced eDiscovery*

At its core, these steps build a machine learning model to determine what documents are relevant to a specific case and, more specifically, to a particular case issue. For each step in this process, there are both mandatory steps and optional settings. I will explain each part of the process's required actions first and then optional steps.

To access the relevancy model, click Advanced eDiscovery in the Compliance Center. Click Review sets and the name of a review set. Click Manage review set and Show relevance.

Within the relevancy module, there will be new navigation. The gray bars along the top are the overall steps in the process. The settings for each step are on the left navigation with the blue bar highlights.

Prepare

The first process step is to prepare. These are simply the steps we need to do to set up our case and case issues appropriately. Our required steps are to run pre-processing on the container of documents and to set up our case issues. Our optional steps are the process advanced settings, process task status, process results, process custodians, set uploads, set up keywords, and set up advanced keywords.

The first required step is to run pre-processing on our containers. Pre-processing prepares the files, so they are ready to go for our machine learning and machine training process later. To do this, click Process on the first gray bar at the top of the page. Click Setup on the left navigation. Make sure you do not click Setup on the gray bar. On this page, we will see a list of all the containers in your review set. A container corresponds to a load of files into the review set. For example, adding a search to the review set will result in one container. Click the name of a container to highlight it in blue. Then click the Process button at the bottom of the page. Eventually, under the Pre-processing column, the bar will turn orange and show as complete (shown in Figure 14-53), and you can move on.

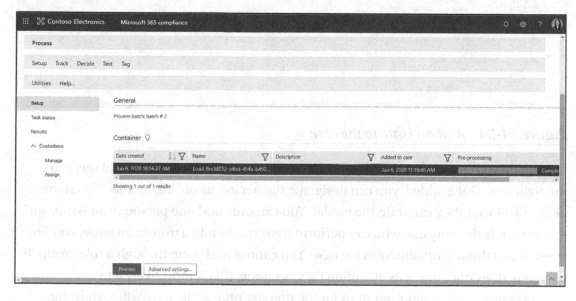

Figure 14-53. Run pre-processing on a container

The other required step in this process is to set up issues. A case issue is the precise legal questions or conflicts you are addressing in the case. The legal department will provide issues for this situation. Click the setup link at the top in the gray bar to access issues. You will need to create issues on this page and assign a person to perform the training. By default, one issue, called Case issue, is created for you. You can click the issue name and then the pencil on the right side of the page just above the issue to edit it, shown in Figure 14-54. To create a new issue, click the plus icon. You can have more than one issue per case and run the train and apply step for each issue. Here you can name the issue, add a description, and add someone to the issue.

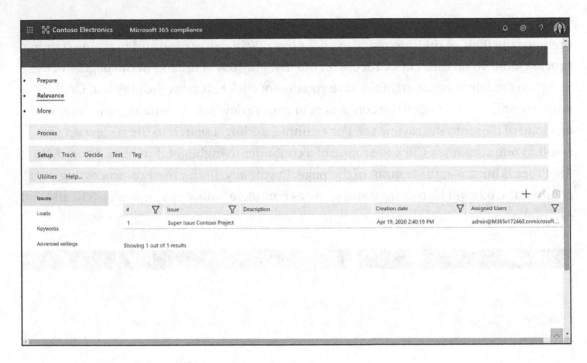

Figure 14-54. *Add an issue to the case*

To add someone, click their name in the left box. Click the arrow to add them to the right box. Once added, you can designate the person as on, off, or idle. This status defines whether they can train the model. You can only add one person to an issue, and this person is the only one who can perform training. To add a user to an issue, you first need to add them individually to the case. You cannot add them through a role group. If someone does not appear as an option for your issue, this is most likely why.

Those are the two required steps for the prepare phase. Next, we will review the optional steps. The first optional step is process task status. To view this page, click Process on the gray bar at the top. Then click Task status on the left navigation. This page shows you the status of whatever tasks you are performing at that time, such as pre-processing or adding files to a case, which we will go over later. If you are unsure if processing was successful, check this page.

The next optional step is results. Click Results in the left navigation. This page will show you the process summary results, how many files it extracted, how many were processed and processed with errors, erroneous file types, and more. It is good to check this page after you run pre-processing, but before you proceed to training to make sure everything worked and you received the expected results.

The next optional step is to set up keywords. Keywords are useful to highlight certain words in different colors, shown in Figure 14-55. When your attorney trains your model, those words will show in a different color to easily see them. This highlight helps them determine what is relevant and not relevant. To set up keywords, click Setup on the top gray bar. Then click Keywords in the left navigation. To add a keyword, click the plus sign located on the right side of the page above the keyword list. You can put multiple keywords in here, separated by a comma. You can choose from a list of colors, which will be the highlight color for those keywords, and then you can select which issue to which these keywords apply. For example, you could have three keywords show as red and one as blue.

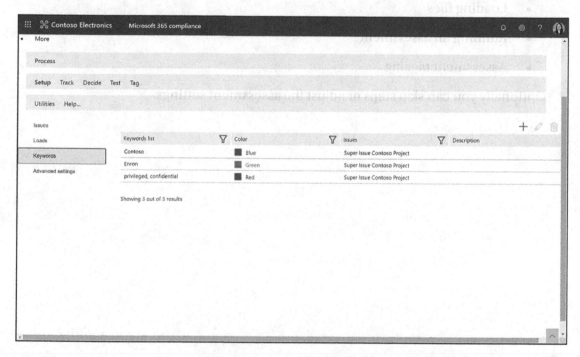

Figure 14-55. *Keywords to highlight during the relevance tagging step*

Finally, the last optional step is to set up advanced settings. Click Setup on the top gray bar and then Advanced settings in the left navigation. Here there are two cost parameters. These parameters are the cost per hour for one of your low-cost attorneys to review the files and the number of files they can review per hour. Once you have trained your model, when you are trying to decide what percent relevancy makes sense for your case, these parameters help you. For example, 35% relevancy means reviewing all the files with a 35 and above relevancy score, which would cost $500,000 based on these cost parameters. This information helps you determine where to set that percent relevancy and even if the case is worth it to pursue or settle based on the costs required to go through discovery.

Train and Apply

Now, we will move on to the train and apply phase of the relevancy process. The mandatory steps in train and apply are

- Tracking your progress
- Loading files
- Running an assessment
- Assessment tagging

Optionally you can skip steps or adjust the assessment settings.

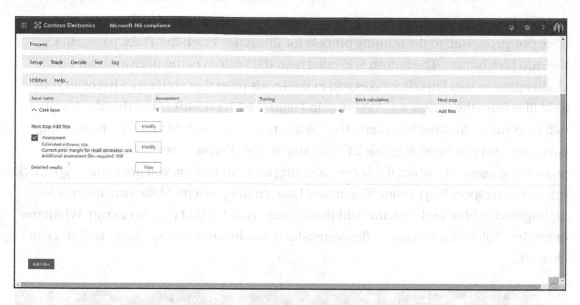

Figure 14-56. *The Track page in the Advanced eDiscovery relevancy module*

First, let us understand how the Track area works. To get to this area, click Track on the gray bar at the top. That click brings you to the Track page, shown in Figure 14-56. The Track page shows you where you are in the train and apply process. You can always come back to this page if you get lost in the user interface. The Track page shows you the next step in this process. Click the issue name to expand it and see the process details.

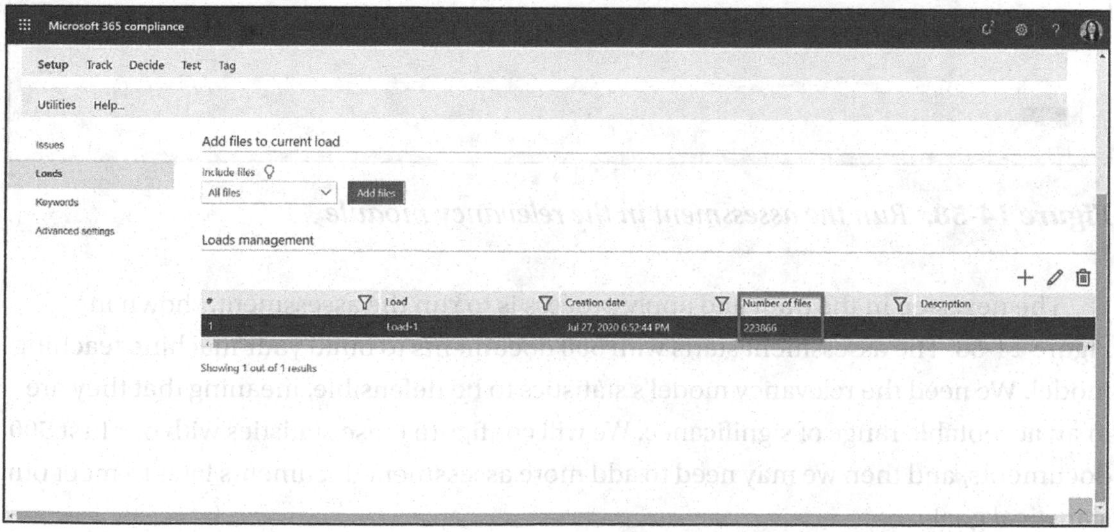

Figure 14-57. *Load files for the relevancy training process*

The first step in train and apply is to load files. Loading files adds the content you have pre-processed to the training process for this issue. From the Track page, click the Add files button. The button is located near the bottom of the page and can be challenging to see. This click takes you to the Loads page that contains a list of all your load files from the review set. As shown in Figure 14-57, please ensure that the Number of files column does not have zero. If it has a zero, you did not do your pre-processing correctly, and you need to go back to that step in the "Prepare" section and run pre-processing again. However, if it shows anything other than zero, you are good to go. Click the row corresponding to your files, under Loads management. Make sure the row is highlighted in blue and click the Add files button. Wait for that process to run. When the operation finishes, it will say, "Files were added to relevance successfully," and you can click OK.

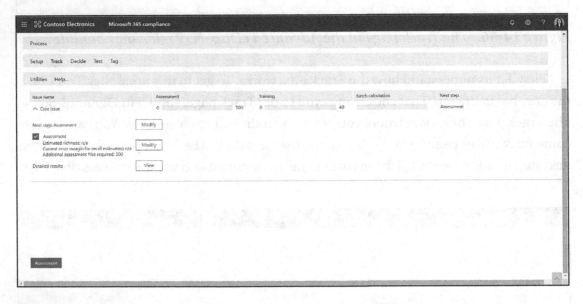

Figure 14-58. *Run the assessment in the relevancy module*

The next step in the train and apply process is to run the assessment, shown in Figure 14-58. The assessment starts with 500 documents to build your machine teaching model. We need the relevancy model's statistics to be defensible, meaning that they are in an acceptable range of significance. We will configure these statistics with our first 500 documents, and then we may need to add more assessment documents later to meet our statistical goals.

The number of documents we need to tag for the entire process depends on various things, such as the assessment's richness. Richness is the number of relevant documents in the sample of 500. If you have a high level of richness, the training will go a lot faster than if you have a low level of richness. If your richness is less than 2%, then this process could take so long that it is just not worth the time. The assessment process's output will determine the estimated richness; the recall level, which is the percentage of relevant documents that we want to find; and an error margin, which we want to be 10% or less. The error margin is determined based on the richness of the data. A higher richness means it is easier for the system to find relevant documents, which means you will have a higher recall level with a lower error margin.

The system selects a random sample of 500 documents from the files in our review set. The best-case scenario is the system will give us additional sets of 500 files to review until we see enough to provide us with an error margin of 10% or less. When we tag things as relevant or irrelevant, we need to be consistent in our assessment and have a high enough number of documents that the machine learning model can understand what is relevant.

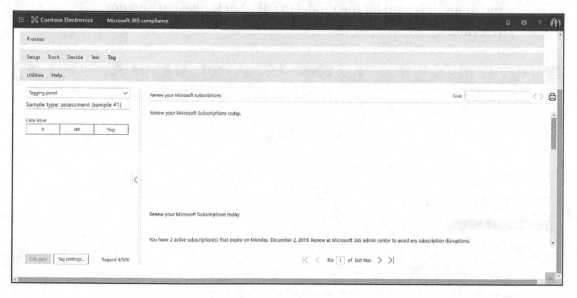

Figure 14-59. Tagging panel in the Advanced eDiscovery relevancy module

Let us start tagging documents. From the Track page, click Assessment to start the evaluation. That click brings you to a screen. The screen displays the file on the right side of the page, and the tagging panel is on the left. View the document and mark it as either

R for relevant or NR for not relevant, or skip if you do not know, shown in Figure 14-59. As a reminder, we defined keywords earlier that the system displays in color to make it easier for them to find these relevant files while they are tagging.

As you tag these documents, follow these tagging best practices:

1. **Be consistent**. If you make errors during training, you need to return to those files to correct them. If you have too many errors, you need to abort and start over. I will cover how you can clear the data and start over later in this section.

2. **Tag the files based on content only**. Do not consider metadata, such as the custodian, a date, or any other file metadata. You should not consider a date range or graphical images when tagging the files. Also, do not consider the formatting of the text. Only consider the actual text and words in the document.

3. **Use the skip tagging option only when necessary**. The relevancy module does not train based on skipped files, and if you pass on too many, it is hard for the model to tell what is relevant and not relevant.

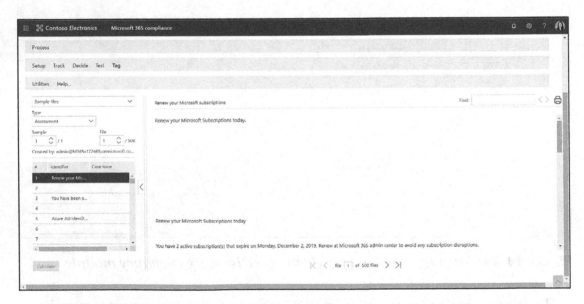

Figure 14-60. *Sample files in the Advanced eDiscovery relevancy module*

You can browse sample files, for example, if you need to go back and correct a tagging error. To do that, select sample files from the dropdown in the upper-left corner of the page, and this will give you a list of all the files in your current set, shown in Figure 14-60. You can find the document in the scroll menu or put the file number in the file field, which will let you jump directly to that file.

Once you review all 500 of the assessment files, the assessment phase will be complete. In the next step, called the training phase, the model will predict what it thinks is relevant and not relevant, and you will start the actual training by telling the model if it is correct.

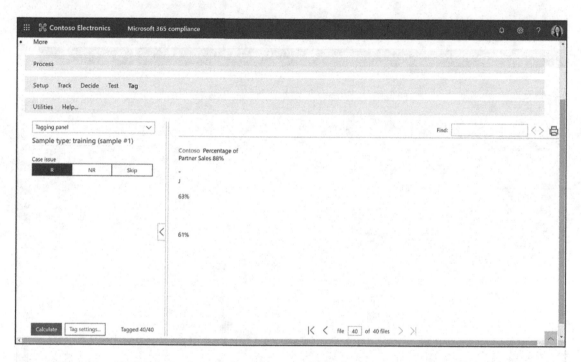

Figure 14-61. *Calculate the statistics to see if you have completed training*

To start, go back to the Track tab and click Training. The process is going to be the same as in the assessment phase. You will go through the batches of 40 documents, and you need to decide whether the file is relevant or not relevant. When you finish the sets of 40 files, click calculate in the lower left of the screen, shown in Figure 14-61. The model will determine whether your training is complete, meaning that we have hit our statistical targets for error margin. If we have not hit our targets, the system will give us another set of 40 documents to review for training.

Eventually, you will hit your statistics goals, which will end the training. The amount of training sets you need to do is going to be entirely different for every case. But once the training bar is all orange and up to 40, the next step is to run the batch calculation.

The batch calculation scores documents on how likely they are to be relevant. Files tagged as relevant or not relevant by the expert will receive a score of either 0 or 100. The batch calculation scores the relevancy of the remaining documents that you did not review on a scale of 0–100. You will then run some reports and view some graphs on the cost to review the rest of the items manually, and you can decide how to proceed from there.

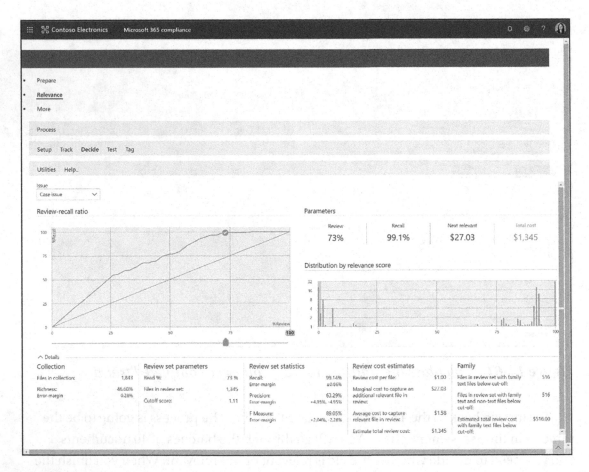

Figure 14-62. *Decide*

Once you have run your batch calculation, you can move on to the Decide tab. The Decide tab gives us the information we need to make a proportional decision about the data. You will see a few charts and sections of data on the page, shown in Figure 14-62. Please keep in mind these numbers are entirely fake and unrealistic because I used a demo environment:

- **Review-recall ratio**: A comparison of results according to relevance scores in a hypothetically linear review. The recall is estimated given the review set size. Move the slider at the bottom of the graph to change the review percentage, which affects the cost information.

    - **Review**: The X-axis is the percentage of files to review based on this cutoff.

    - **Recall**: The y-axis is the percentage of relevant files in the review set.

- **Parameters**: Cumulative calculated statistics about the review set concerning the file population for the entire case. The cost shows the projected cost of discovery based on the parameters you entered in the prepare ➤ advanced settings step earlier in this section. It shows the cost to review one document and for the overall discovery process.

- **Distribution by relevance score**: A graph of the relevance score of the files in the load set.

- **Details**: Data about the file collection (load set), the statistics, parameters, costs, and document families.

These graphs give us a calculation of how much it costs to review a single document. It allows us to decide what percentage of documents we want to review and at what cost. We need to weigh the risk of missing documents based on the case specifics with the cost of reviewing more documents. For example, if it is a litigation case and costs you $100,000 to settle, you will not spend $150,000 to review all the documents. Our machine learning model module that you just built by reviewing those documents will identify what documents are likely relevant and export those for manual review.

Validate and Test

The last step in the relevancy process is to validate our model through testing. We do this test through an illusion sample. We do the test by taking a statistically significant random sample of the unreviewed documents to make sure that we did this process correctly. We want to ensure that the files we think are below our review percentage are, in fact, irrelevant. This test proves to the court that our model is valid.

Start a test by clicking the Test tab in the gray bar at the top of the page. There are two test options:

1. **Test the rest**: Used to validate culling decisions, such as reviewing only files above a specific relevance cutoff score based on the final Advanced eDiscovery results.

2. **Test a slice**: Performs testing like the "Test the rest" test but focuses on a segment of the file set specified by Relevance Read %.

The purpose of the tests is similar for both types. You have decided to only review documents with a relevance score of 35 or higher in our example. We want to make sure that 35 is the correct number. To accomplish this, we will take a random sample of documents with a score of less than 35 and have an expert review them for relevancy. After the review, we will compare the statistics of the test with those of the overall model.

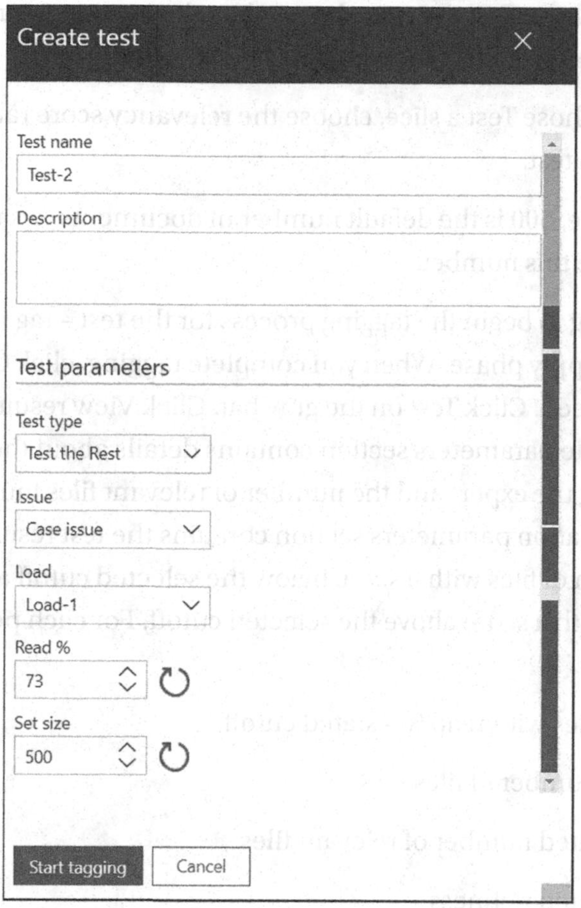

Figure 14-63. *Set up a test to provide our Advanced eDiscovery relevance model's validity*

To run a test, click Test on the gray bar at the top of the page. At the bottom of the page, click the blue button that says New test. A screen, shown in Figure 14-63, appears.

- Enter any name and description for the test.

- Under Parameters, for test type, choose Test the rest or Test a slice.

- For Issue, choose the model you want to test.

- For Load, choose the load set you used when training the model.

- For Read percentage

- If you chose Test the rest, choose the relevance score under which you want to collect the sample.

- If you chose Test a slice, choose the relevancy score range you want to test.

- For Test size, 500 is the default number of documents to sample. You can change this number.

Click Start tagging to begin the tagging process for the test – tag in the same way you did in the train and apply phase. When you complete tagging, click Calculate on the bottom left of the screen. Click Test on the gray bar. Click View results next to your test.

The table's Sample parameters section contains details about the number of files in the sample tagged by the expert and the number of relevant files found in that sample.

The table's Population parameters section contains the test results, including the review set population of files with a score below the selected cutoff and "The Rest" population of files with a score above the selected cutoff. For each population, it displays the following results:

- Includes files with read % – stated cutoff

- The total number of files

- The estimated number of relevant files

- The estimated richness

- The average review cost of finding another relevant file

In this section, we reviewed the relevancy module. There are a couple more settings and things that you can do with it, but those extra settings confuse people when you are just getting started with it. This walk-through helps you understand how relevancy might be useful in your organization, how you can test it out, and, if you do want to use it, how to get started.

Export

The last feature area in Advanced eDiscovery is export. Use export when you want to get files or a summary out of Advanced eDiscovery. Usually, there are two reasons people export files. First is to give them to the opposing party or the person who made the file request. Second is to import them into another eDiscovery system using a load file. There are many reasons you might only want to export an inventory or summary of your files. For example, your legal department might wish to see a manifest of the information. Or you can use this list to comply with a privacy data subject request.

To run an export in Advanced eDiscovery, go to your review set. Click Action in the navigation and then Export. A window will appear that presents you with several options. If you want only to export a subset of documents in your review set, such as those you tagged as relevant, select those items before clicking Export. First, let us go through the steps to export a summary, and then we will go through the options to export files.

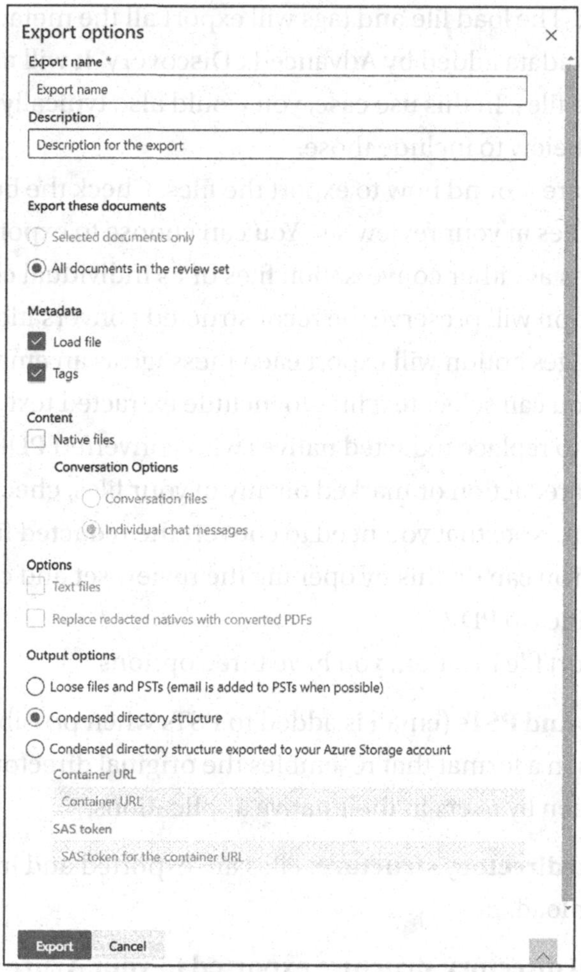

Figure 14-64. *Export options for Advanced eDiscovery*

First, create a name and description for the summary export, shown in Figure 14-64. Under Export these documents, choose from Selected documents only, to export only the subset you selected in the previous step. Or you can choose to export information for all documents. Under Metadata, select the load file option, which will result in your summary report. You can also choose to include any tags you added. Skip the Content and Options sections. For Output options, choose Condensed directory structure. Click the blue Export button. This click starts a job to create the export.

Suppose you would like to import the file metadata and review data into a different eDiscovery system. In that case, you should check the boxes next to load file and tags in the export option box. The load file and tags will export all the metadata associated with the file, including metadata added by Advanced eDiscovery. It will also preserve the tags you have added to the files. In this use case, you would also typically include the files, so follow the directions below to include those.

The next choices are around how to export the files. Check the box next to native files to export all the files in your review set. You can choose to export Teams and Yammer conversations as either conversation files or as individual chat messages. The conversation files option will preserve the reconstructed conversations in a PDF. The individual chat messages option will export each message as an email message.

Under Options, you can select text files to include extracted text versions of native files. You can choose to replace redacted natives with converted PDFs. If you have performed document redaction or marked on any of your files, check this box to preserve the redaction. Note that you need to convert the redacted files to PDF before starting your export. You can do this by opening the review set and choosing Action ➤ Convert all redacted files to PDF.

Then, for the export file location, you have three options:

1. **Loose files and PSTs** (email is added to PSTs when possible): Export files in a format that resembles the original directory structure seen by users in their native applications.

2. **Condensed directory structure**: Files are exported and included in the download.

3. **Condensed directory structure exported to your Azure storage account**: Exports files to your organization's Azure storage account. This option is useful if you want to share the files with someone outside your company or if you already have a process

set up with other people in your organization who wish to access the same blob to get the exported data repeatedly. I go into detail about using this option in the following.

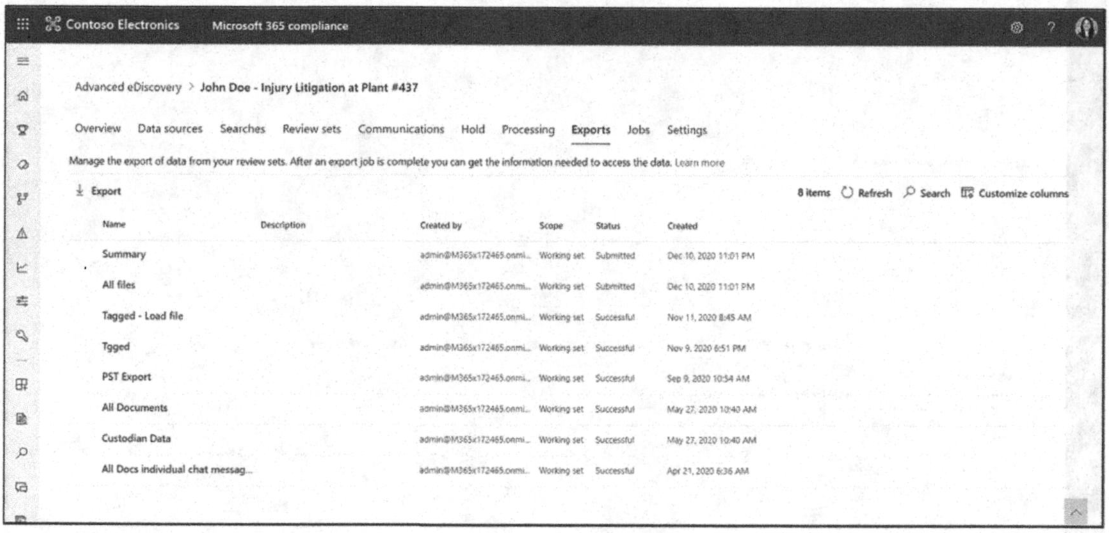

Figure 14-65. *The Advanced eDiscovery Exports tab*

Click the Exports tab to see a list of all the exports you have created, shown in Figure 14-65. Once the status equals successful, you are ready to export your data. To do this, click the export name you want to download and click Export. These exports are available for the life of the case.

If you chose the preceding Loose files and PSTs or Condensed directory structure, you could click a blue Download button. This click starts the download to your local machine.

If you chose the Azure export option, click the export name and copy the URL from the window that appears. You will need to download and install Azure Storage Explorer to access the download. Follow the instructions linked in the pop-up window to download and install Azure Storage Explorer. Once complete, keep Azure Storage Explorer open on your screen.

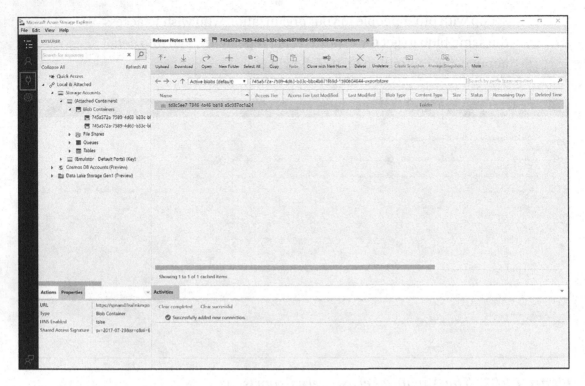

Figure 14-66. *Azure Storage Explorer for Advanced eDiscovery exports*

To add your data location, find a black bar with something that looks like a power plug on the left-hand side of Azure Storage Explorer, shown in Figure 14-66. Click the power plug icon, and then a screen will pop up asking how you want to connect to Azure Storage. Choose Use a shared access signature (SAS) URI. Click Next. On the next screen, you will want to paste the URI that you copied from the Advanced eDiscovery export window. Go ahead and change the display name or keep it as it is.

You will then click Connect, and it will add the storage location to Azure Storage Explorer. To see your files, double-click the folder in the export location. You will then see information such as a summary file, export load file, and then your actual files in separate folders, just depending on the options you chose in the export configuration screen.

Review the Export Files

Now let us review what the exports look like in terms of file structure and content. If you chose Loose files and PSTs export structure, the system organizes the exported content in the following structure:

- **Root folder**: Contains the export information. Unzip it to see the files. The export names the folder as ExportName.zip.

    - **Summary.csv:** Contains export statistics.

    - **Results.csv:** A manifest of the files included in the export, listed in the following.

    - Azure folder ➤ AED export ➤ folder named as export GUID:

        - **Export_load_file.csv:** The metadata file.

        - **Summary.txt:** Information about the export.

        - **Exchange:** This folder contains all content from Exchange in native file format.

        - **SharePoint:** This folder contains all native content from SharePoint in a native file format. There are subfolders for each site or OneDrive.

Next, let us look at files for the Condensed directory structure option:

- **Root folder**: This folder is named ExportName.zip.

    - **Export_load_file.csv:** The metadata file.

    - **Summary.txt:** Information about the export.

    - **Input_or_native_files:** This folder contains all the native files included in your export. If you included redacted PDF files, they are in a separate folder.

    - **Error_files:** This folder contains the following error files if they are included in the export:

        - **ExtractionError:** A CSV file that contains any available metadata of files that were not correctly extracted from parent files.

- **ProcessingError:** This file contains a list of documents with processing errors. This content is item-level, meaning if an attachment resulted in a processing error, the email message that contains the attachment is included in this folder.

- **Extracted_text_files**: This folder contains all the extracted text files generated at processing.

In this chapter, we reviewed every aspect of the Advanced eDiscovery solution. These topics included

- An overview of the eDiscovery process

- Creating a case and setting permissions

  - Configuring case settings

- Managing custodians and holds

  - Fixing processing errors

- Managing custodian communications

- How to run a search

- Working with review sets

  - Managing review set settings and analytics

  - Adding non–Office 365 data to a case

  - Reviewing content in a review set

  - Querying and filtering data in a review set

- Working with the relevancy module

- Exporting data out of Advanced eDiscovery

In the next chapter, we will look at the Data Investigations tool to run an internal investigation, using functionality like Advanced eDiscovery.

CHAPTER 15

Data Investigations

At the time of this writing, *Data Investigations* is in public preview. Please be aware that Microsoft could potentially remove it from the Compliance Center. If that happens, know that you can accomplish the use cases outlined in this chapter using the *Advanced eDiscovery* solution. We point out the similar functionality throughout this chapter.

Data Investigations allow you to search, investigate, and act on data-related incidents. Data-related incident examples can include a data leak, data spillage, or a need to search for and purge messages containing harmful attachments. It could also include an internal investigation for customer information for a GDPR or other data subject request.

For example, a data spill occurs when someone releases a document containing confidential, sensitive, or malicious content into an untrusted environment. When a data spill is detected, it is essential to quickly control the environment, assess the spillage's size and locations, examine user activities around it, and delete the service's spilled data. You can also use it to investigate what happened and take the appropriate actions to remediate the spillage.

Other common scenarios for using Data Investigations include investigating confidential documents emailed to an external recipient, where there was no sensitivity level or protection applied, or if someone shared customer personally identifiable information (PII) in a file inappropriately. Another scenario is a data breach where you want to investigate the breach's data and the extent of the violation.

This chapter will look at how to use the Data Investigations solution to remediate these scenarios. You will notice that Data Investigations appear like the Advanced eDiscovery solution. Microsoft built both solutions using the same technology and user interface. A different team often runs Data Investigations compared to eDiscovery. Therefore, you can set different permissions for the data investigations solution vs. eDiscovery. You can also use Data Investigations to delete data that matches your search and review results, whereas you currently cannot in Advanced eDiscovery.

© Erica Toelle 2021
E. Toelle, *Microsoft 365 Compliance*, https://doi.org/10.1007/978-1-4842-5778-4_15

Permissions and Licensing

To access a Data Investigation in the Microsoft 365 Compliance Center, you need to have the Data Investigation Manager role. This role allows you to create, edit, delete, and control access to data investigations.

Microsoft includes the Data Investigation Manager role in the following role groups:

1. Compliance Administrator

2. Data Investigator

Each person of interest in a data investigation must have one of the following licenses:

- Microsoft 365 E5

- Microsoft 365 E5 Compliance

- Microsoft 365 E5 eDiscovery and Audit

- Office 365 E5

Data Investigations Overview

First, we need to understand the data investigation process.

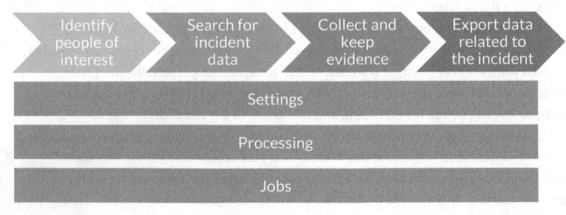

Figure 15-1. *The data investigation process*

There are four steps in this process, shown in Figure 15-1. These steps are as follows:

- **Identify people of interest**: These are the people who may be involved in the incident. Identifying them preserves their information and performs a more in-depth search index on their data.

- **Search for incident data**: This step gathers the evidence for the investigation.

- **Collect and keep evidence**: Adding the search results to evidence preserves the data in a separate location so that you can conduct a full investigation.

- **Export data related to the incident**: If necessary, you can export data you have identified as relevant to the case to pass it off to HR, legal, or another team.

In addition to these four steps, there are three supporting areas on which we rely throughout the entire process:

- **Settings**: Allows us to configure specifics about each of the preceding steps.

- **Processing**: Tracks the advanced indexing status of data sources associated with the investigation. Use this tab to remediate any processing errors so that all data is fully searchable in the inquiry.

- **Jobs**: Track the status of long-running processes triggered by user actions when using and managing investigations.

To access Data Investigations, visit the Microsoft 365 Compliance Center. On the left-hand navigation, click Data investigations.

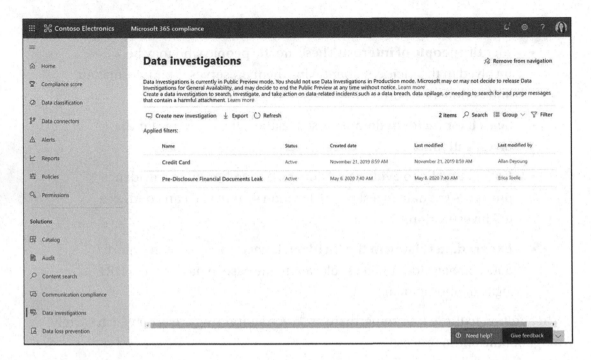

Figure 15-2. The Data investigations overview page

This click will bring you to the Data investigations overview page, shown in Figure 15-2, where you can see a list of all the investigations to which you have access. You can see whether each investigation is active or inactive, the case creation date, the last modified date, and who last modified it. Additionally, you can export this list of cases or refresh the list if the information has changed. You can also see the total number of items in the list, search within the list, group items in the list, or filter items. Now we are going to create a new investigation.

Note   Microsoft built Data Investigations using the same technology as Advanced eDiscovery. Most of the steps and the user interface are the same.

Many of the steps and options in data investigations are the same as Advanced eDiscovery and are covered more in depth in Chapter 14. I will not repeat the information here. As we go through the Data Investigations tool, I will point out where you can visit Chapter 14 for more details.

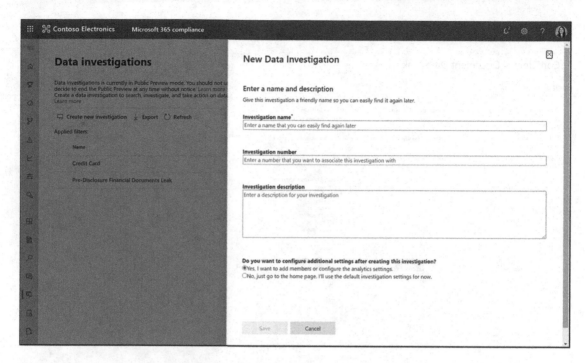

Figure 15-3. *New Data Investigation screen*

To create a new investigation, click Create new data investigation. In this screen, shown in Figure 15-3, you can enter the investigation name, an optional investigation number, and an optional description and then choose to configure additional settings after creating this investigation. I recommend choosing yes and adding members or configuring the analytics settings. Please note that the investigation name must be unique and cannot be the same name as a content search, a Core eDiscovery case, an Advanced eDiscovery case, or a Data Subject Request in your compliance environment.

Settings

Choosing yes brings you to the settings page. The settings page is precisely the same as Advanced eDiscovery. So please see the "Case Settings" section in Chapter 14 for more information.

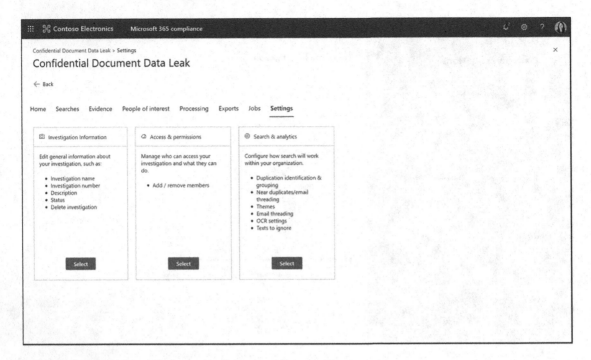

Figure 15-4. *Data investigation settings*

Once you have completed your settings, shown in Figure 15-4, you will be brought to the investigation homepage. On the homepage of the investigation, you can see the recent job statuses and any errors, including password-protected files or unknown file types.

Identify People of Interest

According to our process, the first thing we will do is select people of interest in our case. Use the People of interest tab, shown in Figure 15-5, to add and manage the people you have identified as persons of interest during your investigation of the evidence. When you add people of interest, their data sources, such as their mailbox and OneDrive account, are identified and mapped to the investigation.

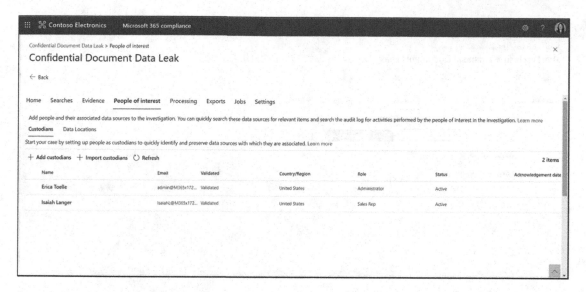

Figure 15-5. *People of interest tab*

This step also preserves the data so the user cannot delete or modify it. This process is technically the same as the Advanced eDiscovery custodian steps. Please see the "Manage Custodians and Holds" section in Chapter 14 for more information on how to add a person of interest to the investigation.

In the next step, you can scope searches by searching only the content locations of these people. You can also view and search the people's audit log activity to further help your investigation on the People of interest tab. You can always add more people of interest throughout the investigation.

Processing

The tool also reprocesses the people of interest's data to perform more in-depth indexing, called advanced indexing. Advanced indexing reprocesses any partially indexed data. Unindexed data can include images or unsupportive file types. Advanced indexing allows us to have more effective searches later in the process. It ensures data is fully discoverable when you run searches to collect data for an investigation. Advanced indexing is also why we want to start with people of interest if they are known. The in-depth indexing will allow our search to be more effective in the next step. Please note that, as always, this advanced indexing is the same advanced indexing in Advanced eDiscovery.

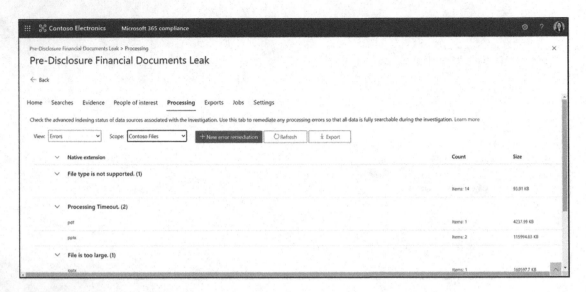

Figure 15-6. *Processing errors*

The Processing tab, shown in Figure 15-6, allows you to monitor advanced indexing status and fix any processing errors using error remediation. Processing will show you any errors that occurred while processing or indexing the content. The feature then allows you to go through a remediation process to resolve those errors. I describe the error remediation process in the section called "Processing and Error Remediation" in Chapter 14.

Search for Incident Data

The next step in our Data Investigations case is the Searches tab, shown in Figure 15-7. Again, this search is the same as Advanced eDiscovery, and we cover the steps in the "Advanced eDiscovery Searches" section of Chapter 14. Specifically, for data investigations, here are some ideas for how you might search for your content.

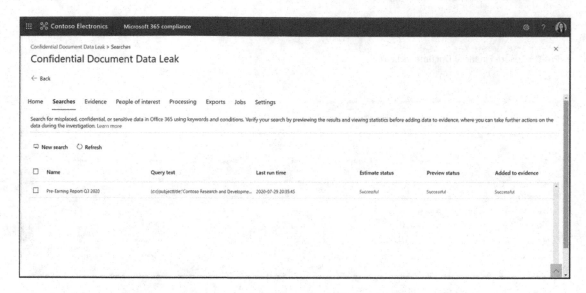

Figure 15-7. *Data investigation search*

Let us say you want to search for a leaked email. First, scope the search to the people of interest you defined in the previous step. Then, you can use the title/subject field to look for the email subject. You can use the date range condition to narrow down the search. You could choose the participants condition to find additional people involved in the email.

When you have completed your search, add it to evidence in the same way you would add a search to a review set in Advanced eDiscovery. I covered this in Chapter 14 in the section titled "Create a Review Set."

Jobs

Jobs track the status of long-running processes that are triggered by user actions when using and managing investigations. For example, when you add a search to evidence, it takes some time to gather the items, ingest them, index them, and construct the conversations.

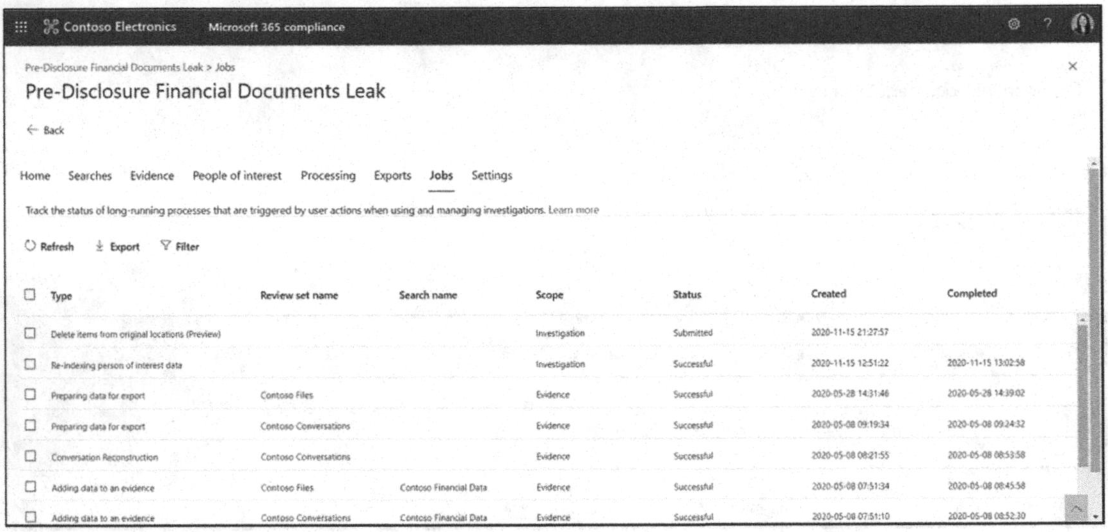

Figure 15-8. *The Data Investigations Jobs tab*

You can view these long-running processes' status, including any errors, on the Jobs tab, shown in Figure 15-8. For more information on jobs, please see Chapter 14.

Collect and Keep Evidence

Click the Evidence tab to access your evidence sets. Use this evidence area to investigate and review the data you collected from Microsoft 365. The data in the evidence set is a snapshot of the search results that you collected previously. Even if you choose to delete data from your production Microsoft 365 environment, a copy of the data will remain in evidence for the duration of your investigation. This process allows you to quickly contain the environment by deleting data located in the live service's original content locations for any time-sensitive investigations.

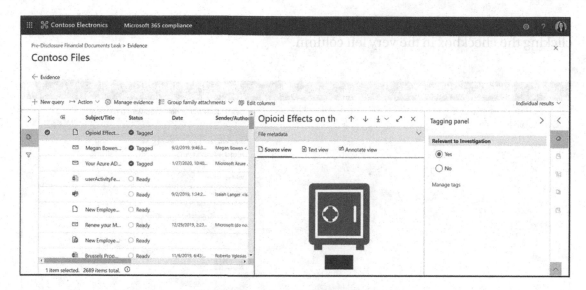

Figure 15-9. *Tag items as relevant to your investigation*

When you add search results to evidence, a process is triggered to extract files, metadata, and text. When this process is complete, the data investigations tool builds a new index of all the data and adds it to an evidence set. Then, you can search and filter your data. You can tag each piece of content as relevant or irrelevant to this data leak or investigation during the review process, shown in Figure 15-9.

If you wanted more information about reviewing information and working with it in the evidence set, you see the section "Manage Review Sets" in Chapter 14.

Delete Items from Their Original Locations

The ability to delete items from their original locations is an action that is unique to data investigations. Specifically, you can delete items from SharePoint, OneDrive, and Exchange. Remember that a copy of the item will still exist in evidence. This action deletes the items from the original content locations.

For this action, the user needs to have the Search and Purge role. The Data Investigator role group already contains the Search and Purge role.

To make it easier to delete the correct data, create a search containing only the items you tagged for deletion. To do this, click New query. Create a title for the search, such as "Items for deletion." Click Add condition, and then select tags. Select the tag that you decided would indicate items tagged for deletion. Click Save.

Now you have a view of all the items you want to delete. Select all the items by clicking the checkbox in the very left column.

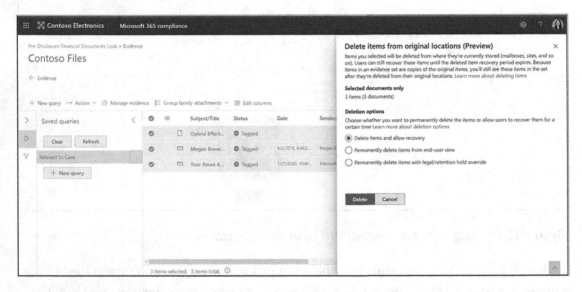

Figure 15-10. *Delete items from their original locations*

Now click Action and then Delete items from original locations. A window will appear. Under the heading Selected documents only shown in Figure 15-10, "3 items (3 documents)" indicates the number of items selected for deletion. The number of documents indicates the total number of items, including any files attached to a parent item. For example, choose one email message, and that message has an attached Word document. The number of items and documents displayed under Selected documents only will only be one item and two documents.

Remember that when you add data to evidence, it separates email messages from attachments, so you have two separate files. Similarly, if there are embedded files in an Office document, they are also divided into multiple files. Suppose you select the attachments of an email or a file attached to a document in SharePoint and OneDrive for deletion. In this case, it will delete both the parent item and the attachments. Similarly, if you select an item with attachments, the parent item and all attachments are deleted.

Under Deletion options, you have three choices. To learn more about the details of how Microsoft 365 deletes content, please see Chapter 8, in the "How Retention Works in Microsoft 365" and "How Deletion Works" sections:

- **Delete items and allow recovery**: Items are soft-deleted. Soft-deleting items means that users can still recover these items. The system respects legal holds and retention policies on the items.

- **Permanently delete items from end user view**: Items are hard-deleted. End users cannot recover the items, but admins can. The system respects legal holds and retention policies on the items.

- **Permanently delete items with legal/retention hold override**: Items are hard-deleted. The system ignores legal holds and retention policies on the items.

Make your selection and click Delete. Deletion is a long-running process, so you can track this job on the Jobs tab. You may receive a status of Partially Successful for the Delete items from original locations job. Several situations can result in this job status.

After the job has completed running, you may receive a job status of Partially Successful. In general, this status indicates that the job ran successfully, but not all items were soft-deleted. Here's a list of reasons that result in partially successful deletions:

- A mailbox item is located in the Recoverable Items folder in the source mailbox.

- Someone purged a mailbox item from the Recoverable Items folder in the source mailbox.

- A document was already located in the first-stage recycle bin in a SharePoint or OneDrive site.

- A document was moved to a different SharePoint site after you added it to the evidence set. In this case, the system won't move the document to the recycle bin on the new site.

- A document was permanently deleted in SharePoint or OneDrive (moved to the second-stage recycle bin) after adding it to the evidence set.

Export Data Related to the Incident

Lastly, you can export content from any data investigation. Again, this is the same as Advanced eDiscovery. Please see Chapter 14 and the section "Export" for more information.

In this chapter, we reviewed how to use Data Investigations to search, investigate, and act on data-related incidents. This tool is similar to Advanced eDiscovery but has a user interface tailored to data investigations. You can also set unique permissions for this solution and bulk delete data from Microsoft 365.

There are four steps in the data investigation process. They are as follows:

- Identify people of interest.

- Search for incident data.

- Collect and keep evidence.

- Export data related to the incident.

Additionally, three areas support the preceding steps. They are

- Settings

- Processing

- Jobs

In the next chapter, we will detail how to use the Data Investigations solution to comply with data subject requests. We will also discuss using the Core eDiscovery solution to complete these requests if you don't own advanced licenses.

CHAPTER 16

The Unified Audit Log

The audit log tracks user and admin activities across Microsoft 365. For example, if you need to find out if a user viewed a specific document or purged an item from their mailbox, you could find that activity in the audit log. You can use the Microsoft 365 Compliance Center to search the Unified Audit Log to view user and admin activity in your organization.

As of March 2021 here are over 650 audit activities available in the audit log with more added frequently. These are the main categories of information:

- User activity in SharePoint Online and OneDrive for Business

- User activity in Exchange Online (Exchange mailbox audit logging)

- Admin activity in SharePoint Online

- Admin activity in Azure Active Directory (the directory service for Microsoft 365)

- Admin activity in Exchange Online (Exchange admin audit logging)

- eDiscovery activities in the Security and Compliance Center

- User and admin activity in Power BI

- User and admin activity in Microsoft Teams

- User and admin activity in Dynamics 365

- User and admin activity in Yammer

- User and admin activity in Microsoft Power Automate

- User and admin activity in Microsoft Stream

- Analyst and admin activity in Microsoft Workplace Analytics

- User and admin activity in Microsoft Power Apps

© Erica Toelle 2021

E. Toelle, *Microsoft 365 Compliance*, https://doi.org/10.1007/978-1-4842-5778-4_16

- User and admin activity in Microsoft Forms

- User and admin activity for sensitivity labels for sites that use
  SharePoint Online or Microsoft Teams

Before you get started with the audit log, you'll need to turn it on. Microsoft is in the process of enabling the audit log by default, but you should check to make sure that yours is on. To do this, visit the Microsoft 365 Compliance Center. In the left-hand navigation, click Audit. If your audit log is not on, there'll be a yellow ribbon across the top asking you if you'd like to turn on the audit log. Click yes. If you do not see this, go ahead and do a quick search to ensure its returning audit activities.

Permissions and Licensing

To view the audit log, you'll need the View-Only Audit Logs or Audit Logs role. By default, the system assigns these roles to the Compliance Management and Organization Management role groups.

The length of time that the system retains the audit record depends on the type of license assigned to specific users. Here are the types of licenses that include audit and the length of time audit activity for a user is kept with a certain license:

- Office 365 F3 – 90 days

- Office 365 E1 – 90 days

- Office 365 E3 – 90 days

- Office 365 E5 – 1 year

- Microsoft 365 Business Premium – 90 days

- Microsoft 365 F1 – 90 days

- Microsoft 365 F3 – 90 days

- Microsoft 365 E3 – 90 days

- Microsoft 365 E5 – 1 year

- Microsoft 365 E5 Discovery and Audit – 1 year

- Microsoft 365 E5 Compliance – 1 year

The system retains records for Azure Active Directory, Exchange, and SharePoint activity by default for one year for users with that license entitlement. You can keep other audit activities for one year if you create an audit log retention policy. We will cover this information in depth later in the chapter.

Lastly, organizations can purchase an additional add-on license to retain audit activities for up to ten years. As of this writing, Microsoft has not yet released the details of this license.

When Do Events Appear in the Audit Log?

Depending on the Microsoft 365 service or feature, audit log events could take up to 30 minutes or 24 hours to appear in an audit log search, shown in Table 16-1 below.

Table 16-1. *Information about when events appear in the audit log*

Microsoft 365 service or feature	30 minutes	24 hours
Defender for Office 365 and Threat Intelligence	X	
Azure Active Directory (user login events)		X
Azure Active Directory (admin events)		X
Data Loss Prevention	X	
Dynamics 365 CRM		X
eDiscovery	X	
Exchange Online	X	
Microsoft Power Automate		X
Microsoft Project	X	
Microsoft Stream	X	
Microsoft Teams	X	
Power Apps		X

(*continued*)

Table 16-1. *(continued)*

Microsoft 365 service or feature	30 minutes	24 hours
Power BI*	X	
Security and Compliance Center	X	
Sensitivity labels		X
SharePoint Online and OneDrive for Business	X	
Workplace Analytics	X	
Yammer		X
Microsoft Forms	X	

*Audit logging for Power BI isn't enabled by default. To search for Power BI activities in the audit log, you have to enable auditing in the Power BI admin portal.

Search the Audit Log

To search the audit log, visit the Microsoft 365 Compliance Center. In the left navigation, click Audit.

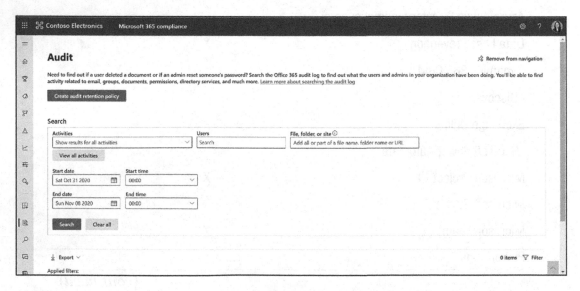

Figure 16-1. *The Microsoft 365 audit log page in the Compliance Center*

Here, you can see the audit log search options, shown in Figure 16-1. The options group user and admin actions together. Select the activities you want to see, or do not select any to show results from all activities. There are about 650 activities currently in the audit log, as of March 2021, with more activities added frequently. You can use the search box at the top of the activity list to narrow down activities, select all activities in a group, or select individual activities.

Here are the other audit log search options:

- **Users**: Leave this field blank to search all users. Otherwise, start typing an email address, and the system will suggest matching accounts. You can then select the accounts for which you want to see activities.

- **File, folder, or site**: Leave this field blank to search all locations. You can also type some or all of a file or folder name to search for the file or folder's activity. You can add a wild card at the beginning of the term to search for everything related to a file, or add the wild card to the end of the location, to return all entries for a site or folder.

- **Start date, start time, end date, and end time**: The system displays these values in UTC format. The maximum range is determined by the user's license, as described in this chapter's "Permissions and Licensing" section. If you're using a maximum range, such as 90 days for E3 licenses, make sure the start time isn't earlier than the current time. Otherwise, you will get an error. If you've recently enabled auditing, the start date can't be before you enabled auditing; otherwise, you'll get an error.

Audit Log Search Results

Your search results have a maximum of 5,000 events displayed. It displays them in increments of 150 events, and you can press Shift + End to load the next 150. We show a sample of the audit log search results in Figure 16-2. If there are more than 5,000 events returned by your search, it will show the most recent 5,000 items. If you see precisely 5,000 results, that's a good indication that there were more than 5,000 results returned by your search.

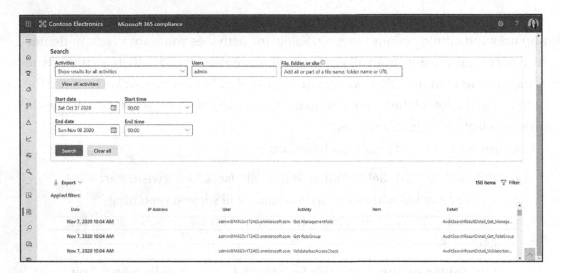

Figure 16-2. *The Microsoft 365 audit log showing search results*

To view all of the items returned by the search, for example, more than 5,000 items, you can export the results and download them to a CSV file. The CSV file can have a maximum of 50,000 items. You have two choices for your export:

1. **Save loaded results**: This choice will export the results displayed on the screen. This option is useful if you're further filtering your results and you're working with less than 5,000 events.

2. **Download all results**: This option downloads everything that met the search criteria up to 50,000 items.

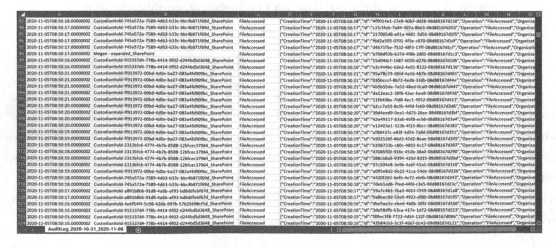

Figure 16-3. *Audit log CSV results*

Again, suppose your download contains exactly 50,000 items. In that case, that's a good indication that your search returned more items than the limit, and you'll want to adjust your search to narrow it down to less than 50,000 items to make sure you're not missing any information. The Download all results option contains the raw data from the audit log, shown in Figure 16-3. This file contains different column names, such as creation date, user IDs, the operation they performed, and an audit data column, which we'll talk about in a moment. You will not see these extra columns of data if you select the Save loaded results option. Instead, you'll only see the information displayed on the screen.

Search Results Information

The audit log search results display audit log activities. You can filter the search results by date range, IP address, user, activity, and detail, a free-form text field. You can also sort by any column. Each activity displays the following information:

- **Date**: The date and time in UTC when the event occurred.

- **IP address**: The IP address of the device used when the system logged the activity. It displays the IP address in either IP V4 or IP V6 address format. For some services, the value shown in this field might be the IP address of a trusted application, for example, Office Web Apps calling into the service on behalf of the user. For admin activity or activity performed by a system account, it doesn't log the IP address for Azure Active Directory–related events. The value displayed in this field is null.

- **User**: The user or service account who has performed the action that triggered the event.

- **Activity**: The activity performed by the user. This value corresponds to the activities that you selected in the Activities dropdown list.

- **Item**: The object that was created or modified as a result of the related activity, for example, the modified or viewed file or the updated user account. Not all activities have a value in this column.

- **Detail**: Additional information about an activity. Again, not all activities will have any information in this section.

Some audit log activities may have additional information available, which you can see by clicking the activity. If you'd like to learn more about the audit log property details that you might see, please visit this link: https://erica.news/AuditLogProperties.

Transform the AuditData Column

When you export audit data to a CSV file using the Download all results option, there's an included column called AuditData. The audit data column contains additional information about each event. This column's data consists of adjacent objects containing multiple properties from the audit record. You can use the JSON transformation tool and the Power Query editor in Excel to split the audit data column into multiple columns so that each property in the JSON object has its own column. This method lets you sort and filter on one or more of the properties.

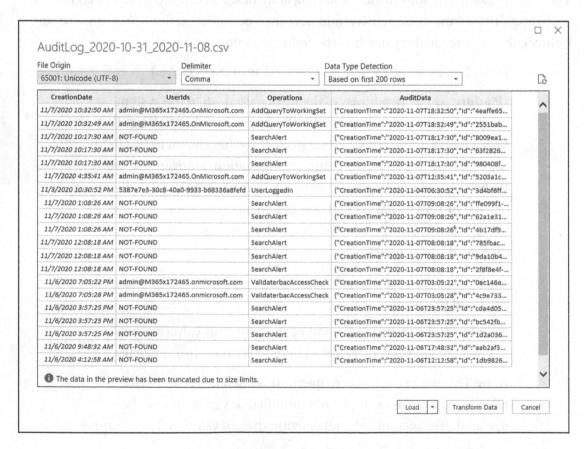

Figure 16-4. *The query table for the first step in the data transformation process*

To do this, open a new Excel file, click the Data tab, and find the Get and transform data section on the left. Within the section, click From Text/CSV. Navigate to your downloaded audit data file. You'll see a table with some sample data, shown in Figure 16-4. Click the Transform Data button. This click will load your data into a query table. Find the audit data column, right-click the column name, and choose Transform and then JSON. This choice will transform the audit data into the word "record." There's an icon with two arrows pointing away from each other to the right of the audit data name. Click this icon to expand all of the data from the audit data column into separate columns.

Figure 16-5. *The list of available columns*

Next, it will show you a list of the available columns, shown in Figure 16-5. Please take the time to deselect some of these columns to include only the information that you need. The deselection will make it much easier to work with your data later. If you get the error that the list may be incomplete, click the Load more link to load all the columns. When you're happy with the columns that you have selected, click Okay.

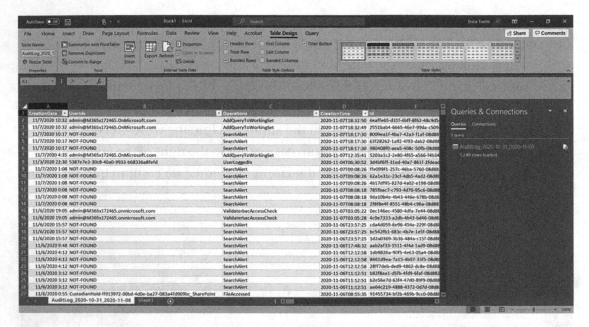

Figure 16-6. Expanded data columns result

You will see all of the columns of data that were previously in the audit data column expanded into their columns, shown in Figure 16-6. When you're happy, click Close and Load to be brought back to your Excel sheet. Now you can work with your audit log data, just as you would any other large amount of data in Excel. You can use things like pivot charts and tables, queries, or other data analysis tools to work with the audit data.

PowerShell and Office 365 Management Activity APIs

Please note that you can use PowerShell to search the Unified Audit Log. You can also programmatically download data from the audit log using the Office 365 Management Activity APIs: https://erica.news/O365MgmtAPIs.

Many people will use these APIs to download their audit data into a separate database if they want to keep it longer than their license allows.

Advanced Audit

Advanced audit capabilities allow you to retain your audit log data for up to one year. You can also buy add-on licenses that keep your data up to 10 years. Additionally, an advanced audit allows you to create and manage audit log retention policies to customize your audit trail length. It also gives you access to additional audit events critical for some data investigations. Finally, advanced audit gives you high-bandwidth access to the Office 365 Management Activity APIs.

Audit Log Retention Policies

Retaining audit records for extended periods can help with ongoing forensic or compliance investigations. Microsoft is also in the process of releasing the capability to maintain audit logs for ten years. The 10-year retention of audit logs supports lengthy running investigations and regulatory, legal, or internal obligations such as records management.

Advanced audit retains all Exchange, SharePoint, and Azure Active Directory audit records for one year. This retention is accomplished by a default audit log retention policy that keeps any audit record that contains the value of Exchange, SharePoint, or Azure Active Directory for the workload property. The workload property indicates the service in which the activity occurred.

All audit log records generated in services that aren't covered by the default audit log retention policy are kept for 90 days by default. You can create a customized audit log retention policy to keep audit records for more extended periods, up to 10 years.

All custom audit log retention policies created by your organization take priority over the default retention policy. For example, suppose you create an audit log retention policy for Exchange mailbox activity with a six-month retention period. In that case, the custom retention period is shorter than the one-year default policy for Exchange mailbox activities. Therefore, the audit activity will be retained for the shorter duration specified by the custom policy.

You can have a maximum of 50 audit log retention policies in your organization. Before you create or modify an audit log retention policy, you must have the organization configuration role Compliance Center.

How to Create an Audit Log Retention Policy

Click the Create audit log retention policy button. A form will appear that asks you to name your audit log retention policy, shown in Figure 16-7 below. You can also add a description, and I recommend adding details for the settings you choose in the following to help you remember the configuration.

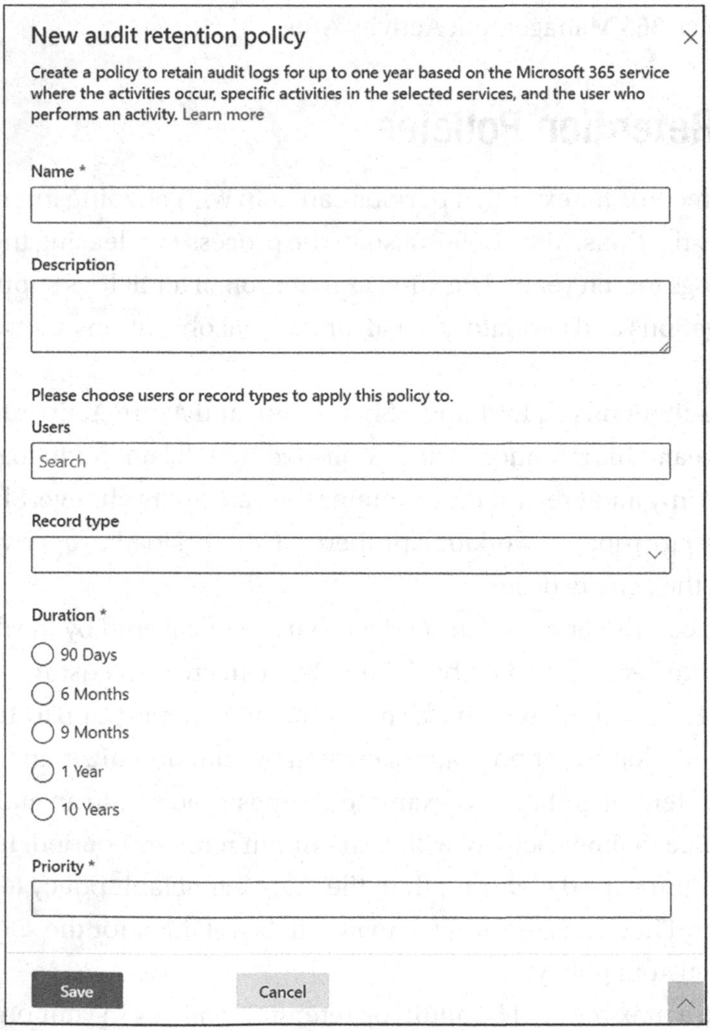

New audit retention policy ✕

Create a policy to retain audit logs for up to one year based on the Microsoft 365 service where the activities occur, specific activities in the selected services, and the user who performs an activity. Learn more

Name *

[   ]

Description

[   ]

Please choose users or record types to apply this policy to.

Users

[Search   ]

Record type

[∨]

Duration *

◯ 90 Days

◯ 6 Months

◯ 9 Months

◯ 1 Year

◯ 10 Years

Priority *

[   ]

[Save]   [Cancel]   ⌃

Figure 16-7. *Create a new audit log retention policy*

For users, you can select one or more users or leave it blank to cover all users. This field is mandatory if you do not assign a record type. Next, select a record type. You can choose one or more options. If you select a single record type, a dropdown field to optionally select activities appears. You can use this list to choose activities from the selected record type. If you choose multiple record types, then the policy will apply to all activities in those categories.

For the audit log retention policy duration, you can choose from the following options:

- 90 days

- 6 months

- 9 months

- 1 year

- 10 years

Lastly, for priority, a higher value equals a higher priority. For example, five is higher than one.

Note that you can also create audit log retention policies via PowerShell.

Access to Crucial Events for Investigations

Crucial events can help you investigate possible breaches and determine the scope of compromise. They can help you to conduct forensic and compliance investigations. Crucial events include information such as when mail items were accessed, when mail items were replied to and forwarded, and when and what a user searched for in Exchange Online and SharePoint Online.

The specific audit log events include

1. MailItemsAccessed

2. Send

3. SearchQueryInitiatedExchange

4. SearchQueryInitiatedSharePoint

5. MailItemsAccessed

The MailItemsAccessed event is a mailbox auditing action triggered when mail protocols and mail clients access mail data. It can help investigators identify data breaches and determine the scope of possibly compromised messages. If an attacker gained access to email messages, the MailItemsAccessed action would be triggered even if there are no other signals.

To search for MailItemsAccessed audit records, you can search for the Accessed mailbox items activity in the Exchange mailbox activities dropdown list in the audit log search tool in the Microsoft 365 Compliance Center.

The Send event is also a mailbox auditing action triggered when a user performs one of the following activities:

1. Sends an email message

2. Replies to an email message

3. Forwards an email message

Investigators can use the Send event to identify emails sent from a compromised account. The audit record for a Send event contains information about the message, such as when someone sent it, the InternetMessage ID, the subject line, and if the message had attachments. This auditing information can help investigators identify email messages sent from a compromised account or sent by an attacker. Additionally, investigators can use a Microsoft 365 eDiscovery tool to search for the message (using the subject line or message ID) to identify the message recipients and the email contents.

To search for Send audit records, you can search for the Sent message activity in the Exchange mailbox activities dropdown list in the audit log search tool in the Microsoft 365 Compliance Center.

The SearchQueryInitiatedExchange event is triggered when a person uses the search bar in Outlook on the Web (OWA) to search for items in a mailbox. Investigators can use the SearchQueryInitiatedExchange event to determine if an attacker who may have compromised an account tried to access sensitive information in the mailbox. The audit record for a SearchQueryInitiatedExchange event contains information such as the actual text of the search query. By looking at the search queries that an attacker may have performed, an investigator can better understand the attacker's intent.

To search for SearchQueryInitiatedExchange audit records, you can search for the Performed email search activity in the Search activities dropdown list in the audit log search tool in the Compliance Center.

A search for items in a SharePoint site triggers the SearchQueryInitiatedSharePoint event. Investigators can use the SearchQueryInitiatedSharePoint event to determine if an attacker found sensitive information in SharePoint. The audit record for this event contains the actual text of the search query. By looking at the search queries that an attacker may have performed, an investigator can better understand the searched file data's intent and scope.

To search for SearchQueryInitiatedSharePoint audit records, you can search for the Performed SharePoint search activity in the Search activities dropdown list in the audit log search tool in the Compliance Center.

High-Bandwidth Access to the Office 365 Management Activity API

Advanced audit also allows you to have high-bandwidth access to the Office 365 Management Activity API. At the publisher level, throttling limits can restrict organizations that access audit logs through the APIs. For a publisher pulling data on behalf of multiple customers, all the customers share the limit. Advanced audit allows a tenant-level limit rather than the publishing limit. The result is that each organization will get its own fully allocated bandwidth quota to access its auditing data.

The bandwidth is not a predefined static limit. The system models it on the combination of factors, including the number of seats in the organization and the fact that E5 organizations will get more bandwidth than non-E5 organizations. Microsoft initially allocates all organizations a baseline of 2000 requests per minute. This limit will dynamically increase, depending on an organization's seat count and its licensing subscription. E5 organizations will get about twice as much bandwidth as non-E5 organizations. There will also be a cap on the maximum bandwidth to protect the health of the service.

In this chapter, we've covered everything in the Audit solution. This information included

- Permissions and licensing

- Performing an audit log search

- Understanding the audit log search results

- Export of audit log data

- Transformation of the AuditData column

- PowerShell and the Office 365 Management Activity APIs

- How the audit log retention policies work

- How to create and manage audit log retention policies

- How to access crucial events

- How to get high-bandwidth access to the Office 365 Management Activity APIs

Index

A

Actions, 41
Activity explorer, 7
  data, 97, 98
  licensing and permissions, 96
  monitoring security and compliance
    events, 99
  page, 98
Advanced audit
  crucial events, 511–513
  high-bandwidth access to Office 365
    Management Activity API, 513
  log retention policies, 509, 511
Advanced eDiscovery, 365
  AI, 401
  bulk remediation process, 424–427
  case creation
    compliance center, 396
    overview page, 397
  case settings, 398–402
  communications, 414
  custodial locations, 404
  custodian activities, 407
  custodian communications (see
    Custodian communications)
  custodian on hold, 406, 407
  custodians in bulk, 408, 409
  data locations on hold, 409
  data sources tab, 403
  export

    Azure Storage Explorer, 482
    file location, 480, 481
    files review, 483, 484
    options, 479
  Jobs tab, 429
  licensing and permissions, 394, 395
  litigation process, 388, 389
  processing errors view, 423
  processing overview screen, 422
  query-based holds, 410–412
  reduce time and cost, 392
  relevancy (see Relevancy process)
  review sets (see Review sets)
  searches
    additional locations, 431
    overview page, 430
    statistics, 432–435
  SharePoint Online and OneDrive for
    Business content on hold, 413
  single file error remediation, 427, 428
Alerts, 302–305
Archive mailboxes
  enabling, 249–251
  licensing and permissions, 248, 249
Artificial intelligence (AI) models, 279, 401
Assign permissions options, 129
Audit logs, 15
Auto-applied retention policy, 68
Auto-apply
  retention label policy

515

E. Toelle, *Microsoft 365 Compliance*, https://doi.org/10.1007/978-1-4842-5778-4

Printed in the United States
by Baker & Taylor Publisher Services

Printed in the United States
by Baker & Taylor Publisher Services